# Public Goods and Public Welfare

# Public Goods and Public Welfare

John G. Head

Duke University Press   Durham, North Carolina   1974

Acknowledgements

I gratefully acknowledge the permission of Macmillan (London) and
the St. Martin's Press and the editors of *Public Finance/Finances
Publiques, Finanzarchiv*, and *Rivista di diritto finaziario e scienza
delle finanze* to reprint the relevant essays included in this volume.

# Contents

# Introduction

The vast extent and growth of the public sector have been perhaps the most important fiscal phenomena of the postwar period. This development had been long in the making, but it nevertheless caught the public economist of the late 1940s unprepared. In the Anglo-American public finance literature of the preceding fifty years the subject of public expenditure had been largely neglected. The need for a limited amount of public spending in areas such as defense, law and order, education and transportation was taken more or less for granted; and attention was focused on the question of the appropriate means of raising the necessary revenue. As a result of the Keynesian revolution of the 1930s, due account was finally taken of the possible role of both revenues and expenditures in stabilization policy. But discussion of the central question of the appropriate nature and extent of public services was not pursued beyond the early insights of Adam Smith, John Stuart Mill, and Henry Sidgwick.

As a result, the public finance response to the problems of a large public sector has been very slow and unsatisfactory. Only now, after almost a quarter of a century of development, are the outlines of a new public finance reasonably clear, with public expenditure taking its rightful place in the center of discussion. In the new public expenditure analysis the early insights of British and continental European writers have been deepened and further developed to provide a comprehensive theory of public spending; and this development at the theoretical level has been accompanied by important advances at the applied level in cost-benefit analysis and program budgeting.

At the theoretical level, three main areas of discussion can be distinguished. The first and most obvious need was to establish a comprehensive set of welfare objectives. The natural approach here would have been to draw upon the findings of modern welfare economics. There was, however, a widespread feeling of dissatisfaction with modern welfare theory on the part of many leading public finance economists. Instead they set about developing their own welfare framework based on a multiplicity of objectives which were felt to be more realistic and more comprehensive. Certain methodological problems have, however, emerged in the interpretation of the resulting multigoal framework some of which are still largely unresolved.

The second major area of discussion has been the theory of market failure. It had long been recognized that public expenditure can be justified only where the failure of the market mechanism to achieve welfare objectives can be convincingly demonstrated. In traditional Pigovian and modern welfare economics a variety of market failure problems had been distinguished, but the general impression remained that such failure was more or less marginal and could hardly serve either to explain or justify the vast public sector of modern democratic society. The new approach in this area was therefore initially to refurbish the nineteenth-century Continental concept of a pure public good or social want, which would provide a case in which the market fails altogether. The detailed analysis of this case by Samuelson and Musgrave provides the seminal core of the modern theory of public expenditure.

The polar case of a pure public good was, however, soon recognized to be too restrictive and unrealistic to serve as the basis for a general theory of public expenditure. Few if any goods or services satisfy the requirements for pure publicness. Much effort has therefore been devoted to the problem of generalizing the public goods concept and integrating it with other market failure concepts into a more general theory of market failure. At the same time, within modern welfare economics, the crucial market failure concept of externality was greatly refined and further developed to complement and ultimately to merge with the modern theory of public goods.

The third major area of discussion and the last to emerge has been the theory of political provision for public goods. It was finally recognized that the demonstration of market failure to achieve welfare objectives provides no guarantee that government will necessarily do better. As a result of contributions by Downs, Buchanan and Tullock and others, the whole area of collective decision-making is now the subject of intensive interdisciplinary study.

The essays reproduced in this volume were written over the ten-year period 1962 to 1971 and deal in detail with various aspects of these developments in modern public expenditure theory. The first essay provides a general survey of all three major areas distinguished above, with particular emphasis on the framework of welfare objectives. It therefore serves as a general introduction to most of the main topics treated in subsequent chapters. This is followed in the second essay by a discussion of some of the basic methodological problems which have emerged in the interpretation of Musgrave's standard multi-goal framework of welfare objectives.

The third essay provides a general exposition of the theory of a pure public good, including the derivation of optimum conditions, market failure analysis and problems of public provision. The fourth and fifth essays explore in detail the much-discussed relationship between the equity and efficiency aspects of public goods supply.

The sixth essay examines Lindahl's voluntary exchange theory of public goods, which has had a crucial influence on the development of the modern discussion. Buchanan's book *The Demand and Supply of Public Goods* represents the culmination of the Wicksell-Lindahl approach and is reviewed in the seventh essay.

The eighth essay is concerned with the precise characteristics of the public goods concept, the ways in which the concept may be generalized, and its relationship to other concepts in the theory of market failure. The ninth essay explores the concept and policy implications of externalities which emerge as a generalization of the public goods concept from the previous essay.

The tenth and eleventh essays are concerned with the concept and policy implications of merit goods, which, in Musgrave's classic formulation, serve to epitomize those market failure problems which lie beyond the scope of the consumer sovereignty concept.

The final essay applies the theory of public goods to the design of a system of multilevel government.

Public Goods and Public Welfare

# 1. The Welfare Foundations of Public Finance Theory

## 1. Introduction

The Robbinsian revolution in the Anglo-American welfare economics literature of the 1930s has had an impact on public finance theory hardly less profound than its superficially more spectacular contemporary, the Keynesian revolution in employment theory.

As with its Keynesian counterpart, this revolution in welfare economics has been faithfully reflected in the public finance textbooks. During the interwar period, the great English texts in public finance theory, by Pigou[1] and Dalton,[2] were beautifully articulated neoclassical structures based firmly on the utilitarian welfare economics of Edgeworth and Pigou. Since the war, however, all the leading texts, from Mrs. Hicks[3] to Musgrave,[4] have exhibited, in various ways and to a greater or lesser degree, the great Robbinsian uneasiness regarding their welfare foundations.[5]

It might perhaps have been expected that the postwar public finance theorist would turn for support to the New Welfare Economics which was erected on the ruins of Old Welfare by Kaldor, Hicks and others. To many practitioners, however, the extremely complicated New Welfare debate of the 1940s seemed inconclusive, and appeared in any case to rage at a very safe and increasing distance from any conceivable practical application. The public finance theorist thus felt compelled to develop his own "post-Keynesian" policy framework based on "broad goals generally accepted by the community"; Musgrave's "multiple theory of the public household" represents a highly

Reprinted without significant change from *Rivista di diritto finanziario e scienza delle finanze* 24, no. 3 (September 1965): 379–428.

[1] A. C. Pigou, *A Study in Public Finance* (London, 1928).
[2] Hugh Dalton, *Principles of Public Finance* (London, 1922).
[3] U. K. Hicks, *Public Finance* (London and Cambridge, 1947).
[4] R. A. Musgrave, *The Theory of Public Finance* (New York, 1959).
[5] It is interesting to observe, however, that the postwar editions of Pigou and Dalton, whilst incorporating entirely new sections on budgetary policies for full employment, show no trace of the revolution in welfare economics.

formalized synthesis of this general approach.[6] Since 1950, as a result of such developments as the theory of second best, confidence in welfare economics as a possible foundation for policy conclusions has, if anything, receded still further, in spite of important work by such outstanding theorists as Baumol, Musgrave, Samuelson, and Buchanan.

The overwhelming feeling of most public finance specialists is therefore that welfare economics is a purely academic exercise quite remote from the burning policy problems of our turbulent age.[7] This widely-held view has, however, never been examined in detail in the public finance literature; welfare economics and the new welfare politics are frequently dismissed with little more than a wave of the hand.[8] It is the aim of the present article to remedy this omission by setting out and analyzing modern welfare theory from the viewpoint of a public finance theorist, paying particular attention to its operational characteristics and specific implications for public policy.

We shall begin (section 2) with an analysis of the New Welfare debate, in which we shall attempt to clarify some of the fundamental problems involved in devising appropriate goals and criteria for policy. Then (section 3) we shall examine the operational characteristics of the New Welfare Economics paying particular attention to those policy implications of greatest interest to the public finance specialist. In section 4 we shall consider to what extent the welfare theory of public policy can be regarded as providing a truly general economic theory of the public household. Finally (section 5) we shall examine the special contribution of welfare politics. Section 6 contains a brief summary of the main conclusions.

## 2. New Welfare Criteria and Their Problems

### 2.1 Robbins and the Wreck of Utilitarianism

Proceeding on the assumptions of interpersonal comparability of utility, equal capacities for satisfaction, and diminishing marginal

---

[6] Musgrave, chap. 1. An earlier version is to be found in his article "A Multiple Theory of Budget Determination," *Finanzarchiv* 17 (1956–57). In the opening paragraph of this article, Musgrave observes that a normative theory of the public household must overcome the serious difficulty that ". . . certain aspects of the problem lead us into the thin air of welfare economics, where as yet the oxygen has been prone to give out before the peak was scaled."

[7] As leading British public finance specialists Peacock and Wiseman have recently remarked, "There is considerable and growing skepticism among economists as to the value of welfare economics as a basis for economic policy. . . ." See A. T. Peacock and J. Wiseman, *The Growth of Public Expenditure in the United Kingdom* (Princeton, 1961), p. 13.

[8] See, for example, ibid., pp. 12–14.

utility of income, utilitarian welfare economics had suggested that public policies should be such as to raise total utility (with the ultimate aim of maximizing utility for the society as a whole).[9]

In his famous essay, Robbins finally swept this theory from the Anglo-American literature with a twofold argument regarding the impossibility of interpersonal comparisons, and the impropriety and dubious logical status of the value judgments hence and otherwise required.[10] Like Myrdal in his celebrated work published two years earlier,[11] he then went on to suggest that the economist should completely abandon prescriptive theory in order to concentrate attention on positive theory where his comparative advantage is greatest.

Robbins's strictures on interpersonal comparisons were widely accepted. Similarly, it should have been obvious that any prescriptive theory must by definition require value judgments. Such a theory cannot, by its very nature, be "proved" or "disproved" in any usual scientific sense; its whole aim is rather to influence policy, and its "validity" must therefore depend upon the strength of the arguments in terms of general acceptability, community advantage, social justice, etc. which can be mustered in support. That the economist should therefore abandon this slippery field is, however, itself a value judgment, and one which has never been generally accepted in practice by the profession.

## 2.2  The Pareto Criterion

In their search for a more satisfactory alternative, the New Welfare pioneers turned for inspiration to the work of Pareto, who had in effect suggested that public policies should be such as to make at least some members of the community better off without making any others worse off (with the ultimate aim of reaching a situation in which it is no longer possible to make anyone better off without making someone else worse off—the so-called Pareto optimum).[12]

This Pareto criterion appears to offer two very important advantages. To begin with, interpersonal comparisons of utility are not required;

[9] For the classic statements of this approach as applied to public finance theory, see Pigou and Dalton. Long before this utilitarian synthesis of the revenue and expenditure sides of the budget by Pigou and Dalton, the various sacrifice theories of equitable taxation were erected on similar foundations.

[10] Lionel Robbins, *An Essay on the Nature and Significance of Economic Science* (London, 1932), chap. 6.

[11] Gunnar Myrdal, *Vetenskap och politik i nationalekonomien* (Stockholm, 1930); translated from the German edition by Paul Streeten as *The Political Element in the Development of Economic Theory* (London, 1953), chap. 8.

[12] Vilfredo Pareto, *Manuel d'economie politique*, 2nd ed., pp. 617–18.

questions of the form "Would an additional $1 yield more utility to A or B?" do not have to be answered. Furthermore, the basic value judgment would seem to be much more generally acceptable and less controversial than the radically egalitarian Old Welfare approach. Who but the pathological would oppose policies from which they themselves must stand to benefit?

Against these two important advantages, however, there seem to be two weighty disadvantages. In the first place, the Pareto criterion would appear to be highly restrictive of the vital reallocative economic functions of government. Even with the most flexible and imaginative (feasible) burden-sharing arrangements, how many projects could be found which would not leave a substantial minority feeling worse off? Still more important perhaps is the fantastic scope for strategic behavior and consequent preference-revelation problems; any single individual, by disguising his preferences in an attempt to obtain an even greater net benefit, may be able to block projects of significant benefit to all. Hence, as a result of adopting only those policies which satisfy the Pareto criterion, the ultimate goal of a Pareto optimum may clearly remain very far from fully achieved, particularly in a dynamic framework.[13]

Moreover, such a criterion is extremely conservative in matters of income distribution; since no one is ever to be made worse off as a result of public policy, grossly undemocratic and potentially explosive inequalities of income are effectively preserved.

The great welfare debate of the 1940s is best regarded as an attempt to retain the advantages of the Pareto criterion whilst avoiding its disadvantages. In the following two sections, we shall consider these attempts in the fields of allocation and distribution in turn.

## 2.3   Allocative Problems

Of the two evident defects of the Pareto criterion, it was the problem of its allocative restrictiveness which most concerned the New Welfare pioneers. In order to overcome this problem, the hypothetical compensation principle was introduced.

### 2.3.1   The Kaldor criterion

Thus Kaldor in his brilliant early contribution suggested that public policies are desirable if, as a result, "it is *possible* to make some

---

[13] A close approach to a Pareto optimum seems likely only over a very long run in a completely unchanging world, i.e., in a pure comparative statics context.

people better off . . . without making anybody worse off."[14] It must therefore be possible to compensate all losers from a policy, but such compensation need not actually be paid.

An obvious variation on this approach, suggested by Hicks,[15] is that a policy is desirable if it would be impossible in the prepolicy situation to make all individuals at least as well off as they will be as a result of the policy.

The difference between these hypothetical compensation criteria and the Pareto criterion can easily be seen with the help of Graaff's actuality locus diagrams.[16]

Thus in the diagrams of Figure 1, for a community consisting of two individuals A and B, we measure A's level of utility along the $X$ axis, and B's level of utility along the $Y$ axis. Utility points 1 and 2 represent the actual pre- and postpolicy positions; and the corresponding actuality loci $L_1$ and $L_2$ show the positions which could be reached by redistributing income in costless lump-sum fashion from utility points 1 and 2 respectively.

For the Pareto criterion to be satisfied, utility point 2 must lie northeast of utility point 1. Such a policy is shown in Figure 1a. For the Kaldor criterion, however, all that is required is that *actuality locus $L_2$* should pass northeast of utility point 1; whilst, for the Hicks criterion, actuality locus $L_1$ should pass southwest of utility point 2. Thus, in Figure 1b, both the Kaldor and the Hicks criteria are satisfied, even though the Pareto criterion is far from satisfied.

It is therefore clear that the hypothetical compensation criteria are allocatively much less restrictive than the Pareto approach, at least as conventionally interpreted. Since it is no longer necessary that no one actually be made worse off, it should be technically possible to devise a far greater number of allocatively desirable policies, though preference-revelation problems undoubtedly remain. Such criteria should therefore offer a much broader and more reliable path to a Pareto optimum.

At the same time, it is evident that the new principle retains at least one advantage of the Pareto criterion in avoiding the need for interpersonal comparisons. Whether an additional $1 would yield more utility to A or to B is a matter of no concern whatever: all we need to know is whether each could or could not be made better off in one situation than in another.

However, in spite of the greater scope for effective performance of

---

[14] N. Kaldor, "Welfare Propositions of Economics and Interpersonal Comparisons of Utility," *Economic Journal*, 1939, p. 550. If all such policies are implemented, a Pareto optimum will of course be achieved.

[15] J. R. Hicks, "The Valuation of Social Income," *Economica*, 1940, p. 111.

[16] See J. de V. Graaff, *Theoretical Welfare Economics* (Cambridge, 1957), p. 76.

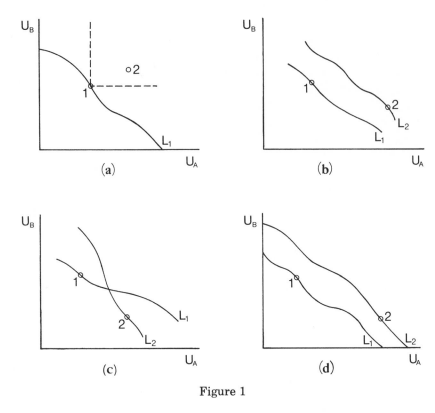

Figure 1

the reallocative economic functions of government allowed by Kaldor-Hicks criteria, it is still far from certain whether, on balance, the arguments in terms of general acceptability, community advantage and social justice are as strong here as in the case of the Pareto approach. In the first place, hypothetical compensation introduces great uncertainty in matters of income distribution; quite drastic, capricious and inequitable redistributions of income could occur. Furthermore, there is a question of rationality and social waste which bears directly on the allocative problems with which we are at present concerned.

### 2.3.2  The Scitovsky double criterion

Thus it was soon pointed out by Scitovsky[17] that the Kaldor (and by implication the Hicks) criterion could lead to a contradiction. If compensation is not actually paid, both the implementation of a policy and its abandonment may simultaneously be desirable. This can be seen from Figure 1c, where $L_2$ passes northeast of utility point 1, whilst

[17] T. Scitovsky, "A Note on Welfare Propositions in Economics," *Review of Economic Studies*, 1941–42.

$L_1$ similarly passes northeast of utility point 2. In this case, the post-policy situation 2 is simultaneously better than and worse than the prepolicy situation 1.

Hence a government systematically adopting all policies satisfying the Kaldor criterion could find itself condemned to continual socially wasteful policy reversals and would soon appear ridiculous. Once these policy implications are properly appreciated, it is clear that the balance of argument may favor the sterile but consistent Pareto criterion.

To avoid this problem, Scitovsky proposed a reformulation of the Kaldor criterion, public policies being desirable only if (a) it would be possible, as a result, to make some people better off without making anyone else worse off, and (b) it would be impossible, by reversing the policy, to make everyone at least as well off. A policy must therefore satisfy *both* the Kaldor and the Hicks criteria. In terms of the diagram, not only must $L_2$ pass northeast of utility point 1, but $L_1$ must simultaneously pass southwest of utility point 2. In this way, all possibility of a contradiction is completely avoided.

The double criterion is clearly allocatively more restrictive than the original Kaldor-Hicks criteria; but it must be remembered that the hypothetical compensation approach is now condemned to silence only in those potentially contradictory cases in which it was so likely to make a complete fool of itself and its practitioners. The reformulated version is therefore likely to command much stronger support than the original Kaldor or Hicks criterion; whilst at the same time the extreme allocative restrictiveness of the Pareto criterion is considerably reduced.

### 2.3.3 The Samuelson criterion

Samuelson[18] has, however, suggested that the Scitovsky criterion is allocatively still not sufficiently demanding. In particular, such a criterion could lead to the adoption of policies which would permanently exclude possibly still better (but on this criterion noncomparable) positions on $L_1$ below the point of intersection with $L_2$.

According to this argument, a policy is unambiguously desirable only if the possibility of reaching still better positions is not thereby excluded. This will be so if, by redistributing in *both* situations, it is impossible to make everyone at least as well off in the prepolicy situation as in the postpolicy situation; or, in terms of the diagram, $L_2$ must lie entirely outside $L_1$. Such a policy is shown in Figure 1d.

This new approach clearly ensures that the possibility of reaching still better positions is not excluded; and, like the Scitovsky, it avoids

[18] P. A. Samuelson, "Evaluation of Real National Income," *Oxford Economic Papers,* 1950, pp. 10–11.

all possibility of a contradiction. Is it, however, a net improvement? The further restriction of the government's reallocative functions could well be considered too heavy a social price to pay in order to avoid all possibility of excluding conceivably superior positions. Thus, although policies may satisfy the Samuelson requirements which cannot satisfy the Pareto criterion, numerous policies satisfying the Pareto criterion will fail to pass the Samuelson test! The Samuelson approach therefore avoids the problems of the hypothetical compensationist criteria, but only at the cost of being allocatively almost as restrictive as Pareto.

## 2.4   Distributional Problems

Throughout the hypothetical compensationist search for an allocatively more satisfactory alternative to the Pareto criterion, the historically basic aim of avoiding interpersonal comparisons of utility remained achieved. All hypothetical compensationist criteria may, however, approve policies involving significant redistribution of income and large losses for some individuals. Since these redistributions are unpredictable and need be in no way related to any widely-held concept of social justice, the general acceptability advantage of the Pareto criterion is apparently largely lost. Why should any individual support a policy from which he may stand to lose substantially, without any guarantee that the major beneficiaries will include the less fortunate sections of the community?[19] The New Welfare literature contains a number of important and ingenious attempts to deal with this problem.

### 2.4.1   The long-run approach

Thus, Hotelling[20] and Hicks[21] have suggested that, if a sufficiently long period is considered, the *sequence* of policies adopted through systematic application of (say) the Kaldor criterion will collectively

---

[19] A number of leading contributors to the New Welfare debate, including Baumol, Reder and Ruggles, have maintained that the hypothetical compensationist criteria do not avoid the need for interpersonal comparisons. This is true only, however, if we employ the term *interpersonal comparisons* in a very special normative sense to mean a comparative evaluation of the welfare significance of the gains and losses of different individuals. This is of course very different from the purely positive question as to whether an additional $1 would yield more utility to A or to B. The confusion here stems from Robbins who uses the term in both senses, at considerable cost in clarity of exposition. It seems preferable to restrict its use to the purely positive sense in which we have employed it above.

[20] H. Hotelling, "The General Welfare in Relation to Problems of Taxation and of Railway and Utility Rates," *Econometrica*, 1938, sec. 4.

[21] J. R. Hicks, "The Rehabilitation of Consumer's Surplus," *Review of Economic Studies*, 1940–41, p. 111.

satisfy the Pareto criterion. The argument is that the redistributive effects of the individual policies will be more or less randomly distributed; the person who loses as a result of one policy is likely to gain from another.

Taking this longer-term view of the hypothetical compensationist criteria, it is apparent that, for each individual, the redistributive gains and losses from particular policies may be expected to cancel one another out. Hence, neglecting the considerably greater distributional *uncertainty* compared with the Pareto criterion, individuals, contemplating ex ante the preparation of a five- or ten-year program as a whole, may be almost as happy distributionally to have the individual policies chosen in accordance with a hypothetical compensationist criterion as with a Pareto criterion.

Against this very considerable ex ante distributional advantage, we would have to recognize that redistributions of income, perhaps involving large losses for some individuals, will in general still occur, especially in the short run as a result of particular policies, but also in any relevant longer period. Thus, in any practical application, the ex ante general acceptability of the long-run hypothetical compensation approach may well give way to a deep and perhaps well justified sense of dissatisfaction on the part of certain minority (or even majority) groups. Furthermore, even from an ex ante point of view, individual attitudes to the distributional uncertainty involved may preclude its general acceptance; and, except in relatively restricted applications, the distributional ethics of a well ordered lottery are anyway not widely accepted in modern civilized communities.

### 2.4.2   Actual compensation

For these reasons it is possible to maintain that all losers should somehow actually be compensated. This is the general position of the "actual compensation" school, which has included such famous practitioners as Baumol, Reder, and Ruggles.[22]

Under this approach, we might seem to be back with the Pareto criterion and its overwhelming allocative disadvantages. As a result of this logical excursion, however, it is possible to see that the Pareto criterion is perhaps allocatively rather less restrictive than the hypothetical compensationists were inclined to imagine. In particular, when we allow for the possibility of package deals and direct compensation, and when we introduce a limited time-dimension (along the

[22] W. J. Baumol, "Community Indifference," *Review of Economic Studies,* 1946–47; M. W. Reder, *Studies in the Theory of Welfare Economics* (New York, 1947); and Nancy Ruggles, "The Welfare Basis of Marginal Cost Pricing," *Review of Economic Studies,* 1949–50.

lines suggested by Hotelling and Hicks) permitting such direct or indirect compensation to take place "within a reasonable period," it is clear that the technical (if not the strategic) causes of the allocative restrictiveness of the Pareto criterion may be significantly reduced (though far from eliminated) at no great distributional cost.

On a more fundamental level, however, neither the long-run arguments of Hotelling and Hicks, nor the actual compensation approach is distributionally satisfactory. Precisely where the redistributive effects of particular policies do average out over time, or where the direct and indirect compensations arranged are most nearly complete, grossly undemocratic and potentially explosive maldistributions of income are most effectively preserved and perpetuated. Neither approach therefore contributes anything at all to avoiding the serious charge that Paretian criteria may be dangerously conservative in matters of income distribution.

### 2.4.3  Little's criterion

For this reason, it is of particular interest to consider Little's suggestion that the basic welfare criterion should include an explicit reference to income distribution.[23] More specifically, he has suggested that "an economic change is desirable . . . if it causes a good redistribution of wealth, and if the potential losers could not profitably bribe the potential gainers to oppose it – always assuming that no still better change is therefore prejudiced."[24] Thus, instead of all policies causing significant redistributions being excluded (as under the actual compensation approach), those allocatively desirable policies which cause "good" redistributions will be permitted. At the same time, the more arbitrary and inequitable redistributions permitted by the hypothetical compensationist criteria will be prevented; either the policy must be abandoned or compensation must be paid.

At first glance this approach would appear to be a very sensible distributional compromise between the hypothetical compensationist and Paretian criteria. But how is a "good" redistribution to be defined?

If, for example, we define a "good" redistribution as one leading to greater equality, Little's criterion, however just and socially beneficial, will be almost as controversial as the Old Welfare approach. Indeed, in some societies, it may be that the only definition of a "good" redistribution which will command very general short-run acceptance will be one which at least allows no absolute losses; and with this we

---

[23] I. M. D. Little, *A Critique of Welfare Economics* (Oxford, 1957), p. 96.
[24] Ibid., p. 109.

are back to Pareto! Alternatively, if we leave the question of definition unanswered, Little's approach, whilst superficially attractive, turns out on closer examination to be merely a verbal smokescreen covering basic disagreements which would inevitably erupt into open conflict if an attempt was ever made actually to apply the criterion. Finally, if the interpretation of "good" and "bad" redistributions is to be left to the "appropriate authority," Little's formulation reduces to the next and much more common approach.

### 2.4.4   The economic aspect approach

According to this approach the economist *qua* economist cannot legitimately or usefully pronounce upon questions of income distribution. Here, more than anywhere else, so the argument runs, the recommendations of the economist impinge crucially upon "non-economic" and highly controversial aspects of social experience, and his claims to unique authority are therefore at their most feeble. The distributional problems we have been discussing may be regarded as providing a conclusive demonstration of this point.

Elements of this approach can be found in the works of almost all hypothetical compensationists. In our earlier discussion, we have treated their tests as sufficient criteria for desirable public policies; and it is certainly true that most of the contributors frequently slipped over into this unconditional terminology. In their more careful moments, however, they explicitly restricted their discussions to the conditions for (or definition of) an increase in the following magnitudes: "aggregate real income," "physical productivity" or "production of wealth" (Kaldor); "real social income" or "productive efficiency" (Hicks); and "potential real income" (Samuelson). By restricting welfare theory to the economic, i.e. allocative (and less controversial), aspects of public policy, it was hoped to avoid distributional problems altogether.[25]

Consistently restricted in this way, New Welfare Economics would clearly be much less controversial and would probably be quite widely accepted. The additional support would, however, be of little real significance, since the satisfaction of New Welfare criteria would no longer be either sufficient or necessary for desirability. To all intents and purposes New Welfare Economics would have abandoned the field of fully fledged prescriptive theory at the risk of becoming a

---

[25] Failure on the part of the hypothetical compensationists consistently to observe this self-denying ordinance undoubtedly accounts for much of the confusion which has attended the welfare debate.

dangerously slippery and misleading exercise in persuasive definitions.[26]

To the public finance theorist, it is of particular interest to observe that the sociopolitical theory of Wicksell and Lindahl provides an unusually fine example of the economic aspect approach as applied to a Pareto criterion. Thus, recognizing the distributional conservatism of the Pareto criterion, both Wicksell and Lindahl insist on attaching important distributional ("sociopolitical") qualifications to their otherwise essentially Paretian theories of the budget. In particular, these latter theories are only to be applied in the presence of a just distribution of property and income. They must therefore remain entirely "hypothetical," since the determination of a just distribution is beyond the competence of the public finance theorist.[27]

### 2.4.5  The social welfare function

Since policies to improve "allocation" also impinge on "noneconomic" aspects of social experience and may be quite controversial, it is clearly only a short step from the economic aspect position to complete acceptance of the "given ends" approach advocated by Robbins, according to which the economist should completely abandon the field of prescriptive theory. This approach was in fact soon formalized in the "social welfare function" theory of Bergson[28] and Samuelson,[29] under which the social welfare function is to be taken as given to the economist by some "appropriate authority." Practitioners of this approach tend, however, to assume that the social welfare function will necessarily exhibit, for example, Paretian characteristics. Thus the irresistible urge to make policy pronouncements has effectively overwhelmed the "given ends" approach; and compensationist policies are presented in the intellectually respectable *wertfrei* garments of the Robbins school. Only the question of distribution is usually left to the "appropriate authority," and like Little's, the theory therefore reduces in practice to yet another (perhaps rather less misleading) variant of the economic aspect approach.

[26] An important part of Little's brilliant work is devoted to the discussion and illustration of this problem; though, as we have seen, his own solution to it is more apparent than real. The definitive analysis of the dangers of persuasive definitions and implicit value judgments in the much wider setting of the history of economic thought is that of Myrdal.

[27] For detailed references and further discussion of the Wicksell-Lindahl approach, see secs. 5.1 and 5.2 below.

[28] A. Bergson, "A Reformulation of Certain Aspects of Welfare Economics," *Quarterly Journal of Economics,* 1937–38.

[29] P. A. Samuelson, *Foundations of Economic Analysis* (Cambridge, Mass., 1947), chap. 8.

## 3.   Applied Welfare Economics and Public Finance Theory

In spite of the very important allocative and distributional problems we have just discussed, it follows from the very nature of prescriptive theory that any of the welfare criteria set out in the preceding section could provide the cornerstone of a *logically* sound prescriptive theory of public policy. But can such criteria ever be applied? Can they really be translated into detailed recommendations for the sort of society we are likely to have to deal with? And can the resulting theory be regarded as a truly general theory of the public household? Welfare economists, like their critics, have been well aware of these crucial operational problems and have made a number of important attempts to deal with them.

### 3.1   Conventional Optimum Conditions Analysis and Its Applications

Thus, for example, a very large and important part of the welfare literature has been devoted to the derivation and discussion of the so-called optimum conditions of production and exchange.

#### 3.1.1   The nature and interpretation of the optimum conditions

For a given (and usually very simple) society, these conditions describe the detailed economic characteristics of a Pareto optimum, i.e. of a situation in which it would be impossible, by reallocating resources, to make any individual better off without making someone else worse off. Thus, taking the simplest case of two individuals (A and B), two commodities (X and Y), and two factors (K and L), and making the usual convexity assumptions, the following three conditions can be distinguished:[30]

(a) An *exchange condition*, requiring that the marginal rate of substitution in consumption between the two commodities should be the same for both individuals, i.e.

$$MRS \frac{A}{XY} = MRS \frac{B}{XY}$$

[30] For an elegant geometrical derivation of these conditions, see F. M. Bator, "The Simple Analytics of Welfare Maximisation," *American Economic Review*, 1957. Also Little, chaps. 8 and 9.

(*b*) A *production condition,* requiring that the marginal rate of substitution in production between the two factors should be the same for both commodities, i.e.

$$MRS \, \frac{X}{KL} = MRS \, \frac{Y}{KL}$$

(*c*) An *overall condition,* requiring that the common marginal rate of substitution in consumption between the two commodities should equal the marginal rate of transformation between them, i.e.

$$MRS \, \frac{A}{XY} = MRS \, \frac{B}{XY} = MT \, _{XY}$$

These three conditions are individually necessary and collectively sufficient for the attainment of a Pareto optimum. For a given society there will, however, be a different Pareto optimum for every conceivable distribution of welfare and hence of factor ownership; the locus of all such Pareto-optimal points is known as a utility possibility function.

The crucial role of optimum conditions analysis in welfare economics is easily seen when it is remembered that the achievement of a Pareto optimum is the ultimate aim of hypothetical and actual compensationists alike. Optimum conditions analysis is therefore to be regarded as an attempt to transform this basic welfare goal into a set of detailed operational requirements.

At the same time, however, it must not be forgotten that the precise welfare status of the Pareto optimum varies significantly under the different approaches. Thus it is only for a thoroughgoing hypothetical compensationist that the achievement of a Pareto optimum may be regarded as necessary and sufficient for maximum welfare; for the other major schools with their various distributional qualifications it is necessary but certainly not sufficient. The interpretation of the welfare significance of the optimum conditions must therefore vary accordingly.

With these distributional reservations, however, we can conclude that public policy should be directed towards the simultaneous satisfaction of the optimum conditions.

### 3.1.2 Optimum conditions analysis and the market mechanism

The precise scope for public policy will, however, depend upon the extent to which these detailed requirements can be met through the market mechanism. In terms of familiar market variables, and assuming no external economies or diseconomies, the optimum conditions set out above require uniform product and factor prices equal (or, in the special case of perfectly inelastic factor supplies, proportional) to marginal costs and marginal value products respectively.[31] Thus it is easy to see that decentralized market institutions of the sort embodied in the traditional concept of perfect competition would be quite capable of ensuring that all these optimum conditions are fully satisfied.[32] Ignoring distributional problems, the economic functions of government should here be confined to enforcement of contracts and similar activities associated with the preservation of the existing "ideal" institutions.

Where the market exhibits monopoly elements, however, it is equally obvious that the necessary price-cost-product relationships can in general no longer be established. It is therefore a legitimate economic function of government to correct the resulting disturbances to the optimum conditions. A special but particularly interesting and important case here is the nonconvexity introduced by decreasing cost phenomena, which renders competitive markets inefficient and at the same time promotes the growth of monopoly elements.[33]

Further problems arise where there are external economies or diseconomies associated with the production or consumption of certain goods.[34] In such cases it is impossible for private economic units, through ordinary private pricing, to appropriate the full social benefits (or be charged the full social costs) arising directly from their activities. As a result a sharp distinction must be drawn between *private* and *social* marginal costs, products and benefits; and the market requirements for a Pareto optimum must now be interpreted strictly in terms of the relevant social magnitudes. Since competitive markets can only establish the corresponding private relationships, the correction of the resulting disturbances to the optimum conditions must be regarded as another legitimate economic function of government.[35]

---

[31] For a detailed demonstration, see Bator and Little.

[32] As Bator rightly remarks (p. 31), "this 'duality' theorem is the kernel of modern welfare economics."

[33] For an excellent discussion of this particular nonconvexity, see Bator, pp. 46–53.

[34] For a very clear statement of the modern external economies and diseconomies doctrine, see F. M. Bator, "The Anatomy of Market Failure," *Quarterly Journal of Economics*, 1958, sec. 2. Further technical refinements can be found in J. M. Buchanan and W. C. Stubblebine, "Externality," *Economica*, 1962. See also chap. 9 below.

[35] It is often said that the output of goods exhibiting external economies should be encouraged, whilst that of goods exhibiting external diseconomies should be discouraged. Such statements should not, however, be interpreted too literally. Thus, in the case of goods exhibiting reciprocal external economies (e.g., where individual A's consumption benefits B and vice versa), it has recently been shown that total output of the product may be overexpanded under the market mechanism. See J. M. Buchanan and M. Z. Kafoglis, "A Note on Public Goods Supply," *American Economic Review*, 1963, sec. 2. This is not, however, the fundamental and damaging criticism of the external economies

### 3.1.3   Applications to public finance theory

From the point of view of the public finance specialist, the usefulness of this attempt to translate the rather vague goals and criteria of theoretical welfare economics into operational standards and detailed recommendations can perhaps best be seen by considering its specific implications for two policy areas of particular interest in public finance, namely pricing policy of nationalized industries and taxation policy. These implications were seen very early, analysed with considerable rigour and discussed at great length by the New Welfare theorists, and it is therefore mainly to them that modern Anglo-American public finance theory owes some of its most important and best-known policy conclusions.[36]

**3.1.3.1** *Pricing policy of nationalized industries.*[37]   Thus, for a world with no external economies or diseconomies, it is an immediate implication of optimum conditions analysis that, if there is perfect competition in the private sector, a nationalized industry should charge that uniform marginal cost price which will equate supply and demand for its product. In the very special case where factor supplies are perfectly inelastic and there are equal degrees of monopoly in private product markets, the nationalized industry should ensure that its price-marginal cost ratio is equal to that obtaining in the private sector.

Where, however, there are imperfections of competition or external economies and diseconomies in the private sector, some optimum conditions will already be disturbed. Only if these disturbances are duly corrected by other means does it still follow that the above pricing policies should necessarily be adopted. Again, if there are external

---

doctrine that it might at first appear. All that is required to rescue the familiar commonsense statement is the recognition that external economies must be interpreted in a relative sense. Thus, if the spillover from A on to B is sufficiently greater than that from B on to A, it is apparent that B's consumption will tend to be relatively overexpanded. Then, assuming that A's consumption is relatively complementary with purely private goods, it is obvious that efficiency may well demand a reduction in total output of the goods exhibiting the external economies and an expansion of the output of purely private goods. A similar situation may arise where there are several different goods exhibiting (nonreciprocal) external economies.

On the most fundamental theoretical level, these phenomena are clearly no more significant for the basic doctrine than the equally important fact that with only one good exhibiting (nonreciprocal) external economies, Pareto efficiency may well require an absolute expansion of the output of relatively complementary private products.

[36] Indeed, Hotelling's pioneering contribution to New Welfare theory was made precisely in the context of an analysis of these public finance problems.

[37] For a useful survey of the lively debate on this subject sparked off by Hotelling's classic article, see Nancy Ruggles, "Recent Developments in the Theory of Marginal Cost Pricing," *Review of Economic Studies,* 1949–50.

economies or diseconomies associated with the nationalized product, marginal social cost-benefit equality must be insisted upon.

In the classic case of a nationalized decreasing cost industry, Pareto-efficient uniform pricing may clearly involve substantial losses. If multiple pricing is impossible, taxation must be employed to cover these losses. Problems of taxation policy therefore arise.

**3.1.3.2** *Taxation policy*.[38] If all optimum conditions are satisfied in the pretax situation, it is an obvious implication of optimum conditions analysis that if revenue must be raised (say to finance the deficit of a nationalized decreasing cost industry) it should be raised in such a way as to leave the optimum conditions undisturbed.

Where factor supplies are elastic, it is apparent that the only taxes which will satisfy this requirement are lump-sum taxes such as poll taxes and taxes on factor rents. Thus, for example, if the supply of effort is elastic, proportional general taxes, such as proportional income and expenditure taxes and a general sales tax, all disturb the leisure-commodity optima by reducing the net real wage below the marginal productivity of labor. An equal revenue excise must also distort, but may be either better or worse than the various general taxes depending upon the precise nature of the excise. With minor modifications, similar arguments apply in the case of an elastic supply of savings or risk-taking.

Only in the special case where factor supplies are perfectly inelastic is the range of nondistorting taxes significantly wider. Here all general taxes (including proportional and progressive income, capital and expenditure taxes, and a general sales tax) will leave the optimum conditions undisturbed.

Where, however, not all optimum conditions are satisfied in the pretax situation, tax policy may legitimately be used to correct the disturbances. In such cases optimum conditions analysis implies that excise taxes with the right distorting effects will be superior not only to the various general taxes but even to a lump-sum tax.

## 3.2 The General Theory of Second Best

We have seen in section 3.1 that conventional optimum conditions analysis enables us to take at least a few uncertain steps in the direc-

---

[38] The New Welfare debate on taxation policy followed very similar lines to that on pricing policy and Hotelling's article was again an important stimulus. This debate has been well summarized in David Walker, "The Direct-Indirect Tax Problem — Fifteen Years of Controversy," *Public Finance/Finances Publiques*, 1955.

tion of establishing operational standards and making detailed recommendations for public policy. In recent years, however, the confidence of New Welfare theorists in optimum conditions analysis as the road to applied welfare economics has been seriously undermined by the development of the general theory of second best.

### 3.2.1  Optimum conditions analysis and feasibility considerations

It had always been evident that optimum conditions analysis takes absolutely no account of feasibility considerations of either an administrative or political character, and admits only those "natural" constraints embodied in relatively simple production functions. Such feasibility considerations are, moreover, obviously of the greatest importance in any actual society, and frequently *prevent* the satisfaction of one or more optimum conditions.

It appears to have been quite widely assumed, however, at least implicitly, that the desirability of satisfying one optimum condition is in practice somehow independent of the satisfaction of all other conditions; a situation in which more optimum conditions are satisfied is superior to one in which fewer are satisfied. According to this view, the welfare significance of optimum conditions analysis is substantially unaffected by feasibility considerations. Policies to satisfy particular optimum conditions can be implemented with confidence until the maximum number of conditions is satisfied. By implication, such a situation can properly be regarded as constituting a second best.

### 3.2.2  The general theory of second best

Bringing together and generalizing from some of the more careful obiter dicta on this subject from tariff and tax policy discussions, Lipsey and Lancaster[39] have shown that these implicit assumptions are in general completely unjustified. Indeed they are able to establish a "General Theorem of the Second Best" according to which "if there is introduced into a general equilibrium system a constraint which prevents the attainment of one of the Paretian conditions, the other Paretian conditions, although still attainable, are, in general, no longer desirable,"[40] i.e. "if one of the Paretian optimum conditions cannot be fulfilled a second best optimum is achieved only by departing from all other optimum conditions."[41]

From this general theorem follows an important negative corollary

[39] R. G. Lipsey and K. Lancaster, "The General Theory of Second Best," *Review of Economic Studies*, 1956–57.
[40] Ibid., p. 11.
[41] Ibid., p. 12.

that "there is no a priori way to judge between various situations in which some of the Paretian optimum conditions are fulfilled while others are not. Specifically, it is not true that a situation in which more, but not all, of the optimum conditions are fulfilled is necessarily, or is even likely to be, superior to a situation in which fewer are fulfilled."[42]

Since feasibility constraints are of such obvious importance in practice, optimum conditions analysis thus appears to be totally irrelevant to the design of a practicable (second best) policy program.

However, it is clear from the Lipsey and Lancaster discussion that the second best program is likely to be extremely complicated and will in general require a remarkable amount of detailed information.

It has therefore seemed to many theorists that, unless optimum conditions analysis can somehow be rehabilitated, all hope of ever applying welfare criteria must be abandoned.[43]

### 3.2.3 An illustration from public finance theory

For the public finance theorist, the propositions of the general theory of second best can readily be illustrated from the field of taxation policy. Thus in section 3.1.3.2 above we saw that, if all optimum conditions are satisfied in the pretax situation and the supply of effort is elastic, the only nondistorting taxes are those in lump-sum form. All other taxes disturb at least the leisure-commodity optima. It is generally recognized, however, that an administratively practicable lump-sum tax (such as a poll tax) is likely to be so inequitable as to be politically unacceptable, whilst an equitable lump-sum tax (levied, say, according to earning capacity) is likely to be administratively impracticable. It is therefore only realistic to concede that feasible taxation necessarily involves the disturbance of at least one set of optimum conditions.

In this situation, it might be (and has often been) suggested on the basis of optimum conditions analysis that the second best will be a general tax (such as an income, capital, expenditure or sales tax) disturbing only the leisure-commodity optima, rather than a system of excises which also disturbs commodity-commodity optima. From the negative corollary, however, it follows that this conclusion is in general completely unfounded; a tax disturbing fewer optimum conditions is not necessarily superior to one disturbing more. The answer in any particular case will depend upon the relationships of relative comple-

[42] Ibid., pp. 11–12.
[43] See, for example, E. J. Mishan, "Second Thoughts on Second Best," *Oxford Economic Papers*, 1962.

mentarity and substitutability between leisure and the taxed commodities.

Regarding the general characteristics of a second-best tax, it follows from the general theorem that such a tax must disturb all optimum conditions. More specifically we can say that a second-best tax
will take the form of a system of unequal excises such that (in the
present case) the highest rates of tax are imposed on leisure-comple-
ments (entertainments, television sets, furs, jewelry, etc.) and the
lowest rates on leisure-substitutes (repair and maintenance services,
time-saving consumer durables, etc.).[44]

It is obvious, however, that the design of a second-best tax will require an extraordinary amount of detailed information regarding complementarity and substitutability relationships. Moreover, the resulting tax is likely to be extremely complicated, e.g., different rates
of excise will usually be necessary on the same commodity when consumed by different people. Such a tax seems likely to be no more feasible administratively and politically than a lump-sum tax!

Instead of the sort of retreat to optimum conditions policies advocated by Mishan, it would, however, seem possible in some cases to
recommend policies representing at least some improvement on the
optimum conditions alternative. Thus, in our present tax-policy example, a set of excises with the highest rates on entertainments,
television sets, furs, jewelry, etc. and the lowest rates on repair and
maintenance services and time-saving consumer durables—but uniform as between different individuals—may frequently represent a
considerable and perfectly feasible improvement on the general income, expenditure or sales tax suggested by a naive application of
optimum conditions analysis.

In certain other cases, optimum conditions analysis may still be
valid and useful. Thus, in the case of two nationalized industries (X
and Y) in close competition, the satisfaction of the X–Y optimum
(through the adoption of a common pricing policy in relation to marginal cost) may clearly be desirable irrespective of the state of the relevant public-private relationships if the elasticity of substitution between public and private products is very low.

As a result of the general theory of second best, it must, however,
be recognized that the problem of translating welfare goals and criteria
into detailed recommendations is vastly more difficult than optimum

---

[44] For the original and definitive demonstration of this point, see W. J. Corlett and D. C.
Hague, "Complementarity and the Excess Burden of Taxation," *Review of Economic
Studies,* 1953–54.

conditions analysis, even with the necessary distributional reservations, might appear to suggest.[45,46]

## 3.3 Public Goods and the New Optimum Conditions Analysis

The decline of confidence, among New Welfare theorists, in the usefulness of optimum conditions analysis as a road to applied welfare economics has coincided somewhat ironically with a growing interest on the part of public finance theorists stimulated by the work of Samuelson and Musgrave in the pure theory of public expenditure.[47]

Basing his theory on the Continental concept of a "public good" which must be consumed in equal amounts by all, Samuelson reaches two extremely important conclusions.

Thus, making the usual convexity assumptions, he is able to show both algebraically and geometrically that the familiar Pareto-optimum condition requiring equality between marginal rates of substitution and marginal rates of transformation no longer holds. Where in the case of two private goods (X and Y) and two individuals (A and B) the condition was

$$MRS_{XY}^{A} = MRS_{XY}^{B} = MT_{XY},$$

what is now required, where one of the two goods is public, is equality between the marginal rate of transformation and the sum of the marginal rates of substitution, i.e.

[45] The literature on the appropriate pricing policy for a nationalized decreasing cost industry provides a further convincing demonstration of this conclusion. Thus, if multiple pricing is not feasible, the absence of a workable criterion for indivisible investment decisions in an uncertain world has been held to justify a return to the inefficient average cost pricing policy which Hotelling in his pioneering contribution had apparently completely discredited! For an excellent critical summary of the pricing policy debate, paying particular attention to this and other related second-best problems, and reaching the depressing "third-best" average cost pricing conclusion, see Little, chap. 11.

[46] It is important to recognize that second-best theory also undermines the logical foundations of such well known techniques of applied welfare economics as cost-benefit ("systems") analysis and index numbers, both of which are operational offshoots of optimum conditions analysis relying for their strict welfare significance (such as it is) upon the validity of the optimum conditions approach.

[47] P. A. Samuelson, "The Pure Theory of Public Expenditure," *Review of Economics and Statistics,* 1954; "Diagrammatic Exposition of a Theory of Public Expenditure," *Review of Economics and Statistics,* 1955; and "Aspects of Public Expenditure Theories," *Review of Economics and Statistics,* 1958; and R. A. Musgrave, especially chap. 1, sec. B and chap. 4, secs. C and D. For a more detailed account of the work of Samuelson and Musgrave, see chaps. 3, 4, and 8 below.

$$MRS_{XY}^{A} + MRS_{XY}^{B} = MT_{XY}.$$

As a result of this striking change in the optimum conditions, it is no longer possible to achieve a Pareto optimum through the decentralized pricing system of a competitive market. More specifically, charging individuals a uniform price equal to the marginal cost of producing a unit of the good (or even "average marginal cost" per individual served by that unit) is not efficient in the case of public goods. What is needed is a highly idealized system of multiple pricing, which no decentralized market mechanism can be expected to provide.

Even with ideal multiple pricing, however, Samuelson emphasizes that the market mechanism will still fail. Since a public good not only can but must be consumed equally by all, those who do not pay cannot be excluded from the benefit. The market will therefore fail because individuals will refuse to contribute and their true preferences will not be revealed.

It is therefore in somehow promoting adequate provision of these public goods that at least some of the proper economic functions of government are to be found.

On closer analysis, it can be shown that Samuelson's public good in fact exhibits, to an extreme degree, special forms of two conceptually quite distinct and independent characteristics, namely joint supply and external economies. Thus it is joint supply which alone accounts for the striking change in the familiar Pareto-optimum conditions and the consequent need for multiple pricing demonstrated by his analysis.[48] It is extreme external economies (complete impossibility of exclusion), however, which account for the total failure of the market mechanism to ensure revelation of true preferences.

It is also apparent that few goods exhibit these special forms of joint supply or external economies to the extreme degree postulated by Samuelson. In fact, however, as Samuelson himself has indicated, the presence of elements of either characteristic is all that is required to support his general conclusions. Thus in the case of elements of jointness, where a given unit of a good, once produced, can be made at least partially available, though possibly in varying degrees, to more than one individual, it is easy to show that a similar strikingly Samuelsonian optimum condition still holds. Similarly, in the case of a good

---

[48] In their otherwise very useful recent contribution to the refinement of the modern external economies and diseconomies doctrine, Buchanan and Stubblebine make no attempt to distinguish between external economies and Samuelsonian joint supply. As a result they appear to demonstrate that the Samuelsonian optimum conditions result from the existence of external economies.

exhibiting external economies (but where exclusion may nevertheless be far from completely impossible), preference revelation problems still arise. A whole host of "goods" including national defense, public health schemes, education, flood control measures, television and radio services, roads, bridges, etc. can be found which will satisfy these less demanding requirements.

In this way then Samuelson has been able to develop a new optimum conditions analysis of direct and immediate interest to the public finance theorist. His concept of a public good, although clearly an extreme case, provides a graphic illustration of compound market failure, whilst at the same time concentrating attention on the important economic fact that some of the best examples of goods exhibiting jointness characteristics also pose extremely difficult price-exclusion problems. The new optimum conditions analysis is, however, no less vulnerable than the conventional analysis to the general theory of second best; Samuelson, for example, recognizes clearly that an ideal solution to the multiple-pricing and preference-revelation problems highlighted by his analysis may well be politically impossible. We shall return to this subject in section 5 below.

## 4. Welfare Economics and a General Economic Theory of the Public Household

The public finance specialist accustomed to working with his own familiar post-Keynesian policy framework may well object that the welfare theory of public policy set out in the preceding section completely ignores some of the most important modern economic functions of government. How can such an academic exercise seriously be put forward as a general economic theory of the public household?

The post-Keynesian approach typically postulates four broad goals "generally accepted by enlightened modern societies," namely equity (including reasonable equality of income and equal treatment for equals), perfect allocation of resources, economic stability (in all its aspects), and an optimum rate of economic growth. Using well known Pigovian and Keynesian theoretical arguments as well as empirical evidence, it is then a relatively simple matter to establish at least a prima facie case for supposing that, in the absence of government intervention, the market mechanism will be completely incapable of ensuring anything approaching continuous full attainment of any of these goals. The promotion of each of the post-Keynesian goals is therefore a legitimate economic function of government. A highly formalized version of this approach is to be found in the first chapter of Musgrave's great work *The Theory of Public Finance,* where the promotion of each goal (with the exception of growth) is assigned heuristically to a different "branch" of the "fiscal department" of the "public household."

Of these post-Keynesian functions, it might appear that welfare theory completely ignores stability and growth, and provides a most unsatisfactory treatment of distribution. This impression seems to be rather widespread amongst public finance specialists, and has undoubtedly contributed significantly to the view that welfare economics is a purely academic exercise quite remote from the burning policy issues of the twentieth century.

## 4.1   Welfare Goals and Post-Keynesian Goals

It is important to recognize, however, that the modern goals of stability and growth are fundamentally questions of allocation and distribution.

Thus involuntary unemployment can quite properly be regarded as essentially a drastic disturbance of work-leisure optima; and, since Keynes, it has been generally agreed that suitable expansionary fiscal and monetary policies can easily be devised which will substantially eliminate the unemployment without loss to the rest of the community, i.e. that anti-slump policies can readily satisfy even the demanding Pareto criterion, at least until high levels of employment are restored.[49] It is also clear that deflationary disturbances have particularly significant and pernicious redistributive effects.

Similarly, the essential welfare features of inflation are the inefficiencies due to speculation and bottlenecks, and the redistributions away from fixed income recipients. It is certainly true that anti-inflationary measures satisfying a Pareto (or even a Kaldor) criterion are much more difficult to devise and implement, but it is generally agreed that such policies do nevertheless exist.

The important effects of economic instability on the balance of payments are likewise significant only for the national and international inefficiencies and maldistributions caused by the necessary measures of control.

Even the great modern policy preoccupation of economic growth is

---

[49] This point is clearly recognized in Reder's classic study of welfare economics. His largely successful attempt to reconcile full employment policy with welfare theory must be accounted a major contribution to New Welfare Economics. See M. W. Reder, pt. 3.

basically a matter of allocation and distribution. Thus, on the one hand, questions of allocation are obviously involved, notably between consumption and investment goods industries, between different types of investment including investment in research and in the development of new products and processes, and between relatively expanding and declining industries. Likewise it is evident that important questions of distribution between present and future generations are also involved. A suboptimal rate of growth thus implies the disturbance of certain optimum conditions which are of strategic importance in the growth process, and/or that insufficient weight is being given to the preferences of future generations.

However, even if it is conceded that the allocative aspects of stability and growth can be dealt with quite adequately within the framework provided by New Welfare goals and criteria, it might still be argued that the extremely important distributional aspects, and indeed the whole post-Keynesian concept of an equitable income distribution, easily become lost in the scholastic refinements of modern welfare theory.

From our earlier discussion in section 2.4 above, it is evident that the treatment of distribution in modern welfare theory is far from fully satisfactory. It may be doubted, however, whether the post-Keynesian approach really advances the discussion. In particular, there is probably very little real agreement in most societies regarding the meaning to be attached to a goal of equity.[50] Similarly, pious platitudes on the distributional evils of inflation frequently obscure a profound indifference to the plight of the less fortunate minority; large and better-protected sections of the community are unwilling either to cooperate in anti-inflationary action or to support adequate protective measures (such as index ties) for fixed income groups. The same problem of public apathy is hardly less important in the case of unemployment.[51]

Thus the post-Keynesian approach of postulating arbitrary distributional goals alleged to be generally accepted by the community only obscures the fundamental distributional problems pointed up by our

---

[50] And this is true not only of the vertical equity concept of reasonable equality, but also of the horizontal equity concept of equal treatment for equals.

Not all exponents of the post-Keynesian approach gloss over these problems. Thus, for example, Musgrave goes to some trouble to stress the difficulties associated with the concept of a proper state of distribution. However, even he is inclined to treat the concept of horizontal equity as a logical problem rather than as a serious problem of conflicting interests. See his chap. 8.

[51] Even the postwar rise of rapid economic growth to preeminence among the goals of economic policy in advanced countries must to some extent be viewed in terms of the struggle by the higher income groups to modify the redistributive policies of the welfare state by securing concessions for private savings and investment.

earlier welfare discussion. The treatment of distribution can therefore hardly be regarded as adequate under either approach.[52]

## 4.2 The Causes of Market Inefficiency

Having demonstrated the fundamental identity of welfare goals and post-Keynesian goals, it is tempting to ask whether it may not be possible to achieve a similar integration of the Pigovian, Keynesian and Samuelsonian theories of why, in the absence of government, the market mechanism is incapable of achieving these policy goals.[53,54]

### 4.2.1 Nonappropriability

According to Samuelson, as we have seen, the basic cause of market inefficiency is the existence of "public goods," which exhibit special forms of two distinct and independent characteristics, namely joint supply and external economies.

It is not difficult to see, however, that Samuelsonian joint supply (or indivisibility of product) accounts for a special but very important category of decreasing cost problems, including the classic example of a bridge. Once a given unit of such a good has been produced to serve one individual, the cost of making that same unit available to other individuals falls to zero, i.e. we have sharply decreasing costs.

Furthermore, it is possible to trace all decreasing cost problems and all types of external economies and diseconomies to a common source in nonappropriability,[55] which we may define as that property of a good which makes it impossible for private economic units, through ordinary private pricing, to appropriate the full social benefits (or be charged the full social costs) arising from their production or consumption of that good. To account for external economies in the narrow modern sense, these benefits need only be interpreted quite narrowly in terms of use or enjoyment of the product itself. Interpreting "full social benefits" in the widest sense, however, it is clear that nonappropriability is also a crucial factor in all decreasing cost problems. In particular, if all other optimum conditions are already satisfied, a decreasing cost

---

[52] To the extent that some consensus on distributional matters does exist, even the Pareto criterion can be interpreted as approving the required redistributions. No separate distributional goal is therefore necessary. See also chap. 5, sec. 2 below.

[53] Since the treatment of distribution is unsatisfactory in modern welfare theory and the post-Keynesian alternative alike, we shall confine our attention to the allocative aspects of the various goals.

[54] The pioneering contribution to this subject is that of W. J. Baumol, *Welfare Economics and the Theory of the State* (Cambridge, Mass., 1952). For a more detailed development of some of the following arguments, see chap. 8, sec. 4.2 in this volume.

[55] The term derives from Sidgwick. See Henry Sidgwick, *Principles of Political Economy*, (London, 1883), pp. 406–7. Musgrave's concept of "impossibility of exclusion" is fundamentally identical.

monopolist, by lowering his price from (say) average cost to marginal cost, could provide *resource-allocation benefits,* in the sense that, as a result of his action, it would be possible to make some people better off without making anyone else worse off. Unless price discrimination is feasible, the monopolist could not, however, charge for these benefits, and would merely incur large losses. Pareto-efficient pricing cannot therefore be expected. It is interesting to observe that the same sort of argument can be applied to all problems of imperfect competition and not only to those involving decreasing costs.

In the same way, nonappropriability may also be regarded as accounting to a considerable extent for problems of economic instability. Thus, in a situation of unemployment, economic units increasing consumption- or investment-spending, or accepting a substantial money-wage cut, can by no means appropriate through private pricing the full social benefits in the form of multiplier and real balance effects on the incomes and profits of other economic units. With the signs changed, a similar argument applies to the inflation case, where again the benefits from reduced inefficiencies of all sorts are not fully appropriable.

Likewise in the case of suboptimal economic growth, the full benefits in terms of rising real incomes resulting from growth-promoting behavior, such as thrift, risk-bearing, and dividend- and wage-restraint, are seldom likely to be fully appropriable from the point of view of the economic unit which must bear the full cost of such behavior.

Competitive depreciation and tariff and export-subsidy wars, including beggar-my-neighbor remedies for unemployment, provide still further examples of cases in which socially responsible behavior fails to receive anything like its just reward.

The fundamental role of nonappropriability in a general theory of market failure is therefore clear: domestic and international misallocation of resources, economic instability and suboptimal rates of growth all stem to an important extent from nonappropriability problems.

### 4.2.2 Numbers

We have seen that nonappropriability prevents private economic units from levying adequate charges for the benefits flowing from their production or consumption of certain goods, and that, as a result, the price mechanism cannot automatically ensure continuous full achievement of even the purely allocative aspects of conventional welfare goals. Market-type agreements may, however, nevertheless be concluded to eliminate many inefficiencies of nonappropriability origin.

Thus, as long as such inefficiencies remain, it must be possible, at least in principle, to devise voluntary contractual arrangements of benefit to all members of the community. In the traditional Pigovian case of smoke nuisance, for example, it may be possible for a laundry suffering from the effects of smoke from a neighboring factory to reach an agreement with the factory management on the installation of a smoke-abatement device.

The appearance of such voluntary contractual arrangements can, however, be relied upon only where the number of economic units, whose agreement is required to eliminate the inefficiency, is relatively small. In these cases, a satisfactory agreement should be technically quite easy to devise and police, the potential advantages should be evident to each party, and the direct and indirect (retaliatory) consequences of failure to cooperate should be clear and unmistakable. Where numbers are large, however, none of these conditions holds and individual economic units may well imagine (rightly or wrongly, depending upon whether others follow their example) that they can enjoy much the same standards of service, profit, income, etc. without cooperating or contributing.

Since the elimination of all inefficiencies in this way is in general quite out of the question, the theory of second best suggests that such agreements as are concluded are at least as likely to reduce as to increase welfare. This becomes even more obvious when it is remembered that voluntary agreements need not be aimed at the elimination of an inefficiency, but may be essentially exploitative or redistributive as in the case of agreements to monopolize!

### 4.2.3  A general theory of market inefficiency

Ignoring distribution, it therefore seems that a general theory of market inefficiency must rest to a very large extent on the twin pillars of nonappropriability and large numbers. Of the most important concepts in modern theories of market inefficiency, only imperfect knowledge (including all forms of uncertainty) and irrational motivation do not appear to be fully accounted for, and even here some part of the problem is undoubtedly ascribable to the above factors. A detailed analysis of these problems can be found in chapter 10.

## 4.3  A General Economic Theory of the Public Household

From the analysis of sections 4.1 and 4.2 above, we can conclude that it is indeed possible to construct a general economic theory of the public household on the foundations provided by modern welfare economics, namely the welfare goals or criteria, and an integrated theory of market failure based largely on nonappropriability problems involving large numbers of economic units. The impression that such a theory must remain seriously incomplete and remote from the more important policy issues is completely unfounded. It is of course true that the treatment of the vital problem of distribution is unsatisfactory, but, as we have seen, the post-Keynesian alternative is if anything even less adequate in this respect.

## 5. Welfare Economics and Welfare Politics

We have shown that it is possible to construct a general economic theory of the public household on the foundations provided by modern welfare economics. But can any actual government be expected to conduct the affairs of its household in the prescribed manner, systematically applying welfare criteria and implementing all (and only) those policies which satisfy such criteria? And, if not, can welfare economics, however detailed and specific in its proposals, really be regarded as operational in any meaningful political sense?

With only a few outstanding exceptions, welfare theorists and public finance theorists had until recent years virtually ignored these fundamental questions. As Peacock has cogently remarked, "More often than not, a statement about the way governments should behave is passed off as a statement about how they actually behave."[56] Thus the apparent implication of the various welfare theories, that, where the market mechanism fails, government can be expected to do better, has gone largely unchallenged (with minor reservations in respect of *means*). Leading exponents of the conservative political tradition have continued to concentrate on completely unconvincing demonstrations of the narrow range of market failure, and on primitive invocations of the threat to "freedom" posed by government intervention (particularly when it takes the form of "direct" controls).

If, however, there is no guarantee that any actual government will behave in the particular manner prescribed by welfare theory, the apparent case for government intervention, based on welfare criteria and market failure, collapses completely; a partial switch of functions to the political mechanism wherever market failure can be demon-

[56] A. T. Peacock, "Economic Analysis and Government Expenditure Control," in A. T. Peacock and D. J. Robertson, eds., *Public Expenditure: Appraisal and Control* (Edinburgh and London, 1963).

strated may reduce rather than increase welfare.[57] In a fundamental political sense, welfare economics would be completely nonoperational. Welfare politics can be regarded as at least the beginnings of an attempt to deal with this crucial objection.[58]

## 5.1 Wicksell

This basic political problem has seldom been more clearly recognized than by Wicksell in his *Finanztheoretische Untersuchungen* of 1896.[59] Thus, with particular reference to Mazzola's brilliant anticipation of Samuelson's optimum conditions analysis of public goods, he points out that the mere derivation of the appropriate optimum conditions (together with the demonstration of market failure) provides absolutely no guarantee that they can or will be satisfied through the political mechanism.[60] And turning to particular forms of government, he quickly dispels any illusions regarding the potential welfare performance of "benevolent" despotisms and conventional parliamentary democracies alike.[61]

Wicksell then proceeds in effect to set up the Pareto criterion (with important sociopolitical qualifications) as the ultimate test for desirable budgetary policies, supporting it by reference to the basic philosophy of democracy and the desirability of avoiding all forms of tyranny (including that of a majority). The rest of his discussion is devoted mainly to the crucial political question of devising legislative procedures to ensure that the Pareto test is systematically applied and all (and only) those policies satisfying this test are implemented. For this purpose he recommends simultaneous voting on each particular item of public expenditure together with the method of financing it, flexible burden-sharing arrangements, and his famous "approximate unanimity" requirement.

[57] For a very forceful recent statement of this point, see J. M. Buchanan, "Politics, Policy, and the Pigovian Margins," *Economica*, 1962.

[58] This objection, far more than any problem of interpersonal comparisons, obviously is extremely damaging to utilitarian welfare economics and hence to the public finance theory erected upon it by Dalton and Pigou. In reading these great neoclassical works one can hardly fail to be struck by Wicksell's penetrating remark of more than a quarter of a century earlier that "even the most recent manuals on the science of public finance frequently leave the impression . . . of some sort of philosophy of enlightened and benevolent despotism."

[59] Knut Wicksell, *Finanztheoretische Untersuchungen* (Jena, 1896). Most of the relevant section is available in English translation by J. M. Buchanan as "A New Principle of Just Taxation" in R. A. Musgrave and A. T. Peacock, eds., *Classics in the Theory of Public Finance* (London and New York, 1958). Subsequent references will be to this latter volume.

[60] Ibid., sec. 2.

[61] Ibid., sec. 3.

It is important to recognize that Wicksell's contribution goes far beyond the brilliant but rather negative insight that a veto right for minorities ensures that budgetary policies failing to satisfy the Pareto criterion will be rejected. In particular he shows an intense awareness of the allocative and distributional problems of the Pareto criterion.

Thus he advocates the use of flexible and imaginative burden-sharing arrangements precisely as a practical political solution to the problem of allocative restrictiveness.[62] His aim throughout is to ensure that all Pareto-desirable policies are in fact implemented; whilst his main apparent concern is with the political application of the Pareto criterion, the ultimate goal of a Pareto optimum remains clearly in view. At the same time he is not unaware that, even in theory, flexible financing arrangements may not represent anything like a complete solution because of preference revelation and strategic behavior problems.[63] He completely fails to see, however, that these latter problems may be considerably exacerbated by the adoption of flexible financing arrangements. In practice then, even Wicksell's Paretian approach is likely to be extremely restrictive of the important reallocative economic functions of government; particularly in a dynamic context, a Pareto optimum must be expected to remain very far from fully achieved.

Wicksell is also extremely sensitive to the problem posed by the distributional conservatism of the Pareto criterion. Thus he is willing to advocate policies satisfying this criterion only if the distribution of property and income is just.[64] If the distribution of property and income is not just, he recognizes that some revision is necessary; but "it would obviously be asking too much to expect such revision ever to be carried out if it were made dependent upon the agreement of the persons primarily involved."[65] The approximate unanimity requirement must therefore be abandoned in such cases. Wicksell does not, however, attempt to specify the nature of a just distribution. As pointed out in section 2.4.4 above, his "New Welfare" theory thus provides an excellent example of the economic aspect approach.

It is interesting to notice that Wicksell's theory of welfare politics has been further developed in a recent article by Buchanan.[66] Most of Buchanan's discussion is devoted to the exposition of a broadly Wicksellian welfare politics (though shorn of Wicksell's crucial sociopoliti-

---

[62] Ibid., pp. 89–90.
[63] See, for example, ibid., p. 117.
[64] Ibid., p. 108.
[65] Ibid., p. 109.
[66] J. M. Buchanan, "Positive Economics, Welfare Economics, and Political Economy," *Journal of Law and Economics*, 1959.

cal qualifications).[67] In the penultimate section (7), however, he points out that in a democratic society some form of majority rule may have to be recognized as a political constraint; an approximate unanimity requirement is likely to be politically unacceptable. Even in this "second best" situation, he suggests that it should still be possible to ensure the political implementation of the Pareto criterion. What is required is that the "political economist" should devise and propose only those policies which satisfy this criterion.

In this approach, Wicksell's unanimity requirement has a very different but still vital role, not as a political measure to guarantee the practical application of the Pareto criterion, but rather as an ex post test to be applied by the politicoeconomic adviser to his own policy proposals. In particular, if, under majority voting, his proposal is rejected or obtains only a simple majority, this constitutes an a posteriori demonstration that the proposal should never have been made; and, if possible, it should be replaced by a Pareto-desirable alternative. Even if policies are not reversible (as with investment decisions under the price mechanism), the political economist can at least build up a fund of practical experience in his difficult task.

In this way Wicksell's welfare politics is transformed by Buchanan into an ingenious but obviously less operational theory of political obligation for economic advisers.

## 5.2  Lindahl

However, the first important and far more intensive development of the basic Wicksellian framework appeared many years earlier with the publication in 1919 of Lindahl's great work *Die Gerechtigkeit der Besteuerung,* later supplemented by two reconsiderations in 1928 and 1959.[68]

---

[67] Buchanan's main concern in this article is to show that, in spite of the persuasive arguments of the neo-Robbinsian "positivists" such as Friedman, the economist still has an important "positive" role in policy formulation, namely in designing and testing policies to satisfy the Pareto criterion. He thus attempts, with the aid of familiar but rather superficial general acceptability and democratic arguments, to insert the Pareto criterion as the given end in a "given ends approach." In this way the fundamentally normative nature of the resulting "political economy" is effectively obscured.

[68] Erik Lindahl, *Die Gerechtigkeit der Besteuerung* (Lund, 1919); "Einige strittige Fragen der Steuertheorie," in Hans Mayer, ed., *Die Wirtschaftstheorie der Gegenwart* (Vienna, 1928); and "Om skatteprinciper och skattepolitik," *Economi Politik Samhälle, Festskrift till Bertil Ohlins 60 – årsdag* (Stockholm, 1959). A salient section (pt. 1, chap. 4, sec. 2) of Lindahl's original work and the whole of his later reconsiderations are available in English translations. See Erik Lindahl, "Just Taxation – A Positive Solution," and "Some Controversial Questions in the Theory of Taxation," in Musgrave and Peacock; and "Tax Principles and Tax Policy," *International Economic Papers,* no. 10 (London and New York, 1960). For a detailed analysis of Lindahl's theory see chap. 6 in this volume, "Lindahl's Theory of the Budget."

In assessing Lindahl's contribution, it is important to remember that Wicksell's discussion had been devoted mainly to the elucidation of the main features of his normative political program. On crucial positive questions regarding the precise functioning and welfare performance of the various forms of political organization (and even of his own consensus system), his treatment is restricted to a few brief penetrating remarks; but, as Buchanan has recently emphasized, "Normative theory must be erected upon and must draw its strength from the propositions of positive science."[69] Even on the normative side, Wicksell's justification of his approach is hardly more than suggestive, and its precise relationship to its more important competitors is left unclear. Lindahl's work is best regarded as a particularly ingenious attempt to fill these gaps in Wicksell's theory and further develop its detailed implications.

Thus, in developing his theory of the budget, Lindahl has three distinct aims. The first is to establish the nature of a "just" system of public expenditure and taxation, i.e. to develop a prescriptive theory of the budget. The second is to determine to what extent budgetary policy in a parliamentary democracy can be expected to satisfy these welfare requirements. The third is to recommend, in the light of his welfare principles and positive analysis, detailed changes in voting procedures and tax legislation, which would facilitate a closer approach to the welfare goal under democratic government.

According to Lindahl, a just budget must satisfy two requirements. The first is that it must establish a just distribution of property. This is the "sociopolitical" (distributional) requirement, which the fiscal theorist must take as given. The second is that, on the basis of this just property order, a Pareto optimum should be established. This is the "purely fiscal" (allocative) requirement handed down from his "higher standpoint" by the public finance theorist. Lindahl's welfare requirements are therefore fundamentally similar to those of Wicksell.

In support of his prescriptive theory, Lindahl offers a number of interesting arguments. To the modern reader perhaps the most startling of these is his attempt to derive not merely the sociopolitical but also the purely fiscal requirement from natural law propositions.[70]

[69] J. M. Buchanan, "Marginal Notes on Reading Political Philosophy," Appendix 1 to J. M. Buchanan and G. Tullock, *The Calculus of Consent* (Ann Arbor, 1962) p. 308.

[70] Thus he points out (1919, German edition, p. 139) that the purely fiscal budget must be regarded as a positive exercise of the economic rights expressed in a just property order. In determining the fiscal budget these economic rights should therefore be safeguarded equally. According to Lindahl, the analysis of his model democracy (to be discussed below) demonstrates that this will be the case only where each individual taxpayer is obliged to contribute to the cost of public services in proportion to their marginal utility to him. In fact, however, when it comes to the point in the model, the detailed content of the purely fiscal principle is simply postulated rather than derived.

In addition, however, he is very concerned to show that his theory is consistent with and more general than the then widely accepted sacrifice and ability-to-pay theories. Thus he makes an ingenious attempt to show that the equal sacrifice principle can be derived from his purely fiscal principle; and he is willing to concede that the minimum aggregate sacrifice principle offers an attractive "economic" solution to the sociopolitical problem.

Although not entirely without value, all these arguments can be shown to be rather vulnerable. None of them, however, is fundamental to the Wicksell-Lindahl position; and the rather widespread impression that Lindahl's prescriptive theory is somehow untenable is completely incorrect.[71]

Lindahl's second distinct objective is to determine to what extent budgetary policy in a parliamentary democracy can be expected to satisfy his welfare requirements and, in particular, the purely fiscal requirement handed down by the public finance theorist. His general approach to this problem is first of all to set up a highly stylized model of the democratic political mechanism, in which the purely fiscal requirement will be fully satisfied.[72] Then, by means of a comparison of the main institutional features of his "model democracy" with those of actual parliamentary democracies, he proceeds to indicate the nature and direction of the departures from the "fiscal optimum," which must be expected in practice.

In the model, budgetary policy regarding the provision of particular public goods is assumed to be determined by bargaining and free agreement between two economically homogeneous groups of satisfaction-maximizing citizens with "equal power." With the aid of his famous diagram, Lindahl then proceeds to provide an extremely suggestive and illuminating positive analysis of the functioning of this model, concluding that equilibrium must indeed be established at a unique fiscal optimum. Closer analysis with the help of market analogies from some of the better known oligopoly theories reveals, however, that it is only on the basis of Lindahl's extremely special "competitive market" interpretation of the "equal power" assumption that achievement of

---

[71] For a detailed demonstration, see chap. 6, sec. 3 in this volume.

[72] As mentioned in n. 70 above, the model is simultaneously intended to serve as a detailed "derivation" of the purely fiscal principle from the more general requirement of fiscal justice, viz. that "all citizens should be able equally to safeguard their economic rights as regards the satisfaction of their public needs." See Lindahl (1919, German edition), p. 139. This double role of the "positive Lösung" has been a major source of the great confusion which has surrounded the interpretation of Lindahl's theory. The problem of interpretation has not been made easier for Anglo-American students by the fact that, of the original work, only the "positive Lösung" has so far appeared in English translation.

the fiscal optimum can be guaranteed.[73] Some approach to a closely related Pareto optimum can, however, quite reasonably be expected.

Lindahl recognizes very clearly that conditions in actual parliamentary democracies diverge in numerous important respects from those of the model. In order to determine to what extent budgetary policy in actual democracies can be expected to satisfy his purely fiscal requirement, he therefore proceeds to examine the probable effect of each divergence on ability to achieve the fiscal optimum. Thus he considers the effects of such important facts of political life as difficulties in evaluating the benefits of public goods, political parties, the existence of more than two parties and of divergencies of interest within parties, the absence of simultaneous voting on the extent and financing of expenditures in a particular area of public activity, and the absence (as under majority voting) of free agreement and equal power. Lindahl's discussion of these divergences is extremely useful and throws light on many of the important problems of positive analysis in this field. Regarding the effects of majority voting (and coercion generally), he suggests that no great departure from the fiscal optimum need occur, owing to the important economic and political costs which any such departure must involve. At the same time, however, he draws particular attention to the danger of overexpansion of the public sector under majority voting.[74] Whilst in most cases his analysis is fundamentally sound, he appears very seriously to underestimate the effects of introducing more parties and divergencies of interest.[75]

Finally, in the light of his welfare principles and positive analysis of welfare performance, Lindahl proceeds to develop in great detail a policy program designed to facilitate a closer approach to his purely fiscal goal. In addition to the Wicksellian recommendations of a limited veto right for minorities, proportional representation and linking of particular taxes to particular categories of expenditure, Lindahl particularly emphasizes the importance in tax legislation of observing a

---

[73] See chap. 6, sec. 4.1 in this volume.

[74] Without the introduction of a political constraint on the possibility of direct redistributions, this danger need not arise. See chap. 6, sec. 4.2.2 in this volume. When such a constraint is introduced, however, the danger of purely redistributive overexpansion (and even of underexpansion) of the public sector becomes very real. Lindahl explicitly envisages such a constraint (1928, p. 225, n. 14). For further analysis of this problem, see chap. 6, sec. 5.2 in this volume; and sec. 5.4.1 below. Also J. M. Buchanan, "Fiscal Institutions and Efficiency in Collective Outlay," *American Economic Review, Papers and Proceedings,* 1964.

[75] At the same time it should be emphasized that, by confining his attention throughout to small numbers of monolithic groups, he very carefully avoids the numbers problem both in his model and in his policy recommendations. It is therefore possible to regard his discussion as representing a considerable advance over Wicksell's in the treatment of numbers. For further discussion, see chap. 6, sec. 4.2.1 in this volume.

very sharp distinction between sociopolitical taxation (for which steep progression may be required) and purely fiscal taxation (for which probably much less progressive ability taxes are most suitable).[76] The main aim of such a separation is to avoid the allocative danger of over-expansion of the public sector pointed up by his positive analysis of the effects of majority voting. He also provides an interesting discussion of the detailed form which the ability taxes should take,[77] and considerably extends Wicksell's discussion of the provision of goods with public aspects but which also confer special benefits on particular classes (the problems of public utility pricing and of special assessments).[78] According to Lindahl, such supplementary "practical" tax principles and proposals are necessary because of important practical and theoretical limitations of the approximate unanimity requirement.

This latter contention represents Lindahl's major departure from Wicksell's normative theory, and it is particularly interesting to notice that in his later reconsiderations his doubts regarding the usefulness of the consensus requirement develop to the point where he abandons it completely as impracticable.[79] Like Buchanan,[80] he therefore accepts majority voting as a necessary constraint, and proceeds to advocate his detailed program as the means by which a closer approach to the fiscal optimum might be secured under majority voting. In this way, however, his normative theory comes perilously close to becoming little more than a theory of political obligation for majority parties.

## 5.3  Downs

Constrained coercion is a fundamental factor in Lindahl's positive theory of welfare politics; whilst on the normative side he looks to small-group bargaining or enlightened (or further constrained) coercion as the political means to a fuller attainment of his fiscal optimum. Considering the important role of economic analogies in Lindahl's discussion, a striking omission is his failure to mention the possibility of competition; but in most actual parliamentary democracies, competition between political parties is surely hardly less evident than political bargaining and coercion.

In Lindahl's theory, political parties are implicitly regarded as

---

[76] This is in fact simply a special "aggregative" application of the principle of linking particular taxes to particular expenditures. Sociopolitical taxes should be linked to sociopolitical (e.g., social security) expenditures, and purely fiscal taxes to purely fiscal expenditures.

[77] German edition (1919), pp. 203–24.

[78] Ibid., pp. 155–78.

[79] See (1959), pp. 13–14.

[80] See above, sec. 5.1.

class parties, seeking only to reflect the true preference of members of their particular social class. Politicians are simply the political representatives of well defined and virtually monolithic socioeconomic groups such as rich and poor, or analogous functional groups such as labor, capitalists and farmers. Such a view, although partly true in most democracies, completely ignores the extremely important and widely recognized fact that most political parties are usually only too ready to compete, where necessary, by making judicious (and not so judicious) sacrifices of conservative or socialist political principle to the god of electoral expediency. It was left to Anthony Downs in *An Economic Theory of Democracy*, published in 1957, to develop a positive theory of welfare politics emphasizing this crucial phenomenon of competition.[81]

Thus Downs analyzes the welfare performance of a majority-voting model characterized by competition for political power between two vote-maximizing political parties. For his politicians, political principles and programs are valued not for themselves but only for their vote-catching potential. His political parties thus have absolutely no interest in the achievement of welfare goals for their own sake. How then can any approach to a welfare goal such as a Pareto optimum be expected? Surely the positive analysis of such a model must indicate the likelihood of large, arbitrary and unpredictable departures from the optimum, and thus confirm, once and for all, the complete political irrelevance of welfare economics.[82]

The analogy with the market mechanism does, however, suggest at least a prima facie case for a careful examination of the welfare performance of the model. Thus conventional economic theory assumes that firms try to maximize profits and thus have no direct interest in welfare goals; and, even in a convex world with no external economies or diseconomies and no public good problems, it is a familiar conclusion of economic analysis that, where there are monopoly elements, a Pareto optimum will not in general be achieved, due to a conflict between Pareto efficiency and the profit motive. Where perfect competition exists, however, this conflict disappears and a Pareto optimum will be achieved.[83] By analogy, is it not possible that competition might achieve a similar reconciliation between vote maximization and Pareto

---

[81] Anthony Downs, *An Economic Theory of Democracy* (New York, 1957).

[82] Downs, chap. 15, provides an excellent critical discussion of the political vacuum in welfare economics.

[83] Where intense competition prevails, the profit maximization and perfect knowledge postulates of perfect competition can be relaxed in favor of the more realistic assumption that, in a world of uncertainty, firms employ conventional rules of thumb such as full cost pricing in an attempt to make large positive profits. In this situation, "natural selection" should be sufficient to limit departures from ex post profit maximization and Pareto optimality. See A. A. Alchian, "Uncertainty, Evolution, and Economic Theory," *Journal of Political Economy*, 1950.

efficiency in the political process, with the government encouraging the production and consumption of just those commodities left under- or overexpanded by the market mechanism?[84]

In fact, however, as Downs's analysis shows, it is only under extremely special conditions that political competition can guarantee the establishment of a Pareto optimum.[85] Thus, even where knowledge is perfect and feasibility considerations can be ignored, it is only where both parties must announce their policies simultaneously that a party with a Pareto-optimal program will necessarily be elected.[86] In this particular case, since for each suboptimal program there will be a number of optimal programs such that everyone is better off, a party clearly maximizes its election chances by choosing one of the optimal programs consistent with its policy on distribution.

Where, however, (say) the government party must by convention announce its policy first, the announcement of a Pareto-optimal program by this party (to ensure maximum support, given its policy on distribution) will no longer force the announcement of an optimal program by its competitor. The opposition can now win a simple majority by adopting any suboptimal program satisfying the essentially redistributive requirement that a majority of voters is made better off than under the government's announced program.

To obtain even these relatively meagre welfare results, however, we have to assume a degree of perfection of knowledge far beyond anything required in the case of the market mechanism for the establishment of a Pareto optimum under perfect competition in a convex world with no public good problems.[87] In particular, we have to assume that political parties have perfect knowledge of the preference fields of all individuals. But how is such knowledge to be obtained in the case of goods with public aspects? As under the market mechanism, preference-revelation problems arise; public statements by interest groups would tend to lead vote-maximizing political parties into underexpansion of public activities. Downs also shows[88] that even the introduction of political bargaining in the particular form of a vote-selling market

---

[84] As Downs puts it (p. 178): "The political parties in our model are not interested per se in making society's allocation of resources efficient; each seeks only to get elected by maximizing the number of votes it receives. Therefore even if the government has the ability to move society to a Paretian optimum, it will do so only if forced to by competition from other parties. . . . Thus the crucial issue is whether interparty competition always forces the government to move society to a Paretian optimum."

[85] For Downs's brilliant analysis of the welfare performance of his model democracy, see ibid., chap. 10.

[86] Ibid., chap. 10, sec. 2B.

[87] On the effects of relaxing the assumption of perfect knowledge and introducing various forms of uncertainty, see ibid., chap. 10, secs. 2C–2F.

[88] Ibid., chap. 10, sec. 2D.

can overcome this problem reasonably satisfactorily only in the very special small numbers case of compulsory collective bargaining between two monolithic groups of vote-buyers and vote-sellers respectively, i.e. essentially the two-party bargaining model of Lindahl's analysis.[89]

Even ignoring the problem of strategic behavior, it is anyway inconceivable that any party could obtain the intricate knowledge necessary for the establishment of the necessary individual marginal equivalences. With knowledge generally recognized to be irremediably defective, the incentive to try to devise optimal programs is also significantly diminished.

Furthermore, there are likely to be vitally important problems of political and administrative feasibility. Thus the complicated system of multiple (discriminatory) taxation required for Pareto-efficiency is likely to be both politically unacceptable and administratively impracticable, as are the costless lump-sum taxes and transfers we have implicitly envisaged as redistributive devices. Again, the promotion of certain activities by some (or all) methods may be unconstitutional.

Hence, for all these reasons, each stemming more or less directly from the existence of various forms of uncertainty, some sort of "second-best" optimum is clearly the very most that competition between vote-maximizing political parties can be expected to produce. Downs's introduction of the vitally important phenomenon of uncertainty, and his analysis of its welfare implications, must be regarded as a contribution to welfare politics hardly less significant than his emphasis on the role of competition.

## 5.4  Buchanan and Tullock

The most important recent development in the field of welfare politics has, however, been the comprehensive analysis provided by Buchanan and Tullock in *The Calculus of Consent*.[90]

Although the positive theories of Lindahl and Downs clearly incorporate many of the most characteristic features of actual parliamentary democracies, they must still seem somewhat Eurocentric to an American in their apparent neglect of such important phenomena as log-rolling and the activities of pressure groups and vested interests. Buchanan and Tullock recognize that such institutions demonstrate

[89] It is interesting to notice that Downs makes only one passing reference to Lindahl in the course of his brilliant exposure (ibid., chap. 15) of the political inadequacy of welfare economics. He is apparently unaware of Lindahl's pioneering contribution to a new welfare politics.

[90] J. M. Buchanan and G. Tullock, *The Calculus of Consent* (Ann Arbor, 1962).

the importance of vote-trading; even where the hypothetical vote-selling market envisaged by Downs is prohibited, a similar effect may be obtained through the bartering of votes on one issue for votes on another. Thus whereas Lindahl stresses the role of bargaining and coercion in a world of monolithic socioeconomic groups and class parties, and Downs highlights the importance of competition between vote-seeking political parties, Buchanan and Tullock emphasize the phenomenon of vote-trading.[91]

### 5.4.1 Log-rolling, redistribution of income and misallocation of resources

Thus the central feature of their discussion is an analysis of the welfare performance of a simple majority voting model characterized by vote-trading.[92]

Consideration of this log-rolling model suggests that small groups of electors will have a considerable incentive to trade their votes on particular issues in such a way as to ensure majority support for tax-expenditure proposals of special advantage to their particular groups. Two main types of proposals are of obvious relevance here, notably expenditure projects conferring special benefits on particular classes but financed out of general taxation, and expenditure projects of general benefit but financed by means of discriminatory taxation. By exchanging their votes on issues of this sort, it is clearly possible for groups together representing (say) 51 percent of the electorate to benefit themselves at the expense of the rest of the community. In this way, both special and general benefit projects will tend to be pushed well beyond the level for which the beneficiaries themselves would be willing to pay. The public sector may thus be extended far beyond the allocative optimum, essentially as an engine of redistribution from minority to majority. Especially where burden-sharing arrangements are rather rigid and embodied in a time-hallowed pattern of taxes, it would seem that, even in the case of pure public goods, the redistributive effect may outweigh the under-expansionary influence of preference-revelation problems.

The important conclusion of the Buchanan and Tullock analysis of

[91] Buchanan and Tullock also point out (pp. 134–35) that the package policies proposed by competing political parties may be regarded as a form of implicit vote-trading between groups of electors. The socioeconomic groups of Lindahl's analysis can likewise be regarded as the product of an explicit or implicit logrolling process. It seems clear, however, that much would be lost if the important political phenomena stressed by Lindahl and Downs were to be completely subsumed in the concept of vote-trading.

[92] Ibid., chaps. 10–12. This analysis is developed initially in terms of a simple example (chap. 10), and then presented more formally (chaps. 11 and 12) with the aid of game-theoretical tools. The independent contribution of game theory to their analysis and results seems, however, to be slight.

simple majority voting and related rules is therefore that the misallocative effects of such political mechanisms flow essentially from
their redistributive potentialities, and take the particular form of overexpansion of the public sector. At the same time they recognize very
clearly[93] that it would be in the interests of all, including the majority, to employ allocatively nondistorting lump-sum taxes and transfers for redistributive purposes, rather than the less direct method of
expanding the size of the public sector. Such lump-sum measures are
not, however, politically or administratively feasible. Indeed, it is a
major point of their analysis that the scope for employing even those
direct redistributive tax-transfer measures which are administratively
feasible is likely to be strictly limited by political considerations (including formal constitutional barriers)[94]; and of course such measures
are anyway likely to be allocatively distorting as Downs emphasizes.[95]

Buchanan and Tullock thus provide a most interesting explanation
and demonstration of the important Wicksell-Lindahl contention[96]
that unequal power and coercion (as under majority voting) are likely
in practice to lead to overexpansion of public activity. Unlike Lindahl,
they do not, however, proceed on these grounds to advocate a sharp
legislative separation of purely fiscal from sociopolitical budgetary
items. Indeed, recognizing the limited scope for direct redistributive
measures, they explicitly oppose such a separation on distributional
grounds.[97] Presumably, however, the allocative costs in the form of
overexpansion of the public sector must be set against this "second-
best" distributional argument.

### 5.4.2 External costs and decision-making costs

Generalizing from their extensive analysis of simple majority voting
and brief consideration of more and less inclusive voting rules, Buchanan and Tullock suggest that overexpansion of the public sector
and hence the misallocative costs of the various voting rules must
diminish steadily as their inclusiveness increases, ultimately falling
to zero where complete consensus is required. From this "external
costs" function[98] it does not, however, necessarily follow that complete

[93] Ibid., especially chap. 13.
[94] Ibid., chap. 13. See also sec. 5.4.4 below.
[95] Downs, chap. 10, sec. 2F.
[96] Wicksell, p. 87; Lindahl (1928), p. 225, n. 14. See also n. 74 above.
[97] Thus they conclude (p. 197) that, "Western governments have opened the way for more
and more effective redistribution which is accomplished indirectly through the tax
financing of public goods and services. By incorporating highly progressive, but nominally general, taxes with special-benefit public services in the fiscal process, the redistribution that is carried out far exceeds that which could be accomplished directly."
[98] Buchanan and Tullock distinguish between reallocative and redistributive external
costs. For the present we shall completely ignore the latter category.

consensus is allocatively ideal and therefore to be preferred to all
other voting rules. Thus, in addition to the external costs in terms of
optimum conditions disturbed or not established, Buchanan and Tullock distinguish the "decision-making costs" in terms of the time and
effort required to reach agreement.[99] In sharp contrast to the external
costs function, they suggest that decision-making costs will be very
high where all must agree and each individual can therefore utilize
an effective veto for bargaining purposes. As the voting rule becomes
less inclusive, so these decision-making costs will fall steadily to negligible levels. By combining these cost functions for any particular activity, subset of activities or complete set of all activities, the voting
rule involving minimum total costs can at least conceptually be indicated.[100] The external and decision-making cost functions ($E$ and $D$)
and the combined (total) cost function ($T$) are illustrated in the diagrams of Figure 2 below.

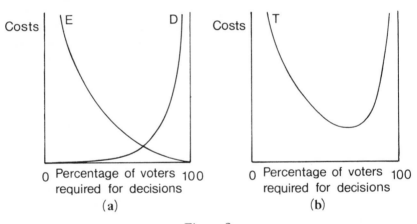

Figure 2

Buchanan and Tullock employ these cost functions to demonstrate
that the fundamental problem of welfare politics is that of choosing
between different voting rules all of which are in general likely to be
imperfect; that majority voting may be preferable to a consensus requirement; that voting rules should ideally vary from one activity to
another; and that the market mechanism (even where it is imperfect)
may be more efficient than any political mechanism for the performance of many economic functions.[101]

[99] See ibid., pp. 68–69. These costs are subsequently discussed in greater detail in chap. 8.
[100] Ibid., pp. 69–72.
[101] For the demonstration of these extremely important propositions, see ibid., especially
chaps. 6 and 14.

Although the distinction between external costs and decision-making costs is a major contribution of the Buchanan and Tullock analysis, it may nevertheless be doubted whether such a sharp separation is either possible or profitable. Thus, taking the case of a unanimity rule to illustrate, Buchanan and Tullock suggest in effect that such a rule, although likely to be extremely costly in terms of the time and effort required to reach agreement, must eventually result in the correction of all misallocations.[102] Where numbers are large, however, such a result is conceivable only over a very long run in a completely unchanging world; only in this case can the mere existence of mutually beneficial policies be said to guarantee their implementation in the face of overwhelming technical and strategic obstacles. Thus, although in a strict comparative statics framework Buchanan and Tullock may be correct, it is important to recognize that over any reasonable period, and especially in a dynamic framework, a Pareto optimum will always be far from fully achieved where unanimity is required; and the costs of such a voting rule must anyway take the form of misallocations and suboptimal agreements as well as "the time and effort required to secure agreement" (i.e. resources devoted to bargaining).[103]

Whether or not the distinction between external and decision-making costs is entirely satisfactory, it does, however, serve to point up the need for a clear distinction between the redistributive misallocations emphasized by Buchanan and Tullock (and also by Lindahl) and misallocations (including resources devoted to bargaining) due to the preference-revelation problems emphasized by Musgrave and Samuelson (and also by Wicksell in his discussion of Mazzola). This corresponds precisely to Downs's distinction between "positive blocking" and "negative blocking."[104]

### 5.4.3 The Pareto criterion and the choice of voting rules

In *The Calculus of Consent* the fundamental problem of welfare politics is for the first time clearly recognized as that of choosing between different voting rules, all of which are in general likely to be allocatively inefficient.[105] But precisely what criterion should be employed in making this choice, and how should it be applied?[106]

---

[102] See, for example, ibid., pp. 88–90.

[103] Their criticisms (ibid., pp. 110–11) of what they regard as the misplaced emphasis by Musgrave and Samuelson on the role of preference-revelation problems in obstructing the achievement of Pareto optima, although interesting, are therefore far from fully justified.

[104] See Downs, p. 177.

[105] Especially chap. 14.

[106] For their highly original discussion of these crucial questions, see ibid., chap. 7.

Following Wicksell, Buchanan and Tullock assert the primacy of the Pareto criterion, though without his important sociopolitical qualifications. Likewise with Wicksell, they observe that a consensus requirement is the only means whereby the political application of such a criterion can be guaranteed. They make a unique contribution, however, in recognizing that this requirement should be applied not as a voting rule, but rather to the choice between different voting rules at the more fundamental level of constitutional decision-making.

At this level, the particular budgetary policies likely to be implemented under a given voting rule need no longer satisfy the Pareto criterion individually. All that is required is that the complete sequence of measures should do so collectively. As long as there is sufficient uncertainty regarding the likely composition of decisive majorities to ensure that, for each individual, the redistributive gains and losses on particular issues can be expected on balance to cancel out, a system such as majority voting may therefore be capable of unanimous adoption. And recognizing the preference-revelation problems associated with the employment of consensus as a voting rule, it becomes apparent that majority voting may be adopted unanimously in preference to a consensus requirement. This theory thus provides a firm logical foundation for the frequent contention (apropos of majority voting) that individuals may agree to be coerced.

It is interesting to observe the close relationship between this ingenious transformation of Wicksell's welfare politics and the extensions of the Pareto criterion suggested in the welfare economics of Hotelling and Hicks.[107] Thus the work of Buchanan and Tullock can quite properly be regarded as spelling out the political implications of this wider Pareto criterion. As a result of these developments in both welfare economics and welfare politics, it is now clear that the Pareto criterion, properly interpreted and applied, need not be unnecessarily restrictive of the crucial reallocative economic functions of government. Indeed, as Buchanan and Tullock have shown, the most Pareto-desirable political mechanism may well result in overexpansion of public activity.

### 5.4.4 The Pareto criterion and the distribution of income

It is an outstanding achievement of Buchanan and Tullock to have shown how, in spite of the preference-revelation problems associated with a unanimity rule, an allocatively satisfactory theory of welfare politics can still be constructed on fundamentally Wicksellian foundations. It may be doubted, however, whether their treatment success-

---

[107] See sec. 2.4.1 above.

fully avoids the distributional problems of a modified Pareto criterion lacking sociopolitical qualifications.[108]

Thus, although under majority voting each individual may *expect* the redistributive gains and losses on particular issues to cancel out, significant redistributions will still occur, especially in the short run; and an ex ante consensus may soon give way to a well justified ex post sense of dissatisfaction.

This point may to some extent be met by the suggestion that, in recognition of the uncertainties involved, certain income-insurance measures may be unanimously embodied in the constitution.[109] Such measures could well include the prohibition of some of the main categories of potentially redistributive legislation, such as nationalization and geographically discriminatory taxation.

More fundamentally, however, it is precisely where the redistributive effects of particular policies do average out over time that undemocratic and potentially explosive maldistributions of income are most effectively perpetuated. It was of course precisely in recognition of this problem that Wicksell and Lindahl attached crucially important sociopolitical qualifications to their otherwise Paretian theories, and it is difficult to see how some such qualification can be avoided; distributional ethics based solely on individual attitudes to risk are unlikely to be widely accepted in modern civilized communities. Hence, although as Wicksell himself concedes, "one can scarcely proceed cautiously enough in such matters," the widely-held political, social and moral objections to distributional conservatism cannot simply be ignored.

## 6. Conclusions

On the basis of the above analysis, the following conclusions are suggested:

(*a*) To the public finance theorist in search of a truly general and fully operational prescriptive economic theory of the public household, New Welfare Economics, in itself, offers no more than a theory of political obligation. Since the aim of a theory of political obligation is to influence policy, its usefulness or "validity" must depend upon the persuasiveness of the arguments which can be mustered in support. Examined from this point of view, the great debate over welfare criteria during the 1940s can be seen as an attempt to retain the general ac-

---

[108] See secs. 2.4.1 and 2.4.2 above.
[109] Buchanan and Tullock develop this point in some detail in chap. 13.

ceptability advantages of the Pareto criterion whilst avoiding its evident disadvantages in terms of allocative restrictiveness and distributional conservatism. As a result of that debate, it is clear that the problem of allocative restrictiveness can largely be overcome in ways which entail no great distributional cost. Distribution, however, is ultimately a problem of conflict, and none of the ingenious attempts by New Welfare theorists either to solve or to avoid this problem can be regarded as adequate.

(b) New Welfare goals and criteria, in themselves, appear rather remote from any practical policy application. Optimum conditions analysis (including such operational offshoots as systems analysis and index numbers) may be regarded as an attempt to translate the basic New Welfare goal of a Pareto optimum into detailed recommendations and operational criteria for policy. Ignoring distributional complications, optimum conditions analysis suggests that public policy should be directed towards the correction of disturbances to the optimum conditions, resulting from the existence of monopoly elements (including decreasing cost problems) and external economies and diseconomies. From the point of view of the public finance specialist, the usefulness of optimum conditions analysis can readily be seen by considering its detailed implications for pricing policy of nationalized industries and taxation policy.

When feasibility considerations are admitted into the formal framework of optimum conditions analysis, the comparative simplicity of its policy implications unfortunately disappears; and the resulting theory of second best has led to an understandable decline of confidence among New Welfare theorists in the usefulness of optimum conditions analysis and its derivatives.

In the public finance world, however, this decline of confidence has been more than offset by recent developments in the theory of public expenditure. Thus Samuelson and Musgrave have pioneered a new optimum conditions analysis based on the Continental concept of a public good which must be consumed in equal amounts by all. This concept of a public good, although clearly an extreme case, provides a graphic illustration of compound market failure, and serves to focus attention on the important economic fact that some of the best examples of goods exhibiting Samuelsonian joint supply also pose extremely difficult price-exclusion problems.

(c) Among public finance specialists, there is a widespread impression that the welfare theory of public policy is little more than an academic exercise quite remote from such burning post-Keynesian policy issues as stability and growth. On closer examination, however, it appears that it is perfectly possible to construct a general economic theory of the public household on the foundations provided by modern welfare economics, namely the welfare goals or criteria and an integrated theory of market failure based largely on nonappropriability (or price-exclusion) problems involving large numbers of economic units. The treatment of distribution is admittedly unsatisfactory, but the post-Keynesian multiple theory of the public household is, if anything, even less satisfactory in this respect.

(d) As it stands, however, this general economic theory of the public household still offers no more than a detailed theory of political obligation for "enlightened" governments. If there is no guarantee that any actual government will behave in the particular manner prescribed by welfare (or post-Keynesian) theory, the apparent case for government intervention, based on welfare criteria and market failure, collapses completely. An analysis of the welfare performance of differing political mechanisms is therefore required if welfare economics is to become operational in the most fundamental political sense. Although much still remains to be done in this field, it is clear that the highly original contributions of such pioneers as Wicksell and Lindahl and of more recent writers, such as Downs and Buchanan and Tullock, have provided at least the foundations of a comprehensive theory of welfare politics.

# 2. Welfare Methodology and the Multibranch Budget

## 1. Introduction

The welfare framework of public finance theory is now well established, indeed stereotyped. Public finance measures are analyzed for their effects on four objectives, equity, efficiency, stability, and growth. In Musgrave's elegant formulation, this framework is heuristically institutionalized, with each objective (except growth) assigned to a specific "branch" of the "fiscal department" of government.[1]

This stereotyped public finance response to the fundamental welfare doubts of the post-Robbins period has received little critical attention in the literature.[2] By contrast, the more self-conscious struggles of the welfare economists to achieve a satisfactory formulation and interpretation of welfare objectives have been widely criticized.[3] However, it is easy to see that the four goals of the public finance framework can readily be reduced to the familiar questions of allocation and distribution which have absorbed the welfare literature.[4] The same basic problems of formulation and interpretation are therefore common to both.

Several recent developments in public finance suggest the need for a careful reexamination of the conventional public finance framework. One is the increasing interest in certain applications of welfare economics to public finance theory, notably in the theory of public goods.[5] Another is the appearance, within the accepted framework, of the con-

Reprinted without significant change from *Public Finance/Finance Publiques* 23, no. 4 (1968): 405–24.

[1] See R. A. Musgrave, *The Theory of Public Finance* (New York, 1959), chap. 1.
[2] A notable exception is to be found in Buchanan's review of Musgrave. See J. M. Buchanan, "The Theory of Public Finance," *Southern Economic Journal*, 1960.
[3] For a recent survey by the present writer, see chap. 1, sec. 2 in this volume.
[4] See, for example, chap. 1, sec. 4.1, above.
[5] See, especially, P. A. Samuelson, "The Pure Theory of Public Expenditure," *Review of Economics and Statistics*, 1954; and "Diagrammatic Exposition of a Theory of Public Expenditure," *Review of Economics and Statistics*, 1955. These basic articles have since given rise to a large and rapidly-growing body of literature.

troversial concept of a merit good.[6] Finally there are the important
writings of Buchanan, spanning welfare economics and public finance
theory, which explicitly raise serious doubts regarding the adequacy
of the standard normative framework.[7]

We shall begin, in section 2, with a general discussion of the basic
purposes which a welfare framework might be expected to serve. In
the light of this discussion of welfare methodology, we shall then attempt, in section 3, to clarify some apparent obscurities and inconsistencies in the standard formulation of the multibranch budget.
Section 4 contains a brief summary of the main conclusions.

## 2.  The Purpose of Welfare Theory

It is clearly impossible to formulate or interpret a framework of
welfare objectives until the purpose of welfare theorizing has been
firmly established. A given welfare framework may be regarded as
satisfactory or unsatisfactory depending upon the criterion of assessment employed. Robbins, for example, criticized the received welfare
theory of his day in terms of criteria appropriate to the assessment of
positive theory.[8] Such criteria might evidently be regarded as quite
inapposite in a welfare context.

It might therefore have been expected that the New Welfare pioneers would give explicit attention to the purpose of welfare theory and
to the problem of devising suitable criteria for the assessment of
alternative welfare theories. In fact, however, they were so completely
obsessed with devising a welfare framework less vulnerable to Robbins's objections, that these more general questions were virtually
ignored. Even in the later literature this central problem of welfare
methodology has received remarkably little explicit attention.[9]

It seems obvious, however, that there are a number of possible approaches to the problem of formulating and interpreting a welfare

---

[6] See Musgrave, pp. 13–14; also see chap. 10 in this volume.

[7] In addition to the important paper by Buchanan cited in n. 2 above, see in particular
his "Positive Economics, Welfare Economics, and Political Economy," *Journal of Law
and Economics*, 1959; and "The Relevance of Pareto Optimality," *Journal of Conflict
Resolution*, 1962.

[8] See L. Robbins, *An Essay on the Nature and Significance of Economic Science* (London,
1932), chap. 6.

[9] Some of the more important exceptions would include the papers by Buchanan cited
in n. 7 above. Also G. C. Archibald, "Welfare Economics, Ethics, and Essentialism,"
*Economica*, 1959; and A. Bergson, "On Social Welfare Once More," in his *Essays in
Normative Economics* (Cambridge, Mass., 1966).

framework, corresponding to the different views which may be taken of the ultimate purpose of welfare theory.

## 2.1   An "Ethical" Framework

One possible view is that the purpose of welfare theorizing is the derivation of ethically-desirable policy proposals. According to this view, the welfare framework might ideally be expected to provide the foundation for a complete *ethical* ordering of all possible economic situations. Armed with this information, the welfare economist would then be in a position to provide comprehensive and identical counsel on economic policy matters to legislators, government officials, interest groups and ordinary citizens alike. If consulted, say, on the desirability of a capital gains tax in a given situation, he would presumably hope to offer the same "ethically-impelling" advice to a right-wing or left-wing legislator, to a civil servant, to a business or union representative, to a shareholder or a wage-earner.

The criterion for assessment of a welfare framework must here be straightforwardly ethical. The objectives in question would be assessed by the welfare economist in terms of ultimate ethical criteria, which might include such broad considerations as general acceptability, social justice, rationality, social consequences, etc. Suitably weighted and adapted to appeal to his audience, these would then constitute the arguments which he would put forward by way of ultimate justification for his counsel.

Although the theorist would of course wish his counsel to be of maximum influence on all levels, he does not here seek general acceptability for its own sake. It is not therefore especially likely that he would employ the Pareto test or Wicksellian consensus as a single ultimate criterion of assessment.[10] Thus, for example, even in the absence of any far-reaching consensus of opinion, he might nevertheless include an objective of reasonable equality of income in his welfare framework, justifying this inclusion in terms of the intrinsic injustice and dangerous social consequences of greater inequality. Similarly, he might wish to base his concept of allocative efficiency, not on overt preferences, but on a "normalized" set of consumer preferences adjusted for certain effects of ignorance and irrationality. Thus, even in the absence of a general consensus, he might favor a sumptuary excise on tobacco, on the grounds that consumers are ignorant and irrational in their attitudes to the health hazards involved. If it is desired to provide compre-

---

[10] An extreme individualist might of course advocate a purely Paretian framework on primarily ethical grounds.

hensive counsel on all conceivable policy issues, these controversial questions cannot simply be ignored or set aside.

The difficulties with this approach to the welfare framework are immediately evident. As the literature amply demonstrates, different welfare economists employ different ultimate ethical criteria, and there is no absolutely impelling standard to which an appeal can be made. No determinate welfare framework can therefore be expected to emerge.

Another obvious problem is that the policy counsel based on a given ethical framework, however ethically desirable, may simply be quite unacceptable to large numbers of potential clients. The proponent of this approach might, as a result, despair of counselling vested interests, and reserve the benefits of his advice for the impartial government official or civil servant. Even here, however, his ethical framework may prove quite unacceptable. This approach is therefore particularly vulnerable to objections in terms of acceptability and political feasibility.

Nevertheless it seems clear that the desire to offer ethically-desirable policy counsel is in itself perfectly legitimate.[11]

## 2.2 An "Acceptable" Framework

A somewhat different view is that the purpose of welfare theory is the derivation of *acceptable* policy proposals. According to this view, the welfare framework should, if possible, provide the foundation for a generally acceptable ordering of all conceivable economic situations. Here again the welfare economist could hope to offer comprehensive and identical counsel to all. However, in contrast to the straightforwardly normative approach discussed in section 2.1 above, the purpose here is seen to be the provision of policy advice which will necessarily be accepted by the union leader, business man, government official or legislator to whom it is offered.[12]

A fundamental problem with this approach is that, where individual values conflict, no generally acceptable ordering of all possible economic situations can be constructed. In a given situation, for example, an objective of greater equality may be supported by some and op-

---

[11] Utilitarian welfare economics provides perhaps the best example of a welfare framework which seems primarily "ethical" in purpose. Some modern welfare theorists attach special distributional strings to otherwise essentially Paretian criteria. Such modifications no doubt frequently reflect the influence of ethical considerations.

[12] As we have already seen, general acceptability may also be a very powerful, though not necessarily decisive, consideration in the design of an ethical framework, particularly for an individualist. In the present context the emphasis is on acceptability, relevance or influence for its own sake.

posed by others. In this situation a policy of, say, more progressive taxation is clearly not generally acceptable – but neither is the status quo. Such conflict may obviously prevail over significant areas of policy.

Two alternative responses to this problem may be considered.

(a) The "flexible" alternative. Since the central problem in designing a comprehensive and acceptable welfare framework is to be found in the conflicting values of different individuals and groups, one obvious response might be to offer different counsel to different individuals based on a welfare framework acceptable to each. Progressive income taxation might be recommended to a left-wing legislator, labor leader or wage-earner, a value-added tax to a right-wing legislator, business man or shareholder. A medical association representative might be counselled on the types of taxation needed to control tobacco consumption – or on the alternatives to a national health scheme. An adherent of minimum sacrifice doctrine would be counselled on the need for radical levelling legislation.

In this approach no attempt is made to compromise or criticize the conflicting values of different individuals and groups. The welfare theorist simply takes his client as he finds him, whether democrat or dictator, racist, misanthropist, etc. Only the information problem remains of "reading off" and formalizing the social welfare function or welfare framework for each client. It therefore appears that the objective of providing acceptable counsel on economic policy can in principle be substantially achieved.

Possible objections to this approach are not difficult to imagine. The role of the welfare theorist is essentially reduced to that of a Robbinsian technician, grinding out the policy implications of what must frequently be mere prejudice and vested interest. Moreover the potentially infinite variety of relevant welfare functions makes the development of a coherent body of welfare doctrine virtually impossible. For these reasons, the theorist may choose to restrict the range of welfare functions which he will regard as admissible, rejecting, say, all those which attach a negative value to the welfare of others; or he may choose to ignore his client's views on matters which are "none of his business"; or he may offer counsel acceptable only to the "true statesman" or government official. Any such "ethical" restriction must, however, narrow the range of those who will find his counsel relevant or appealing.[13]

(b) The "partial" alternative. The other obvious response to the problem of conflicting values in attempting to devise an "acceptable" wel-

---

[13] Some flavor of this general approach may perhaps be detected in the rather ambiguous formulations of the social welfare function school. Bergson's recent discussion provides a reasonably clear example.

fare framework is, of course, simply to restrict the chosen objectives to those on which different individuals and groups are agreed. Identical counsel can then be offered to all on what may still be a fairly wide range of fundamentally noncontroversial policy issues. The counselling service is not, however, comprehensive. Where individual values conflict, no advice can be offered.

Here it seems evident that the Pareto test, properly interpreted, must provide the appropriate criterion for assessment. Objectives such as full employment and efficient resource allocation may be generally accepted. There may also be certain (perhaps very wide) limits to the degree of inequality of income which is regarded as tolerable. To the extent that such generally accepted objectives exist, they can quite properly be included in the welfare framework. Other objectives on which no such consensus exists should be excluded. These might well include reasonable equality (somehow specified), horizontal equity, and most adjustments of individual preferences for the effects of ignorance and irrationality. The appropriate set of welfare objectives is in effect simply an elaboration of the Pareto test.[14]

The obvious disadvantage of this approach is, of course, its lack of comprehensiveness. On crucial policy issues where individual values conflict, it provides no guidance whatsoever. In some societies such conflict may prevail over wide areas of policy. The political economist may thus find himself unable to offer counsel on many of the most burning issues of economic policy.

## 2.3   A "Useful" Framework

It is not of course necessary to demand that a set of welfare objectives should provide the foundation for impelling counsel on policy matters. A very different view of the purpose of welfare economics is that it should provide useful or interesting information for policy rather than impelling counsel. Thus the political economist might properly investigate the policy implications of an objective such as horizontal equity. As a result he might be able to demonstrate that perfect horizontal equity requires full taxation of capital gains under the personal income tax. This finding need not, however, be regarded as either an

---

[14] In the welfare literature the best example of this approach is to be found in the work of Baumol, especially *Welfare Economics and the Theory of the State* (Cambridge, Mass., 1952). This approach, in which the Pareto test is in effect regarded as a sufficient criterion for policy, should be sharply distinguished from one in which the Pareto test is treated as both necessary and sufficient. From an acceptability point of view, the latter application of the Pareto test ignores the possible unacceptability and even explosive character of the status quo. It must therefore be justified on other, e.g. ethical or political, grounds. For an interesting example of this latter approach, see Buchanan, "Positive Economics, Welfare Economics, and Political Economy."

explicit or implicit policy recommendation. The proposition "horizontal equity requires full taxation of capital gains" is in itself purely positive, and should not be confused with the purely prescriptive proposition "a capital gains tax should be imposed." According to this view, a set of welfare objectives should merely provide the foundation for the derivation of information which will be "useful" or "interesting" in policy discussions.

Here it seems clear that a much less demanding criterion can be employed in assessing a given welfare framework. A sufficient condition for approval would presumably be that a significant number of individuals, or even a few prominent or relatively influential persons, should share the objective in question. An objective of reasonable equality should therefore qualify without difficulty — and one of great inequality. An objective of allocative efficiency based on the overt preferences of consumers would likewise be perfectly acceptable — and one in which these preferences were subject to prior adjustment for certain effects of ignorance and irrationality.

One possible objection to this approach is that, although the resulting propositions are positive in form, they inevitably carry strong moral overtones. Horizontal equity, for example, is a value-loaded term, and it is therefore only too easy to infer, from the original positive proposition stated above, that a capital gains tax should in fact be imposed.

A further problem is that the criterion of "usefulness" leaves the welfare framework hopelessly indeterminate. Any number of objectives or sets of objectives could satisfy such a simple requirement. In the interests of developing a coherent body of welfare doctrine it might therefore be felt desirable to narrow the choice somewhat by raising the standard of "usefulness" in the direction of "general acceptability."

Neither of these problems would seem, however, to preclude a positivistic approach to the development and interpretation of a framework of welfare objectives.[15]

## 2.4   A "Political" Framework

A common characteristic of all of the preceding approaches to welfare theory is the lack of any explicit attention to the political process. Economic policies must, however, be implemented through a political

[15] In the modern welfare literature this approach was first developed clearly and explicitly by Archibald. It could also be argued that, in their more careful moments, this is perhaps what the hypothetical compensationists may have had in mind. Little explicitly considered such an interpretation of the hypothetical compensationist school, and in this context developed his well-known critique of nominally positive but value-loaded propositions. See I. M. D. Little, *A Critique of Welfare Economics* (Oxford, 1951), chap. 6. See also the exchange between Little and Archibald in *Economica* (1964).

mechanism. It might therefore be made a prime requirement of a welfare framework that it should provide the foundation for *politically operational* policy proposals. It might even be required that no policies other than those consistent with the chosen welfare framework should be politically operational.

The obvious criterion for assessing a given welfare objective would here seem to be that it should be possible to specify a political mechanism or voting system under which all and only those policies consistent with the given welfare objective are actually implemented. Thus if, for example, the Pareto test is taken to constitute the welfare framework, it must be shown that there is some feasible voting system capable of ensuring the implementation of all and only those policies satisfying the Pareto test. Following Wicksell, it might be suggested that a voting system of relative unanimity could provide a close approximation to this result.[16] Similarly, if provision is made in the welfare framework for some adjustment of individual preferences, for example in the fields of equity and growth, it must be shown that there is a feasible political mechanism capable of making these particular desired adjustments—and no others.

This criterion for assessing a welfare objective might seem to be very demanding. It is interesting, however, to observe that it is still insufficient to guarantee actual political implementation of the resulting policy proposals. Suppose, for example, that an advocate of the Pareto test can show that a voting rule of relative unanimity would ensure the effective political implementation of Pareto-desirable policies. Depending upon the requirements for constitutional change, it may, however, simply be impossible to secure the necessary switch from an existing system of, say, majority voting (or military dictatorship!) to relative unanimity.[17]

[16] It should be noted, however, that it is not sufficient to be able to show that a minority veto will effectively exclude policies not satisfying the Pareto test. It must also be shown that large number problems and possible strategic behaviour will not obstruct the implementation of policies which do satisfy the Pareto test; and this is much more doubtful.

[17] The best example of this general approach is to be found in the work of Buchanan; see especially "Positive Economics, Welfare Economics, and Political Economy." Thus, for example, Buchanan has particularly emphasized the point that a voting rule of relative unanimity would ensure the political implementation of the Pareto test, and has claimed this as a decisive operational advantage of this particular welfare criterion. He has also recognized the problem of securing the necessary constitutional change. It should be noted that the Pareto test is here interpreted as both a necessary and sufficient criterion for policy. See n. 14 above.

In more recent writings, Buchanan has switched his advocacy of the Pareto test and the consensus requirement to the constitutional level rather than the level of detailed economic policy decision-making. Interpreting the welfare criterion in this way, however, it would appear that the welfare theorist would in effect withdraw from counselling on virtually all the burning policy issues of the day, restricting his activities to counselling on constitutional changes and on those other changes, if any, where individuals can be persuaded to adopt a "properly constitutional attitude."

There is an obvious temptation under this approach to define the welfare objective directly in terms of some convenient political process, such as an existing system of majority voting.

## 2.5 A Relativistic View of Welfare Methodology

We have now seen that the problem of formulating and interpreting a framework of welfare objectives can be approached in a number of quite distinct ways, depending upon the view which is taken of the purpose of welfare theorizing. Thus the purpose of welfare theorizing may be seen to be the generation of ethically desirable policy proposals. Alternatively the emphasis may be placed on the acceptability of the counsel offered to individual clients. Or, again, the political implementation of the proposals may be regarded as all-important. Finally, and more modestly, the attempt may be made to provide useful information rather than impelling counsel on policy matters. The criterion to be employed in assessing a given welfare framework must clearly vary with the approach adopted.

The relativistic view of welfare methodology taken here is that any of these approaches to welfare theory is perfectly legitimate. It is true, as we have seen, that each can readily be shown to suffer from certain difficulties and disadvantages: ethically desirable policies are not necessarily either acceptable to one's client or politically operational; acceptable policies may not be ethically desirable, etc. As far as possible, no doubt, a multipurpose framework should be employed. Where desiderata conflict, however, there seems to be no obvious reason why the primary emphasis should be placed on one purpose rather than another.

## 3.  Implications for the Multibranch Budget

The previous discussion of welfare methodology should enable us to clarify some important obscurities and ambiguities which are to be found even in Musgrave's classic formulation of the multibranch budget. The purpose to be served by this standard welfare framework in public finance theory is usually far from clear. Musgrave, for example, is explicit that his framework is not meant to describe what actually "goes on in the capitals of the world." It is to be a "normative" or "optimal" theory.[18] Beyond this, however, there is no systematic

---

[18] See Musgrave, p. 4.

discussion of the appropriate criterion for the development, assessment or interpretation of such a theory. The only general guidance we are offered is that "the framework of a normative theory of public economy . . . depends upon the political and social values of the society it serves . . .";[19] and the precise nature of this dependence can only be inferred with some difficulty from his subsequent detailed discussion. Other presentations of the multibranch framework are typically even less satisfactory in this respect.

Generally speaking it is probably true to say that the three- or four-goal framework is intended implicitly to serve several purposes at once, "ethical," "acceptable," "political," and "useful." The primary emphasis may, however, vary quite markedly from one presentation to another. In accordance with the relativistic view of welfare methodology taken here, any of these approaches, or any combination of them, may be regarded as perfectly legitimate. Certain apparent obscurities, ambiguities and inconsistencies can, however, be considerably clarified when considered explicitly in the light of the various purposes which a welfare framework might be intended to serve.

## 3.1   Problems of the Distribution Branch

A useful point of departure for our discussion is provided by the criticism, levelled against Musgrave's formulation of the standard public finance framework, that there is a fundamental philosophical inconsistency in the treatment of the various objectives. Thus Buchanan has argued that, whereas Musgrave's theory of the allocation branch is firmly based on the acceptance of individual values, his discussion of the distribution and stabilization branches is somewhat ambiguous and could easily be interpreted as introducing "external" norms.[20] Hence, for philosophical consistency, "it seems clear that if individual valuations are to count in the determination of the share of resources to be devoted to the public sector, they should also be counted in determining the amount of redistribution that is to be carried out through the fiscal process and also in determining the degree to which stabilization objectives are to be promoted by fiscal activity. Consistent application of the individualistic approach would extend the theory of the allocation branch to the other two budgets; there would, for this purpose, be no need for a three-part breakdown."[21]

It is certainly true, as we have seen, that the familiar three- or four-

---

[19] Ibid.
[20] See Buchanan, "The Theory of Public Finance," pp. 235–36.
[21] Ibid., p. 236.

goal framework can readily be reduced to the two traditional welfare objectives of equity and efficiency. It is also true that the equity objective in public finance is frequently formulated in what appears to be a somewhat arbitrary and authoritarian fashion with no clear and explicit foundation in individual values – though there is usually some rather woolly reference to "generally accepted standards of equity." Musgrave, for example, whilst recognizing the great difficulties involved in specifying the distributional objective, seems clearly unwilling to rely on the unadjusted preferences of individuals in this field. Instead he looks, perhaps somewhat optimistically, to the political process to provide a satisfactory solution.[22] In his discussion of public goods (or "social wants"), he therefore follows Wicksell and Lindahl in basing his concept of optimal supply on acceptance of individual tastes for public goods, combined with a preexisting ideal distribution of income somehow brought about by the operations of the distribution branch.[23] Similarly in Samuelson's theory of public expenditure, we find the acceptance of individual preferences for public goods combined with the apparently arbitrary equity requirement that the distribution of income should be "swung to the ethical observer's optimum."[24] The basic philosophical dichotomy observed by Buchanan thus seems to be a characteristic feature of the orthodox modern theory of public goods.

Following Buchanan, it certainly seems reasonable to ask why, if individual preferences for public goods can be accepted, individual values in the field of income distribution cannot likewise be accepted. One obvious answer is that individual values in matters of income distribution are too liable to be based on envy, prejudice, and self-interest to provide an adequate ethical foundation for the operations of the distribution branch. This attitude certainly seems to be implicit in much traditional public finance discussion of the distribution question, as for example in the various sacrifice theories of equitable taxation right through to Henry Simons's celebrated view that "the case for drastic progression in taxation must be rested on . . . the ethical or aesthetic judgment that the prevailing distribution of wealth and income reveals a degree (and/or kind) of inequality which is distinctly evil or unlovely."[25] In theorizing of this sort, the primary emphasis is evidently placed on what we have termed an "ethical framework." Problems of acceptability, political implementation, and even usefulness are regarded as secondary.

A rather different argument for special treatment of equity is that

[22] See Musgrave, pp. 17–22.
[23] Ibid., pp. 9–12.
[24] See Samuelson, "The Pure Theory of Public Expenditure," p. 388.
[25] See H. C. Simons, *Personal Income Taxation* (Chicago, 1938), pp. 18–19.

here, more than in any other area of policy, individual values are in obvious conflict. In contrast to the situation in the allocation branch, individual values cannot therefore provide the foundation for a generally acceptable distributional objective. The theorist may respond to this problem by taking a purely relativistic view of equity, standing ready to adjust the concept to fit the prejudices of his client; or he may choose to narrow the range of his counsel to exclude all distributional issues except those where a substantial degree of consensus can realistically be claimed to exist. The first of these responses is perhaps to be diagnosed in Samuelson's public expenditure theory in the somewhat empty formalism that the distribution of income is to be "swung to the ethical observer's optimum." The second is no doubt to be seen in the increasingly sharp distinction drawn between the two concepts of horizontal and vertical equity, and the remarkable analytical attention devoted to the former concept in the modern tax policy literature — though it could well be argued that there is in fact no far-reaching consensus on horizontal equity either.

In view of the problem of conflicting values it could also be argued that in the field of equity, if nowhere else, the public finance theorist should aim to provide "useful information" rather than an impelling program of reform. He might therefore quite appropriately grind out the implications of a number of "interesting" objectives such as horizontal equity, equal sacrifice, minimum aggregate sacrifice, capacity to pay, etc., hoping thereby to provide positive information which may be useful in policy discussions, without attempting, perhaps overambitiously, to develop a normative program. This modest approach to the distribution question is not common in the literature, though some of the best recent discussions of the traditional public finance objectives of tax equity could perhaps be interpreted in this way.[26]

At least until recently there has been even less evidence in the public finance literature of any explicit concern over the problem of political implementation. There seems, nevertheless, to have been some awareness that the problem of political implementation may be especially acute in the case of conventional equity objectives. This awareness may to some extent account for the tendency, observable for example in Musgrave, to define the equity objective in terms of the results of some convenient and reasonably acceptable political process such as majority voting.[27] By contrast, the objectives of allocation and stabilization are usually defined quite independently of the results

[26] Musgrave's discussion of the ability-to-pay tradition provides a good example. See Musgrave, chap. 5.
[27] See, for example, R. A. Musgrave, "A Multiple Theory of Budget Determination," *Finanzarchiv*, 1956–57, pp. 336–37.

of a political process, even though it is recognized that they too must ultimately be achieved (if at all) through some suitable voting mechanism. A somewhat similar dichotomy is, of course, already to be observed in Wicksell, whose analysis represents the classic attempt to develop a truly political framework for public finance theory. Thus Wicksell explicitly exempts distributional adjustments from the rule of relative unanimity which is to apply to all other policy proposals; for distributional adjustments, some form of majority voting appears to be envisaged.[28] Even where heavy emphasis is placed on the development of a politically operational framework, special treatment of the distribution problem can therefore still be observed; though the reason for such special treatment is no doubt usually to be traced back to the feeling that individual values cannot provide the basis for an ethically desirable or even widely acceptable equity objective.

## 3.2   Problems of the Allocation Branch

As we have seen, there is considerable truth in the charge that there is a fundamental philosophical inconsistency in the orthodox modern theory of public goods and, more generally, in the standard welfare framework of public finance theory. This argument should not, however, be pressed too far. In particular it ignores the controversial concept of a merit good (or "merit want") which plays a significant role in Musgrave's analysis of the allocation branch.[29]

In contrast to his discussion of public goods (or "social wants") where individual tastes are accepted without question, Musgrave employs the merit goods concept to epitomize those cases in which the concept of allocative efficiency might properly be based, not on overt preferences, but on a "normalized" set of consumer preferences adjusted for certain effects of ignorance and irrationality. In an earlier version of his multiple theory, he seems to have considered assigning this controversial function of adjusting consumer preferences to a separate branch.[30] In his more comprehensive discussion in *The Theory of Public Finance,* however, the concept is firmly, and more logically, established in the allocation branch.

It is not therefore correct to argue as a general proposition that Musgrave accepts individual preferences without question, even in the

---

[28] See Knut Wicksell, "A New Principle of Just Taxation," in R. A. Musgrave and A. T. Peacock, eds., *Classics in the Theory of Public Finance* (London and New York, 1958), pp. 108–9. Even here Wicksell is reluctant to depart too far from the consensus requirement, which, in this area, has the advantage of "preserving a certain desirable stability in social relationships."

[29] See Musgrave, *The Theory of Public Finance,* pp. 13–14.

[30] See Musgrave, "A Multiple Theory of Budget Determination," p. 341.

allocation branch. On the contrary, he introduces doubts and qualifications, which, although perhaps less important, are precisely analogous
to those which afflict the typical public finance treatment of the distribution branch. On a more careful reading it appears that even the
polar category of public goods or social wants should not be immune
from these reservations, if it can be shown that the preferences in
question, e.g. for military spending, are based on ignorance and subject
to waves of irrational prejudice. Indeed, in Musgrave's analysis, the
merit goods problem is explicitly associated with both distributional
and social wants problems.[31] Health and education seem to provide the
best examples of services in which all of these problems are combined.
It is also interesting to notice that, as in his discussion of the distribution branch, Musgrave shows considerable uneasiness in his treatment
of merit goods, tending here again to look to the political process for a
ready-made solution.[32]

It should not, of course, be thought that Musgrave is alone in extending his reservations regarding individual preferences from the distribution to the allocation branch. A corresponding symmetry of
treatment is to be found, for example, in recent welfare discussions by
Bergson and Rothenberg;[33] and a similar attitude is familiar from the
writings of such authors as Scitovsky and Galbraith.[34]

Both in the standard public finance framework as formulated by
Musgrave, and also in the welfare framework of a writer such as
Bergson, we therefore find that the overt preferences of individuals
are not regarded as sacrosanct, even for purposes of the allocation
branch. In spite of the obvious logical symmetry with the distribution
branch, the case for incorporating a merit goods or preference adjustment concept in the allocation branch analysis is, however, much less
well understood and less widely accepted in the literature. It may
therefore be useful to reconsider, in the light of our previous discussion
of welfare methodology, how the inclusion of such a controversial concept might be interpreted and justified.

One very obvious answer is that overt preferences may diverge from
the individual's true preferences or "real interests." In certain types of
complex choices, the information available to the individual may be
hopelessly inadequate. Some adjustment of his overt preferences for

---

[31] For a detailed analysis of these relationships, see "On Merit Goods," chap. 10, sec. 3 in
this volume.
[32] See Musgrave, *The Theory of Public Finance*, p. 14.
[33] See Bergson; also J. Rothenberg, "Consumers' Sovereignty Revisited and the Hospitability of Freedom of Choice," *American Economic Review, Papers and Proceedings*
(1962).
[34] See, for example, J. K. Galbraith, *The Affluent Society* (Boston, 1958); and T. Scitovsky,
*Papers on Welfare and Growth* (London, 1964), pt. C.

the effects of ignorance may therefore be justified. Again, the possibility of irrationality in certain types of choice, or with certain types of individuals, can readily be demonstrated. The Pigovian argument regarding the reversibility of the defective telescopic faculty provides an excellent example. It might also be argued that the individual's expressed preferences are biased by the effects of advertising, much of which is misleading rather than informative. For reasons such as these, it may be felt that unadjusted overt preferences cannot provide the basis for an ethically-appealing concept of allocative efficiency. The inclusion of a merit goods or preference adjustment concept in the analysis of the allocation branch is no doubt usually to be interpreted in this way. Musgrave's discussion provides an obvious example. Here the primary emphasis is on the development of an "ethical framework."

Alternatively it might be recognized that, however the economist might feel about such matters, many people and organizations do in fact hold strong views about the uninformed or irrational character of other people's preferences. The medical profession, for example, might feel strongly that, in view of the long-term hazards to health, the continued large-scale consumption of tobacco products must reflect preferences based on ignorance, advertising, and/or irrational motives which, if revealed, might possibly be regarded as unacceptable by the individual himself. Similarly an educated elite might regard a lack of interest in education as irrational. If "acceptable" counsel is to be offered on these issues, the existence of such strong views can hardly be ignored.

Whilst this is undoubtedly true, an obvious problem is that, as in the case of equity, individual views on these matters may be in sharp conflict. Is it really possible to design an acceptable welfare framework incorporating merit goods considerations? One possible response to this problem is for the theorist to open a purely formal merit goods account in the allocation branch, leaving the details to be filled in to fit the views of each particular client (medical association, teachers' association, etc.). In terms of the formalism employed at least partly for this sort of purpose by social welfare function theorists in the distribution branch, it is not only the distribution of income but also the allocation of resources which must at least to some extent be left open for final adjustment to the "ethical observer's optimum." There is perhaps some flavor of this approach to be detected in Scitovsky's suggestion that "if the economist feels incompetent to make such judgments himself, he should at least admit their legitimacy and provide the analytical framework to help others to make these judgments."[35]

[35] See Scitovsky, p. 249.

Another possible response to the problem of conflicting views on merit goods is for the theorist simply to narrow the range of his counsel to those merit goods issues on which a reasonable consensus can be achieved. Thus, in a particular society, it may be fairly generally agreed that high tobacco consumption is based on ignorance and irrational motives. Where such agreement exists, an acceptable welfare framework incorporating some adjustment of overt preferences is clearly possible. In some societies, of course, the range of agreement on important merit goods issues may be quite limited. In these cases no guidance is provided, and comprehensiveness is sacrificed to acceptability. However, such an interpretation of the preference-adjustment concept may nevertheless appeal to those who would be reluctant to provide a framework for the indulgence of every whim and prejudice of their clients on the subject of other people's preferences, but who would likewise shrink from the explicit value criticism characteristic of the ethical approach. This seems to be the essential logic of Buchanan's position.[36]

In view of the extremely controversial character of the merit goods concept and the possibly very narrow area of consensus on important merit goods issues, there is also much to be said for a purely positivistic approach. Recognizing that significant and influential groups in the community regard, say, health and education as services which should be expanded beyond the level for which low-income beneficiaries would be willing to pay, these might simply be labeled merit goods. The theorist might then analyze the requirements for efficiency in the provision of merit goods, hoping thereby to provide useful and interesting information for policy decision-making. At the same time he would make it clear that he is not arguing that merit goods should be provided for, efficiently or otherwise. In this way the policy implications of strong views on the uninformed or irrational character of other people's preferences can be rigorously analyzed by the public finance theorist, without any prior indulgence in slippery value criticism and without any commitment as to the desirability or acceptability of such objectives. There seems to be little evidence of this interpretation of the adjusted preference concept in the literature, though it may well offer the most fruitful and least controversial avenue for further development.

Little attention has likewise been paid to the important question of political implementation. It is easy to see, however, that in the conventional, primarily ethical, formulation, a program of provision for merit goods must in general stand little or no chance of political implementation.[37] An awareness of this basic problem has probably

36 See Buchanan, "The Theory of Public Finance."
37 For a detailed analysis, see chap. 10, sec. 6 in this volume.

contributed to the extreme uneasiness which, as we have seen, is evident in even the best and most forceful discussions. A tempting "political" solution is of course to define the merit goods objective in terms of some convenient political process, the appropriate adjustments in individual preferences being those considered desirable by, say, a simple majority of voters. Musgrave in fact seems ready to employ majority approval as a necessary, though perhaps not a sufficient, criterion.[38] A somewhat similar approach is developed in more detail by Lindahl who sees a "normalized" set of minority preferences as the appropriate foundation for an objective of allocative efficiency to be achieved under a regime of majority voting.[39]

It appears therefore that the inclusion of a merit goods or preference adjustment concept in the allocation branch analysis can be interpreted and justified in a number of different ways corresponding to the alternative purposes which the multibranch framework might be expected to serve. The precise formulation of the concept will vary with the approach adopted.

## 4   Conclusions

The main results of the above analysis can be briefly summarized as follows:

(a) The problem of formulating and interpreting a framework of welfare objectives can be approached in several quite distinct ways depending upon the view which is taken of the ultimate purpose of welfare theorizing. The primary purpose of welfare theory may be alternatively viewed as the development of "ethically-desirable," "acceptable," or "politically operational" policy proposals, or simply the provision of "useful" or "interesting" information for policy decision-making. Beyond a point these desiderata no doubt conflict, and there seems to be no reason why the primary emphasis should not be placed on one purpose rather than another.

(b) The main purpose to be served by the familiar multibranch budget of public finance theory is usually far from clear. Some apparent obscurities, ambiguities and inconsistencies in the formulation of this standard framework can, however, be considerably clarified

---

[38] Musgrave, *Theory of Public Finance,* notes (p. 14) that, in the case of social wants, "majority rule is a necessary evil to approximate the desired result, not a principle desired as such. In the case of merit wants, however, the very purpose may be one of interference by some, presumably the majority, into the want pattern of others."

[39] See Erik Lindahl, "Tax Principles and Tax Policy," *International Economic Papers,* no. 10 (London and New York, 1960), sec. 3.

when considered explicitly in the light of the various purposes on which the primary emphasis might be placed. Thus we find that what might appear to be a basic philosophical inconsistency in the special treatment generally accorded to the distribution branch can be interpreted and justified in a number of different ways according as the emphasis is placed on "ethical," "acceptable," "useful," or "political" considerations. Similarly the uncertain status of the controversial merit goods or preference adjustment concept in the allocation branch can also be considerably clarified when the alternative purposes to be served by the multibranch framework are explicitly considered.

# 3. The Theory of Public Goods

## 1. Introduction

Surveying the Anglo-American public finance literature of the past fifteen years, one can hardly fail to be struck by the increasing attention devoted to the theory of public expenditure, or, as it has come to be known, the theory of public goods.

Those of us whose public finance studies date from any but the most recent period probably retain a general impression of the overwhelming emphasis placed on taxation theory and fiscal policies for economic stability, along with a close examination of fiscal institutions. Public expenditure was traditionally treated descriptively, with the support of scattered theoretical insights gleaned from Adam Smith or from the welfare economics of Pigou.

Following influential contributions by outstanding theorists such as Samuelson, Musgrave and Buchanan, this traditional emphasis is now changing; and public expenditure theory has become a major preoccupation of the public finance specialist. It is the aim of this paper to discuss some of the main developments in this important and rapidly expanding field.

## 2. The Theory of Public Goods

The central contribution to the modern discussion is to be found in Samuelson's "pure theory of public expenditure" presented in three short papers in the mid-1950s.[1] Although this theory has now been in

Reprinted with some corrections and minor changes from *Rivista di diritto finanziario e scienza delle finanze* 27, no. 2 (June 1968): 209–36. This paper was originally presented at the Conference on Economic Policy, University of Queensland, August 1967.

[1] P. A. Samuelson, "The Pure Theory of Public Expenditure," *Review of Economics and Statistics,* Nov. 1954, pp. 387–89; "Diagrammatic Exposition of a Theory of Public Ex-

circulation long enough to have achieved the status of a classic, and has been interpreted and reinterpreted on a number of occasions, both by Samuelson himself and by other writers,[2] it is still the source of considerable confusion in the literature.

The theory is based on the traditional Continental concept of a "public good" which, to quote Samuelson, "differs from a private consumption good in that each man's consumption of it . . . is related to the total . . . by a condition of *equality* rather than of summation."[3] Thus, for a private good such as bread, the total $X$ equals the sum of the separate consumptions $X^A$ and $X^B$ of the two persons A and B, i.e. $X = X^A + X^B$; whereas, for a public good, like national defense, each person's consumption $Y^A$ and $Y^B$ is identically equal to the total $Y$, i.e. $Y^A = Y^B = Y$.

The modern analysis of this concept has three main objectives which should be clearly distinguished. The first is to derive the requirements for optimal provision of a public good. This is the normative theory of public goods. The second is to show that no decentralized market mechanism can be expected to satisfy these requirements. This is the theory of market failure in public goods. The third is to indicate the fundamental character of the problems involved in attempting to ensure optimal provision for public goods through the political mechanism. The analysis thus consists of three distinct stages, the first two of which effectively constitute a welfare economics of public goods, and the last a welfare politics of public goods.

penditure," *Review of Economics and Statistics,* Nov. 1955, pp. 350–56; and "Aspects of Public Expenditure Theories," *Review of Economics and Statistics,* Nov. 1958, pp. 332–38. Musgrave's important contribution follows essentially similar lines, though with significant differences of detail and emphasis. See R. A. Musgrave, *The Theory of Public Finance* (New York, 1959), especially chap. 1, sec. B, and chap. 4, secs. C and D. These modern developments can be traced back directly to the renaissance of the benefit theory in the Continental literature of the 1880s. For extracts from some of the most important contributions to this earlier literature, see R. A. Musgrave and A. T. Peacock, eds., *Classics in the Theory of Public Finance* (London and New York, 1958). Of particular importance are those by Mazzola, Sax, Wicksell, and Lindahl.

[2] Both Samuelson and Musgrave have reexpounded and further developed their respective theories at a recent meeting of the International Economic Association. See P. A. Samuelson, "Pure Theory of Public Expenditure and Taxation," and R. A. Musgrave, "Provision for Social Goods," subsequently published in J. Margolis and H. Guitton, eds., *Public Economics* (London, 1969). For an earlier (1962) attempt by the present writer, see "Public Goods and Public Policy," chap. 8 in this volume. An outstanding contribution to the literature, and the first book-length treatment of the subject in English is J. M. Buchanan, *The Demand and Supply of Public Goods* (Chicago, 1968). See chap. 7 below.

[3] Samuelson (1955), p. 350. Musgrave provides an essentially equivalent definition of a public good as one which "must be consumed in equal amounts by all." See Musgrave (1959), p. 8.

## 2.1   Optimal Provision for Public Goods

The derivation of the requirements for optimal provision of public goods is simply a variant of the familiar Paretian optimum conditions analysis for a world of private goods. The two-dimensional diagrammatic treatment is in fact somewhat simplified by the introduction of a public good.[4]

Thus, in geometrical terms, the first step (which Samuelson omits as it is unaffected by the introduction of a public consumption good) is to derive the production possibility locus or transformation schedule from the given factor endowments and the production functions. This yields the familiar optimum production condition that the relative marginal factor productivities should be the same in all uses. The second step, with which Samuelson is particularly concerned, is to derive the utility possibility locus (or locus of Pareto-optimal points) from the production possibility locus and the preference maps. This yields the crucial overall *MRS-MT* relationship.

Following Samuelson we therefore begin in Figure 1 (iii) with a production possibility locus $xy$ showing transformation possibilities between a private good $X$ and a public good $Y$, and reflecting the conventional assumption of generalized diminishing returns. It is assumed that public goods enter the preference functions of individuals in the same way as private goods; and the indifference maps relating $X$ and $Y$ for the two individuals A and B are shown in Figure 1 (i) and Figure 1 (ii) respectively. From the definition of a public good we know that each person's consumption of the public good is identically equal to the total produced. Once the output of the public good in Figure 1 (iii) or the consumption of either person in Figure 1 (i) or Figure 1 (ii) is fixed, the horizontal position in the other diagrams is therefore fixed at the same level.

Each Pareto-optimal point shows maximum (ordinal) utility for A for given levels of utility for B. To derive one such point, let us suppose that B's utility is to be held at the level represented by indifference curve $b_1 b_1$. What then is the highest indifference curve which can be reached by A?

To answer this question we plot $b_1 b_1$ on Figure 1 (iii) and subtract

---

[4] For simplicity, we shall follow Samuelson's geometrical derivation (1955). The two-person, two-good case considered in the geometrical analysis can readily be generalized to the multiperson, multicommodity case. See idem (1954). Throughout our discussion, except where otherwise noted, we shall have a multiperson community explicitly in mind.

For the corresponding geometrical analysis for a world of private goods, see F. M. Bator, "The Simple Analytics of Welfare Maximisation," *American Economic Review,* Mar. 1957, pp. 22–59.

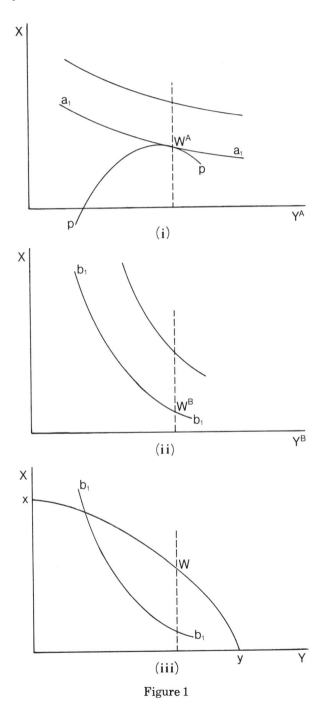

Figure 1

it vertically from $xy$ to obtain the quantities of $X$ and $Y$ which can be made available to A consistent with holding B on indifference curve $b_1b_1$. The resulting opportunity curve $pp$ is then drawn in Figure 1 (i). As it was obtained by vertical subtraction of $b_1b_1$ from the transformation curve $xy$, the slope of $pp$ must equal $MT - MRS^B$.

Of the points on the opportunity curve $pp$, it is obvious that person A would prefer the point $W^A$ where an indifference curve $a_1a_1$ is tangent to $pp$. The tangency condition is therefore

$$MRS^A = MT - MRS^B$$
or
$$MRS^A + MRS^B = MT$$

Having determined A's preferred consumption of the public good at $W^A$, the fact that the public good must be fully and equally consumed by all then allows the determination of the corresponding point for B at $W^B$ on $b_1b_1$ and the production point $W$ on $xy$.

Other Pareto-optimal points could be derived in the same way by setting B's utility at a higher or lower level, obtaining the corresponding lower or higher opportunity curve for A and finding the indifference curve for A which is tangent to it. In this way the complete set of Pareto-optimal points or utility possibility locus can readily be derived. This is shown as the curve $UU$ in Figure 2 where A's utility is measured along the horizontal axis and B's utility is measured along the vertical axis. At all points on the locus the same Samuelsonian tangency condition must of course be satisfied.

We thus find that the familiar Pareto-optimum condition for a world of private goods,

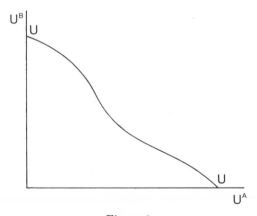

Figure 2

viz. $$MRS^A = MRS^B = MT$$

is radically altered when one of the two goods is public.

In accordance with his well-known predilection for the social welfare function approach to welfare economics, Samuelson then proceeds to determine a unique "best state of the world" where a social welfare contour touches the utility possibility locus. Like the first step, this third and final step in the analysis is of course the same in a world of public goods as for a world of private goods. Those who, like myself, would hesitate to follow Professor Samuelson in this third step of the analysis for a private goods world, would likewise prefer to part company with him at this same stage of public goods analysis. By restricting ourselves, in the hypothetical compensationist tradition, to the allocative aspects reflected in the derivation of the utility possibility locus, we can avoid losing sight of the main result, namely the new optimum conditions, in the empty formalisms of the social welfare function treatment of the distributional aspects.[5]

## 2.2   Market Provision for Public Goods

Can the market mechanism be expected to satisfy the crucial $\Sigma MRS = MT$ condition for optimal provision of public goods? To answer this question we must first attempt to spell out the requirements in terms of ordinary market variables.

### 2.2.1   Optimal public goods supply and market variables

In terms of ordinary market variables the condition $MRS^A + MRS^B = MT$ would appear to be satisfied by the following:

For the private good X,

(1) $$P_X = MC_X,$$

and, for the public good Y,

(2) $$P_Y^A + P_Y^B = MC_Y,$$

[5] Samuelson's use of the social welfare function approach in his public goods analysis appears to have misled Musgrave, and no doubt others, into thinking that the introduction of a public good introduces a welfare indeterminacy which does not exist in a private goods world and which requires the strong value judgments of the social welfare function for its resolution. See Musgrave (1959), pp. 8, 12, 84. In fact, however, the same strong value judgment is of course required to select a unique optimum on the utility possibility locus for a private goods world. In his latest treatment (1969) it seems that Musgrave now concedes this point. For a detailed discussion of equity and efficiency interrelationships in public goods analysis, see chaps. 4 and 5 below.

where $P_Y^A$ and $P_Y^B$ are the prices of the public good to persons A and B, and are chosen in such a way that

(3)                                 $$MRS_{YX}^A = \frac{P_Y^A}{P_X},$$

and

(4)                                 $$MRS_{YX}^B = \frac{P_Y^B}{P_X},$$

so that

$$MRS^A + MRS^B = \frac{P_Y^A + P_Y^B}{P_X} = \frac{MC_Y}{MC_X} = MT.$$

Thus we see that, in terms of ordinary market variables, Pareto-optimal provision of public goods requires in general a set of differential prices to individual consumers summing to marginal cost.

It is important to notice that the differential prices to individual consumers need not necessarily be uniform over quantities purchased by a single individual. In the case of the services of a public good, re-trading is not generally possible, and all that is strictly required for efficiency is a set of *marginal* prices summing to marginal cost. The prices of inframarginal units of public good purchased by a single individual may thus be varied within wide limits, analogous to the two-part tariffs, block tariffs and the "ideal" of perfect discrimination familiar from the literature on public enterprise pricing.[6]

Once a particular Pareto-optimal pricing rule has been specified, we find in general that each point on the utility possibility locus trans-lates back into a specific pattern of factor ownership. In our present market context the pattern of factor ownership may presumably be taken as given. If then we can specify, for example, uniform pricing over quantities purchased, there will be a unique set of Pareto-effi-cient differential prices to individual consumers and a unique Pareto-optimum corresponding to the given pattern of ownership of factors. It is the distribution of welfare and not the efficiency of the solution which varies from one optimal pricing rule to another.

In the special case of price uniformity over quantities purchased by a single individual, and if in addition we assume constant opportunity

[6] This point has recently been developed with reference to the problem of peak load pricing which has much in common analytically with the theory of public goods. See the ex-cellent discussion by J. M. Buchanan, "Peak Loads and Efficient Pricing: Comment," *Quarterly Journal of Economics,* Aug. 1966, pp. 463–71. This analysis is applied to the case of public goods in his book *The Demand and Supply of Public Goods.*

costs, it is interesting to observe that the unique Samuelsonian optimum can be presented in the following different ways, all essentially
equivalent, and linking up some of the major pre- and post-Samuelson
contributions to the public goods literature:

   i.   In Figure 3 (i), we present the unique Pareto optimum in fundamental Bowen-Samuelson terms by plotting the slopes of the indifference curves ultimately reached by A and B against quantities of
the public good to yield the curves $MRS^A$ and $MRS^B$. These curves
are summed vertically to produce the curve $\Sigma MRS$. The (constant)
slope of the transformation schedule is similarly plotted as the line
$MT$. The Pareto-optimal output of public good is then shown by the

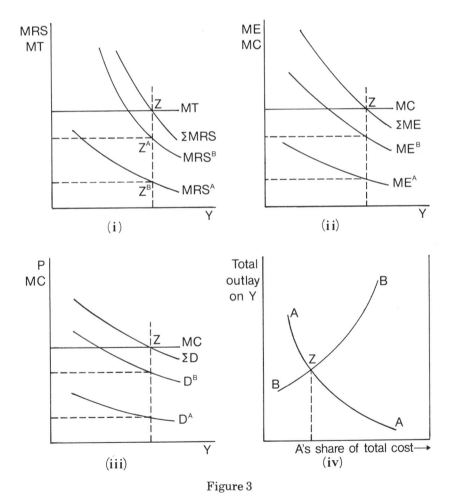

Figure 3

point of intersection $Z$ of $\Sigma MRS$ and $MT$, with $MRS^A$ and $MRS^B$ at $Z^A$ and $Z^B$.[7]

ii.   In Figure 3 (ii), we present the same unique optimum in terms of Hicksian marginal evaluation curves, $ME^A$ for A and $ME^B$ for B, obtained by plotting the slopes of successive indifference curves along the relevant opportunity line for each person. The unique optimum $Z$ is here shown where $\Sigma ME$ (the vertical summation of $ME^A$ and $ME^B$) cuts the constant opportunity cost curve $MC$ (identical to $MT$). This presentation has recently been employed by Buchanan.[8]

iii.   In Figure 3 (iii), a generalized Marshallian presentation in terms of summed demand schedules is employed.[9] $D^A$ and $D^B$ are the demand (Samuelsonian "pseudo-demand")[10] schedules for A and B which are then summed vertically to yield $\Sigma D$. $Z$ is then the point where $\Sigma D$ cuts the marginal (and average) cost curve $MC$.

iv.   The Marshallian presentation can readily be translated into an even more celebrated alternative due to Lindahl.[11] For this purpose, in Figure 3 (iv), we plot the total money cost of the quantity of public goods which each individual would demand at various percentage shares of total cost against these percentage shares, measured from left to right for A and right to left for B. This yields the "constant share demand schedules" $AA$ and $BB$ for A and B respectively. The unique optimum based on the given pattern of factor ownership (with uniform prices and hence cost shares over quantities purchased) is then the point of intersection $Z$ of the "demand schedules" $AA$ and $BB$, Lindahl's famous $P$ point.

Both the generalized Marshallian and Lindahl diagrams can be rigorously derived from the underlying indifference maps,[12] and their fundamental identity with the Bowen-Samuelson and Buchanan devices in this special case is therefore clear.

[7] See Samuelson (1955), p. 354. This presentation was first employed in the pioneering contributions of Bowen. See H. R. Bowen, "The Interpretation of Voting in the Allocation of Economic Resources," *Quarterly Journal of Economics*, Nov. 1943, pp. 30–32; and *Toward Social Economy* (New York, 1948), pp. 176–78.

[8] See, for example, J. M. Buchanan and W. C. Stubblebine, "Externality," *Economica*, Nov. 1962, pp. 371–84; and more extensively in *The Demand and Supply of Public Goods*.

[9] Bowen's presentation, though analytically quite distinct, has occasionally been interpreted in this way. See, for example, Musgrave (1959), pp. 75–76. The same technique has conventionally been used to present the solution to the analytically related peak load pricing problem. See, for example, P. O. Steiner, "Peak Loads and Efficient Pricing," *Quarterly Journal of Economics*, Nov. 1957, pp. 585–610.

[10] See Samuelson (1969).

[11] See E. Lindahl, "Just Taxation—A Positive Solution," in Musgrave and Peacock, pp. 169–70.

[12] For a derivation of the Lindahl diagram from the underlying indifference maps, see L. Johansen, "Some Notes on the Lindahl Theory of Determination of Public Expenditures," *International Economic Review*, Sept. 1963, pp. 347–49.

If we cannot assume uniform pricing over quantities for each individual, but some other nonuniform pricing rule can nevertheless be specified, a Marshall-Lindahl presentation of the unique optimum is no longer possible. Demand schedules cannot be drawn. The resulting unique optimum can, however, still be shown in the Bowen-Samuelson and Buchanan diagrams. If no particular pricing rule can be specified in advance, the link between the pattern of factor ownership and the distribution of welfare (or position on the utility possibility locus) is snapped, and even the Bowen-Samuelson and Buchanan diagrams break down.[13]

As there seems to be some confusion on this point in the literature, it is also important to emphasize that the $\Sigma MRS = MT$ condition in no way implies that the public good must be made available at a uniform price of zero to all consumers.[14] On the contrary, as we have seen, differential marginal pricing to individual consumers is in general required, and it is not necessary that these marginal prices should be uniform over quantities purchased by a single individual. The essential point here is of course that, whilst a zero price provides one perfectly efficient method of rationing a given public goods supply, as in the case of an existing durable public good (e.g. an existing Polaris system), it is completely incapable of solving the crucial production problem of how much to produce.

### 2.2.2 Market failure in public goods supply

Can the market mechanism be expected to generate a set of differential marginal prices summing to marginal cost as required for Pareto-optimal provision of a public good? To answer this question it is helpful to distinguish clearly between two very different characteristics of the public good concept as defined by Samuelson, namely joint supply and external economies.

**2.2.2.1** *Joint supply.* The first and perhaps the most obvious implication of Samuelson's equal consumption concept ($Y^A = Y^B = Y$) is that the services of a public good are in joint supply, in the special sense that, once a unit of the service is made available to one in-

[13] Except in the case of zero income-elasticity of demand for the private good. In this special case there will be only one Bowen-Samuelson *MRS* curve for each individual regardless of the pricing rule followed. This exception was noted by Samuelson (1955), n. 9. A presentation in terms of marginal evaluation curves, however, remains impossible.

[14] See, for example, the lively exchange between Minasian and Samuelson on this issue: J. R. Minasian, "Television Pricing and the Theory of Public Goods," and P. A. Samuelson, "Public Goods and Subscription TV: Correction of the Record," *Journal of Law and Economics*, 1964.

dividual, a service unit of the same quality *can* be made available to other individuals at no extra cost. A unit of Polaris submarine deterrent, once made available to A, can be made fully and equally available to B. The services to A and B are therefore joint products.[15,16] (We shall ignore, for the present, the impossibility in some cases of withholding the service from B if it is made available to A; we shall assume that prices can be charged.)

It is easy to see that it is this joint supply characteristic which accounts for the radical change in the optimum conditions and the consequent need for differential marginal pricing to individual consumers. If, when a service unit is made available to A, a descriptively identical unit *can* be made available to B without extra cost, it is clear that (ignoring possible cases of negative marginal evaluation) full and equal consumption is necessary for Pareto optimality. The requirement of differential pricing then follows at once from the fact that consumers with different tastes or marginal evaluations for the good must be brought into utility-maximizing equilibrium at the same level of consumption.

In the economics literature the concept of joint supply is of course more familiar from the traditional Marshallian examples of the joint supply of two descriptively different goods such as meat and wool from

[15] This application of joint supply terminology was first developed in detail by the present writer in "Public Goods and Public Policy," chap. 8 in this volume. It has been further discussed by C. S. Shoup, "Public Goods and Joint Production," *Rivista internazionale di scienze economiche e commerciali,* Mar. 1965, pp. 254–64. For a more comprehensive discussion and generalization of the concept, see J. M. Buchanan, "Joint Supply, Externality and Optimality," *Economica,* 1966.

The same characteristic is referred to in various ways by other writers. In his original articles, Samuelson himself refers to joint supply on one occasion (1955, p. 355), but also refers to *jointness of demand,* as well as to the generalized market failure concept of *external effects.* Musgrave in *The Theory of Public Finance* employs the term *joint consumption,* and in his most recent treatment (1969) he modifies this to *nonrivalness in consumption.* The use of joint demand, joint consumption or nonrivalness in consumption seems very misleading with its unfortunate implication that the public good characteristic is a special and extreme case of complementarity in demand like left and right shoes! In his I.E.A. paper (1969) Samuelson fixes on the term *consumption externality* which seems to imply that the jointness stems essentially from consumption of the product. It is easy to see from the Polaris example that this is far from necessarily the case.

[16] As has been pointed out on a number of occasions, the pure public good concept can readily be generalized in its joint supply aspects by relaxing the assumption that the public good provides service units of the same quality or in the same quantity to all individuals. This enables us to cover the multitude of important cases such as the fire station which benefits A, who lives nearby, more than B who lives further away. See, for example, chap. 8 below, p. 169; Musgrave (1969); and, for a comprehensive analysis, Buchanan (1966). In his most recent analysis (1969) Samuelson draws no clear distinction between this phenomenon of differing quality services and the taste differences for identical quality service units which are an essential feature of his original treatment. The two phenomena are analytically equivalent, however, only if the "composition of the input unit" (e.g. the location of the fire station) is fixed. See Buchanan (1966).

a common "input unit" sheep.[17] It is also well known that Pareto-optimal supply of strictly joint products in general requires divergent prices for the different products summing to the marginal cost of the "input unit." If the two products are D and E, the requirement is

$$P_D + P_E = MC,$$

where $P_D$ and $P_E$ are the prices of D and E, and $MC$ is the marginal cost of the "input unit." In these Marshallian cases, more meat or more wool for one individual means correspondingly less meat or less wool for another. Each product can also readily be traded between different consumers. Uniform pricing both over individuals and over quantities is therefore required for each product. It is then only a short step to the familiar conclusion that a perfectly competitive market can ensure Pareto-optimal provision of goods which are in joint supply in the conventional Marshallian sense.

In the analogous Samuelsonian case of joint supply, however, we have seen that differential marginal prices to individual consumers are in general required; the individual with the higher marginal evaluation should pay more. Here it seems clear that a perfectly competitive market must fail, as the consumer with a relatively high marginal evaluation can always turn to alternative suppliers. Perfect competition is simply not capable of generating marginal prices which discriminate between different consumers of a given product.

Since perfect competition fails due to the existence of competing sources of supply, it may be interesting to consider whether conferring a legal monopoly on one producer might perhaps lead to some improvement. Assuming the conventional profit maximization motive, it is clear that the monopolist would choose if possible to discriminate perfectly, both as between different consumers and over quantities, in order to appropriate the full amount of consumer surplus. Though it may be distributionally objectionable, such a pricing policy would lead to a unique Pareto optimum.

But is perfect discrimination likely to be feasible in the case of a public good? As direct retrading of the services enjoyed by different consumers is not possible, discrimination is in principle quite conceivable. (We continue to assume of course that the service can readily be withheld from those who do not pay.) For practical purposes, however, the informational demands placed on the monopolist are tremendous. He must in effect have full knowledge of the preference maps of all potential consumers; and this information is likely to be

---

[17] Shoup has suggested the term *multiple-user products* for the joint products in the public goods case to distinguish them from the *multiple-commodity products* of the conventional Marshallian case. See Shoup, p. 257.

particularly difficult to obtain in what are effectively bilateral negotiations with individual consumers each of whom has every incentive to disguise both his marginal evaluation and his consumer surplus. At best our monopolist will therefore find himself reduced to seeking some rough objective index of marginal evaluation, such as income, to determine marginal price, with perhaps a simple "block tariff" system for inframarginal units. Thus, whilst the monopolist may perhaps be expected to improve somewhat on the performance of a decentralized (i.e. competitive) market mechanism, the information problem sets an important limit to any such improvement.

**2.2.2.2** *External economies (and diseconomies).* In the previous section we have shown that even if the services of a public good could easily be withheld from those who do not pay, the joint supply characteristic creates differential pricing requirements for Pareto-optimal provision which no decentralized market mechanism can be expected to satisfy.[18] It is this joint supply characteristic and the consequent change in the optimum conditions which has been particularly emphasized by Samuelson.

There is, however, a further quite distinct characteristic of the public good, which is that the associated services cannot be withheld from those who do not pay. Once a unit of service is made available to one individual, a service unit of similar quality not only *can* but *must* be made available to all other individuals. Full and equal consumption by all individuals is not merely a necessary condition for Pareto optimality (ignoring negative marginal evaluations); it holds by definition of a public good (i.e. $Y^A = Y^B = Y$). This characteristic has been particularly stressed by Musgrave who refers to it as "impossibility of exclusion."[19]

It is interesting to notice that the two public goods characteristics of joint supply and impossibility of exclusion, although conceptually quite distinct, are nevertheless frequently associated in practice, as in the example of defense services. This relationship is not of course entirely accidental, as exclusion difficulties are usually inherently greater in the case of jointly supplied services. There are, however, many exceptions, as can be seen from the obvious exclusion possibilities in the example of the jointly-supplied services of a bridge, and the exclusion problems frequently encountered in the scramble to

[18] In his original discussion Musgrave (1959, p. 10, n. 1) misses this essential point, arguing instead that in cases of Samuelsonian joint supply (or "joint consumption") "entrance fees can be charged, different amounts can be consumed by various people, and the service can be provided through the market. Demand schedules can be added horizontally." His more recent treatment (1969) seems more satisfactory in this respect.
[19] See Musgrave (1959), p. 8.

exploit a scarce natural resource or crowded facility with no jointness characteristics in the relevant range.[20]

The impossibility of withholding some part of the benefits of an activity from those who do not pay is of course precisely the definition of the neoclassical concept of external economies. The impossibility of exclusion which characterizes a public good is therefore simply an extreme case of external economies, such that, when one individual consumes a unit of service, an identical-quality service unit is consumed by all other individuals without payment.[21] In the case of Polaris submarine deterrent, for example, the defense-producing firm is completely unable to charge for any part of the given-quality service unit fully and equally consumed by all individuals. This can therefore be regarded as an extreme case of external economies of Scitovsky's producer-consumer variety.[22] The same is true of the draining of a malarial swamp. Alternatively, we might envisage a case such as that of a vaccination against some communicable disease, which when consumed by A provides similar protection to B. Although it seldom quite fits in practice, this case clearly provides in principle an example of extreme external economies of Scitovsky's consumer-consumer variety. Here the producing "public health firm" can readily exclude a single consumer of an injection of vaccine, but once the health benefit has been made available to one consumer, all others enjoy a similar-quality service unit without paying.

[20] For a more detailed discussion of these relationships, see chap. 8 below, pp. 172–75. In his original treatment of these problems, Musgrave (1959, p. 10, n. 1) maintained that exclusion problems necessarily entail joint supply. He has now reversed his position (see 1969).

In his excellent recent discussion of the joint supply characteristic, Buchanan (1966) also attempts to demonstrate that the existence of exclusion problems necessarily implies the existence of joint supply. In fact all he shows is that exclusion problems will not be "observed," unless joint supply (either Marshallian or Samuelsonian) is privately profitable. Where exclusion problems are not "observed," market failure is of course even more striking.

[21] As the case of the special joint supply characteristic, it is therefore obvious that the public good concept can readily be generalized in its nonexclusion aspects. See, for example, chap. 8 below, pp. 171–72. Thus, in one dimension, it may be recognized that only a part of the benefit is strictly nonexcludable, e.g., the "general" as against the "vocational" aspects of education. In another dimension, it may be recognized that exclusion is seldom literally impossible for any aspect of a service, but only more or less difficult and uneconomic. It should be noted in this latter connection that some degree of excludability may be achieved either through the adoption of a "pricing system" (such as tolls, or complicated legislation on property rights) which may be very costly to the supplier and/or the consumer, or through the employment of a relatively inefficient but more readily excludable technology (such as locks and nightwatchmen rather than police patrols etc.). The vast body of literature on external economies is effectively concerned with these more general cases.

[22] See T. Scitovsky, "Two Concepts of External Economies," *Journal of Political Economy,* Apr. 1954, pp. 143–51.

In the producer-consumer cases where no part of the service produced can be withheld from any consumer who does not pay, it seems obvious that a perfectly competitive market will produce little or nothing, at least in large-number cases. Market failure is virtually complete. The position is essentially the same in the corresponding consumer-consumer cases.

In our analysis of the joint supply characteristic, we saw that conferring a legal monopoly on one producer might reasonably be expected to improve market performance, at least if we ignore the information problem. Thus the omniscient monopolist can proceed to design and announce the set of differential prices which will simultaneously ensure Pareto-optimal public goods supply and maximum monopoly profit. Where price-exclusion is impossible, however, this efficient price set is completely unenforceable. Little or nothing will be produced, and market failure is again virtually complete. Here then nothing whatever can be gained by conferring a legal monopoly on a single producer.

It thus seems clear that of the two characteristics of a public good, impossibility of exclusion is much the more potent cause of market failure. Samuelson's repeated emphasis on joint supply as the essential characteristic of a public good seems therefore somewhat misleading; although of course it is certainly true, as we have seen, that some degree of market failure can still be demonstrated even in the complete absence of price-exclusion problems.[23]

For completeness it is interesting to notice that a further public goods characteristic, impossibility of rejection, must be distinguished, where, as explicitly envisaged by Samuelson,[24] some individuals may place a negative marginal evaluation on the public good, e.g. the Quaker attitude to defense.[25] To satisfy the equal consumption requirement in such cases, the services of the public good not only can and must be fully and equally available to all, they must actually be consumed fully and equally by all, including those who would prefer, if possible, to consume less than the total amount available, even at a zero price. This further characteristic of nonrejectability can be ignored only if we explicitly restrict the public good concept to services which represent "goods" and not "bads" over the relevant ranges for all individuals. By contrast, of course, nonrejectability becomes the

[23] Musgrave also now appears to regard joint supply (his "non-rivalness in consumption") as the "essential" characteristic of the public good (1969). This is also Buchanan's position. Perhaps the Samuelson position is best understood as implying that exclusion problems are in fact of little practical importance; or that, where they are important, they are almost invariably associated with jointness problems.

[24] See Samuelson (1955), n. 1; and (1969).

[25] This characteristic has also been noted independently by Carl Shoup.

essential concept for a pure "public bad" like the fallout from nuclear testing.

Impossibility of exclusion and impossibility of rejection frequently go together, as illustrated by the example of defense. The two characteristics are not, however, necessarily related, as can easily be seen from the example of TV services, where (if we ignore the possibility of descramblers) it is clear that the service is effectively nonexcludable but readily rejectable (by switching off the set).

Just as impossibility of exclusion is easily seen to be an extreme case of external economies, so impossibility of rejection is simply an extreme case of external diseconomies. Pareto optimality here requires negative marginal prices for those individuals with negative marginal evaluations. In this respect also market failure can readily be predicted.

**2.2.2.3** *The exchange mechanism and large numbers.* We have seen that neither a competitive market mechanism nor a legal monopoly can possibly be expected to generate and enforce the set of differential marginal prices summing to marginal cost as required for Pareto-optimal provision of a public good. Instead of analyzing the performance of some conventional and arbitrarily-chosen market regime, assumed somehow to have been imposed on the community, we could alternatively consider the more general question as to whether any completely voluntaristic system of market-type agreements could ensure Pareto-optimal provision of public goods.[26] This more general formulation serves to focus attention on the crucial role of large numbers in market failure analysis, particularly in relation to the nonexclusion characteristic.

Thus, as Wicksell was the first to recognize,[27] where the number of economic units in the community is large, no completely voluntaristic system of market-type agreements can reasonably be expected even to approximate Pareto-optimal provision of public goods. As Wicksell puts it: "If the individual is to spend his money for private and public uses so that his satisfaction is maximized, he will obviously pay noth-

---

[26] This more general framework has been consistently employed by Buchanan, most notably in his book *The Demand and Supply of Public Goods.*

[27] In his critique of Mazzola's brilliant anticipation of Samuelson's optimum conditions analysis for public goods. See K. Wicksell, "A New Principle of Just Taxation," in Musgrave and Peacock, pp. 80–82. In the relevant modern literature the role of large numbers was first analyzed in a more general setting by Baumol in *Welfare Economics and the Theory of the State* (Cambridge, Mass., 1952), chap. 11. Since then it has been noted on a number of occasions. See, for example, Musgrave (1959), pp. 9, 80. Two recent contributions are of particular interest, notably M. Olson, *The Logic of Collective Action* (Cambridge, Mass., 1965), chap. 1, and J. M. Buchanan, *Public Finance in Democratic Process* (Chapel Hill, N.C., 1967), chap. 9 (and similarly in *The Demand and Supply of Public Goods*).

ing whatsoever for public purposes . . . Whether he pays much or little will affect the scope of public services so slightly, that for all practical purposes he himself will not notice it at all."[28] Thus, even though it must in principle be possible to design an agreement on public goods supply such that all individuals receive significant net benefits, no single individual or small number of individuals has any obvious incentive to contribute. In a sense, therefore, it can quite properly be said that, under a large-number voluntaristic system (of which the conventional market regimes considered earlier constitute special cases), the individual (a) has no incentive to reveal his true preferences for public goods, or, perhaps more precisely, (b) is not motivated to do the signalling of his tastes needed to achieve a Pareto optimum.[29]

To avoid possible confusion, it should, however, be emphasized that individual behavior here is not "strategic" or "interdependent" in the familiar sense of attempting to influence the behavior of others. The "false signals" and "masked preferences" referred to in this context describe behavior which is to all intents and purposes completely independent; the existence of other individuals is essentially ignored.[30] As Wicksell concludes, the real problem here is how effective consultation or interaction between individuals can be secured.[31]

The position in the large-number group is to be sharply contrasted with that in the small-number group. Where numbers are small, the contribution of a single economic unit is no longer imperceptible in

[28] Wicksell, p. 81.

[29] This preference-revelation terminology plays a prominent part in the standard modern expositions of the theory by Samuelson and Musgrave. From a careful reading of both authors, it is quite clear that statement (b) in the text provides the more precise rendering – it is in fact a slightly modified version of a formulation by Samuelson (1954, p. 388). The confusion revealed by Sharp and Escarraz should therefore have been unnecessary. See A. Sharp and D. R. Escarraz, "A Reconsideration of the Price or Exchange Theory of Public Finance," *Southern Economic Journal,* 1964. Sharp and Escarraz also miss the crucial point relating to the effects of large numbers.

From Samuelson's discussion it is also clear that preference-revelation problems are not restricted to those which result from the existence of large numbers. Thus it is only Musgrave who might appear to link the preference-revelation problem exclusively with the large numbers case. Even Musgrave, however, recognizes clearly the possible role of more conventionally "strategic" behavior in obstructing the achievement of a Pareto-optimum in a small-number context. See (1959), pp. 79–80.

Again in contrast to Samuelson, Musgrave appears to associate preference-revelation problems with impossibility of exclusion rather than joint supply. But, as we have already seen in our earlier analysis of the joint supply characteristic, preference-revelation problems are here again a potent cause of market failure. Thus, even where exclusion is possible, the legal monopoly fails precisely because of the multitude of small-number preference revelation problems (of a bilateral monopoly character) facing the producer in a joint supply situation.

[30] This point has been particularly stressed by Buchanan. See, for example, (1967), p. 114. On a careful reading, however, the standard discussion of the large-number case, such as Musgrave's (1959, p. 80), seems reasonably clear in this respect.

[31] See Wicksell, p. 82.

relation to the total. If our large-number community could somehow be welded into just a few monolithic economic units, a voluntaristic system could quite reasonably be expected to perform much more efficiently. Thus, even with independent behavior between economic units, the supply of public goods will be considerably increased because of the larger size of the basic economic unit.[32] Over and above this, however, the perceptibility of the behavior of each economic unit is likely to facilitate the process of consultation or interaction necessary for Pareto-desirable agreements on public goods supply. The contribution of "others" to projects of joint benefit is no longer likely to be independent of own-contribution. Genuinely strategic or interdependent behavior aimed at influencing the behavior of others is here the rule; and "false signals" and "masking of preferences" will be employed strategically by each economic unit in an attempt to minimize own-contribution and extract maximum net benefit from the interaction process. Some rough approach to Pareto-optimal public goods supply can, however, quite reasonably be predicted, especially when we remember the smaller organizational costs and less formidable information problems involved in small-group agreements.[33]

In general, however, it seems necessary to consider the large-number case in the public goods context. Since a pure public good provides the same service to all economic units without any capacity limit, the efficient size of the sharing group is literally infinite; and efficiency requires an agreement effectively embracing all individuals. At the other extreme we have what we might call the "club good," the joint benefits of which extend only to a very limited subset of individuals, as in the case of a swimming pool or golf course. As our analysis suggests, the club good may be fairly efficiently supplied through a voluntaristic system of market-type agreements.[34] The club good thus constitutes the central concept for an economic theory

[32] If the public good is inferior for one or more individuals, it is even possible that public goods supply may be overexpanded under independent adjustment in these small-number cases. The possibility of overexpanded consumption of a public good under independent adjustment has been noted in the literature on "impure" public goods. See J. M. Buchanan and M. Z. Kafoglis, "A Note on Public Goods Supply," *American Economic Review*, June 1963, p. 411. The prime cause in their discussion would appear to be the phenomenon of "nonseparability," or some other unusual combination of complementarity and substitutability relationships on the production or consumption side.

[33] Analogously, some approach to the maximization of joint profits through a similar process of small-number interaction is a familiar assumption of modern oligopoly theory — just as the breakdown of cartel arrangements where numbers are large is a familiar theme of empirical studies. For a more detailed discussion and comparison of interaction in small and large-number groups, see especially Olson, chap. 1.

[34] It is interesting to notice that perfect competition may closely approximate Pareto-optimal provision of a "club good" through optimal replication of the facility in question. See, for example, Samuelson (1969).

of clubs or voluntary associations; whereas the public good provides the paradigm case for the theory of the state.[35,36]

Although the large-number framework is generally relevant in the public goods context, it is important to notice that significant elements of the small-number case may exist even where the number of economic units is literally large. Thus private organizations, such as a few large firms, may coexist with many small units such as households. These large firms may find themselves in an effective small-number situation in relation to public goods supply, with own-contribution highly significant in relation to the total. Thus, even though households remain in an effective large-number framework, substantial amounts of public good may be provided voluntaristically through the action and interaction of large economic units.[37] For the virtually complete failure of the voluntaristic system envisaged by Wicksell, large numbers must therefore be understood to imply that no economic unit should be so large that own-contribution becomes significant or perceptible in relation to the total.[38]

## 2.3   Political Provision for Public Goods

We have now shown that, in general, neither a conventional market regime of perfect competition or monopoly, nor a generalized market regime of voluntary agreements, can be expected to approximate Pareto-optimal provision for public goods.

In the final stage of the analysis, it is recognized explicitly that the demonstration of market failure in public goods is not sufficient in itself to justify public expenditure on public goods. Where the market fails, there is no guarantee that government can do better.[39]

---

[35] This crucial distinction was apparently very clearly recognized by Lindahl, who particularly emphasizes the "all-inclusive" aspect in his discussion of the appropriate definition of a public good. See E. Lindahl, *Die Gerechtigkeit der Besteuerung* (Lund, 1919), pp. 57–58.

[36] For further discussion of club goods and optimal sharing arrangements, see J. M. Buchanan, "An Economic Theory of Clubs," *Economica,* 1965. As the discussion is extended to goods for which optimal "club size" is large, we approach the theory of "coercive organizations" such as unions, local governments etc. Olson's discussion is primarily concerned with the problems of the larger functional economic groups.

[37] It should be noted, of course, that few if any of these larger private economic units are themselves likely to be organized on anything like a fully voluntaristic basis.

[38] In a more general setting this point has been clearly recognized by Baumol and Olson. It is easy to see that small-number elements are likely to become increasingly important as we move further and further away from the paradigm case of full and equal consumption represented by the pure public good.

[39] This fundamental problem is very clearly recognized in the standard modern expositions of the theory by Samuelson and Musgrave. See especially Samuelson (1954), pp. 388–89. Musgrave (1959, chap. 6) devotes a full chapter to the problems of the political mech-

### 2.3.1  The consensus ideal

As Wicksell had so clearly seen, the central problem is to secure through the political mechanism the effective consultation and interaction on public goods supply which, as we have shown, must in general be lacking under a completely voluntaristic market-type system.

It is obviously true that political decisions, however they are reached, explicitly embrace and bind all units in the relevant jurisdiction. However, there is the evident danger, under a simple coercive system like majority voting, that the Pareto-desirable properties of voluntary exchange agreements may be completely lost. Wicksell himself therefore suggested the closest possible political approach to a purely voluntaristic system, namely a voting requirement of (relative) unanimity or minority veto.[40] Any proposal failing the Pareto test is thereby effectively excluded. But can such an approach avoid the imperceptibility problem of a purely voluntaristic system in a large-number setting?

Wicksell seems to have thought that the possibility of vetoing any proposal for public goods supply creates an artificial increase in perceptibility. In other words possession of the veto somehow increases the individual's feeling of involvement with the rest of the community.[41] Even if this is true, however, it may be of little real advantage as the individual may begin to behave strategically, vetoing even overwhelmingly Pareto-desirable proposals in an attempt to extract an even larger net benefit from his negotiations with the community.[42] But in the large-numbers case the community as such does not exist and cannot respond. Since nothing can be provided in the face of the veto, even the limited public goods supply which might be achieved under a voluntaristic market-type system may not therefore be possible.

If, on the other hand, the individual recognizes that the possession

---

anism, though he appears to miss some of the central issues. The problem was also recognized in principle by the public goods pioneers, Sax, De Viti De Marco, and Mazzola, all of whom were, however, inclined to take rather too sanguine a view of the performance of the democratic political mechanism. In the public goods literature, serious analysis of this problem began only with Wicksell. The central contributions to date are surveyed in rather more detail in chap. 1, sec. 5 above.

[40] See Wicksell, especially pp. 87–97.

[41] This suggestion is based on Buchanan's perceptive analysis of the Wicksellian scheme. See, for example, (1967), chap. 9; and *The Demand and Supply of Public Goods*.

[42] The consideration of numerous alternative financing arrangements, as suggested by Wicksell (pp. 89–90), would of course greatly increase the apparent scope for strategic behavior. Probably in an attempt to overcome this problem, Wicksell modified his unanimity requirement to one of "approximate" unanimity. This should certainly help, but some of the advantages of unanimity may be lost in the process.

of the veto does not bring him into any genuine bargaining relationship with the rest of the community, Wicksellian consensus is likely
to degenerate into a system of purely voluntaristic behavior. Each individual contracts out of the consultation process, in effect leaving
his proxy to support only those public goods proposals under which his
own contribution is zero.

Wicksell's pioneering contribution to the political theory of public
goods was further developed by Lindahl, who takes a two-group bargaining model to epitomize the Wicksellian consensus ideal.[43] With the
aid of some further assumptions he then attempts in effect to demonstrate the Pareto optimality and determinacy of public goods supply
in this particular model. As we have already seen, even a purely voluntaristic market-type system can reasonably be expected to produce
some approach to Pareto optimality in the small-numbers case; and
Lindahl's small-number Wicksellian model should presumably perform about equally well, the only difference here being that nothing
can be provided without the explicit agreement of both parties. Relaxing his various assumptions one by one, Lindahl then proceeds to
employ his basic model as a tool for analyzing the effects of such real-
world phenomena as large numbers, general-fund financing and majority voting.[44] In his analysis of the large-number case, he envisages
the effective factoring-down of the system into a set of intersecting
small-number agreements: groups A and B bargain together and agree
to confront C etc.[45] Without a suitable set of "generalized club goods"
to hold the conceptual bargaining pyramid together, it seems, however, that such factoring-down is illegitimate. The classic dilemma
remains that the basic voting unit is not motivated to do the signalling
of his tastes needed to achieve a Pareto optimum.

### 2.3.2  Majority-voting models

As the Wicksell-Lindahl ideal fails to overcome the preference-
revelation problems of public goods supply, and since such systems
are anyway almost unknown in practice, it may be interesting to
consider finally the performance of a familiar system such as majority
voting. On this subject the original Wicksell-Lindahl discussions offered little more than a few brief though penetrating remarks.[46]

---

[43] See the extracts in Musgrave and Peacock, pp. 168–76, 214–32. Lindahl's extremely
influential contribution is analysed in detail in chap. 6 below. See also Musgrave (1959),
pp. 74–80; and Johansen.
[44] It is interesting to observe that essentially the same approach is employed in the first
modern book-length discussion of the theory of public goods. See Buchanan, *The Demand
and Supply of Public Goods.*
[45] See Lindahl, in Musgrave and Peacock, p. 173.
[46] See especially Wicksell, p. 87, and Lindahl, pp. 174–76, 224–26.

Two major models of majority voting have so far been applied to the problem of political provision for public goods.[47]

**2.3.2.1** *The log-rolling model.* Perhaps most in the spirit of the Wicksell-Lindahl insights is the contribution of Buchanan and Tullock, who consider a model of direct democracy in which individuals may trade their votes on one issue for votes on another.[48] Analysis of this log-rolling model suggests that small groups of electors will have an incentive to trade their votes on particular issues in such a way as to ensure majority support for budgetary proposals of special advantage to their particular groups.

The sort of proposal most obviously relevant in our present context is the provision of public goods financed by discriminatory taxation. A low-income coalition, for example, might be formed to support a public health program to be financed by a steeply progressive surtax. Also of some significance here is the fact that individual tastes for public goods may vary; low-income groups may prefer health, high-income groups defense. Defense outlays supported by (say) proportional taxation may therefore offer a discriminatory package attractive to the higher-income groups.

In this way then the Buchanan and Tullock analysis seems to suggest that public goods supply will be pushed well beyond the allocative optimum, essentially as an engine of redistribution from minority to majority. This was precisely the Wicksell-Lindahl conclusion.[49] As Wicksell remarked: ". . . it is like a game of roulette where the players win and lose in turn but the money finally ends up with the bank."[50]

The overexpansion result is, however, far from generally valid. This is particularly easy to see if we suppose, for example, that majority voting is introduced, not into a political vacuum, but to succeed a Pareto-efficient benevolent despotism. In this situation it is clear that a reduction in the existing Pareto-optimal public goods supply used to finance an appropriately discriminatory tax cut is, in principle, just as attractive to a given coalition as the corresponding overexpansion package. Further and more restrictive assumptions are therefore required to generate an overexpansion of public goods.[51]

---

[47] The work of Arrow is in itself of rather limited relevance to the general problem of efficiency in public goods supply, and will not be considered here. For an interesting application of Black's techniques to some artificially restricted problems of public goods supply, see Buchanan, *The Demand and Supply of Public Goods.*

[48] See J. M. Buchanan and G. Tullock, *The Calculus of Consent* (Ann Arbor, 1962), chaps. 10–12.

[49] For references, see n. 46 above.

[50] Wicksell, p. 87.

[51] Another possibility which, however desirable, seems much more remote, is that redistributive techniques will be confined to direct tax-transfer measures and not extended to indirect measures involving public goods.

However, the central welfare conclusion that there is a strong presumption against any close approach to Pareto-optimality still holds.

**2.3.2.2** *The competitive model.* The other majority-voting model which has been applied to the problem of public goods supply serves to highlight further difficulties. Thus Anthony Downs has analyzed the provision of public goods in a parliamentary democracy characterized by competition for political power between two vote-maximizing political parties.[52] In this model, politicians have no direct interest in the welfare implications of particular policies but only in their vote-catching potential.

Downs then proceeds to show that it is only where all information problems are assumed away that some approach to Pareto-optimal public goods supply can be expected. On this unrealistic assumption, competition for votes will tend to force each party to propose Pareto-optimal provision for public goods, since, for each nonoptimal proposal, there will be many optimal proposals capable of attracting unanimous support.

The information requirements of such a system are, however, overwhelming.[53] The political parties become in effect two competing sets of omniscient planners. In order, for example, to design a Pareto-optimal benefit tax program in terms of the volume and mix of public goods and the corresponding set of differential marginal tax-prices, each party must have full knowledge of voter preference maps for public and private goods, and must also have full knowledge of the effects of alternative policies. Neither of these requirements seems likely to be even approximately satisfied. In the case of voter preference maps we encounter a strategic-behavior problem analogous to that facing the legal monopolist under Samuelsonian joint supply,[54] namely that the various subsets of voters have an obvious incentive to understate their preference for public goods in an attempt to minimize their share of the tax cost.

Equally important, however, is the further requirement that voters should be able to recognize a Pareto-optimal program when they see one. For this it is necessary that voters should have full information regarding program content, and should be able to determine the effects of given policies on their own welfare positions. In fact we know that voter information in both respects is rudimentary. It is here also that the Galbraith point regarding the distorting effects of advertising

---

[52] See A. Downs, *An Economic Theory of Democracy* (New York, 1957), chap. 10; and "Why the Government Budget is Too Small in a Democracy," *World Politics,* 1959–60.

[53] For a more detailed discussion of these problems, see the references in the preceding footnote.

[54] See pp. 79–80 above.

on the public-private preferences of voters can be fitted into the formal model. Due to high-pressure advertising of private goods, voters will tend to underestimate the relative benefits of public goods and choose a suboptimal supply of public goods in preference to an optimal supply.[55]

Note, however, that there is no sign of the fundamental market failure problem that, since nothing can be charged, nothing will be provided. Possession of the tax power completely obviates the financing problem posed by impossibility of price exclusion.

### 2.3.3 General implications

Analysis of the sort which we have been discussing clearly provides strong support for the conclusion of modern public goods analysis that, although serious market failure in public goods supply can readily be demonstrated, it should not too readily be assumed that government can do better. Some political decision processes may clearly be more efficient than others, and there is an obvious need in this area for a more general theory of constitutional choice. Even here some beginning has been made, notably by Buchanan and Tullock in *The Calculus of Consent,* and, of course, on a more general level, in the theory of games.[56]

## 3.   Towards a Generalized Theory of Public Goods

As it stands, the modern theory of public goods is perhaps best regarded as a significant parable of public policy. As Samuelson himself has emphasized,[57] the public good concept was chosen not for its realism but rather to provide a polar theory of public expenditure to set against the equally unrealistic Walrasian model of private expenditure. It was hoped that the polar formulation of public expenditure theory would yield theoretical and empirical insights comparable to

---

[55] See Downs (1959–60), p. 552. Other factors may of course work in the opposite direction, e.g., relative unawareness of the tax cost of public goods where outlay taxation is employed.

[56] The need for careful analysis of these problems is clearly recognized by Samuelson in his original contributions. However, in his most recent discussion (1969), he takes a somewhat bleak view both of past achievements and of future prospects in this field. Thus, on past achievements, he remarks that "a corrosive nihilism seems needed to puncture the bubble of vague and wishful thinking in these matters"; whilst on future prospects for applying game theory in this area, he comments that "game theory, except in trivial cases, propounds paradoxes rather than solves problems."

[57] See, especially, idem (1955), p. 350.

those of the Walrasian system; and recent developments have already gone a considerable way towards justifying this hope.

The polar concept of a pure public good can in fact very readily be generalized to encompass the complete spectrum of goods characterized by elements of Samuelsonian joint supply and/or external economies. In this way the theory can easily be extended to cover all of the central issues of public expenditure policy. In the process the theory of public goods inevitably merges with the traditional Anglo-American theory of market failure stemming from Sidgwick and Pigou and based mainly on the generalized external economies concept.[58]

If the polar theory is to be really useful, it should reliably indicate both the structure and analytical results of the generalized theory. This seems in fact to be the case. Thus the first stage of the analysis should provide a generalized normative theory of public expenditure incorporating the distributional considerations, uncertainties and irrationalities ignored for simplicity in our treatment of the polar case.[59] In the second stage, a theory of market failure in generalized public goods can be presented in which the degree of market failure ranges from virtual collapse in the polar case, through serious and significant (in cases like public health and education), to the more marginal cases familiar from the Pigovian theory. In the final stage of the analysis, the problems of political provision are considered, with the general conclusion that, in view, particularly, of the overwhelming information problems involved, political action is probably justified only where a significant degree of market failure due to price-exclusion problems can be demonstrated.[60]

---

[58] For a detailed discussion, see chap. 8 below.

[59] For some discussion of the role of these neglected factors, see "On Merit Goods," chap. 10 in this volume.

[60] It is particularly interesting in this connection to notice the increasing attention being devoted to the informational requirements of alternative policies to correct market failure in the more "marginal" cases discussed in the more conventional Pigovian literature. See especially O. A. Davis and A. B. Whinston, "On Externalities, Information and the Government-Assisted Invisible Hand," *Economica*, 1966.

# 4. Equity and Efficiency in Public Goods Supply

## 1. Introduction

In the ten years since it was first published, Musgrave's classic work *The Theory of Public Finance* has proved a fruitful source of provocative ideas for the developing theory of public goods.[1] No aspect of Musgrave's discussion has, however, created so much confusion and controversy as his treatment of the relationship between equity and efficiency in public goods supply. The relationship between the distribution and allocation aspects of public goods supply has, of course, long been the subject of controversy in the public goods literature. The first serious discussion of the subject was Wicksell's.[2] Wicksell's formulation was further elaborated and somewhat modified by Lindahl.[3] Lindahl's discussion was in turn severely criticized by Myrdal.[4] Much the most comprehensive analysis of the problem is, however, to be found in Musgrave.[5] It is the aim of the present paper to explore and clarify this crucial relationship by means of a detailed critique of Musgrave's analysis.

Reprinted without significant change from *Public Finance/Finance Publiques* 25, no. 1 (1970): 24–37.

[1] R. A. Musgrave, *The Theory of Public Finance* (New York, 1959).

[2] K. Wicksell, *Finanztheoretische Untersuchungen* (Jena, 1896). The relevant section is available in an English translation by J. M. Buchanan as "A New Principle of Just Taxation," in R. A. Musgrave and A. T. Peacock, eds., *Classics in the Theory of Public Finance* (London and New York, 1958), especially pp. 108–9.

[3] E. Lindahl, *Die Gerechtigkeit der Besteuerung* (Lund, 1919). One relevant section (pt. 1, chap. 4, sec. 2) and the whole of a subsequent reconsideration in 1928 are available in an English translation. See E. Lindahl, "Just Taxation – A Positive Solution" and "Some Controversial Questions in the Theory of Taxation," in Musgrave and Peacock.

[4] G. Myrdal, *Vetenskap och politik i nationalekonomien* (Stockholm, 1930). Myrdal's book is available in an English translation by Paul Streeten as *The Political Element in the Development of Economic Theory* (London, 1953). The critique of Lindahl is in chap. 7, pp. 176–85.

[5] Musgrave, chaps. 1 and 4.

## 2.   Indeterminacy in Optimal Public Goods Supply

In *The Theory of Public Finance* Musgrave distinguishes two major problems which government must overcome in attempting to ensure an optimal supply of public goods:

1. In contrast to market supply of private goods, there is the problem that individuals will not reveal their true preferences for public goods.

2. Again in contrast to market supply of private goods, there is no unique optimum for the government to aim at.[6]

Analysis of this second problem will provide a useful starting point for a discussion of some more general questions regarding Musgrave's treatment of the equity and efficiency objectives.

Basically it seems clear that Musgrave's second proposition is incorrect. In welfare maximization analysis for *both* a private goods world *and* a world with a public good, we obtain a utility possibility locus or infinite set of Pareto-optimal points corresponding to different distributions of welfare. In *both* cases the choice of a unique optimum or *optimum optimorum* requires the strong value judgments of a social welfare function.[7]

How then does Musgrave obtain this strange result? Fundamentally it derives from his particular method of separating the distribution and allocation functions of government. Following Wicksell and Lindahl, Musgrave suggests that the first step in welfare maximization should be the establishment of an ideal distribution of income. Then, on the basis of this ideal distribution of income, the government should proceed to supply public goods in accordance with individual preferences, defined in terms of the Pareto criterion as requiring that no one should be made worse off.[8]

In Figure 1, for a community consisting of two persons A and B, we measure A's level of utility along the horizontal axis and B's level of utility along the vertical axis. In diagrammatic terms the two-step procedure evidently implies, at the first step, that from the infinite set of points, represented by the actuality locus *LL,* which can be reached by lump-sum redistributions in the initial situation with no public goods supplied, the government should choose the most equitable. To do this, a social welfare function is required, and the initial distribu-

---

[6] Ibid., p. 8.

[7] Compare, for example, Bator's well known diagrammatic analysis of welfare maximization for a private goods world with Samuelson's diagrammatic analysis for a world with a public good. See F. M. Bator, "The Simple Analytics of Welfare Maximisation," *American Economic Review,* 1957, especially pp. 28–29; and P. A. Samuelson, "Diagrammatic Exposition of a Theory of Public Expenditure," *Review of Economics and Statistics,* 1955, especially p. 353 and chart 4, p. 352.

[8] See Musgrave, pp. 17 and 81–82.

tive optimum $Z$ is determined where a social welfare contour $W_1W_1$ just touches the actuality locus $LL$. At the second step, according to Musgrave, public goods should be supplied in accordance with individual preferences, defined, following Pareto, in terms of a restriction to north-easterly movements. As a result we see that optimal public goods supply is necessarily indeterminate between points $K$ and $M$ on the utility possibility locus $UU$.[9]

This procedure is, however, very curious. In order to determine the ideal initial distribution, it is clearly necessary to draw on the strong value judgments supplied by the social welfare function. But if the social welfare function is available to select the initial distributive optimum $Z$, why should it not be available to select the welfare maximum $W^*$ on the utility possibility locus $UU$? Musgrave contrasts this situation with that of market supply of private goods, but without a social welfare function there is in general no unique optimum here either.

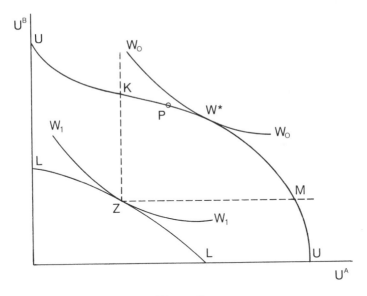

Figure 1

## 3.   Formal Inadequacy of the Wicksellian Framework

What Musgrave's argument about welfare indeterminacy really shows is the existence of a formal flaw in his Wicksellian two-step

[9] For Musgrave's analysis, see pp. 81–84.

procedure for welfare maximization. The existence of an ideal initial
distribution at $Z$ evidently provides no guarantee that the *final* distribution of welfare after public goods have been provided will likewise be ideal. The provision of public goods must in general affect the
distribution of welfare, and the central equity concern in welfare
maximization analysis should obviously be the selection of the final
distributive optimum $W^*$ on the utility possibility locus, rather than
the selection of an initial distributive optimum at $Z$.[10]

Even in *The Theory of Public Finance,* Musgrave shows complete
awareness of this formal inadequacy, but argues that the advantages
of the Wicksellian approach outweigh its disadvantages.[11] However,
in his more recent Biarritz paper, Musgrave attempts to reformulate
the two-step procedure in order to remove or reduce this formal inadequacy.[12] Following Wicksell and Lindahl he assumes that, for
Pareto efficiency, public goods will be supplied at differential tax-
prices corresponding to individual marginal evaluations of the public
good, i.e. so-called voluntary exchange pricing. Given the distribution
of income or pattern of factor ownership, he argues that the application of such a pricing rule will produce a *unique* Pareto optimum
corresponding to the unique optimum under competitive pricing in a
world of private goods and private property. It would therefore appear
that the two-step procedure could be freed from welfare indeterminacy
and distributional inadequacy by assuming an ideal initial distribution of income *plus* the application of the voluntary exchange pricing
rule.

Musgrave appears, however, to overlook an important ambiguity
in voluntary exchange pricing. In particular, voluntary exchange
strictly requires only *marginal* tax-prices equal to marginal evaluation for each individual. Tax-prices for inframarginal units of public
goods may be varied within certain limits analogous to the multipart
tariffs and the perfect discrimination concept familiar from discussions
of public enterprise pricing.[13] Following Lindahl, but not Wicksell,
Musgrave apparently assumes uniform pricing over quantities to each
individual.[14] As is clear from Lindahl's own discussion, such an
assumption is, however, very arbitrary, and is introduced as an alleged
requirement of equity or "equal power" precisely in order to resolve

[10] This point was first recognized by Myrdal, pp. 183–84. See also Samuelson, p. 354, n. 9.
[11] Musgrave, pp. 84–86.
[12] R. A. Musgrave, "Provision for Social Goods," International Economic Association Conference, Biarritz, Sept. 1966, subsequently published in J. Margolis and H. Guitton, eds.,
*Public Economics* (London, 1969), pp. 129–34.
[13] See, for example, J. M. Buchanan, *The Demand and Supply of Public Goods* (Chicago,
1968), pp. 39–40.
[14] This assumption is quite evident from his discussion. See Musgrave (1969), pp. 129–34.

the same indeterminacy problem which has troubled Musgrave.[15] It seems clear that the assumption of uniform pricing over quantities, required to ensure determinacy under voluntary exchange provision of public goods, is on a completely different level of institutional arbitrariness from the competitive pricing assumption required to produce uniqueness in a private goods world.

Even if we follow Lindahl and assume uniform pricing over quantities, the unique optimum generated on the basis of an ideal initial distribution of income or factor ownership still fails to satisfy the requirements for a welfare maximum. It is the final distribution of welfare which is of central concern, and the existence of an ideal initial distribution obviously still fails to guarantee the achievement of the welfare maximum at $W^*$.[16] Musgrave recognizes this problem but suggests that at least the scope of the distributional problem is in this way reduced.[17] This is, however, an illusion, since the total redistributive problem remains unaffected. The same strong value judgments are simply applied in two stages, first to reach $Z$, and then to move from Lindahl's $P$ point to the welfare maximum at $W^*$. The central point, however, is that the clean two-step separation of distribution and allocation aspects is not achieved; Lindahl's $P$ point and the welfare maximum $W^*$ do not in general coincide.

To remedy this residual inadequacy, Musgrave redefines the "ideal initial distribution" to be that distribution which, on the basis of the Lindahl tax-pricing rule, will produce the welfare maximum at $W^*$.[18] With this device, first considered by Myrdal in 1930 and finally adopted by Lindahl himself in 1959,[19] the problem of reconciling the

---

[15] See Lindahl, in Musgrave and Peacock, pp. 168–69. After noting the analytical similarity between his political model of voluntary exchange and the familiar economic problem of isolated exchange, Lindahl remarks (ibid., p. 168) that "theoretical economics generally regards price formation in the case of isolated exchange as an indeterminate problem. The same appears, at first sight, to hold of the distribution of public expenditure among the beneficiaries." However, "the indeterminacy of the price problem in the case of isolated exchange is to some extent due to the assumption that the exchange does not take place once and for all, but happens gradually, *different prices being charged for the units successively exchanged*. But in considering the taxpayers' approval of public expenditure, it is more natural to make the opposite assumption" (italics mine). The assumption of uniform prices or cost shares is then introduced as a requirement of equity or "equal power" (ibid., p. 169): "If the economic rights to which the individuals are entitled under a given property order are to be safeguarded in equal measure, everyone should pay the same price for the same units of cost both in the area of the private economy and of public finance." As he then comments, "the economic aspect of the problem thereby becomes a good deal more determinate."

[16] See the references to Myrdal and Samuelson in n. 10 above.

[17] See Musgrave (1969), p. 131.

[18] Ibid., p. 132. In general, such an initial distribution will not, of course, correspond to $Z$ in Figure 1 above. It is not therefore an "ideal initial distribution" in any normal sense.

[19] See Myrdal, p. 183; and Lindahl, "Om skatteprinciper och skattepolitik," *Ekonomi Politik Samhälle* (Stockholm, 1959), translated as "Tax Principles and Tax Policy," *Inter-*

Wicksellian two-step procedure with the requirements of welfare maximization is evidently completely solved in a purely formal sense. It seems clear, however, that the price of this reconciliation is very high. Specifically, there is an intrinsic indeterminacy in any formulation of the welfare maximization problem in terms of an ideal initial distribution of income, which can be avoided only on the basis of very arbitrary institutional assumptions.

## 4.  Possible Advantages of the Wicksellian Framework

Why then does Musgrave make such heroic efforts on behalf of such a recalcitrant two-step maximization procedure? In the course of his two discussions he offers a number of interesting reasons which we shall consider in turn.

1. The first is that "unless the state of distribution is given [to begin with], individuals cannot translate their preferences, whether for private or public wants, into a pattern of effective demand."[20] Crucially related to this argument is the point in his Biarritz paper that the Wicksellian procedure, appropriately reformulated, "suggests a method of pricing for social goods which is analogous to that of pricing for private goods . . . ,"[21] viz., differential tax-prices corresponding to marginal evaluation for each individual, or "voluntary exchange pricing."

In fact, however, the standard social welfare function approach to the welfare maximization problem with public goods suggests at least equally clearly the possibility of voluntary exchange pricing. In Samuelson's analysis, for example, the possibility of voluntary exchange pricing follows rather directly from his elegant derivation of the allocative requirement $MRS^A + MRS^B = MT$. A basic point which Musgrave appears to overlook, but which is obvious in Samuelson's more general formulation, is that, as we have already noted, there are an infinite number of voluntary exchange pricing solutions varying in their treatment of inframarginal units.

---

*national Economic Papers,* no. 10, 1960, p. 11. Myrdal warns that such a definition is "circular," which of course it is. Lindahl, however, seems untroubled by this problem. It is interesting to notice that Musgrave also recognizes the possibility of such a redefinition at one point in *The Theory of Public Finance,* p. 77, n. 1, but it is not reflected in his discussion in the text.

[20] Musgrave (1959), p. 17.

[21] Musgrave (1969), p. 132.

Even more important, however, is that Musgrave overlooks the fact that voluntary exchange pricing is not a necessary condition for optimal public goods supply. As Samuelson has emphasized in his Biarritz paper, optimal voluntary exchange pricing effectively requires omniscience on the part of the policy-maker.[22] Thus, from his knowledge of individual preference functions and the transformation function, the policy-maker must in effect derive the utility possibility function and, by applying the social welfare function, select the welfare maximum $W^*$. He can then work backwards, as suggested by Lindahl and Musgrave, on the assumption, say, of uniform prices or cost-sharing to the ideal initial distribution of numeraire private good and the appropriate set of tax-prices. However, as Samuelson points out, if the policy-maker is able to do this, the whole operation is essentially a pointless charade. Any "initial distribution" and set of tax-prices would be perfectly acceptable, since the supply of public goods can simply be set at the optimal level corresponding to $W^*$, and distribution can then be swung to the $W^*$ optimum by means of a suitable system of lump-sum taxes and subsidies.[23]

It would therefore seem that Musgrave's first set of arguments for the Wicksellian framework is inadequate. It may be true, as Musgrave suggests, that unless the state of distribution is given, individuals cannot themselves translate their preferences for public goods into a pattern of effective demand. This translation may, however, be performed for them by an omniscient policy-maker.

2. The second set of arguments offered by Musgrave is that his Wicksellian two-step procedure should serve to minimize the inefficiencies which result when distributional and allocative considerations are combined.[24] Following the two-step procedure, it is obvious that the ideal initial distribution should as far as possible be achieved by means of a tax-transfer mechanism rather than through the supply of public goods.[25] Once the ideal initial distribution has been established, public goods should then be provided in accordance with individual preferences, either through a voluntary exchange system of tax-prices, or, we should now add, by some other allocatively efficient procedure.

In the absence of feasibility problems, Musgrave is obviously right that the supply of public goods should not be used as an engine of re-

---

[22] See P. A. Samuelson, "Pure Theory of Public Expenditure and Taxation," in J. Margolis and H. Guitton, eds., *Public Economics* (London, 1969), sec. 3.

[23] See Samuelson (1969), Appendix. This possibility is also clear from his original discussion. See idem, "The Pure Theory of Public Expenditure," *Review of Economics and Statistics*, 1954, p. 388.

[24] See Musgrave (1959), pp. 40–41, and (1969), pp. 132–33.

[25] See Musgrave (1959), p. 18, and (1969), pp. 132–33.

distribution; and the Wicksellian two-step procedure which isolates the problem of establishing the ideal initial distribution of income from the problem of public goods supply certainly facilitates recognition of this point and suggests some possible policy procedures.

At first glance, however, it would seem that Samuelson's social welfare function approach is equally satisfactory in this respect. Thus, for example, Samuelson has long emphasized the point that an efficient redistributive policy ideally requires the use of a system of lump-sum taxes and transfers.[26] In fact his social welfare function approach to public goods supply suggests a two-step procedure for welfare maximization somewhat analogous to the Wicksellian approach, in which, at the first step, the supply of public goods is explicitly set at the $W^*$ level, and the distribution of income or numeraire private good is then "swung to the ethical observer's optimum" by means of a suitable set of lump-sum taxes and subsidies.[27] We therefore see that in the absence of feasibility problems and with an omniscient policy-maker, the reformulated Wicksellian framework and the social welfare function framework suggest a somewhat similar dichotomy of redistributive and reallocative policies.

When the hopelessly unrealistic assumption of an omniscient policy-maker is abandoned, however, the Wicksellian framework and the emphasis on voluntary exchange pricing in Musgrave's discussion may find some policy justification. In the absence of omniscient policy-making the central problem emerges that individuals have an incentive to disguise their true preferences for public goods in an attempt to obtain a more favorable tax-price or cost-sharing arrangement.[28] Under these conditions the feasible best allocative solution may well require the establishment of a rigid set of tax-price institutions, perhaps roughly proportional to income and constant over quantities, against which individuals can be expected to reveal their preferences for public goods through their choice of a political party at periodical elections under a regime of, say, majority voting.[29]

For best results this "tax constitution" should be designed, following Lindahl's suggestion, to approximate at least roughly the relevant

---

[26] See, for example, Samuelson (1954), p. 388. Like Musgrave, Samuelson recognizes of course that the ideal system of lump-sum taxes and transfers will not in general be feasible. In contrast to Musgrave, however, he goes on to recognize that, as a result, public goods supply may under certain circumstances provide the feasible-best redistributive device. See Samuelson (1955), "concluding reflection" (iv)a, pp. 355–56.

[27] See Samuelson (1954), p. 388.

[28] This, of course, is the first of the two major problems in ensuring efficient political provision of public goods distinguished by Musgrave, and set out on p. 94 above.

[29] If tax-prices are rigidly set in advance, individuals cannot hope to obtain a more favorable tax-price or cost-sharing arrangement by strategic concealment of their true preferences.

marginal evaluations for public goods of the different income groups.[30] Under these circumstances the apparent implication of the social welfare function approach that any old set of tax-prices will do, since its redistributive effects can subsequently be corrected by an appropriate set of lump-sum taxes and subsidies, is evidently quite inapposite and misleading; the use of an appropriate tax-price system is central to the achievement of a feasible best allocative solution.

Similarly, there is an evident need, if possible, to draw a sharp distinction in the tax constitution between these "purely fiscal" tax-prices and any prior "sociopolitical" taxes which may be required for purely redistributive purposes. A sharply progressive personal income tax, for example, which combines the two functions, will tend to produce allocatively excessive demands for public goods by the lower income groups and allocatively deficient demand by the higher income groups. Under a lower-middle income coalition, public goods supply will therefore tend to be overexpanded, whilst under a middle-upper income coalition, public goods will tend to be underexpanded.[31] For best results it is evidently true, as Wicksell and Lindahl first suggested, that the two functions should, if possible, be substantively separated on the most practical policy level, and not merely, as a heuristic device, in the mind's eye of the theorist.

Note, however, that this "operational" version of the voluntary exchange approach differs in certain crucial respects from the voluntary exchange theory from which it derives. In particular there is no question of genuinely simultaneous determination of the volume of public goods supplied and the cost-sharing arrangement or set of tax prices, which Wicksell, Lindahl and Musgrave have all maintained is an "essential condition for any adequate theory of the public household."[32] Although the operational version is in some sense suggested by the theory, the essential condition of simultaneous determination of public goods supply and cost-sharing is abandoned for preference-revelation purposes in favor of a prior setting of tax-prices or cost shares.[33]

[30] Lindahl argues that differences in marginal evaluations are likely to be due to differences in incomes rather than differences in tastes for public goods. He therefore regards income taxation, with an appropriately chosen rate-structure, as providing a suitable tax constitution for public goods supply. See, for example, Lindahl, in Musgrave and Peacock, pp. 228–29.

[31] See, for example, chap. 6, sec. 5.2 below.

[32] Musgrave (1959), p. 62.

[33] In Wicksell's original formulation, genuinely simultaneous determination of tax shares and public goods supply, and flexibility of burden-sharing arrangements, are seen as operational requirements for an efficient solution. When cost shares are variable, however, individuals may behave strategically in order to obtain more favorable cost-sharing arrangements, and their true preferences for public goods may not therefore be effectively or economically revealed.

Whether or not Musgrave had this particular policy justification in mind is doubtful.[34] The whole approach is, however, very fully spelled out by Lindahl and the central preference-revelation point is clearly stated by Bowen.[35] A more recent version of the same general approach is to be found in Buchanan, though with a completely different treatment of the redistributive aspects.[36]

3. This brings us to the third and most general set of reasons which Musgrave puts forward to justify his Wicksellian two-step separation of functions. Here Musgrave makes the point that "the kind of reasoning that deals with the efficient allocation of resources in terms of a given pattern of individual demand is not applicable to the problem of the Distribution Branch; the problem is ill-adapted to solution by the customary tools of economic analysis."[37] Since the customary tools of economic analysis are best fitted to handle the problem of allocative efficiency in public goods supply, it is proper for the economist to concentrate on this problem.[38] In principle, however, the distribution question is presumably of equal importance in welfare maximization, and to avoid losing sight of it completely Musgrave advocates the formal device employed by Wicksell and Lindahl of explicitly postulating prior policies to establish an ideal distribution. What of the social welfare function approach employed by Samuelson? According to Musgrave, "following Samuelson's formulation, the entire state of distribution is determined along with the allocation of resources between social and private wants, thus combining the problem of the Allocation and Distribution Branches into one."[39]

Musgrave is obviously right in suggesting that the treatment of distribution is more difficult than the treatment of allocation, and this is well recognized in the Wicksell-Lindahl approach which he develops. It is also recognized, however, in most of the modern literature on

[34] Musgrave obviously regards the two-step procedure both as a heuristic device to promote "orderly thinking about the basic issues of budget policy" (1959, p. vii) and as an aid to efficient policy design. As to the latter, however, and apart from the point that a tax-transfer mechanism should be used for redistributive purposes, he provides no clear formulation or rationale of voluntary exchange pricing as an operational procedure for allocatively efficient public goods supply.

[35] Lindahl (1919, pt. 3, chap. 4) explores at some length the details of a practical tax constitution based mainly on ability taxes and calculated to provide a good approximation to the voluntary exchange ideal. The rationale of such a system in terms of preference revelation is not, however, clear in Lindahl, and was first stated by Bowen. See H. R. Bowen, "The Interpretation of Voting in the Allocation of Economic Resources," *Quarterly Journal of Economics*, 1943–44, p. 45.

[36] See, especially, J. M. Buchanan, *Public Finance in Democratic Process* (Chapel Hill, N.C., 1967), chap. 19.

[37] Musgrave (1959), p. 85.

[38] Ibid., p. 89.

[39] Ibid., p. 84.

welfare economics. Typically, the allocation objective is the subject of sophisticated analytical treatment, whilst the distribution objective is treated in a purely formalistic fashion.[40] Specifically, Musgrave is incorrect in implying that the social welfare function approach provides an integrated treatment of the two problems. As developed by Samuelson and others, the social welfare function approach actually provides strikingly dichotomous treatment of the distribution and allocation aspects, concentrating the full fire-power of modern welfare analytics on the allocation problem, whilst providing the most perfunctory treatment of distribution, which is passed over with the empty formalism that it should be "swung to the ethical observer's optimum."[41]

It appears therefore that the Wicksellian framework advocated by Musgrave is just one of a common class of welfare theories which concentrate attention on the allocation function whilst keeping a foot in the door for the more controversial function of income redistribution.

This familiar approach has, of course, been strongly criticized in the recent literature, notably by Buchanan who maintains that there is a philosophical inconsistency involved in the dichotomous treatment of the distribution and allocation functions.[42] According to Buchanan, the Pareto criterion provides the appropriate welfare framework for public goods analysis. In this framework all functions, distribution as well as allocation, are subjected to the uniform and philosophically consistent rule of the Pareto criterion. Although Buchanan has demonstrated that the Pareto test may be much less conservative in matters of income distribution than had originally been assumed, it is nevertheless possible to argue that the Pareto criterion provides a very inadequate framework for the operations of the distribution branch.[43] As Musgrave puts it, "there is no simple set of principles, no uniform rule of normative behaviour that may be applied to the conduct of public economy. Rather we are confronted with a number of separate, though interrelated, functions that require distinct solutions."[44]

[40] For a survey and critique of the treatment of the distribution problem in modern welfare theories, see, for example, chap. 1 in this volume, sec. 2.4.

[41] Samuelson (1954), p. 388.

[42] See, in particular, J. M. Buchanan, "The Theory of Public Finance," *Southern Economic Journal*, 1960, pp. 235–36; and, more recently, "What Kind of Redistribution Do We Want?" *Economica*, 1968, pp. 188–90.

[43] See, for example, chap. 2, sec. 3.1, above. Indeed it could be argued that the Pareto criterion is inadequate even for purposes of the allocation branch. See chap. 2, sec. 3.2. On the distribution question, see also K. Klappholz, "What Redistribution May Economists Discuss?" *Economica*, 1968.

[44] Musgrave (1959), p. 5.

## 5.  Conclusions

The main results of the above analysis can now be summarized briefly as follows:

1. On the most fundamental level, there is no indeterminacy in optimal public goods supply which we do not find in a world of private goods. Musgrave's suggestion to the contrary derives from a formal flaw in the original formulation of his Wicksellian two-step procedure for welfare maximization. In particular the establishment of an ideal initial distribution in no way guarantees that the final distribution of welfare after public goods have been supplied will likewise be ideal. This difficulty is, however, surprisingly hard to eradicate without abandoning not only the spirit but even the form of the two-step procedure. Thus a formal solution is possible only if the "ideal initial distribution" is defined in terms of the welfare maximum achieved after public goods have been supplied; and even this can be done only on the basis of some institutionally quite arbitrary voluntary exchange pricing assumption.

2. The advantages claimed by Musgrave for the Wicksellian framework over the standard social welfare function approach, as employed, for example, by Samuelson, are for the most part illusory. The Wicksellian framework, either as originally formulated or in Musgrave's somewhat convoluted reformulation, is simply a slight variation on the social welfare function approach. Thus the two approaches offer a similar dichotomous treatment of distributional and allocative aspects; and under omniscient policy-making the procedures they suggest for welfare maximization are likewise equivalent. The one advantage of the Wicksellian formulation, overlooked by Wicksell and Musgrave, is that it serves to suggest what, in the absence of omniscient policy-making, may well be the feasible best operational procedure for welfare maximization with public goods.

# 5. Public Goods and Separation of Branches

One of the most controversial topics in the public goods debate of the past ten years has been the relationship between the equity and efficiency aspects of public goods supply. Much of the confusion and controversy on this topic can be traced to Musgrave's classic formulation in *The Theory of Public Finance* (1959), which is based on the pioneering contributions of Wicksell and Lindahl. In a previous paper published in this review (see chap. 4), I have therefore attempted to clarify certain aspects of this relationship by means of a detailed critique of Musgrave's formulation, including the revised version contained in his stimulating Biarritz paper of 1966 (1969). Harold Hochman's wide-ranging comments (1970) on my paper appear to blur some crucial issues, and, on other issues, reflect an apparent lack of awareness of my own position as developed in detail in earlier papers. Some further discussion may therefore be useful.

In the following section I shall abstract from the possibility of Pareto-desirable redistribution which I shall then discuss in section 2.

## 1. Equity-Efficiency Interrelationships

1. Following Musgrave, my original paper explores the possibility and desirability of a two-step welfare maximization procedure under which an ideal initial distribution of income is first established, and public goods are then supplied in accordance with individual preferences. Hochman seems to have no fundamental objections to my analysis of the main issues involved, though he makes a number of references to a recent paper by McGuire and Aaron (1969), which appeared after my own paper was already complete. Some of these references are, however, extremely misleading.

Reprinted without significant change from *Public Finance/Finance Publiques* 25, no. 4 (1970): 546–55.

Thus, for example, he states that: "If Lindahl's solution is applied by the allocation branch, the distribution branch can couch its judgments in terms of post-transfer *income* and arrive at the same overall conclusion as it would in a world of private goods alone" (1970). In fact, of course, even if the Lindahl solution is applied, the "overall conclusion" regarding the ideal initial distribution will be very different from that in a world of "private goods alone," as I have pointed out in my paper (see chap. 4 above, n. 18).[1] The same point is in fact explicitly noted by McGuire and Aaron (1969, pp. 38–39).

*If* the ideal initial distribution were the same, with and without public goods (supplied in accordance with the Lindahl solution), a genuine two-step maximization procedure and corresponding "separation of branches" would be conceptually possible. Unless we make some extremely restrictive assumptions, however, this is not generally the case; and Hochman is therefore quite wrong in concluding that "it would make no difference whether the distribution branch reasons, procedurally, like Musgrave, starting with an adjustment along Head's interior or private goods frontier (*LL*), or like Samuelson, who starts on the exterior frontier (*UU*), invokes a social welfare function and works backward to *LL* to determine the distribution of private goods consistent with the social optimum" (1970).

2. The "conceptual separation of functions" actually attempted by McGuire and Aaron is much more limited in scope (1969, pp. 35–36). They note that, under constant costs, the Lindahl solution would impose a tax on each individual equal to his valuation of public good in terms of private good (*MRS* × quantity). A given ideal initial distribution of income (measured in terms of private good), established by the distribution branch, is therefore unaffected by the activities of the allocation branch in the performance of its "purely fiscal function" of supplying public goods. On this basis McGuire and Aaron argue that distribution and allocation functions can therefore be separated in the sense that, if the distribution branch first determines an ideal initial distribution of private good in the light of the utility possibility frontier *UU* based on both private and public goods, the allocation branch could simply be instructed to find the Lindahl solution (which is here the welfare maximum). The result, they argue, is a two-step maximization procedure in which the allocation branch is freed from any concern with distributional problems. This, they suggest, may be "convenient."

---

[1] In his introductory section Hochman (1970) refers, somewhat ironically, to "an additional complication, which Head does not discuss, for the provision of public goods generates income effects, which in themselves alter individual preferences for private goods and, therefore, affect the welfare connotations of any particular ex ante distribution of income."

In fact, even this modest separation is a complete illusion. The ideal initial distribution cannot be found unless the distribution branch computes the full Lindahl solution by working backwards, on the Lindahl assumption of uniform prices (over quantities), from the chosen maximal point on the utility possibility frontier to the appropriate initial distribution of private good. The price of relieving the allocation branch of any distributional responsibility is therefore effectively to impose the full computational burden of both functions on the distribution branch. It is hard to see how this could possibly be "convenient"!

As a result of these analytical inadequacies both the Hochman discussion and the McGuire and Aaron paper tend to obscure the essential point that the "conceptual separation of functions" offered in Musgrave's Biarritz paper is in no sense a genuine separation. Under the proposed procedure the allocation and distribution branch budgets must be simultaneously determined. Implementation in accordance with a two-step procedure is possible only after the two steps have in effect been taken together. This is precisely the point of Myrdal's fundamental objection that the concept of the ideal initial distribution becomes "circular" in this approach (1953, p. 183). It is also clear from Samuelson's recent analysis (1969, sec. 3).

3. A somewhat similar confusion permeates another elegant recent contribution to the public goods literature by Winch (1969). Winch begins by arguing that "since optimum allocation depends on the chosen distribution, and cannot be the subject of independent value judgments, it is necessary that distribution be decided first" (p. 495). In fact, however, the choice of a maximal point on the utility possibility frontier simultaneously determines both optimal allocation and ideal distribution. Winch goes on to suggest (p. 498) that the relevant distributional value judgments can be embodied in a tax structure which would guarantee an ideal distribution of private good for each possible volume of public good. If all preference functions are known, this could, of course, be done, though it would serve no obvious purpose. It is, however, a central point of Winch's analysis that the distributionally ideal tax structure can be specified even if public goods preferences are unknown (p. 503). This goes far beyond the modest claims of McGuire and Aaron, and implies the possibility of a genuine two-step separation of distributional and allocative functions.

As Grove (1970) has recently demonstrated, however, such independent determination of a distributionally ideal tax structure is possible only if the social welfare function is separable in terms of private and public goods. For the two-person, two-good case, this requires that the ratio of the marginal social significance of private good for the two persons should be independent of the volume of the public good.[2] Winch appears to recognize this point (p. 498), but he evidently fails to appreciate what a severe and arbitrary restriction is thereby imposed on the Paretian social welfare function which he employs. As Samuelson has emphasized from the outset (1954, 1955, 1958, 1969), no genuine separation of distributional and allocation aspects is conceptually possible except in very special cases.[3]

4. The question of conceptual separability must, of course, be clearly distinguished from that of operational separability. On this issue, Hochman, again quoting McGuire and Aaron, argues that the separation of issues which is allegedly possible at the conceptual level fails at the operational level due to nonrevelation of individual preferences for public goods. And it is certainly true, as I emphasize in my own paper (see chap. 4 above, p. 99), that perfect practical implementation of the Lindahl-Musgrave two-step procedure requires full knowledge of all preference functions. From the preceding discussion it should, however, be clear that preference-revelation problems are not "the sole reason for a necessary breakdown of the allocation-distribution distinction in public goods supply," as McGuire and Aaron would have us believe (1969, p. 36).

In the paragraph from which Hochman quotes, McGuire and Aaron contrast the implementation problems of the two-step procedure in the public goods context with the corresponding problem in a world of private goods (1969, p. 39). From the point of view of informational requirements and preference-revelation problems this contrast is, however, less striking than is often assumed. Even in a world of private goods the determination of the welfare maximum involves the application of the social welfare function to select a point on the utility possibility locus; but to derive the utility possibility locus individual

---

[2] Let the social welfare function be written as

$$(1) \; W = W(X_1^1, X_1^2, X_2),$$

where $X_1^1$ and $X_1^2$ represent consumption of the private good by persons 1 and 2, and $X_2$ is the volume of the public good fully and equally consumed by both. Under the condition stated in the text, the welfare function is separable and can be rewritten as

$$(2) \; W = \phi[f(X_1^1, X_1^2), X_2],$$

which can be maximized in two stages. See Grove (1970), p. 242. For Paretian welfare functions commodities cannot, of course, enter as independent arguments, but corresponding requirements can readily be stated for this case (Grove [1970], p. 244).

[3] The best known special case in which a meaningful conceptual separation of issues is possible is, of course, the partial equilibrium case in which the marginal utility of private good is constant. In this case the optimum output of the public good is independent of the distribution of the private good. As a result the allocation branch operation can proceed independently of the distribution branch, with the ideal distribution determined at the second stage in the light of the allocation branch decision. See Samuelson (1969), Appendix, Section A.

utility functions must be known. Assuming that the market mechanism is employed to solve the allocation problem, the fact remains that each individual has an incentive to misrepresent the utility implications of any prospective redistribution of private goods in an attempt to obtain a more favorable net redistribution. The two-step procedure remains "viable," but on a strict interpretation, welfare maximization by this procedure requires full knowledge of individual utility functions, as in the public goods case.[4] In this context, even Samuelson's classic papers are somewhat misleading.

5. The remainder of Hochman's section I is devoted essentially to summarizing some of the main arguments developed in my own paper and we seem to be in substantial agreement on most issues, both conceptual and operational.

## 2. Pareto-Desirable Redistribution

1. Amongst the reasons put forward by Musgrave for the separation of the distribution and allocation branches is the fundamental methodological argument that "the kind of reasoning that deals with the efficient allocation of resources in terms of a given pattern of individual demand is not applicable to the problem of the Distribution Branch; the problem is ill-adapted to solution by the customary tools of economic analysis" (1959, p. 85). I examine this argument in section 4 (3) of my paper (see chap. 4), pointing out that Musgrave's dichotomous treatment of allocation and distribution aspects is in fact characteristic of much "New Welfare" theory including the Bergson-Samuelson social welfare function approach, which provides only the most perfunctory and formalistic treatment of the distribution problem. Hochman agrees with this view, and argues that a more satisfactory analysis of the distribution problem can be provided within the Paretian framework of the allocation branch. The latter half of his paper is devoted to exploring this possibility, along the lines of his recent Leningrad paper with Rodgers (1970).

2. Hochman argues that my discussion does not contemplate the possibility of Pareto-desirable redistribution. In fact, however, I explicitly refer to it (see chap. 4, p. 103). My views on this particular issue were set out in more detail in my earlier paper "On Merit Goods" (see chap. 10 below). The implications of Hochman's discussion are particularly unfortunate as our views correspond so closely.

[4] A similar problem arises in determining the ideal distribution of private goods in the Winch model (1969).

Thus, for example, on the possibility of benevolent patterns of utility interdependence, I argued as follows: "The main relatively pure non-appropriability problem in a distributional context would appear to stem from the possibility that members of the middle- and upper-income groups may derive altruistic satisfaction from increased consumption by the lower-income groups. A member of the upper-income group unilaterally transferring income to the lower-income groups may thus provide altruistic benefits to other high-income individuals. As a result, private philanthropy will tend to be restricted because of nonappropriability problems, even though any given high-income individual might be willing to contribute significantly more for the benefit of the low-income group if other high-income individuals would agree to do likewise. If the number of economic units is large, however, voluntary cooperation is likely to be of only very limited adequacy. It may thus be possible to justify a substantial redistributive tax-transfer system for the benefit of the lower-income groups imposing proportionate sacrifice on all members of the higher-income groups" (see chap. 10, pp. 236–37 below).

Similarly, on the possible role of risk and uncertainty:

". . . individual uncertainty concerning the future may play an important role in the formulation of conceptions of the proper state of distribution and the need for redistributive measures. The individual's own future income, not to mention that of his family, is usually subject to a considerable degree of uncertainty. Even in relatively stable societies, incomes of individuals of the same age, and even of similar educational background and other socioeconomic characteristics, show considerable dispersion. In societies which have been ravaged by great wars, revolutions, depressions, hyperinflations, and other political and social upheavals, such uncertainty may clearly be intense. At least to a substantial degree, such income-uncertainty is likely to be privately unavoidable and uninsurable; and in a society in which most individuals are risk-averters, this uncertainty may be reflected in redistributive government policies and mildly egalitarian conceptions of the proper state of distribution, either of income in general or of particularly important commodities (as in the case of merit goods). Thus an economic policy objective of a proper state of distribution may to some extent reflect individual attitudes towards privately unavoidable and uninsurable risk" (see chap. 10, p. 225).

3. Like Hochman, I argue that both of these factors are likely to be of considerable practical significance. To date, however, it must be admitted that there is little more than intuition and casual observation to support this contention. Thus, for example, we have little if any idea regarding the proportion of actual budgetary redistribution which

can be assigned to the Pareto-desirable category. Following a recent suggestion by Musgrave (1970), Hochman has argued in his Leningrad paper with Rodgers (1970) that all redistribution in kind falls in this category, since transfer recipients themselves would presumably not choose to restrict their own choices in this way. This is, however, far from completely convincing. Thus it could equally well be argued that these transfers are largely coerced; the beneficiaries choose redistribution in kind because political resistance is less and a greater net transfer can therefore be achieved in this way (Shoup, 1969, p. 75). The restriction on individual choice involved may well be negligible by comparison, even where it exists at all. As Musgrave remarks in a more careful passage, "there is no simple test by which the two components may be distinguished in practice" (1970, p. 992).

4. Like Hochman, I am critical of the more traditional approaches to the distribution question, both on operational grounds and because of their authoritarian implications. There appears, nevertheless, to be a significant difference of emphasis between us. Hochman asks rhetorically: "Can individualistic and elitist concepts of polity co-exist, as they do in Head's discussion, in a logical symbiosis?" (1970). My answer is that, in spite of the difficulties which arise once we venture outside the Paretian framework, "it is still possible to argue that uncritical acceptance of individual preferences, including attitudes to risk and uncertainty, cannot provide an adequate welfare framework for public finance theory, least of all in the field of equity" (see chap. 10, p. 228). This is also my conclusion in the more abbreviated discussion of my "Equity and Efficiency" paper (see chap. 4, p. 103). Hochman's views are not entirely clear, but he seems to lean more in the direction of Buchanan's position, which he quotes with approval.

My arguments in support of this conclusion are set out in more detail in a previous paper published in this review (see chap. 2). To recapitulate briefly, I would argue that there are various possible approaches to the choice of an appropriate welfare framework: "ethical," "acceptable," "positivistic," and "political." The Pareto criterion represents just one variety of "acceptable" approach. If the Pareto criterion is accepted, it follows, of course, that the only legitimate redistributions are those which are based on individual preferences. From an ethical point of view, however, it might well be objected that individual preferences in matters of income distribution are too liable to be based on envy, prejudice and self-interest to provide a fully adequate ethical foundation for the operations of the distribution branch. Even from an acceptability point of view the Pareto criterion is inadequate, since individual values conflict sharply on matters of equity. "General acceptability" is achieved only by ignoring the distributional preferences of the lower income groups. Thus, whilst the concept of Pareto-desirable redistribution may often take us a good way towards an adequate normative conception of the distributional objective, judged by ethical or acceptability standards, it can hardly be regarded as fully adequate from either point of view.[5]

5. It is, of course, not only in the distribution branch that we meet reservations and qualifications regarding the adequacy of a welfare framework based on a naive concept of consumer sovereignty or individual preferences. Musgrave, for example, introduces his concept of merit wants to epitomize those cases in which the concept of allocative efficiency might properly be based, not on overt preferences, but on a normalized set of consumer preferences adjusted for certain effects of ignorance and irrationality (1959, pp. 13–14). Hochman suggests that this concept also might well be brought within the scope of the efficiency criterion. Here again I have explored the various possibilities in previous papers (see chaps. 10 and 11). Briefly, I would argue that many of the ignorance and irrationality problems epitomized by the merit wants concept can indeed be brought within the scope of a very broadly defined concept of consumer sovereignty or Pareto efficiency.[6] I would very much doubt, however, whether the sort of "particular-commodity interdependence" envisaged by Hochman takes us very far in this direction. As Hochman's own discussion indicates, it is more directly relevant to the subsidiary distributional and social wants aspects of the merit wants concept.

# References

M. A. Grove, "On Musgrave's Separation of the Tasks of the Public Household," *Western Economic Journal,* Sept. 1970, pp. 241–45.

J. G. Head, "On Merit Goods," *Finanzarchiv,* Mar. 1966, pp. 1–29. [Chap. 10 below.]

J. G. Head, "Welfare Methodology and the Multi-Branch Budget," *Public Finance/Finances Publiques,* no. 4, 1968, pp. 405–24. [See chap. 2 above.]

J. G. Head, "Merit Goods Revisited," *Finanzarchiv,* Mar. 1969, pp. 214–25. [See chap. 11.]

---

[5] The Paretian framework is no better from a "positivistic" or "politically operational" point of view. See chap. 2 in this volume.
[6] As in the case of the distribution branch I would not, however, regard such an approach as fully adequate. For the relevant arguments, see chap. 2, sec. 3.2 and chap. 11, sec. 3 in this volume.

J. G. Head, "Equity and Efficiency in Public Goods Supply," *Public Finance/Finances Publiques,* no. 1, 1970, pp. 24–37. [See chap. 4.]

H. M. Hochman, "Professor Head on Equity and Efficiency: Comment and Addendum," *Public Finance/Finances Publiques,* no. 4, 1970, pp. 536–45.

H. M. Hochman and J. D. Rodgers, "Is Efficiency a Criterion for Judging Redistribution," Institut International de Finances Publiques, Leningrad Conference, Sept. 1970.

M. C. McGuire and H. Aaron, "Efficiency and Equity in the Optimal Supply of a Public Good," *Review of Economics and Statistics,* Feb. 1969, pp. 31–39.

R. A. Musgrave, *The Theory of Public Finance* (New York, 1959).

R. A. Musgrave, "Provision for Social Goods," in J. Margolis and H. Guitton, eds., *Public Economics* (London, 1969), pp. 124–44.

R. A. Musgrave, "Pareto Optimal Redistribution: Comment," *American Economic Review,* Dec. 1970, pp. 991–93.

G. Myrdal, *The Political Element in the Development of Economic Theory* (London, 1953).

P. A. Samuelson, "The Pure Theory of Public Expenditure," *Review of Economics and Statistics,* Nov. 1954, pp. 387–89.

P. A. Samuelson, "Diagrammatic Exposition of a Theory of Public Expenditure," *Review of Economics and Statistics,* Nov. 1955, pp. 350–56.

P. A. Samuelson, "Aspects of Public Expenditure Theories," *Review of Economics and Statistics,* Nov. 1958, pp. 332–38.

P. A. Samuelson, "Pure Theory of Public Expenditure and Taxation," in J. Margolis and H. Guitton, eds., *Public Economics* (London, 1969), pp. 98–123.

C. S. Shoup, *Public Finance* (Chicago, 1969).

D. M. Winch, "Pareto, Public Goods and Politics," *Canadian Journal of Economics,* Nov. 1969, pp. 492–508.

# 6.  Lindahl's Theory of the Budget

## 1.  Introduction

The upsurge of interest in the theory of public expenditure, which has been such a feature of the Anglo-American public finance literature during the past decade, has served to draw attention to Lindahl's subtle neoclassical synthesis of the diverse strands of the benefit theory.[1]

Thus, in the course of his important recent contributions to public expenditure theory,[2] Samuelson has had occasion to refer in some detail to the prior analysis of Lindahl.[3] Musgrave, in *The Theory of Public Finance*,[4] provides a revised version of the detailed critique of Lindahl contained in his celebrated article on "The Voluntary Exchange Theory of Public Economy."[5] English translations of both an important part of Lindahl's original (1919) exposition and the whole of a later reconsideration in 1928[6] have appeared under the auspices

Reprinted with some corrections and minor changes from *Finanzarchiv* 23, no. 3 (October 1964): 421–54. The author is indebted to Professor C. S. Shoup of Columbia University for valuable help and encouragement.

[1] Erik Lindahl, *Die Gerechtigkeit der Besteuerung* (Lund, 1919).

[2] Paul A. Samuelson, "The Pure Theory of Public Expenditure," *Review of Economics and Statistics*, 1954; "Diagrammatic Exposition of a Theory of Public Expenditure," *Review of Economics and Statistics*, 1955; "Aspects of Public Expenditure Theories," *Review of Economics and Statistics*, 1958. For a detailed discussion of Samuelson's theory, see chap. 3 above.

[3] Samuelson (1955), p. 354.

[4] R. A. Musgrave, *The Theory of Public Finance* (New York, 1959), pp. 73–86.

[5] R. A. Musgrave, "The Voluntary Exchange Theory of Public Economy," *Quarterly Journal of Economics*, 1938–39. For another interesting critique (of English origin) see A. T. Peacock, "Sur la théorie des dépenses publiques," *Economie appliquée*, 1952, secs. 4 and 5. Also L. Johansen, "Some Notes on the Lindahl Theory of Determination of Public Expenditures," *International Economic Review*, 1963. This paper was already complete and had been submitted for publication when Johansen's excellent analysis became available. Although our discussions run parallel in some respects, there are significant differences in scope and emphasis.

[6] Erik Lindahl, "Einige strittige Fragen der Steuertheorie," in Hans Mayer, ed., *Die Wirtschaftstheorie der Gegenwart* (Vienna, 1928).

of the International Economic Association in *Classics in the Theory of Public Finance.*[7] Finally, encouraged by the revival of interest in his work, Lindahl himself was moved in 1959 to publish a second reconsideration,[8] devoted mainly to a detailed analysis of Myrdal's penetrating and influential criticisms,[9] which, although published as early as 1930, are still the most damaging to have emanated from his own country over the intervening 30 years. This second reconsideration has also now appeared in English translation in *International Economic Papers.*[10]

Although both the original exposition and two reexpositions are now available in English, it must be admitted that Lindahl's theory does not make particularly easy reading in any language. Description and prescription are almost inextricably interwoven in his discussion; words such as *is, must, ought,* and *should,* sometimes appear to be used almost interchangeably. His basic diagram, even with the axes reversed as by Musgrave, seems almost bizarre to those brought up in the conventional techniques of modern value theory. Thus, in spite of Myrdal's brilliant early work, Musgrave's careful discussions, and Samuelson's illuminating "obiter dicta," it is very doubtful whether the precise nature of the theory is as yet at all generally understood and its merits and defects properly appreciated.

It is the aim of this article to disentangle the descriptive and prescriptive strands of Lindahl's theory and subject them to critical reexamination in the light of more modern theories of value and welfare economics. We shall begin (section 2) with an outline of the main features of his analysis, distinguishing sharply between the prescriptive and descriptive strands. Then (section 3), in the light of modern welfare economics, we shall examine his prescriptive theory. Following this (section 4), we shall employ some familiar tools of modern value theory to analyse his descriptive theory of budgetary policy in a democracy. Finally (section 5), we shall make a few comments on his policy recommendations. Section 6 contains a brief summary of the main conclusions.[11]

[7] Erik Lindahl, "Just Taxation — A Positive Solution," and "Some Controversial Questions in the Theory of Taxation," in R. A. Musgrave and A. T. Peacock, eds.. *Classics in the Theory of Public Finance* (London and New York. 1958).

[8] Erik Lindahl, "Om skatteprinciper och skattepolitik," *Economi Politik Samhälle, Festskrift till Bertil Ohlins 60 — årsdag* (Stockholm, 1959).

[9] Gunnar Myrdal, *Vetenskap och politik i nationalekonomien* (Stockholm, 1930). Myrdal's book is available in an English translation of the German edition by Paul Streeten, *The Political Element in the Development of Economic Theory* (London, 1953).

[10] "Tax Principles and Tax Policy," *International Economic Papers,* no. 10 (London and New York, 1960).

[11] Except where otherwise indicated, all references will be to the relevant English translations.

## 2. An Outline of the Theory

Both in the original exposition of his theory and in his two subsequent revisitations, Lindahl has three distinct aims. The first is to establish the nature of a "just" system of public expenditure and taxation, i.e. to develop a prescriptive theory of the government's budget.[12] The second is to determine to what extent budgetary policy in a parliamentary democracy can be expected to correspond to these ethical principles. The third is to recommend, in the light of his results, changes in voting procedures and tax legislation, which would facilitate a closer approach to the ideal under democratic government.

### 2.1  A Just System of Public Expenditure and Taxation

According to Lindahl, a just system of public expenditure and taxation must satisfy two fundamental requirements.

The first is that, under it, any injustices in the existing distribution of property must be corrected; "property owned without a just title must go to the community."[13] Thus it is the sociopolitical function of taxation[14] to establish a just "initial" distribution of property. This is not, however, an aspect of justice to which the "fiscal theorist" has much to contribute, in spite of the "higher standpoint" provided by his deeper understanding of economic interrelationships.

The second is that "the rest of the tax burden must be distributed in accordance with the thus established just system of property."[15] "But if taxation is to correspond to any particular property structure, it must by and large reflect the individual valuations [of public expenditure] conditioned by that structure."[16] More specifically, "the marginal tax for each individual must not exceed the estimated marginal utility to him of government expenditure"[17]; or, more positively, expendi-

---

[12] And hence, by implication, of economic policy generally.

[13] Lindahl (1919), quoted by Myrdal, p. 178.

[14] As the titles of his three expositions clearly indicate, Lindahl's attention tends, in traditional public finance fashion, to be concentrated mainly on the tax side of the budget. Where necessary, however, we could easily restore the balance without too much disturbing the spirit of his discussion by reading "public expenditure and taxation" for taxation. In the present very important context, we could therefore envisage a sociopolitical category of expenditures as well as of taxes; at least some of the social security and social service outlays of many countries should be regarded as falling in this category.

[15] Ibid.

[16] Idem (1928), p. 227.

[17] Idem (1959), p. 9.

ture on each public good should be pushed to the point where, for each individual, the utility to him of the last unit of public good is equal to the sacrifice represented by the tax-price he must pay for each unit (and the sum of these tax-prices is just sufficient to cover the cost of production).[18] This is the "purely fiscal" requirement which a just system of public expenditure and taxation must satisfy.

Since the determination of the just initial distribution of property is beyond the competence of the fiscal theorist, his "purely fiscal" theory of the second requirement must remain entirely "hypothetical" in the sense that it must proceed on the assumption that a just distribution of property has somehow already been established.

In addition to employing the obvious natural law justification for his concept of justice, Lindahl is much concerned to show that his theory is completely consistent with the then widely accepted sacrifice and ability-to-pay theories, but is in fact more general than these. Thus he proceeds to show that the equal sacrifice principle can be derived from his "purely fiscal" principle; and, at the cost of seeming to abandon his entirely "hypothetical" approach, he is willing to concede that the minimum aggregate sacrifice principle offers a very attractive "economic" solution to the sociopolitical problem.[19]

## 2.2 Budgetary Policy in a Parliamentary Democracy

Lindahl's second objective is to determine to what extent budgetary policy in a parliamentary democracy can be expected to conform to these requirements of justice, and in particular to the "purely fiscal" principle handed down from his higher standpoint by the public finance theorist.

His general approach to this problem is first of all to set up a highly stylized model of the democratic political mechanism, under which the "purely fiscal" requirement will be fully satisfied. Then, by means of a

---

[18] According to Myrdal (pp. 180 and 182), this "more positive" interpretation of the purely fiscal requirement is the main respect in which Lindahl manages to improve on the normative theory of his famous teacher Wicksell, who "emphasized the negative aspect, viz. that no citizen, not even the marginal taxpayer, should pay for more than the utility which he receives from the services of the state. But Lindahl realized that this condition leaves open many possible tax distributions of which only one can be 'just.'"

Wicksell is concerned initially to lay down a criterion for desirable budgetary policy, rather than a goal or welfare maximum. The whole aim of his argument for the adoption of more flexible and imaginative burden-sharing arrangements is, however, precisely to ensure that all desirable projects will in fact be implemented; it is therefore clear that his criterion is intended to lead to a Pareto optimum, though not in general to the unique Lindahl optimum.

[19] For Lindahl's intricate analysis of these issues, see, for example, "Einige strittige Fragen . . . ," pp. 226–32.

comparison of the institutional features of his "model democracy" with those of actual parliamentary democracies, he proceeds to indicate the nature and direction of the probable departures from his "fiscal optimum," which must be expected in practice.

### 2.2.1 The model

In Lindahl's model democracy there are just two economically homogeneous groups of satisfaction-maximizing citizens, A (the relatively rich) and B (the relatively poor). Political power is assumed to be equally distributed between the two groups in the sense that they are equally able to safeguard "the economic rights to which they are entitled under the existing property order."[20] To isolate the "purely fiscal" aspects of the problem, this "existing property order" is assumed to be given.[21] Finally, on the basis of these assumptions, the pattern of public expenditure and taxation is assumed to be determined "by free agreement between the two groups"[22]; the political situation is therefore analogous to a market situation of isolated exchange[23] or bilateral monopoly, or, more precisely, to joint supply of two products where the demand for each product is monopsonistic.[24] The public expenditures in question are assumed to be on pure public goods which must be consumed in equal amounts by all; this is sufficient, though not necessary, to ensure that they cannot be efficiently supplied through the market mechanism.[25]

In order to show that, on these assumptions, the fiscal optimum will necessarily be achieved, Lindahl introduces the following diagram.[26]

Along the $X$ axis we measure, from left to right, A's percentage share in total public expenditure on any one public good or branch of public activity (e.g. defence), this share increasing from zero at point $O$ to 100 percent at $M$. Along the $Y$ axis we measure total public expenditure on the activity in question.

Assuming that the individuals comprising the two groups are able to evaluate the benefits from public goods, we can now proceed to draw

[20] Idem (1919), p. 172.

[21] Ibid., p. 173, n. 4. In the context of the model, Lindahl is concerned to abstract from the moral justification for the existing property order. An alternative procedure would have been to assume explicitly that the existing property order is not only given, but also ideal. Myrdal (p. 181) seems incorrect, however, in suggesting that Lindahl does in fact do this.

[22] Lindahl (1919), p. 168.

[23] Ibid.

[24] Idem (1928), pp. 220–22, and especially n. 12, p. 223.

[25] On this point, see chap. 8 below. One of the most important flaws in Lindahl's exposition is the absence of a clear discussion of this crucial pillar of his prescriptive theory.

[26] Idem (1919), p. 170.

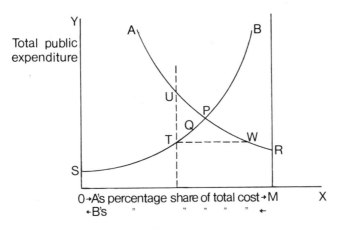

Figure 1

up two "demand schedules" *AR* and *BS*, for A and B respectively, showing the amounts of public expenditure which each group "is prepared to sanction" at the various cost shares, assumed constant over quantities for each group. At any given cost share, "as in the private economy," each group of identical satisfaction-maximizing economic men would wish to see public expenditure pushed to the point where, for each individual member of the group, marginal utility equals price and total utility is therefore maximized. The two schedules therefore represent "the monetary expression of the marginal utility of total public activity for the two parties."[27] Regarding the shape of the schedules, Lindahl suggests that, for each group, as cost shares increase, so the amount of public expenditure desired will diminish.

From this description it is obvious that *P*, the intersection point of the two curves, represents Lindahl's fiscal optimum, since it is only at *P* that the utility of the last unit of public good produced is simultaneously equal to the tax-price for each and every individual member of both groups. Is there, however, any reason for supposing that the fiscal optimum will in fact be reached, and equilibrium established at point *P* in this model democracy?

To show that it must, Lindahl bids us consider first the case in which cost shares are initially set well to the left of *P*, say at 50 percent for each group. In this situation, he suggests that the level of expenditure initially agreed upon will be represented by point *T*. At this cost share, group A would like to see public expenditure pushed to the level rep-

[27] Ibid., pp. 169–70. On the derivation of Lindahl's demand schedules from the "underlying" indifference curves, see Johansen.

resented by point $U$, but this is not possible, since B would not be willing at this price to contribute the balance of total cost. However, at the given cost ratio, both groups would prefer the level of public expenditure represented by $T$ to any smaller outlay; a "provisional equilibrium" will therefore be established at $T$.

At $T$, as we have seen, A's desire for public goods is far from satisfied. Since B will only approve a higher level of public expenditure if its own cost share is reduced, A will therefore offer to bear a greater share of the burden; "the equilibrium position is thereby shifted closer to the intersection point of the two curves. . . . But the shift of the equilibrium position towards $P$ continues smoothly only so long as A's growing sacrifice—and it grows in a double sense, by virtue both of the increase in public expenditure and of the increase of A's share in the cost—is more than compensated by the greater utility due to the expansion of collective activity. Once these two factors become equal, as for instance at point $Q$, A has reached the equilibrium position most favorable to itself."[28]

Symmetrically, if A's cost share is initially set well to the right of $P$, say at $M$, where A is bearing 100 percent of the total, we could describe the movement to "the equilibrium position most favorable to B." Lindahl suggests that, since group B is relatively poor, this will "probably" be at $R$. Starting with initial cost ratios between those represented by $Q$ and $R$, it seems impossible to say what will happen beyond the establishment of a "provisional equilibrium" at the point on $QPR$ corresponding to that ratio. One party would like to see an expansion of public expenditure at a cost ratio more favorable to itself; the other would like to see a contraction at a more favorable ratio. In the light of this analysis, Lindahl concludes that the "possible equilibrium positions" must lie on $QPR$. However, "which of the possible positions—which lie on the curve $QPR$—will eventually lead to equilibrium, is mostly a matter of the extent to which each party is able to defend its own interests."[29]

At this point, just when indeterminacy between $Q$ and $R$ seems inevitable, Lindahl introduces his equal power assumption as a sort of deus ex machina to ensure that ultimate equilibrium must in fact always be established at $P$ and the fiscal optimum therefore necessarily achieved. Thus, "it is not difficult to see what equilibrium position corresponds to a situation in which both parties have equally safeguarded the economic rights to which they are entitled under the existing property order. . . . Equilibrium will be established at the inter-

[28] Lindahl (1919), pp. 170–71.
[29] Ibid., p. 171.

section point of the two curves, where both parties can exchange up to saturation, and where therefore the money value of the net gain that both parties together derive from public activity is maximised."[30] He therefore concludes that in his model democracy "the price of collective goods . . . by and large tends to correspond to marginal utility for each interested party."[31]

Just as the political situation is analogous to a market situation of isolated exchange or bilateral monopoly, so Lindahl observes that the fiscal optimum has its market counterpart; "in the case of market exchange, where free competition leads to a price at which all market parties can exchange up to saturation, we can also state as a general rule that the overall satisfaction of wants of all individuals, as valued by them in money terms, is maximised."[32,33]

### 2.2.2 The model versus parliamentary democracy

Lindahl recognizes, however, that conditions in actual parliamentary democracies diverge in numerous respects from those assumed to exist in his model. It cannot therefore be expected that the fiscal optimum will in fact be reached in practice. By comparing the main features of the model with those of actual democracies, he then proceeds to indicate the nature and direction of probable departures from the optimum.

According to Lindahl, some of the more significant divergences in practice from the conditions of the model are as follows:

(a) In the first place, the individual may find the benefits from many important public services particularly difficult to evaluate. "People are usually unable to appreciate the full implications of these very intricate matters, and must hence be content to guess the value of the advantages. In so doing, they are highly subject to the influence of public opinion. Individual evaluation is, thus, a complicated process and a function of many factors."[34]

It should also be borne in mind that the satisfactions in question may

[30] Ibid., p. 172. "Equal power" is thus defined implicitly in terms of ability to exchange up to saturation. The rights under the existing property order which are to be safeguarded equally are therefore the rights to exchange up to saturation, i.e. the rights to maximize total utility, given the "budget restraint" of the existing property order. As Lindahl himself puts it (ibid., p. 173), "any given property order means in the first place that each individual can satisfy his wants in the measure of their money value to him."

[31] Ibid., p. 173.

[32] Ibid., p. 172, n. 3.

[33] And to round off the analogy with isolated exchange, he notes (ibid., p. 173 n. 5) that "such an equilibrium position must be regarded as the ideal one also in the case of isolated exchange."

[34] Idem (1928), p. 218.

include those of an altruistic as well as of a narrowly self-interested nature. This does not, however, substantially affect the argument.[35]

(b) It must also be recognized that there may be more than two political groupings, and that each group will seldom be economically homogeneous. Although he clearly and explicitly recognizes these possibilities, Lindahl does not seem to consider that they are likely to constitute an independent source of divergences from the fiscal optimum and the individual values on which it is based.[36]

(c) In a parliamentary democracy, however, individual preferences can find effective expression only to the extent that they are accurately reflected in the programs of political representatives. In practice, groups A and B must therefore be regarded as the supporters of political parties A and B respectively.

Lindahl suggests, however, that in a democracy, political programs cannot diverge too long or too far from individual valuations, since, in various ways, "the politicians will have their error brought home to them."[37] The ultimate check here is provided by regular general elections. At least in a comparative statics analysis, this divergence can therefore be more or less ignored.

(d) Legislative procedures seldom provide, as in the model, for simultaneous voting on the extent and financing of expenditures in a particular area of public activity, let alone on detailed items within that given area. "If Parliament were presented only with the totals of the tax bill and of public services, each party would feel that it had failed to receive adequate return for the last unit of tax paid. . . . There is only one way to avoid a contraction of public services harmful to all; each must undertake to pay a greater share than the other towards the cost of those services which each finds most useful."[38] Since budgetary procedures in actual democracies do not provide for such "specialisation of the budget," underexpansion of the public sector would have to be expected.

(e) Finally, and most important, it is not the case in actual democracies that the pattern of public expenditure and taxation is determined by "free agreement" between groups with "equal power." Under majority voting, full political power is formally vested in the representatives of the majority group, who may well consider it unnecessary to enter into negotiations with the minority.

Turning to the effects of this divergence on the fiscal equilibrium, Lindahl suggests that "the coercive element due to the preponderance

---

[35] Ibid., p. 217.
[36] See, for example, his discussion (1919), p. 173.
[37] Idem (1928), p. 219.
[38] Idem (1919), pp. 173–74.

of power obviously has the same effect as if the weaker parties now attached greater values to the public goods. In our diagram [assuming A is the majority party] the new equilibrium is best found by moving the old one along A's price curve, say to point $U$; B's net gain decreases in proportion with the magnitude of the coercive element."[39]

Even in this case, however, individual values are still overwhelmingly important, though they are now to be interpreted as the individual values of the majority. Furthermore, the majority party cannot in general afford completely to ignore the desires of the minority, because of the "economic" and "political" costs which this would involve. Some account will therefore be taken of the extent to which (in the opinion of the majority) minority groups stand to benefit from particular activities.[40]

What will be the cumulative effect of all these divergences from the conditions assumed in the model? Lindahl recognizes that, as a result of these divergences, the fiscal optimum will not be fully achieved in actual parliamentary democracies. He is very concerned to stress, however, that the analogy between budget determination and price formation in the market is still useful and important; "the analogy of price formation in the public and the private economy is not unduly qualified by the above-mentioned shift in the equilibrium position as a result of an uneven distribution of power and of other factors."[41]

## 2.3  Implications for Voting Procedures and Tax Legislation

The analysis of sections 2.1 and 2.2 above has obvious and important policy implications for voting procedures and tax legislation, which Lindahl is not slow to spell out.

(*a*) In the first place, even a rather imperfect democratic form of government offers better prospects of an approach to fiscal justice than totalitarian or absolutist forms, however "benevolent."[42]

(*b*) The performance of actual parliamentary democracies can, however, be considerably improved in various ways.

(i) First, a more accurate reflection of individual preferences, and particularly of minority interests, should be sought by the adoption of the system of proportional representation in the selection of parliamentary representatives at general elections. Minority preferences

[39] Ibid., p. 175.
[40] See, for example, ibid., pp. 175–76; (1928), p. 232; and (1959), pp. 21–22.
[41] Idem (1928), p. 226.
[42] Idem (1919), German edition, p. 145.

are effectively ignored under the more usual systems of a simple plurality or preferential voting.[43]

(ii) Second, to avoid serious distortions due to the attempt to solve both the sociopolitical and the "purely fiscal" problem simultaneously under a single fully-integrated progressive personal income tax, tax legislation should observe a clear distinction between taxes intended to perform these two very different functions. Thus, a division of these two types of revenue between central and local government might be considered; or, if an efficient division of expenditure functions makes this impossible for the reasons mentioned in (iii) below, the progressive personal income tax should be sharply divided into a basic (proportional or mildly progressive) fiscal tax and a progressive surtax.[44]

(iii) Third, to avoid the problem discussed under (d) in section 2.2.2 above, some degree of specialization of the budget could be attempted by linking particular taxes to particular categories of public expenditure.[45]

(iv) Finally, a closer approximation to the "free agreement and equal power" assumptions of the model might profitably be attempted. In particular, the standard democratic procedure of simple majority voting on "purely fiscal" matters should be modified to allow a limited veto for minorities.[46]

# 3.  The Prescriptive Theory of the Budget

Turning now to a detailed examination of the foregoing theory, we have seen in section 2.1 that Lindahl's prescriptive theory lays down two requirements for a "just" system of public expenditure and taxation. The first is that it should establish a just "initial" distribution of property; and the second is that, on the basis of this just distribution of property, expenditure on each public good should be pushed to the point where, for each individual, the utility of the last unit of public good is equal to the tax-price he must pay for each unit. Thus, on the basis of a just property order, public expenditure should be pushed in

[43] Ibid., p. 146.

[44] Idem (1928), pp. 231–32, and (1959), pp. 22–23.

[45] Idem (1919), German edition, pp. 148–49.

[46] Ibid., pp. 146–49. Lindahl's position on this question is, however, completely reversed in his most recent reconsideration. See 149, n. 125 below. In his original discussion he seems not to have noticed the inconsistency between this Wicksellian recommendation (and the related demand for flexible burden-sharing arrangements) and his own advocacy of ability taxation (such as a proportional or mildly progressive income tax) as a practical solution to the "purely fiscal" problem. See also secs. 3.3 and 5.1 below.

each direction to the point where, in relation to that property order, the satisfaction of each individual is maximized; it would therefore be impossible to make someone better off without making someone else worse off, and the situation is thus Pareto-optimal. It is only on the second requirement, however, that the public finance theorist, from his higher standpoint, is particularly well qualified to speak.

We shall now proceed to examine this prescriptive theory in the light of modern welfare economics.

## 3.1   The Hypothetical Nature of the "Purely Fiscal" Principle

The central feature of Lindahl's prescriptive theory is his insistence that the prior establishment of a just distribution of property is a necessary condition for budgetary justice, and, at the same time, that the determination of this just initial distribution of property is beyond the competence of the public finance theorist. In handing down, elaborating and advocating the second "purely fiscal" principle, the public finance theorist must therefore proceed on the explicit assumption that the sociopolitical requirement is satisfied, a just property order having somehow already been established; it is only in the presence of a just property order that he would necessarily suggest that public expenditure should be pushed to the point where, in relation to the given property order, the satisfaction of each individual is maximized.

Lindahl's contention that the determination of the ideal distribution is beyond the competence of the fiscal theorist should be perfectly acceptable to the modern welfare economist. It is indeed a fundamental tenet of "New Welfare" theories, that the economist qua economist cannot usefully pronounce upon questions of income distribution; after a long period in which discussions of income distribution in the Anglo-American public finance literature were effectively dominated by the various pseudoscientific sacrifice theories, it was finally accepted by the end of the 1930s that scientific economic analysis can shed little light on the question. We can now see, however, that this same conclusion was reached much earlier in the Continental literature, not merely by Pareto from whose analysis the more recent Anglo-American discussions derive, but also, on the other side of the political spectrum, by Lindahl's direct intellectual antecedents, Wicksell and Wagner,[47] in their influential sociopolitical principle, subsequently taken over with minor modifications by Lindahl.

[47] See, for example, Wagner, in Musgrave and Peacock, p. 14, and Wicksell in ibid., p. 108.

Rather less familiar, perhaps, is his apparent reluctance to recommend a tax-expenditure program for the establishment of a Pareto-optimum, except on the basis of an ideal initial distribution of property. His attitude is, nevertheless, entirely typical of the more radical reforming branch of economic liberalism in the latter half of the nineteenth century. Modern welfare theories, by contrast, have their roots in a product of the conservative branch of the same liberal tradition, namely Pareto. Thus Pareto was perfectly willing to recommend policies to "improve resource allocation" (make someone better off and no one worse off) on the basis of the *existing* distribution of income, whether "just" or not; Paretian welfare economics was not therefore "hypothetical," even in theory.[48]

Modern welfare economists have not, however, adopted the Pareto criterion without misgivings. Even when the possibilities of compensation, "package deals" and longer-run interpretations of the criterion are allowed for, it must still be regarded as highly restrictive even in matters of "allocation," and extremely conservative in matters of income distribution. A government rigorously applying such a criterion is likely to find itself relegated to the role of a passive observer of the turbulent stream of economic history, unable, by virtue of its self-imposed Pareto-constraint, to divert this stream into socially more desirable channels; at the same time, in the absence of a supplementary sociopolitical principle, grossly undemocratic and potentially explosive inequalities of income are effectively preserved.

For these reasons, some of the most important contributors to "New Welfare Economics," especially in their more careful moments, have contrived to attach "sociopolitical" strings to "allocatively" rather less restrictive Paretian criteria.[49] Perhaps the outstanding example of this approach is Little's criterion,[50] according to which an economic policy is desirable if, by redistributing in the prepolicy situation, it would not be possible to make everyone as well off as in the postpolicy situation, and any resulting redistribution of income is good. The generic relationship between Lindahl's approach and that of these modern theorists is thus quite clear; the more radical branches of modern welfare theory have more in common with Wagner, Wicksell, and Lindahl than with Pareto.[51]

[48] For an excellent discussion of economic liberalism in the nineteenth century, see Myrdal, chap. 5.

[49] For a useful critical discussion of some of the devices employed, see Paul Streeten, "Recent Controversies," Appendix to Myrdal, pp. 212–16; and I. M. D. Little, *A Critique of Welfare Economics*, 2nd ed. (Oxford, 1957), chaps. 6 and 7.

[50] Little, p. 109.

[51] This resemblance would be even more striking had these modern theorists been more concerned with spelling out the requirements for a welfare maximum (or, in Lindahl's terminology, a situation which is "truly just"), rather than with the development of criteria for desirable piecemeal changes.

## 3.2  The Ideal Initial Distribution of Property

Lindahl's precise formulation of the sociopolitical requirement in terms of a just "initial" distribution of property has, however, been the subject of important interrelated criticisms, first by Myrdal, and more recently by Samuelson.

### 3.2.1

Myrdal's first objection is that the concept of a just initial distribution is extremely artificial; it would never be possible in practice to determine the prebudget distribution of property, and it would therefore be impossible to decide precisely what (and whether) prior redistributions are necessary to satisfy the sociopolitical principle. As he expresses it, ". . . the scope of taxation and of public activity in a modern community is very wide. Even if it were narrower, it would be quite impossible to make even a rough guess of what ownership conditions would be in their absence. Yet such a guess would be a necessary condition for deciding what socio-political taxation should precede fiscal taxation."[52]

This argument should be reasonably acceptable to modern public finance theorists, who are only too familiar with the formidable problems involved in statistical studies of redistribution through the budget.[53] Only the roughest quantitative imputation of tax burdens (let alone expenditure benefits) is usually possible, and this imputation is anyway completely "hypothetical" in that it is concerned only with "direct" effects, no attempt being made to compute that distribution of income which would obtain in the complete absence of government.[54]

It might be thought that this problem could be largely overcome by a reasonable reinterpretation of Lindahl's sociopolitical requirement to apply to the current distribution of property as affected by the current (presumably suboptimal) government budget; in this way, the need for imputing the indirect effects of the budget could be avoided.[55]

---

[52] Myrdal, p. 183.

[53] For an excellent example of such a study and references to earlier attempts, see A. H. Conrad, "Redistribution through Government Budgets in the United States, 1950," in A. T. Peacock, ed., *Income Redistribution and Social Policy* (London, 1954).

[54] For a critical discussion of such studies, see A. R. Prest, "Statistical Calculations of Tax Burdens," *Economica*, 1955.

[55] In his final "reconsideration," devoted mainly to answering Myrdal's criticisms, Lindahl employs precisely this defense, arguing (1959, p. 11) that in his theory, "the distribution of property *before* taxation does not refer to any hypothetically impossible [impossible hypothetical?] situation without government activity, but quite simply to the distribution of property which, with the accompanying taxation, does in fact prevail at the moment when the taxation for a future period is being planned."

Myrdal, however, anticipating this possible defense, carries his objection still further, and suggests that, "It is clearly circular to assume that socio-political corrections should be applied to the *actual* situation of which purely fiscal taxation of whatever kind is one of the causes."[56] At least in principle, however, it seems that the suggested reinterpretation involves no circularity and no blurring of the distinction between the sociopolitical and fiscal principles.

### 3.2.2

Granted that the concept of a just initial distribution, properly interpreted, is not inconceivable, nor even nonoperational, we come to a second important objection, raised by Samuelson and emphasized by Musgrave, that, contrary to the impression left by his diagram, Lindahl's particular formulation leaves the just system of public expenditure and taxation indeterminate; starting with a just "initial" distribution of welfare, there will in general be an infinite set of budgetary policies, each of which will satisfy the second "purely fiscal" requirement.[57] The basic point here is that, starting from a suboptimal prepolicy situation with a given distribution of welfare, there is still an infinite set of Pareto-optimal postpolicy situations with distributions such that, as compared with the prepolicy situation, someone has been made better off and no one worse off.

It is important to recognize, however, that this indeterminacy is not peculiar to Lindahl's prescriptive theory. Most modern welfare theories in both the "hypothetical compensationist" and "actual compensationist" traditions exhibit a similar indeterminacy, and this has seldom been considered an important defect.[58] Of the modern welfare theories, only the Bergson-Samuelson "Social Welfare Function" approach is clearly determinate; only here then could we expect only one tax-expenditure system to be "truly just."

Furthermore, it seems only reasonable to interpret Lindahl's "just initial distribution of property" in terms of a given pattern of factor ownership or initial endowment of private good. On Lindahl's assumption that cost shares are constant over quantities of public good for each group, there will, however, be only one Pareto-efficient pattern

---

[56] Myrdal, p. 183.

[57] Samuelson (1955), p. 354, and Musgrave, pp. 8 and 80–84. Musgrave's diagrammatic demonstration of this point, though based on Samuelson's, is more directly relevant to the present discussion in that it incorporates the assumption of an ideal pre-(fiscal) policy distribution of income.

[58] Indeed Samuelson is rather more concerned to point out the inadequacy of Lindahl's diagram as an expositional device than to criticize his prescriptive theory on grounds of indeterminacy. Musgrave, however, clearly regards the existence of multiple optima as a significant flaw.

of inputs and outputs, and commodity and factor prices, corresponding to the just distribution of property.[59] Lindahl's concept of a unique fiscal optimum is then no more unreasonable than the concept of a unique equilibrium situation in the general equilibrium theory of a perfectly competitive economy.[60]

### 3.2.3

This brings us to Myrdal's second major objection to Lindahl's formulation. This objection appears to be levelled at the purely fiscal principle, but, as we shall see, it is also intimately related to Lindahl's interpretation of the sociopolitical principle.

As Myrdal puts it: "Granted the assumption of a just distribution, why should the correct tax be determined by marginal utilities?" For "taxation and the public activity corresponding to its expenditure will *ipso facto* alter the entire economic situation. This should, according to the theory, increase the total utility of each. But it will increase individual utilities by *unequal* amounts."[61] Hence, "even if we assume that the distribution before fiscal taxation is just, it would certainly no longer be just after taxation. . . . For even if subjective value theory could evolve a political rule, this would have to aim at a maximisation or a just distribution of *total* utilities and not of marginal utilities."[62]

This criticism bears particularly heavily on Lindahl's ingenious attempt to show that his theory does not necessarily conflict with Edgeworth's minimum aggregate sacrifice principle, and that it is in a sense more general, as it applies whatever the appropriate initial distribution of income or property; the latter, he is willing to concede, should perhaps be determined by "scientific economic analysis" in accordance with the minimum aggregate sacrifice principle.[63] Myrdal's argument, with its implicit advocacy of minimum aggregate sacrifice and "Old Welfare" principles generally, demonstrates conclusively that this attempted reconciliation is incomplete, since the sacrifice theorist would in general be interested in the post- (purely fiscal)

---

[59] See Johansen. Very special and totally unrealistic assumptions, such as that the traditional "satiability" (or diminishing marginal utility) postulate does not apply to private goods, are not therefore required to ensure a unique optimum. The possibility of employing this latter assumption is mentioned (unfavorably) by Samuelson (1955), p. 354, n. 9.

[60] Lindahl's theory can therefore quite properly be regarded as a very special variety of the Bergson-Samuelson "Social Welfare Function" approach. See, however, chap. 4, pp. 96–97 above.

[61] Myrdal, p. 184.

[62] Ibid., pp. 184–85.

[63] Lindahl (1928), pp. 230–31.

policy distribution as well as, and indeed rather than, the "initial" or prepolicy distribution.[64,65]

It is not, however, true to suggest, with Myrdal, that Lindahl's "purely fiscal" principle is therefore "entirely arbitrary" and "remote from canons of abstract justice"; nor can we agree that "if subjective value theory could evolve a political rule, this would *have to* aim at a maximisation or a just distribution of *total* utilities and not of marginal utilities."[66] This is very clear in the light of modern welfare discussions, the whole aim of which has been to develop a prescriptive theory of economic policy which does not depend upon the interpersonal comparisons and controversial value judgments of Old Welfare theories of the sort which Myrdal, in the passages quoted, seems to regard as the concrete embodiment of the "canons of abstract justice." The main result of these modern discussions has in fact been to establish Lindahl's "purely fiscal" principle, in the generalized form of the Pareto-optimum (and with or without sociopolitical qualifications), as the cornerstone of the New Welfare Economics![67,68]

---

[64] Both Myrdal (p. 185) and Samuelson (1955, p. 354, n. 9) have emphasized quite rightly that this objection cannot satisfactorily be met by the artificial and unrealistic assumption that any redistributions due to "purely fiscal" policy will necessarily be small and their social significance can therefore be neglected.

[65] Though there is little warrant for it in Lindahl's two earlier discussions, it may be possible to reinterpret his sociopolitical principle as requiring an ideal post- (fiscal) policy distribution of property. Samuelson (1955, n. 9) indicates that this is how the correct distribution should be defined; and even Musgrave, who actually adopts the Wicksell-Lindahl concept of an ideal initial distribution himself, seems ready (pp. 84–86) to concede the case in principle for requiring an ideal postpolicy distribution.

In his recent discussion of Myrdal's criticisms, Lindahl does in fact avail himself of this defense. As he puts it (1959, p. 12), "Just taxation always implies that the distribution of property *after* taxes is just." [My italics.] Anticipating this defense in his critique, Myrdal asks (p. 183), "Must this [sociopolitical] condition be fulfilled *before* or *after* taxation? Clearly not after taxation, for the theory would then be circular. Taxation would indeed be just, but only because it would be one of the causes of an ex hypothesi just situation." Lindahl (p. 11) rightly denies the validity of this circularity charge; "to take account of the distribution of property after tax simply means that one anticipates the effects of [purely fiscal] taxation . . . the questions of just distribution of property and just taxation are solved *simultaneously*."

If we are willing to reinterpret the sociopolitical principle in this way, Lindahl's attempted reconciliation with the minimum aggregate sacrifice principle could easily be made complete; but it would be Old Welfare Economics which had swallowed the benefit theory rather than vice-versa. Perhaps this is what Myrdal meant by "circularity" in this context.

[66] Myrdal, pp. 184–85. (First set of italics mine.)

[67] Lindahl (1959, p. 10) is willing to concede all that is strictly necessary here. Thus he admits that, ". . . even if there is agreement about what is meant by a just distribution of property it is still possible within certain limits to arrive at different, but all logically defensible, conclusions about just taxation."

[68] In spite of the rather widespread impression to the contrary, however, it could still be argued that Old Welfare theories are superior to the New Welfare theories which have swept them from the textbooks. The only relevant sense in which any prescriptive theory

## 3.3   The "Purely Fiscal" Principle and Ability to Pay

We have seen that Lindahl's attempt to reconcile his sociopolitical principle with Edgeworth's minimum aggregate sacrifice principle fails. Is his even more ingenious attempt[69] to reconcile the "purely fiscal" principle with the ability-to-pay theory of taxation (which he equates with the equal sacrifice principle) any more successful?

Lindahl bases his argument on the assumption that ability or capacity (i.e. incomes) rather than interests (i.e. tastes) are likely to be the major determinant of the money value of the marginal utility of public goods; incomes vary far more from individual to individual than do tastes for public goods.[70] Thus, as an approximation, he suggests that the money value of the marginal utility of public goods will vary roughly in proportion to income. Charging each individual a tax-price for public goods equal to their marginal utility to him in terms of money (as required by the fiscal principle) will therefore require taxation which is roughly proportional to income, i.e. taxation according to ability.[71]

Assuming with Lindahl that individuals have the same tastes for public goods, i.e. that their conventional downward-sloping marginal utility schedules for any given public good are identical[72] (and independent of the amount of private goods enjoyed), it follows that, for pure public goods consumed in equal amounts by all, the marginal utility of public goods must, at the fiscal optimum, be equal for all individuals (and not merely equal to the tax sacrifice for each person

---

of economic policy can be "proved" or established is that of persuading people to speak, vote or fight for the policies deriving from it; it is therefore the task of the prescriptive theorist to muster arguments in terms of general acceptability, "abstract justice," social benefits, etc. in support of his theory. If the full implications of both approaches were generally understood, it is far less obvious than is sometimes assumed, that a majority could be found to support the professionally more fashionable New Welfare approach.

[69] Lindahl (1928), pp. 228–30. For an equally famous variation on the same theme, but for public goods without jointness characteristics, see Antonio de Viti de Marco, *First Principles of Public Finance*, book 2, chap. 2, especially secs. 2, 3, and 8.

[70] As Lindahl expresses it (ibid., pp. 217–18), "Since differences in the interests of individuals are of less significance than differences in their capacity, the latter must be considered the most important factor in determining the value of public services; interest is only some sort of modifying factor."

[71] Thus (ibid., p. 222) "it would hardly seem extravagant to say that taxation proportional to income – provided that the ratio correspond to valuation – is a result of the same laws of price formation which govern the private economy."

[72] In his recent reexposition (1959, p. 16, n. 19) Lindahl remarks: "The equal interest of individuals in government services can also (perhaps more correctly) be expressed by saying that they have the same indifference maps regarding expenditure for private and public purposes."

individually, as we have stated the condition hitherto).[73] Thus it is easy to see that, in this very special case, the marginal tax sacrifice must also be equal for all individuals. Obviously, however, this is not sufficient to ensure that taxing individuals in proportion to the money value of the marginal utility of public goods will impose equal (total) sacrifice as required by Lindahl's (then standard) interpretation of the ability-to-pay theory. This would be so only in such extremely special cases (common enough in the literature!) as that in which the marginal utility of income (or private good) schedules are not merely identical, but are also of unit elasticity; in this particular case, proportional income taxation would equalize not only marginal tax sacrifice but also total sacrifice for all individuals.[74]

From this discussion it should be obvious that, in the general case, taxation in proportion to the money value of the marginal utility of public goods will neither be proportional to income nor impose equal (total) sacrifice.[75] The attempted reconciliation is therefore incomplete.

In fact, Lindahl himself concedes this incompleteness. He recognizes very clearly, for example, that tastes for public goods are not identical, but he insists quite reasonably that it is often politically and administratively simply not possible to take account of such idiosyncracies.[76] Like many eighteenth- and nineteenth-century economists (including Adam Smith), but much more explicitly, Lindahl therefore advocates ability taxation as a practical solution to the "purely fiscal" problem of charging for public goods at least roughly on the basis of individual preferences or benefits; "the benefit principle is the general one, the ability principle a practical norm for meeting the cost of subjective advantages."[77,78]

---

[73] According to Musgrave (p. 77, n. 1), Myrdal maintains incorrectly that, at the fiscal optimum, the marginal utility of public goods must be equal for all individuals. At least in the English translation, however, Myrdal makes no such suggestion. It is apparent from our discussion that, precisely in Lindahl's special case, Myrdal would have been quite correct!

[74] Lindahl (1959, p. 16) envisages a rather different special case in which the unit elasticity assumption is not required. Instead, the tax-price charged for successive units of public good supplied to each individual is assumed to be varied in such a way that the method of financing each unit (and not only the marginal unit) imposes the same sacrifice on all individuals. It is interesting to notice that, in his earlier expositions, Lindahl explicitly excludes the possibility of differential pricing for different units of the public good supplied to the same individual, in order to ensure the existence of a unique optimum. See chap. 4, pp. 96–97 above.

[75] Lindahl is well aware that proportional income taxation may not impose equal sacrifice. In proceeding, as we shall see, to advocate the equal sacrifice or ability principle as a practical solution to the "purely fiscal" problem, he is very careful not to commit himself to any particular rate-structure. See, for example, (1959), p. 17, n. 20.

[76] See, for example, idem (1928), pp. 228–29, and (1959), pp. 14–16.

[77] Idem (1928), p. 228. Lindahl also stresses (ibid., p. 232, and 1959, p. 18) the onesidedness of the ability principle (as usually interpreted) in leaving the volume of taxation (and public expenditure) indeterminate.

[78] It is important to remember that not all economists advocated ability-to-pay as a dis-

## 3.4 The Place of Value Judgments in Public Finance Theory

Myrdal's final and most fundamental objection to Lindahl's theory is that it is not the business of the economist or public finance theorist to make value judgments and elaborate prescriptive theories of economic policy based on these value judgments. Like Robbins in his famous essay published two years later,[79] he argues that the comparative advantage of the economist lies elsewhere, and more specifically in the field of descriptive or positive theory; in the particular case of the public finance specialist, he considers that this field is the theory of "incidence in the widest sense" or the "study of the *effects* of various possible tax systems."[80]

Along with other factors, the Myrdal-Robbins point of view has undoubtedly had great influence in turning the attention of economists, including public finance theorists, towards the more intensive development of the positive side of their science. It is impossible, however, to overlook the fact that some of the most famous contributors to descriptive theory were directly responsible for the great revival of interest in welfare economics during the 1940s. The names of Hicks, Kaldor, and Samuelson, for example, are now inextricably associated with the New Welfare Economics which they did so much to establish.

That the economist or public finance theorist should refrain from developing prescriptive theories based on even the most explicit value premises is itself a value judgment, and one which, although apparently revered in principle, has never been generally accepted in practice by the profession;[81] and recommendations based on explicit

tributional principle in its own right. Most of those who did so were anyway ultimately concerned with its effect in maintaining the existing distribution of income; and of these the more radical (including J. S. Mill and Sidgwick) insisted with Wicksell and Lindahl that this "existing distribution" should be just. Taking this consideration together with the obvious fact that the ability theory will not "maintain" the existing distribution of income (in any relevant welfare sense) unless the benefits from public goods are related to ability in the way assumed by Lindahl, it becomes clear that the close relationship he claims to exist between the benefit and ability theories is much less contrived and artificial than, for example, Musgrave (p. 78) seems to imagine.

[79] Lionel Robbins, *An Essay on the Nature and Significance of Economic Science* (London, 1932), chap. 6.

[80] For Myrdal's detailed application of his general argument to the particular case of public finance theory, see his pp. 185–90.

[81] It is important to notice that Lindahl himself also accepts the theoretical validity of the point; and in nevertheless proceeding to reject it because of the "higher standpoint" provided by the scientist's deeper understanding of causal interrelationships, he is very much concerned to make his value premises explicit. In his more careful moments, he shows at least as much awareness of the precise logical status of the prescriptive aspects of his theory as do most modern economists.

and implicit value premises somehow still manage to emerge from the writings of even the most uncompromisingly Robbinsian economists, including Robbins and Myrdal themselves. The latter have argued extremely persuasively in favor of their (theoretical) position,[82] but it is still far from obvious that the relevant comparison of all arguments which could be mustered on both sides would show that this position could command majority support, either among public finance theorists or economists generally. Certainly it is not logically incumbent upon the public finance theorist to abandon attempts to develop a prescriptive theory of public expenditure and taxation, and many would consider this all the support that Lindahl's attempt requires on this most fundamental level.

## 4.  The Descriptive Theory of Budgetary Policy in a Parliamentary Democracy

Turning next to his descriptive theory, we have seen that Lindahl's main aim here is to determine to what extent budgetary policy in a parliamentary democracy can be expected to satisfy his "purely fiscal" requirement of budgetary justice. As we saw in section 2.2, his approach is first of all to set up a stylized model of the democratic political mechanism under which his fiscal optimum will necessarily be established. Then, by comparing the characteristics of the model with those of actual parliamentary democracies, he proceeds to indicate the nature of the departures from the optimum, which must be expected in practice. We shall now proceed to examine these two stages of his analysis in turn.

### 4.1  The Model

With his model democracy, Lindahl apparently succeeds where numerous Continental writers of the late nineteenth century had tried and failed, namely in applying the new tools of marginal utility analysis to the development of a descriptive theory of budgetary policy; one of the best of these earlier attempts[83] had already been effectively demolished more than 20 years earlier by his teacher Wicksell.[84]

However, in spite of the high degree of stylization of the model, in

[82] For Myrdal's brilliant argument, see his chap. 8.
[83] By Mazzola. See Musgrave and Peacock, pp. 37–47.
[84] See Wicksell, in Musgrave and Peacock, pp. 80–82.

which the pattern of public expenditure and taxation is assumed to be determined by "free agreement" between two large and economically homogeneous groups with "equal power," serious doubts have from time to time been expressed as to whether his "positive solution" to the problem is strictly valid; is it really true that the fiscal optimum will necessarily be attained and equilibrium established at the single intersection point $P$ of the two "demand schedules" in Figure 1?

### 4.1.1  Multiple optima

We have already encountered Samuelson's objection that, with Lindahl's particular formulation of the sociopolitical requirement in terms of a just initial distribution of property, the fiscal optimum is indeterminate, in the sense that, starting with this ideal initial distribution of welfare, there will in general be an infinite set of Pareto-optimal budgetary policies leading to an infinite set of postpolicy distributions of welfare such that someone has been made better off and no one worse off.[85]

This objection, if valid, would usually be regarded as far more serious for Lindahl's descriptive theory of the functioning of the model than it could possibly be for his prescriptive concept of budgetary justice; equilibrium at a unique fiscal-optimum point $P$ would seem to be logically impossible.

However, it is precisely in the context of the descriptive theory of the model that the validity of this objection seems most doubtful. We have argued in our earlier prescriptive discussion of this same point that it would be perfectly reasonable to interpret Lindahl's "just initial distribution of property" in terms of a given pattern of factor ownership or initial endowment of private good. If we do this, we see that, on Lindahl's assumption that cost shares are constant over quantities for each group, there will be only one Pareto-efficient pattern of inputs and outputs, and commodity and factor prices, corresponding to the just distribution of property. This interpretation seems even more reasonable in our present descriptive context, since Lindahl is here assuming only a "given" initial distribution; questions as to its desirability, and whether it is not the post- (purely fiscal) policy distribution of welfare that we should be interested in, do not arise. Thus we do not have to consider the possible (but in our present context superficial) "Old Welfare" objection that a truly just initial pattern of factor ownership can only be determined from a just post- (purely fiscal) policy distribution of welfare. The existence of a unique fiscal optimum corresponding to point $P$ can therefore quite reasonably be assumed.

[85] See above, sec. 3.2.2.

### 4.1.2   Some Cournot-Bertrand analogies

Even if we can reasonably assume that there is a unique fiscal optimum which can be represented by the single intersection point $P$ in Lindahl's diagram, this is not of course to imply that, in his model democracy, equilibrium will in fact necessarily be established at this point.[86]

Denying that the fiscal optimum will in fact be achieved, Musgrave, for example, suggests that, in Lindahl's case of two groups of taxpayers, ". . . we must have a solution analogous to the Cournot view of duopoly pricing."[87] Thus, "following the Cournot case, we suppose that A and B both disregard the effect of their votes upon the other's cost share."[88] In terms of our example (in section 2.2.1 above) in which cost shares are initially set well to the left of $P$ at 50 percent for each group, Musgrave argues that ultimate equilibrium will eventually be established at Lindahl's "provisional equilibrium" point $T$. "Given the assumption that both disregard the effects of their bidding on price, there is nothing in the mechanism of adjustment that makes for a change in cost shares. . . ."[89] Musgrave seems, however, to overlook the deus ex machina of "equal power."

Strictly speaking, Musgrave's analogy seems more in the tradition of Bertrand than of Cournot. By analogy with Cournot, let us suppose that each group takes the other's quantity demanded (rather than cost share) as given and independent of its own demand, with the volume of public expenditure initially set at Lindahl's "provisional equilibrium" level $T$. In this case, but for the equal power assumption, it seems that cost shares will be indeterminate between $T$ and $W$. Introducing the equal power assumption, perhaps it would be reasonable to assume that equilibrium will ultimately be established at some point $J$ in the neighborhood of half way between $T$ and $W$.[90]

Finally, it may be worth considering a mixed Bertrand-Cournot case of the sort investigated by Stackelberg, where one group takes the

[86] As we have seen, Lindahl is much concerned, in his original expositions, to stress the analogy between the functioning of his model democracy and the workings of the market mechanism. It may therefore be of particular interest to analyze his model in the light of some of the better known oligopoly theories. The analysis contained in the following sections is based on Fellner's modern classic in the field of oligopoly theory, *Competition Among the Few* (New York, 1949).

[87] Musgrave, p. 79.

[88] Ibid.

[89] Ibid.

[90] It may be this sort of Cournot process which Musgrave has in mind when he suggests (p. 79, n. 2) that equilibrium may well be established at a similar point $J$, below (in terms of Lindahl's diagram) the frontier $SPR$. It should be noted that Musgrave is incorrect in suggesting (ibid.) that his own frontier $UDY$ corresponds to Lindahl's locus of "possible equilibrium positions" $QPR$.

other's price as fixed, and the other takes quantity as fixed. Thus, by analogy, group A may take cost shares as fixed, and B the volume of public expenditure. Then if, as in our earlier example, we start from a point at which cost shares are temporarily set at 50 percent for each group "with A to move," it is apparent that A, trying to maximize its utility, will propose the level of outlay $U$; for outlay $U$, B (to maximize its utility) will offer to bear that proportion of total cost represented by the point of intersection between $BS$ and the horizontal through $U$, and so on in a convergent cobweb to the fiscal optimum at $P$. With the "price-quantity" assumptions of A and B reversed, the bargaining process becomes unstable, and we obtain the divergent budgetary cobweb $TW$ ...

It has long been recognized, however, that these Cournot-Bertrand assumptions are completely inadequate as a foundation for the small-group theories which they are designed to support. It is most unrealistic, precisely where numbers are few, to suggest that each firm will assume that its own price or output will have no effect on the price or output of its competitors. Moreover, the firms will soon learn in the course of the "competitive" process that their assumptions are unfounded.[91] Similarly, precisely where numbers are small (as in Lindahl's model where we are considering just two large groups of taxpayers), it is quite unacceptable to suggest that political groupings will assume that the cost share which some other party would be willing to bear is fixed and independent either of the volume of public expenditure or of their own preferences for public goods as revealed in the course of the bargaining process; and a fortiori it would be absurd to assume, as in the Cournot analogy, that the various groups take the volume of public expenditure as given and independent of their own cost share.[92]

### 4.1.3  Leadership equilibria

As a first step in the direction of realism, we might therefore assume instead that only one group acts in this unrealistic fashion. Thus, by analogy with the "leadership" approach to duopoly theory,[93] we might assume that only group B takes cost shares as fixed. Group A, by contrast, is much more sophisticated; realizing that B takes cost shares as given, and knowing the levels of public expenditure which B

---

[91] And this basic flaw cannot be removed by the introduction of "conjectural variation." For an excellent critique of these classical duopoly theories, see Fellner, chap. 2.

[92] Although the three analogies from classical duopoly discussions are grossly unrealistic as descriptive theory, we shall see that the Bertrand analogy has much to commend it as a policy conclusion.

[93] See Fellner, chap. 2.

will desire at any given cost ratio, group A offers to bear that proportion of total cost which will maximize its own level of utility. In terms
of Lindahl's diagram (Figure 1, p. 119), A will offer to bear the cost
share represented by Lindahl's point $Q$, and ultimate equilibrium will
be established at $Q$. Similarly, by reversing the roles of A and B, we
find that equilibrium will be established at "the equilibrium position
most favourable to B," which will be situated somewhere along $PR$
to the right of $P$ (probably at $R$, according to Lindahl).

The determination of the precise position of these "leadership
equilibria" in Figure 1 is not entirely clear from Lindahl's exposition,
even with the help of the algebraic analysis supplied by Wicksell. It
may therefore be useful to provide a demonstration using more conventional demand and supply curves.[94]

In Figure 2, we measure the quantity of public good in physical units

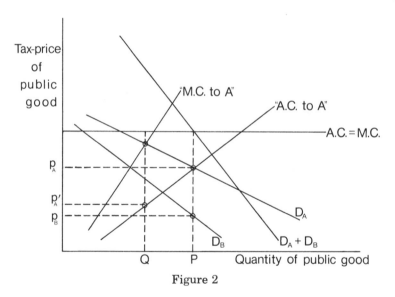

Figure 2

along the $X$ axis, and the tax-price of the good (both to A and B separately and to A and B combined) along the $Y$ axis. $D_A$ and $D_B$ are the
demand schedules of A and B respectively, showing the amounts which
they would like to see produced at different tax-prices; $D_A + D_B$ shows
the total tax-price which the two groups combined would then be pay-

[94] This demonstration was suggested by Bowen's more conventionally Marshallian geometrical exposition of a prescriptive theory of public expenditure very similar to Lindahl's. See H. R. Bowen, *Toward Social Economy* (New York, 1948). For an alternative
demonstration using indifference curves, see Johansen.

ing for each of these desired levels of output. We assume that the public good is produced under conditions of constant costs ($A.C. = M.C.$).

As in Lindahl's diagram, the fiscal optimum must be such that the utility of expenditure on the last unit of public good produced is simultaneously equal to the tax-price for each individual member of both groups, with the combined unit price being just sufficient to cover the cost of producing that unit (and hence of the total output of public goods).[95] This is clearly the case at output $P$, where $p_A$ and $p_B$ are the tax-prices to be paid by A and B respectively.

To obtain the leadership equilibrium for A, we construct a new schedule which we shall call "average cost to A." This schedule shows how the minimum unit tax-price which A must pay rises with rising output of the public good, assuming that B takes price as given and is free to maximize utility along $D_B$; it is obtained as the difference between the constant cost schedule and B's demand schedule $D_B$, and must intersect A's demand schedule $D_A$ at the fiscal-optimum output $P$. From this schedule of "average cost to A" we can now derive the corresponding schedule of "marginal cost to A," showing the additional or incremental cost to A of each additional unit of public good.

On the leadership assumption that A knows B is taking cost shares and the implied unit price as given, A will offer to bear that proportion of total cost which will result in the output of the public good being pushed to the point where the additional cost to A of the last unit of public good is just balanced by its marginal utility.[96] This will clearly be at output $Q$, and the unit tax-price to A must be $p'_A$.

A similar leadership equilibrium can be established for B. It is easy to see that this will in general be such that B will be paying some positive unit price for the public good; it will not in general be at Lindahl's point $R$ where B is contributing nothing.

In contrast to the Cournot-Bertrand analysis, neither party in these leadership cases is acting on assumptions which in the course of the "competitive" process will continually be shown to be completely unfounded. As Fellner puts it with reference to leadership equilibrium in the Cournot case: "As long as the leader has both the desire and the

---

[95] In a partial equilibrium analysis, the assumption of constant costs is necessary to ensure that charging each group a uniform tax-price per unit of public good equal to the utility to that group of the last unit of public good produced, with the sum of these tax-prices being just sufficient to cover the cost of producing that unit, will also be just sufficient to cover the cost of producing the total output of public goods.

The problem here was first recognized by Samuelson when, in a footnote reference to Lindahl, he asks (1955, p. 354, n. 8) whether Lindahl's intersection point $P$ is to be interpreted as the point at which the unit cost or the marginal cost of the public good is covered.

[96] Compare Lindahl's description (1919, pp. 170–71) of the point $Q$ "most favourable to A."

power to make his own output a parameter from the follower's point of view, any change in the assumptions about what the follower will do in these circumstances will prove erroneous; and so will any change in the follower's assumptions. . . ."[97] It is this which constitutes the superiority of the leadership approach.

Nevertheless, in spite of this advance, the leadership theory is still far from satisfactory. As Fellner asks: "Why should the leader have the desire and the power to act in this fashion? If he is more powerful than the follower, why should he be more powerful in this completely arbitrary sense of the term? His rival's reaction to some other behaviour might result in higher profits to both firms. Why should he not try to test this?"[98] Moreover, if we make the assumption that both parties are more or less equally knowledgeable and sophisticated in these matters, we encounter Stackelberg's important conclusion that, in the vast majority of cases, both parties will be striving for "leadership" with the apparent consequences of indeterminacy and disequilibrium.[99]

These objections are of immediate and obvious relevance for a pure leadership analysis of Lindahl's model with its crucial equal power concept. As is evident from Lindahl's own discussion,[100] leadership equilibrium at $Q$ or $R$ is completely contrary to any reasonable interpretation of his equal power assumption that both groups are equally able to defend their economic rights under the existing property order. But with "equal power" (in any normal sense), indeterminacy and mutually costly disequilibrium would seem likely.

### 4.1.4  Qualified joint maximization

Recognizing that it is in general completely unrealistic to assume such a vast "sophistication differential" as seems to be required by the concept of leadership equilibrium, and that even where such a differential exists, there is no reason why leadership should take this particular form, modern theories of oligopoly have usually turned to some variant of Fellner's concept of "qualified joint maximization."[101]

Thus, even where power is unequal, and some form of leadership is likely, it is now generally agreed that the leader will use his power to force the other party to set up reaction functions more nearly consistent with maximization of joint profits. As Fellner puts it: "If the aggregate industry profit is not maximised and the less-than-maximum profit is divided in some fashion, it is always possible to give *every*

[97] Fellner, p. 68.
[98] Ibid., pp. 68–69.
[99] For a detailed discussion of Stackelberg's brilliant analysis, see Fellner, chap. 3.
[100] See above, sec. 2.2.1.
[101] For Fellner's development of this concept, see especially chap. 4.

*single participant* more than he actually gets, by changing the quasi-agreement to a basis on which the aggregate industry profit *is* maximised."[102] Hence, ". . . if one firm has the power to force the other firm into anything, why should it not prefer to force its rival into something more favourable for the powerful firm, and possibly also for the weaker firm"?[103] Where power is more equally distributed, a similar argument again suggests the likelihood of a cooperative solution.

Where numbers are few, some form of "cooperation" to achieve maximum or near-maximum joint profits is therefore extremely likely; such cooperation should be technically quite easy to organize, the potential advantages should be evident to each party, and the possible direct and indirect (retaliatory) consequences of failure to cooperate will usually be both obvious and serious. For various reasons relating mainly to the effects of uncertainty, complete coordination will usually be out of the question;[104] a rough approximation to joint maximization can, however, quite reasonably be expected.

This qualified joint maximization approach is of obvious applicability in Lindahl's model democracy. In any situation short of a Pareto optimum, it must always be possible, by suitable budgetary adjustments, to make both groups better off. This is as true of the leadership equilibria at $Q$ and $R$ as it is of any other suboptimal situation. Thus even without the somewhat embarrassing help of Lindahl's deus ex machina of equal power, some approach to a Pareto optimum can reasonably be expected. If, for example, power is unequally distributed and some form of leadership must be assumed, there is no reason to suppose that the leadership group will accept the follower's demand schedule as an effective constraint on its own satisfaction-maximizing behavior. Rather, the leadership group may be expected to use its power in order to try to modify the follower's reaction function in such a way as to increase its own (and possibly also the follower's) utility by raising public expenditure towards a Pareto-optimum level such as that indicated by Lindahl's intersection point P.

Without the equal power assumption, however, equilibrium cannot in general be expected at the particular point $P$, and the fiscal optimum will not therefore be achieved. Thus, under leadership by A, it is only reasonable to suppose that A will use its greater power not only to raise the output of public goods towards the optimum, but also and at the same time to secure a more favorable distribution of total cost than that represented (for example) by $P$. This possibility is evident from Figure 2, where, on the basis of familiar consumer surplus arguments,

[102] Ibid., p. 130.
[103] Ibid., pp. 118–19.
[104] Ibid., chaps. 5 and 6.

it is obvious that $p_A$ and $p_B$ are not to be regarded as the maximum prices which A and B would be willing to pay on an "all or nothing" basis for the fiscal-optimum output of public goods. In terms of Lindahl's diagram, if "coordination" is complete, we should therefore expect equilibrium at a Pareto optimum point somewhere in the western sector $APS$, between the demand schedules and to the left of $P$. Since the pattern of public expenditure and taxation is assumed to be determined by free agreement, the precise position of this point must be limited by the requirement that B should not be worse off than in the pre-(fiscal) policy situation.

The above argument can conveniently be illustrated using a Samuelsonian utility possibility function diagram.

In Figure 3 we measure A's level of utility along the $X$ axis, and B's

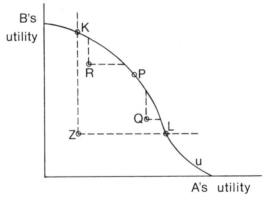

Figure 3

level of utility along the $Y$ axis. The utility possibility function, $u$, shows, for given tastes, technology and factor endowment, the maximum levels of utility of A for given levels of utility of B; it is therefore the locus of Pareto optimum points for the society under consideration.

In the complete absence of (purely fiscal) policy by government, a private exchange economy cannot in general achieve a Pareto optimum because of the existence of public goods;[105] we shall suppose that this pre-(fiscal) policy situation is represented by point Z. The pure leadership equilibria will then be represented by sub-optimal points such as $Q$ and $R$ for A and B respectively, where, at $Q$, A is getting most of the benefit from the existence of government, whilst at $R$, B is getting most of the benefit. Lindahl's fiscal optimum will in turn be repre-

---

[105] For a full discussion and generalization of this point, see chap. 8 below.

sented by the Pareto-optimal point $P$ somewhere on $u$ southeast of $R$ and northwest of $Q$.

Under leadership, say by A, it is apparent that A could do better than the pure leadership equilibrium at $Q$. The joint maximization approach would therefore suggest that A will use its power to secure an expansion of the output of public goods in order to reach some point on $u$ to the right of $Q$. Since we are assuming that the budget is to be determined by free agreement, this point cannot be below $Z$.

The crucial role of Lindahl's assumption of "equal power" in the very special and precise sense of "ability to exchange up to saturation, given the budget restraint of an initial endowment of factors," should now be quite clear; without it, there can be no guarantee that the fiscal optimum will in fact be achieved and equilibrium established at $P$. The most that can be said on the assumption of free agreement alone (in any normal sense) is that, with perfect "coordination," equilibrium will be established on $u$, somewhere between $K$ and $L$.

With the help of other and less arbitrary interpretations of equal power, determinacy may be possible at specific points other than $P$ on $u$.


## 4.2   The Model versus Parliamentary Democracy


As we have seen,[106] Lindahl recognizes very clearly that actual parliamentary democracies differ from his model democracy in a number of important respects. In order to determine to what extent budgetary policy in a parliamentary democracy can be expected to satisfy his "purely fiscal" requirement of budgetary justice, he therefore proceeds to examine the probable effect of each of these differences on ability to achieve the fiscal optimum.

Our analysis of Lindahl's model in the light of some of the more widely known oligopoly theories has already provided us with a considerable amount of information relevant to the determination of the effects of departures from the special assumptions of the model; as we saw, most of these theories embody assumptions, which, in one way or another, are at variance with those of the model. Since Lindahl's analysis of the first, third and fourth divergences is reasonably non-controversial, we shall confine our remarks to the second and fifth.[107]

---

[106] See above, sec. 2.2.2.

[107] We do not wish to suggest, however, that the first three divergences are in any sense less important. Downs's analysis in *An Economic Theory of Democracy* (New York, 1957), with its emphasis on the effects of imperfect knowledge (including all forms of uncertainty), effectively provides a most valuable amplification of Lindahl's analysis of the effects of the first and third divergences.

### 4.2.1  The crucial importance of numbers

Lindahl seems to consider that the existence of more than two parties, or divergences of interest within parties, cannot affect the performance of the model; "in this case, too, it is correct to say that the price of collective goods is chiefly determined by their marginal utility for the different interested parties."[108]

In this passage, Lindahl appears completely to ignore the problem of numbers, which, together with the existence of elements of nonappropriability (supplied by his public good assumption),[109] is the sine qua non of his "purely fiscal" ("New Welfare") foundation for the economic functions of government.[110] This role of numbers in obstructing cooperative solutions to non-appropriability problems in the market has in fact its precise political counterpart in the obstruction of cooperative solutions to preference-revelation problems in the political process.[111] In the case of the services of a pure public good for example, "individuals and small groups will know that . . . the supply to them of this service 'equally available to all' will depend overwhelmingly upon what the rest of the community is induced or forced to contribute, and only to the slightest extent on their own contributions. Each therefore has an enormous incentive to try to minimize his own contribution by understating his true preferences in public statements, bargaining, voting or other political activity relevant to the determination of the sharing of the burden. With large numbers behaving in this way, there is clearly a grave danger of underexpansion of the serv-

---

[108] Lindahl (1919), p. 173.

[109] For a discussion of the nonappropriability pillar of New Welfare theories of the economic functions of government, and the place of the public good concept in such theories, see chap. 8 below.

[110] In particular, the economic cooperation needed to overcome nonappropriability problems in the market is much more likely to be forthcoming if numbers are small, both because it is technically easier to organize, and also (and mainly) because the potential benefit to each economic unit is so much greater and more evident, and the direct and indirect (retaliatory) consequences of failure to cooperate or "contribute" are so obviously likely to be disastrous.

   Where numbers are large, individual economic units may well imagine (rightly or wrongly, depending upon whether others follow their example) that they can enjoy much the same standards of profit, service etc. without cooperating or contributing. Where numbers are small, however, they will seldom be so sanguine. David Hume, in *A Treatise of Human Nature* (London: Everyman Library, 1952), 2:239, makes this same point with particular clarity in his well-known example of the relative ease with which two neighbors may agree to drain a meadow, compared with the problem facing a thousand persons attempting to secure such an agreement.

[111] This market analogy should be obvious from our earlier analysis of Lindahl's model in the light of modern oligopoly theory. The problem, as numbers increase, of achieving stable "qualified joint maximization" solutions through bargaining and quasi-bargaining under unilateral and bilateral oligopoly is a familiar theme of modern value theory.

ice when provided 'free' by government."[112] It was in fact precisely this argument with which Wicksell demolished even the relatively refined benefit theory of Mazzola, which was amongst the best of the earlier attempts to apply the new marginal utility concept to the development of a descriptive theory of budgetary policy.[113]

It is apparent that Lindahl's model of a "cooperative" democracy avoids these Wicksellian strictures only by virtue of the assumption of so few completely monolithic political groupings. As soon as this assumption is relaxed, there is nothing in the requirement of "free agreement," reasonably interpreted, which can guarantee the achievement of the fiscal optimum through "government" any more than through the market. Lindahl's model becomes no more effective in securing fiscal justice than that of Mazzola.[114,115]

In short, just as it is the growth of numbers which has so vastly ex-

---

[112] See chap. 8, p. 174 below. In the case of a pure public good this problem is due as much to jointness as to external economies.

[113] Wicksell, in Musgrave and Peacock, pp. 81–82.

[114] It is interesting to notice that Wicksell's own "New Principle" or "consensus solution" is equally vulnerable to this same argument.

Wicksell emphasizes that his "New Principle" is something of a misnomer, since his aim is to show that the old benefit principle is not only a theoretical ideal, but can also be applied in practice. His critique of the benefit theory therefore goes well beyond, and in fact rejects, the usual superficial objections, (a) that the benefits to individuals from public goods are not capable of evaluation by the individuals themselves, let alone by the government, and must therefore be assessed "collectively"; or (b) that the theory can be applied only where price-exclusion is possible, and prices can therefore be charged (though, as Samuelson has shown, only a very special system of multiple pricing will in general be efficient in the case of public goods). His concern is rather to devise legislative procedures to facilitate the implementation of the principle in the innumerable cases where the benefits can be assessed by the individuals themselves, but prices (or at least efficient multiple prices) cannot conveniently be charged and tax-finance must therefore be used. For this purpose he recommends budget specialization (i.e., simultaneous voting on each particular item of public expenditure together with the method of financing it), flexible burden-sharing arrangements, and his famous "approximate unanimity" requirement.

It is curious that Wicksell hardly seems to notice the vulnerability of his "consensus solution" to this problem to his own criticisms of Mazzola. Indeed the consensus solution is much more vulnerable to these criticisms than is majority voting; only a relatively small number of "political units" disguising their preferences (in an attempt to secure a more favorable distribution of the burden) would be able to block projects of evident benefit to all. Being effectively a political device for the implementation of a pure Pareto criterion, the approximate unanimity requirement must at best be regarded as extremely restrictive of the reallocative economic functions of government; even with the most flexible and imaginative (feasible) burden-sharing arrangements, how many projects could be found which would not leave a substantial minority feeling worse off? Where numbers are large, however, such a requirement is likely to prove completely disastrous.

[115] In the absence of remarkably perfect knowledge, Downs's model democracy would encounter similar difficulties; public statements by interest groups may tend to mislead vote-maximizing political parties into underexpansion of public services.

tended the scope for market inefficiency of nonappropriability origin, so the same process has enormously increased the difficulty of finding cooperative economic and political correctives. In a modern society, what is required for the effective performance of the economic functions of government without coercion is a considerable degree of political centralization supported by a carefully integrated multilevel structure of "government" in the widest sense.[116]

It is extremely interesting to notice that it is precisely this sort of government which Lindahl envisages in extending his model to take account of more than two parties and divergences of interest within each party.[117] Thus he interprets "free agreement" to require bargaining between pairs of the smallest economic units, which, having reached an optimal agreement between themselves, then bargain collectively with other pairs, and so on up the multilevel "government" hierarchy until we reach the two-group bargain at the top which he explicitly discusses in his model. Further assumptions are, however, clearly required to hold this conceptual bargaining pyramid together in the face of large-number problems.

### 4.2.2  Coercion

Lindahl does not for one moment pretend, however, that in actual parliamentary democracies the pattern of public expenditure and taxation is determined by free agreement between parties with equal power. On the contrary, as we have seen,[118] he goes to some trouble to stress the importance of coercion in the context of majority voting, and suggests that ". . . the coercive element due to the preponderance of power obviously has the same effect as if the weaker parties now attached greater values to the public goods."[119] In the diagram (Figure 1, above), assuming A to be the majority party, B's demand schedule is in effect moved vertically upwards, and the new equilibrium is therefore to be found by moving along A's demand schedule from $P$ to (say) $U$.

In the light of our analysis of section 4.1.4 above, the justification for Lindahl's general approach to this problem is obvious. In the absence of free agreement and/or where power is unequally distributed and some form of leadership must be assumed, there is no reason to

---

[116] The close relationship between the reasons for market failure and the problem of finding efficient political correctives should be evident from Buchanan's careful but largely unsuccessful search for differences in the relative rationality of the two mechanisms. See J. M. Buchanan, "Social Choice, Democracy, and Free Markets," and "Individual Choice in Voting and the Market," *Journal of Political Economy,* 1954.

[117] Lindahl (1919), p. 173.

[118] See above, sec. 2.2.2.

[119] Lindahl (1919), p. 175.

suppose that the leadership group will accept the follower's demand schedule as an effective constraint on its own utility-maximizing behavior. Rather, the leadership group may be expected to use its preponderance of power in order to modify the follower's reaction function in such a way as to raise the level of public expenditure and thus increase its own (and possibly also the follower's) utility. With A as leader, the effect is therefore indeed as if B's schedule were to be moved vertically upwards, B now "maximizing utility" for given cost shares at higher levels of public expenditure than before.[120]

In terms of Lindahl's diagram, however, the new equilibrium is not in general to be found by moving along A's demand schedule from $P$ to (say) $U$. At any point on A's demand schedule other than $P$, a Pareto optimum will not in general be achieved, and it would be possible, by suitable budgetary adjustments, to make both parties better off; it is the whole point of the "qualified joint maximization" approach that these adjustments will tend to be forthcoming. As argued in section 4.1.4, equilibrium is to be expected at a Pareto-optimum level of output of public goods, with cost shares more favorable to A than those at $P$. Under complete coordination, we should therefore expect equilibrium at a Pareto-optimum point in the western sector ($APS$) of Lindahl's diagram, somewhere to the left of $P$ and between the two demand schedules; or, in terms of Figure 3, on $u$, somewhere to the right of $Q$.[121] This is not of course Lindahl's fiscal optimum, but it is a rather closer relative (and much more "acceptable" to many modern welfare theorists) than his own discussion might appear to indicate.

# 5.  The Policy Implications

In the light of his prescriptive and descriptive analysis, Lindahl is able to reach a number of policy conclusions, relating mainly to ways in which a closer approach to the fiscal optimum might be facilitated

---

[120] As Fellner puts it (p. 124) in the duopoly discussion from which our joint maximization analogy was drawn: *"In a sense,* the [new reaction functions] may be said to express followers' individual profit maximisation but *not* simply 'for alternative values of the leader's variable.' *They express profit maximisation given not merely the leader's values but given also his assumed willingness and power to accept certain reaction functions and refuse others."*

[121] Under free agreement this point could not of course be below $L$. Even without free agreement, and specifically in the case of majority voting, Lindahl would still argue that there are strict limits to these "purely fiscal" redistributions (and to any prior sociopolitical redistributions for that matter) set by the political costs of irresponsible exercise of power, and/or by the economic (misallocative) costs of feasible redistributive devices. For references, see p. 123, n. 40 above.

in actual parliamentary democracies.[122] Here we shall concentrate attention on those of greatest interest to the public finance theorist, namely his recommendations regarding tax legislation. According to Lindahl, the "purely fiscal" requirement can best be met by ability taxation (say, a proportional or mildly progressive personal income tax), whilst the sociopolitical principle may well require steep progression (such as might be secured through, for example, a very progressive surtax); on no account, however, should these two types of taxes be merged in (say) a single integrated progressive income tax, if serious distortion of "purely fiscal" policy is to be avoided.

## 5.1   Ability Taxation versus Flexible Burden-Sharing Arrangements

With his recommendation of ability taxation to satisfy the "purely fiscal" requirement, Lindahl breaks sharply with Wicksell. One of the most striking features of Wicksell's discussion is his persuasive advocacy of more flexible and imaginative burden-sharing arrangements as an essential prerequisite of more (fiscally) efficient budgetary procedures. Lindahl's recommendation of ability taxation to cover the cost of subjective advantages is in direct conflict with this approach.

As we have seen in section 3.3 above, Lindahl recognizes that tastes for public goods are not identical, but nevertheless advocates the ability basis as frequently offering the closest approach to benefit taxation which is likely to be politically and administratively practicable.[123] Wicksell's objection to this "pragmatic realism" would be that in this way many projects, which, with imaginative burden-sharing arrangements, could satisfy his Pareto criterion and receive approximately unanimous support, may fail to receive even a simple majority; because of the rigid insistence that everyone should contribute to the cost (say) in proportion to income, those whose benefit is less than this will oppose the project. The fiscal optimum may therefore be far from fully achieved.

Where numbers are large, however, Lindahl's "second-best" approach

---

[122] Lindahl's contention that even an imperfect democratic form of government offers the prospect of a closer approach to the fiscal optimum than do totalitarian or absolutist forms is also based largely on the analysis of his model. It is thus a rather more explicit variant of the traditional argument from the public finance literature of the late nineteenth century (e.g., Mazzola, Sax, and De Viti de Marco) that some approach to such a fiscal optimum is a necessary condition for political equilibrium in a parliamentary democracy. For a more recent and more complete analysis of this problem, see Downs, chap. 10.

[123] Lindahl is even willing to argue (1928, pp. 228–29) that differences in minority tastes should not count, because they may offend the sense of justice of the majority.

may nevertheless be well justified. As we have seen in section 4.2.1 above, if numbers on any level of the political hierarchy are effectively large, understatement of true preferences for public goods must be expected in public statements, bargaining, voting or any other type of political activity considered in any way relevant to the determination of cost shares. Since, in one way or another, the large numbers case frequently applies in actual parliamentary democracies, the existence of fairly rigid burden-sharing arrangements embodied in a time-hallowed pattern of taxes may promote rather than hinder fiscally efficient policy-making in a democracy.[124] This rather negative advantage must, however, be set against the positive case for greater flexibility so brilliantly argued by Wicksell.[125]

## 5.2 The Separation of "Purely Fiscal" from Sociopolitical Taxation

Although Lindahl does not hesitate to recommend rigid burden-sharing arrangements for "purely fiscal" purposes, he is very concerned that these arrangements should be as appropriate to their "purely fiscal" purpose as possible. Since, in his opinion, ability taxation comes closest to satisfying the purely fiscal requirement, whilst steep progression seems to be required by the socio-political principle, he insists that tax legislation should observe a very sharp distinction between these two types of taxes; not only should sociopolitical taxes not be used for "purely fiscal" purposes, but on no account should they even seem to be so used (as may being the case where both categories are formally combined in a single progressive income tax).

---

[124] For a very clear statement of this argument, see H. R. Bowen, "The Interpretation of Voting in the Allocation of Economic Resources," *Quarterly Journal of Economics,* 1943–44, p. 45.

[125] An equally important (and logically related) break with Wicksell is to be observed in Lindahl's recent criticisms (1959, pp. 13–14) of the approximate unanimity requirement. In particular, he recognizes the danger that a minority may use its veto to block allocatively desirable legislation in order to secure a shift in cost shares to its own advantage. As indicated in n. 114, above, this point becomes of crucial importance where numbers are large, Wicksell's consensus approach being much more vulnerable to the numbers problem than is majority voting. Lindahl's other and less important objections are (a) that even genuine differences in minority tastes for public goods ought not to count, because they may offend the sense of justice of the majority, and (b) that an approximate unanimity requirement is too restrictive for sociopolitical purposes. The first point seems of no great ethical weight, whilst the second is stressed at least as strongly by Wicksell (pp. 108–09) who advocates approximate unanimity on "purely fiscal" questions only.

Lindahl is inclined to regard his position on the consensus issue as his major departure from the Wicksellian tradition. As he expresses it (ibid., p. 17), "My position can be characterised as an attempt to maintain the benefit principle, while abandoning as impracticable Wicksell's requirement of a large majority."

To the modern reader, Lindahl's suggestion that a fully integrated progressive personal income tax should be divided into a basic proportional or mildly progressive (fiscal) tax and a steeply progressive (sociopolitical) surtax may at first glance seem completely artificial and pointless. The justification for it is, however, simple and of the greatest practical as well as theoretical interest.

Once a fully integrated and steeply progressive personal income tax becomes established (as it has done in many countries) as the foundation of a modern tax system, opposing right- and left-wing pressures tend to ensure that increases or reductions in rates must in some sense "maintain" the existing progressiveness of the tax; the rate-pattern thus eventually becomes a social institution almost as respectable and inviolable as the Church or the Monarchy. Wherever this occurs, it is almost inevitable that, under majority voting, the output of public goods tends to be overexpanded under left-wing governments whose supporters would be bearing less than their fiscal-optimum share of the cost due to the progressiveness of the tax system. Similarly, under right-wing governments, underexpansion of the public sector would have to be expected.[126]

These tendencies have been clearly visible in the postwar experience of the highly developed English-speaking democracies. Introduced under (relatively) left-wing governments and/or in the mildly egalitarian and revenue-hungry climate of the war and immediate post-war periods, heavy and steeply progressive personal income taxation seems to have sent down remarkably deep roots. By the time these progressive tax systems were inherited by the (relatively) right-wing governments of the 1950s, they had become social institutions too respectable to be tampered with (at least overtly). Even without the support of conservative political philosophy, the almost inevitable consequence was then only too likely to be an economically and socially extremely dangerous stagnation of the public sector, due to the fact that, under rigid progression, the effective performance of the "purely fiscal" functions of government would impose an undue burden on the rather wealthier supporters of right-wing governments. The failure to observe a clear distinction between sociopolitical and "purely fiscal" taxation may thus have been one important factor contributing to the widely observed Anglo-American (and Australasian) phenomenon of public poverty in the midst of private affluence.[127]

---

[126] After a long period of social democratic government in Sweden, Lindahl is much more concerned to stress the former rather than the latter possibility.

[127] For a celebrated exposure of this phenomenon, see J. K. Galbraith, *The Affluent Society* (New York and London, 1958).

## 6.  Conclusions

The main conclusions of our analysis can be summarized as follows:

(*a*) Examined in the light of modern welfare economics, Lindahl's prescriptive theory of the budget appears to be reasonably sound in most respects and has much in common with some of the more radical variants of New Welfare theory. His attempts to reconcile his approach with the various sacrifice theories are, however, incomplete (though not entirely without value).

(*b*) Analyzed with the help of market analogies from some of the better known oligopoly theories, Lindahl's model democracy appears unable to achieve his fiscal optimum, except on the basis of what, in a political context, seems a highly arbitrary "competitive market" interpretation of his "equal power" assumption. Some approach to a closely related Pareto optimum can, however, quite reasonably be expected.

(*c*) Lindahl's analysis of the effects of divergences from the special conditions of the model is in most cases useful and interesting. He appears, however, very seriously to underestimate the effect of large numbers of "parties."

(*d*) His major policy recommendations in the field of tax legislation appear to be not only of great theoretical interest, but also of considerable practical importance.

# 7. A Voluntary Exchange Theory of the Public Economy

## 1. Introduction

The modern theory of public goods owes its development above all to three outstanding figures: Samuelson, Musgrave, and Buchanan. Samuelson gave us the first rigorous derivation of the optimum conditions for public goods supply. To Musgrave we owe our appreciation of Lindahl's pioneering contribution and the stimulating general analysis of social wants in *The Theory of Public Finance*. Buchanan has now provided us with the first systematic book-length presentation of the subject in English. Indeed the only comparable attempt to develop a comprehensive theory of public goods is Lindahl's *Die Gerechtigkeit der Besteuerung* published 50 years ago.

From the outset, a characteristic of the modern development has been the emphatic rejection of what was described by Musgrave as the "voluntary exchange theory" of the public goods pioneers, notably Lindahl.[1] By contrast, the most striking feature of Buchanan's exposition is that the theory of public goods is developed explicitly as a voluntary exchange theory of the public economy.

In broad outline Buchanan's procedure is first, to develop a theory of public goods equilibrium under voluntary exchange in a two-person model. At the second step, this theory is extended to a large-number model. At the third and final step, the voluntary exchange context is broadened, and the provision of public goods through political institutions is examined.

A review of James M. Buchanan, *The Demand and Supply of Public Goods*. Rand McNally and Company, Chicago 1968. Pp. ix + 214. Reprinted without significant change from *Finanzarchiv* 29, no. 1 (February 1970): 112–21.

[1] See especially Musgrave's classic critique of thirty years ago, "The Voluntary Exchange Theory of Public Economy," *Quarterly Journal of Economics*, Feb. 1939.

## 2.  Voluntary Exchange in a Two-Person Model

As for Lindahl, the analysis of public goods equilibrium under voluntary exchange between two parties plays an important role in Buchanan's exposition.

### 2.1

Thus, in chapter 2, he begins with the provision of a pure public good in a highly simplified world of equals. Constant opportunity costs are assumed throughout the discussion. Under independent adjustment he shows that each person will equate his own marginal rate of substitution to his marginal rate of transformation. This will not, however, represent an equilibrium situation, since, for a public good, each person will place some value on the other's activity in producing the public good; the production of a public good generates a Pareto-relevant external economy. Both persons may therefore gain from exchange agreements to extend public goods production. Gains from trade are fully exhausted only when the summed marginal rates of substitution equal the marginal rate of transformation.

For Buchanan this model serves to expose the basic motivation for voluntary agreements on public goods supply, viz. the existence of potential gains from trade. In contrast to Lindahl, he deliberately treats the question as to how trade takes place in a rather perfunctory fashion. Assuming away the problem of strategic behavior and implicitly assuming that units of public good are traded *seriatim*, he concludes that equilibrium will be reached when gains from trade are exhausted. The Samuelsonian conditions ($\Sigma MRS = MT$) are therefore derived as conditions for public goods equilibrium in a small-number voluntary exchange model, rather than as conditions for Pareto efficiency in a welfare context.

### 2.2

This analysis is further developed in chapter 3, where the assumption of a world of equals is relaxed. Retaining the crucial implicit assumption that units of public good are traded successively and incrementally, Buchanan shows that, in contrast to familiar competitive private goods trade, public goods trade generates differential marginal prices to the two persons. In spite of their differing marginal evaluations, both persons must be brought into equilibrium at the same level of public goods consumption. A set of differential marginal prices equal to marginal evaluation for each person is therefore required.

Buchanan also emphasizes the further difference from competitive private goods trade, that equilibrium no longer requires uniformity of marginal prices over quantities purchased by a single person. Unless the arbitrary assumption of marginal price uniformity is made, ordinary demand schedules cannot be derived from preference functions and initial endowments to determine a unique equilibrium. The position of equilibrium will depend upon the precise way in which prices vary over the units successively exchanged, which determines how the gains from trade on inframarginal units will be distributed. Since this cannot be predicted, public goods equilibrium exhibits an indeterminacy which is absent in the familiar case of competitive trade in private goods.

It is, of course, precisely for this reason that Lindahl, in contrast to Wicksell, explicitly introduced the assumption of constant cost-shares (and hence unit prices) over quantities for each party in his celebrated model. Buchanan in fact discusses this case in the final section of chapter 3, but appears to overlook the problem emphasized by Lindahl that, with the particular method of bargaining envisaged, there is no mechanism to drive the parties to the unique equilibrium at the Lindahl $P$ point (Buchanan's point $X_1$, Figure 3.3, p. 45). In Buchanan's Figure 3.3, the bargaining would cease at the public goods quantity $OX_0$, since for Tizio there are no further gains from trade to be realized within the price-uniformity convention. To achieve the public goods output $OX_1$, it is evidently insufficient to abstract from strategic behavior. The deus ex machina of "equal power" in the special sense of "ability to exchange up to saturation" is required.

Basic to Buchanan's analysis of the voluntary exchange process is the assumption that units of public goods are traded *seriatim* as in a private goods market. If this assumption is relaxed, and no arbitrary restrictions are imposed on the method of bargaining, it remains true that gains from public goods trade will be exhausted only when the summed marginal rates of substitution equal the marginal rate of transformation. The Samuelsonian conditions therefore still hold as conditions of equilibrium. However, the traditional voluntary exchange requirement of differential marginal prices equal to marginal evaluation for each person is no longer necessary. Thus, for example, the two parties might bargain simultaneously over the two variables, public goods quantity and unit price, and achieve an agreement which exhausts all gains from trade but involves no equality of marginal evaluation and marginal price in any meaningful sense.

## 2.3

In chapter 4 Buchanan relaxes the assumption of a pure public good, "equally available to all," and provides a detailed discussion and generalization of the public goods concept, which he had left perhaps rather too vague in the preceding chapters. For Buchanan the central characteristic of a public good is jointness of supply, closely analogous to, but not identical with, the familiar Marshallian concept. He makes occasional references to the other crucial characteristic of impossibility of exclusion, but does not clearly bring out or sufficiently emphasize the important distinction involved.

In the case of a pure public good, joint supply holds in the special sense that all persons (here two) in the relevant group are jointly supplied with equal quantities of homogeneous-quality consumption services. Few if any services could satisfy this polar requirement, but the joint supply concept can readily be generalized, as Buchanan himself had already demonstrated in detail in earlier papers.[2] As he shows, even a pure private good such as bread can be treated as a special case of joint supply, by treating "my consumption of bread" as a service "available to all." Even here a Samuelsonian requirement ($\Sigma MRS = MT$) still holds as an equilibrium condition, though all marginal rates of substitution except my own are zero. In the general case the input unit for a public good will provide individuals with differing service quantities (some of which may be zero) of varying "quality," e.g. the fire protection received from a fire station of fixed location. Moreover, the proportions enjoyed by different individuals will be variable rather than fixed, e.g. the location of the fire station can be varied. Buchanan explores the further condition for equilibrium required in the latter case; but, in contrast to his previously cited paper, he provides no formal statement of the condition for the two person case. He also correctly observes that most of the traditional examples of public good externalities, e.g. defense, are of Scitovsky's production-consumption variety; though, as he shows, it is easy to provide important examples of the consumption-consumption variety from such areas as health and education. Production-production and consumption-production examples could also be supplied. For any of these cases to constitute "externalities" in the relevant sense, it is, of course, essential to add the characteristic of nonexcludability to the joint supply characteristic.

Once this generalization of the public goods concept is accom-

---

[2] See especially J. M. Buchanan, "Joint Supply, Externality, and Optimality," *Economica*, Nov. 1966.

plished, what if anything is left to distinguish "public good externalities" from the traditional Pigovian concept of externality? Pigou himself draws no distinction, but simply includes classic public goods examples, such as lighthouses, along with (say) the improved climate for surrounding farm land resulting from afforestation, and of course the negative externality of smoke nuisance. In contrast to Samuelson, Buchanan implicitly ignores the possibility of negative marginal evaluation; a public good is available to all, but is, by implication, readily rejectable by those whose marginal evaluations are negative in the relevant range. All external diseconomies would therefore seem, somewhat arbitrarily and unrealistically, to be ruled out. Cases in which the services to different persons are quite different in nature, as distinct from quantity or quality, are also implicitly ruled out. Although, from an analytical point of view, this distinction too seems rather arbitrary, this is nevertheless the criterion that most public goods theorists have probably had in mind.

## 3.  Voluntary Exchange in a Many-Person Model

Having analysed the nature of public goods equilibrium in the two-person model, Lindahl goes straight on to suggest that the same results will hold without essential qualification for the large-number model. This contention has been severely criticized by modern writers, notably Musgrave, and this criticism is accepted and very effectively formulated, but not acknowledged, by Buchanan in chapter 5. The argument is simply that, when numbers are large, any single individual will recognize that public goods supply is virtually independent (both directly, and indirectly through possible effects on the contributions of others) of his own contribution to any voluntary exchange agreement. The consultation and interaction necessary to realize the available gains from trade in public goods is not therefore forthcoming. Consequently little or nothing will be provided under purely voluntary exchange. As Buchanan emphasizes, such a failure to contribute reflects strictly independent behavior, in contrast to strategic withholding of contributions which we should expect in a realistic small-number setting. In contrast to Buchanan's apparent conception, this distinction is, however, already clearly drawn in Musgrave's standard discussion, though admittedly not in Samuelson.

There appears therefore to be a striking difference in the results of voluntary exchange as between small- and large-number models. Buchanan maintains that it is only the large-number model which is relevant for public goods analysis. This seems reasonable for a pure public good which provides equal quantities of homogeneous-quality consumption services to all persons without capacity limit. Buchanan, however, employs a generalized public goods concept, as developed in chapter 4, in which the number of persons jointly benefiting from a particular production unit may be few, or in which the spill-over benefits may be widely spread but of negligible amount. Small-number elements may therefore be of considerable significance. In the more realistic institutional setting (including political parties, as well as private institutions such as large firms), it is even more evidently the case, as Musgrave points out, that both small- and large-number problems may exist side by side. It is only for the polar case of a pure or near-pure public good in an atomistic institutional setting that small-number equilibrium analysis is completely irrelevant.

One might therefore wonder whether Buchanan is really justified, in his earlier analysis of small-number voluntary exchange, in explicitly ignoring strategic behavior problems. If the large-number case were the only one relevant in generalized public goods analysis, the strategic aspects of small-number interaction might well be regarded as irrelevant and hence ignored, as Buchanan argues. Indeed it would then be difficult to justify the whole voluntary exchange methodology of small-number bargaining which Buchanan adopts in his early chapters; the existence of potential gains from trade can be demonstrated equally well in the large-number model, and the equilibrium conditions of the small-number model are simply irrelevant. In fact, however, both types of problem seem relevant and interesting to the public goods theorist. Buchanan's criticisms of Lindahl-type analysis are not therefore entirely justified; though it remains true, as others have pointed out, that Lindahl's generalization to the large-number group is erroneous.

Having shown that in the important case of large-number public good externalities, the process of voluntary agreement is quite incapable of realizing the available gains from trade, Buchanan turns to the puzzling question as to why Wicksell thought that the political analogue of voluntary exchange, namely a system of minority veto, could do better. This question is puzzling not least because of the fact that Buchanan himself regards the two-person voluntary exchange models of his early chapters as equivalent to a two-person Wicksellian consensus model. Moreover, this is precisely how Lindahl formulates his own pioneering small-number analysis, not as a voluntary exchange model in the strict sense, but as a small-number political system based on Wicksellian consensus between homogeneous political groupings. In this way he had hoped to be able to develop the embryonic positive analysis embedded in Wicksell's discussion.

Why then is the large-number consensus system to be so sharply distinguished from the large-number "voluntary exchange" model? Buchanan makes a truly ingenious attempt to rationalize the approximate consensus requirement in a large-number model, but it seems clear that much of the argument applies almost equally well to a pure voluntary exchange system. The argument ultimately relies crucially on an alleged social-psychological involvement effect produced by possession of the veto; but this is far from completely convincing. Since possession of the veto does not bring the individual into a true bargaining relationship with the rest of the community, the consensus system could easily degenerate into the sort of independent adjustment equilibrium predicted for the voluntary exchange model. (This is particularly evident when it is remembered that in Wicksell's discussion the use of the veto cannot prevent the rest of the community from reaching a purely voluntaristic agreement on some rejected proposal). The "Wicksellian gap" between consensus and voluntary exchange thus remains largely inexplicable. For this reason also it is impossible to accept Buchanan's contention (e.g., pp. 6–7) that Wicksellian consensus can usefully be regarded as a political "ideal" analogous to the familiar market "ideal" of perfect competition. A Downsian democracy of competing vote-maximizing political parties would seem to provide a much closer political analogue to the market "ideal."

## 4.  Voluntary Exchange and the Political Process

Having demonstrated that there are large potential gains from public goods trade in the many-person model which cannot be realized through purely voluntary exchange institutions, Buchanan goes on to emphasize that individuals will have an incentive to propose institutional changes which may enable such gains to be achieved, at least in part. Thus, for example, it may be possible to agree on coercive political institutions such as majority voting, if not Wicksellian consensus, as a change in trading rules which will effectively embrace and bind the potential "drop-outs" under voluntary exchange.

### 4.1

To introduce his discussion of political provision for public goods, Buchanan first discusses in chapter 6 the special case of a world of public goods or public "issues," with no private good to play the crucial role of numeraire. Since side-payments are effectively ruled out, trading possibilities are severely restricted. As Buchanan points out, such a world is quite unfamiliar to the economist; but such models, rightly or wrongly, tend to dominate the analysis of voting processes in traditional political science. Buchanan shows how the scope for agreement expands as the number of public issues increases, and analyses and compares the results of a number of variants of consensus and majority-voting rules along lines pioneered by Black and Arrow. In this analysis differences in "decision-making costs" under the different voting rules are virtually ignored, and the emphasis is on possible "external costs."

In the following chapter, Buchanan attempts to apply essentially the same analysis to specifically budgetary issues, viewed as decisions involving the two "public issues" of public outlay and tax-share. The analytical setting here is precisely Lindahl's, viz. a two person Wicksellian consensus model with tax-shares assumed constant over public goods quantities for each party. As in his analysis of this same model in the purely voluntary exchange setting of chapter 3, Buchanan again finds the Lindahl $P$ point to be an appealing equilibrium solution. Indeed, in spite of Wicksell's evident distaste for such rigidities as constant tax-sharing over quantities, the $P$ point is presented by Buchanan as "the uniquely determinate *Wicksellian solution* to the problem of public goods allocation and tax-sharing" in this particular model (p. 135, italics added). Why not freely acknowledge that this is the well known Lindahl solution? It is, however, far from clear, in the absence of an assumption that units of public good are traded incrementally, that the Lindahl solution is any more likely than the infinity of other possible solutions which fully exhaust the potential gains from public goods trade.

With the addition of some further rigidities to the tax-sharing arrangements, the two-person Lindahl model is then extended along the lines of chapter 6 to accommodate a third person. In this context majority voting as well as consensus can readily be examined. As in the previous chapter, majority voting appears a more potent procedure for exhausting gains from trade than one might gather from the strict vote-trading analysis of *The Calculus of Consent*. In contrast to the two-person model, there appears to be no Lindahl-type consensus solution. Buchanan fails to explain that this is due simply to the additional rigidities in burden-sharing arrangements which he builds into the three-person model.

It is interesting to observe that the analytical framework of chapter 6 actually contributes little or nothing to Buchanan's conclusions in the consensus cases. As he explicitly recognizes, the two "public issues" of tax-sharing and public goods quantity are treated quite asymmetrically. Sharp conflicts between preferred tax-sharing arrangements are essentially ignored in the analysis of agreement on public goods quantity; and the analysis follows strict Wicksell-Lindahl lines.

## 4.2

The models just discussed ignore decision-making costs and focus attention on the operation of particular voting rules in the context of a single political decision. When these assumptions are relaxed and we compare the operation of different voting rules over a whole series of budgetary decisions, we find that individuals may unanimously choose majority voting as a means of realizing the potential gains from public goods trade, because of the much lower decision-making costs involved. The relevant analysis here was, of course, set out in detail by Buchanan and Tullock in *The Calculus of Consent*. With this argument, perhaps the major traditional objection to voluntary exchange theory is effectively undermined.

Buchanan then proceeds to show how the same general analysis can be used to explain the emergence of specifically fiscal institutions, notably the rigid tax institutions deplored by Wicksell, which, with their ability-to-pay characteristics, pose a formidable challenge to the claims of voluntary exchange theory to provide a realistic theory embracing both sides of the budget. In particular, the existence of an established (formal or informal) "tax constitution" avoids the heavy decision-making costs involved, even under majority voting, in devising a new set of acceptable cost-sharing arrangements for each fiscal period. Moreover, precisely under majority voting, a suitably chosen tax constitution may serve to reduce the inefficiencies or "external costs" produced in each period by less-than-unanimous decision-making. Thus, as Lindahl suggested, a system of proportional income taxation may provide a cost-sharing arrangement, uniform over the volume of expenditure, which roughly approximates marginal evaluation, at least if we abstract from differences in public goods preferences. Buchanan adds the further point, first noted by De Viti, that over a whole series of unpredictable budgetary decisions the individual may well expect the mix of public goods supplied to offer him about the same benefits as everyone else; differences in public goods preferences can therefore quite properly be neglected. Unanimous agreement may thus be possible on an efficiency-promoting tax constitution based essentially on the traditional "ability" criterion of the elasticity of the marginal utility of income schedule. In this way the challenge to voluntary exchange theory represented by the existence of rigid ability-based taxes can be effectively met. As against the original Wicksellian formulation, it seems likely that the combination of majority voting and a suitably-chosen tax constitution represents a more effective set of public goods trading rules than consensus and flexible burden-sharing.

## 4.3

An equally important aspect of the formal or informal public finance constitution in any society concerns the choice of goods and services to be provided publicly. Purely voluntary exchange, i.e. market-type institutions, function well for private goods provision; potential gains from trade are more or less fully realized. The political process here offers no basic advantages and can match market provision only by the adoption of marketing techniques, as under Lange-Lerner socialism.

The use of the term *public goods* suggests that it is these which will be chosen for public provision; but in Buchanan's discussion, as we have seen, the public goods concept is completely generalized to embrace even the purely private good as a special case. To analyse the problem, Buchanan therefore draws up a classification of public goods according to two characteristics: degree of indivisibility and size of interacting group. As he shows, market-type institutions perform reasonably well not only for purely private goods, but also for small-number public-good externalities, as implied by his earlier analysis of small-number voluntary exchange models.

In the light of his earlier analysis of the large-number voluntary exchange model, it is, however, surprising that he does not bring out more clearly the drastic failure of the market in the large-number model of a pure public good. Even more than in earlier sections of the book, the analysis here seems blurred by his failure to draw a clear distinction between the two major public goods characteristics of joint supply and impossibility of exclusion. Instead, these two characteristics are apparently lumped together under the portmanteau term *indivisibility,* which conceals more than it reveals in a public good context. Thus a particular service may show a considerable degree of "indivisibility" due to extreme joint supply, in the sense that, if the service is supplied at all, it could be fully and equally enjoyed by all without extra cost. However, unless the further characteristic of impossibility of exclusion applies, a market mechanism (a legal monopoly, or even perfect competition) may function tolerably well, though of course not perfectly. The comparison between public and private provision may then be close and difficult, as Buchanan implies. If, by contrast, price-exclusion is also impossible, market techniques fail disastrously in what Buchanan calls their allocation and financing functions. It is here that the political process offers the basic advantage that the chosen tax constitution acts as a readily enforceable, though no doubt far from perfect, pricing scheme.

The general conclusion would therefore seem to be that the fiscal constitution may be expected to assign more or less exclusive jurisdiction to the political process for the provision (not, of course, the production) of services which approximate the Samuelsonian polar case such as defense. It will also assign at least coordinate jurisdiction to the public sector in cases where significant exclusion problems exist, as in the fields of health and education. These conclusions suggest that the heavy emphasis on the joint supply characteristic of public goods in Buchanan (and also in Samuelson) is in some respects dangerously misleading.

## 5.  Some Methodological Reflections

Methodologically the most striking feature of Buchanan's voluntary exchange formulation is that the theory of public goods is presented as a strictly positive theory of the public economy in a society based ultimately on free agreement. The relevance of the theory to any actual society will of course depend on the degree to which this "liberal" assumption applies. For many highly developed democratic societies the theory is at least highly suggestive. Contrary to Buchanan, it is not, however, entirely surprising that the theory, in Lindahl's original formulation, had little impact on the Continental literature, for example in Germany where, in spite of a perceptive and broadly sympathetic review by Georg von Schanz in *Finanz-Archiv,* it was found too unrealistic. As we have already indicated, Buchanan's more sophisticated treatment effectively meets some formidable objections to the Lindahl formulation; and the underlying liberal premise is presumably more relevant now than in the political climate of the interwar period.

Buchanan's positive theory of public goods stands in sharp methodological contrast to the normative formulations of the theory to be found in Musgrave and Samuelson. The general reason why the standard public finance discussions have concentrated primarily on the application of welfare economics to public goods and have left the positive side of the theory rather neglected is, of course, that the positive aspects require the development and application of political theory. Few public finance specialists have shown either the capacity or inclination to cross this traditional border. Public finance has, however, always been recognized as a border discipline, and the recent excursions to which Buchanan has contributed so much should be warmly welcomed.

Buchanan is critical of the Musgrave-Samuelson discussions, not merely for their somewhat meagre positive contribution, but also for their defective normative formulation. According to Buchanan, there is a methodological inconsistency involved in first deriving a set of Pareto-efficient points on the basis of individual preferences for public and private goods, and then introducing what he calls "external criteria" in the form of a social welfare function to select a unique optimum optimorum. Instead he suggests that normative theory should end with the derivation of the conditions for Pareto-efficiency. Interpreted in this way, it is interesting to notice that the analytical content of normative theory is very similar to that of Buchanan's voluntary exchange theory, though the basic positive-normative distinction, of course, remains. As in the case of Lindahl's "positive Lösung," the analysis of the two-party consensus model can then serve simultaneously as a derivation both of equilibrium conditions and of fiscal norms. However, in a general normative framework, it could reasonably be argued that the problem of equity cannot and should not be ignored. This is at least formally recognized not only in the social welfare function formulations of Musgrave and Samuelson, but also in the pioneering contributions of Wicksell and Lindahl.

## 6. Conclusion

*The Demand and Supply of Public Goods* is an important new landmark in the development of the theory of public goods. The book brings together a number of Buchanan's important and original contributions to the subject and welds them into a systematic statement of the theory. As the foregoing discussion indicates, it is possible to disagree with some significant details of analysis and emphasis, but any possible ambiguities and inconsistencies are more than offset by important new insights. More than any other fiscal theorist over the postwar period, Buchanan has helped us to view fiscal phenomena, as he himself puts it, "through a different window." This book represents in many respects the culmination of these efforts.

# 8. Public Goods and Public Policy

## 1. Introduction

One of the most interesting developments in the Anglo-American public finance literature of recent years has been the appearance, under the formidable aegis of Professor Samuelson, of a prescriptive theory of public expenditure based on the alien Continental concept of a "public good."[1]

The concept of a "public good," which first flourished in the Italian, German and Scandinavian literature on public expenditure theory of the late nineteenth century,[2] never really penetrated the English-speaking countries, where prescriptive theories of public expenditure and economic policy generally were founded on such concepts as external economies and diseconomies and consequent divergences between private and social cost-benefit calculations, imperfections of competition including those due to decreasing cost phenomena, and inequities in the distribution of income. The main lines of this largely independent English development can be found very firmly laid down in Pigou's great classic, *The Economics of Welfare*. Although the occasional article did appear in which the "public good" concept was employed or referred to,[3] its precise relationship to its more familiar

Reprinted without significant change from *Public Finance/Finances Publiques* 17, no. 1 (1962): 197–219.

[1] P. A. Samuelson, "The Pure Theory of Public Expenditure," *Review of Economics and Statistics*, 1954; "Diagrammatic Exposition of a Theory of Public Expenditure," *Review of Economics and Statistics*, 1955; and "Aspects of Public Expenditure Theories," *Review of Economics and Statistics*, 1958.

[2] Extracts from some of the most important contributions by Mazzola, Wicksell, Sax and others can be found in English translation in R. A. Musgrave and A. T. Peacock, eds., *Classics in the Theory of Public Finance* (London and New York, 1958).

[3] See, for example, F. Benham, "Notes on the Pure Theory of Public Finance," *Economica*, 1934; R. A. Musgrave, "The Voluntary Exchange Theory of Public Economy," *Quarterly Journal of Economics*, 1938–39; H. R. Bowen, "The Interpretation of Voting in the Allocation of Economic Resources," *Quarterly Journal of Economics*, 1943–44, and *Toward Social Economy* (New York, 1948), chap. 18; and (in French) A. T. Peacock, "Sur la théorie des dépenses publiques," *Economie Appliquée*, 1952.

Pigovian rivals was barely discussed, let alone made clear, and it remained, for most of the English-speaking economic world, yet another mystery in the Pandora's box of Continental esoterica.

Stimulated by the researches of Professor Musgrave, Samuelson has now opened this still far-from-empty box, and has set loose upon an ill-prepared literature a fully fledged mathematical theory of public expenditure, based upon this concept alone. This theory, it is probably fair to say, is still, eight years and two reexpositions later, something of an enigma to most economists, though it is nevertheless felt to be of considerable importance. In the course of his three articles, Samuelson refers to external economies, along with certain other considerations, as important elements in any completely general theory of public expenditure, but, except perhaps to the specialist, the precise relationship between the various concepts remains unclear.

It is the aim of this article to examine the meaning of the public good concept as it appears in Samuelson's theory, and relate it to the more familiar Pigovian and Keynesian theories of public policy. In this way we hope to be able to show the place and importance of the concept in a general prescriptive theory of public policy.

We shall begin (section 2) with a brief outline of Samuelson's theory. Then (section 3) we shall set out in some detail the main characteristics of the public good concept on which the theory is based. Finally (section 4) we shall try in various ways to relate these characteristics, both to one another and to the more familiar concepts of modern theories of market inefficiency.

## 2.   Samuelson's Theory of Public Expenditure

In the following quotation from his original mathematical exposition in 1954, Samuelson provides what appears to be a singularly clear definition of the public good concept, which is to provide the foundation of his normative theory of public expenditure, viz.

"I explicitly assume two categories of goods: ordinary *private consumption goods* $(X_1,...,X_n)$ which can be parcelled out among different individuals $(1, 2,...,i,...,s)$ according to the relations

$$X_j = \sum_1^s X_j^i;$$

and *collective consumption goods* $(X_{n+1},..., X_{n+m})$ which all enjoy in common in the sense that each individual's consumption of such a good leads to no subtraction from any other individual's consumption of that good, so that

$$X_{n+j} = X^i_{n+j}$$

simultaneously for each and every i[th] individual and each collective consumption good."[4]

In his geometrical reexposition in 1955 we find a similar definition of a "public consumption good," which "differs from a private consumption good in that each man's consumption of it . . . is related to the total by a condition of *equality* rather than of summation."[5]

On the basis of this definition, and making the usual convexity assumptions, Samuelson shows algebraically and geometrically that the familiar Pareto-optimum condition of welfare economics, requiring equality between marginal rates of substitution and marginal rates of transformation, no longer holds. Where, in the case of two private goods and two individuals 1 and 2, the condition was $MRS^1 = MRS^2 = MT$, what is now required, where one of the two goods is "public," is equality between the marginal rate of transformation and the *sum* of the marginal rates of substitution, i.e., $MRS^1 + MRS^2 = MT$.

Thus, given the same "New Welfare" value judgment, that the goal of economic life should be a situation in which it is impossible to make someone better off without making someone else worse off, i.e., a Pareto optimum, the characteristic features of the allocation of resources which will achieve this goal will change with the introduction of public goods.

Samuelson points out that this change in the Pareto-optimum conditions with the introduction of public goods has disastrous implications for "duality," i.e., for the ability of a competitive market to compute these conditions, even under otherwise ideal circumstances. In particular, charging individuals a common price equal to the marginal cost of producing a unit of the good (or even "average marginal cost" per individual served by that unit) will not be efficient in the case of public goods. Highly idealized multiple pricing will be required if output of these goods is to be optimal, but "no decentralized pricing system can serve to determine optimally these levels of collective consumption."[6]

Furthermore, circumstances are otherwise far from ideal. As Samuelson expresses it, "one could imagine every person in the community being indoctrinated to behave like a 'parametric decentralized bureaucrat' who *reveals* his preferences by signalling in response to price

[4] Samuelson (1954), p. 387.
[5] Samuelson (1955), p. 350. For one of the clearest of many similar definitions in the traditional Continental public good literature, see that of Sax, in Musgrave and Peacock, p. 183.
[6] Samuelson (1954), p. 388.

parameters or Lagrangean multipliers, to questionnaires, or to other devices. But . . . by departing from his indoctrinated rules, any one person can hope to snatch some selfish benefit in a way not possible under the self-policing competitive pricing of private goods."[7] "It is in the selfish interest of each person to give *false* signals, to pretend to have less interest in a given collective consumption activity than he really has."[8] In short, even with ideal multiple pricing, the market will fail because true preferences will not be revealed.

It is, therefore, in somehow promoting adequate provision of these public goods, that at least some[9] of the proper economic functions of government are to be found.[10] Samuelson warns, however, that these functions are not likely to be easy to perform efficiently, and emphasizes in particular that the benefit theory offers no perfect practical solution.

## 3.   The Characteristics of a Public Good

Turning now to detailed consideration of the public good concept on which this theory is based, it appears that Samuelson's public good has two main characteristics, "jointness of supply," "indivisibility" or "lumpiness" on the one hand, and external economies on the other.

## 3.1   "Jointness"

The first and most obvious implication of the equal consumption requirement ($X_{n+j} = X_{n+j}^i$ for each and every individual) is that Samuelson's public good is in joint supply, in the special sense that, once produced, any given unit of the good can be made equally available to all. Extension of the supply to one individual facilitates its extension to all. Supply of a given unit to one individual, and supply of the same

[7] Ibid., p. 389.
[8] Ibid., pp. 388–89.
[9] The apparent implication of the first article, that all legitimate governmental functions must be of this sort, is considerably modified in "concluding reflection" (iv), pp. 355–56, of the second.
[10] Samuelson speaks of "public expenditure and regulation" and "economic functions of government" as well as public expenditure, and it is clear that all expenditure and therefore, by implication, the necessary revenue-raising activities and hence all economic functions of government are, at least potentially, under consideration. Such outlays as those required to support the multifarious activities of a central bank, price control or import-licensing authority, etc., would therefore be included. As we shall see below, the services of such agencies can indeed quite properly be regarded as "public goods."

unit to other individuals, are clearly joint products.[11] Alternatively we could describe this characteristic as a special type of lumpiness or indivisibility of product.[12] As we shall see,[13] it is this "jointness" which alone accounts for the change in the Pareto-optimum conditions and the consequent need for a highly idealized system of multiple pricing referred to above, a need which a competitive market cannot meet.

Are there many goods which would appear to fall into this category? In his first article Samuelson offers no example. In the second, he instances an outdoor circus and national defense. In the third a battleship and a television program are mentioned. None of these, nor any of a host of other traditional governmental activities seems, however, to satisfy this very stringent requirement to perfection. "Capacity limits" are usually met well before the good has become equally available to all, this applying alike to roads, bridges, hospitals, courts, police, and even flood control measures, irrigation, national defense, and public health schemes such as vaccination programs and draining of malarial swamps. Furthermore, even before capacity limits in any strict sense are encountered, quality variations usually occur. Crowded roads and other facilities are usually regarded as giving inferior service to that provided by the same "goods" less fully utilized.

Under pressure on this particular point from such critics as Enke and Margolis,[14] Samuelson admits in his second article that his public good concept is properly to be regarded only as an "extreme polar case," which the student of public expenditure can set against the "logically equally-extreme category of a private good," in order to bring out the essence of the case for government activity. Accordingly he reformulates the theory with this change of emphasis, to avoid the apparent overstatement of the original article.

It is, however, no more than a change of emphasis. "To deny that most public functions fit into my extreme definition of a public good is not to grant that they satisfy the logically equally-extreme category of a private good . . . Indeed I am rash enough to think that in almost every one of the legitimate economic functions of government that

[11] Samuelson uses the term *joint supply* only once, on p. 355 of his second article, to describe this property. He also refers to *jointness of demand,* traditionally reserved for "bacon and eggs" type phenomena. Musgrave uses the term *joint consumption.* I have preferred *jointness of supply* which is closest to traditional usage. Lindahl (see Musgrave and Peacock, p. 221) uses a joint supply analogy to good effect in his derivation of the "optimum conditions" for the public good case.

[12] This is common usage in traditional public good discussions. Mazzola, Sax and Bowen, for example, all use the term *indivisibility* to describe public goods.

[13] See below, sec. 4.2.1.

[14] S. Enke, "More on the Misuses of Mathematics in Economics: A Rejoinder," *Review of Economics and Statistics,* 1955; and J. Margolis, "A Comment on the Pure Theory of Public Expenditures," *Review of Economics and Statistics,* 1955.

critics put forward there is to be found a blending of the extreme antip-
odal models."[15]

"Jointness" thus remains an essential characteristic of a public
good, though it is now to be understood in the less extreme sense that
a given unit of the good, once produced, can be made at least partially
available, though possibly in varying degrees, to more than one individual. Only beyond a point does additional consumption by one person imply the need for a corresponding reduction in consumption by
others.

The presence of public good elements in this sense is quite sufficient to cause the change in the Pareto-optimum conditions and consequent failure of market catallactics described in section 2.[16] Modified in this way, the public good concept, and hence the theory of public
policy based on it, thus becomes much more realistic and important.
A whole host of activities, including all those listed earlier and many
more, can be found which will satisfy this less demanding requirement.

## 3.2   External Economies

The second important characteristic of Samuelson's public good is
that it gives rise to external economies. In his first article he speaks of
the "external economies or jointness of demand intrinsic to the very
concept of collective goods" and the "external effects basic to the very
notion of collective consumption goods." Describing his theory in the
second article, he states that "it explicitly introduces the vital external
interdependencies that no theory of government can do without,"
and in the third that it "is the natural model to formulate so as to give
strongest emphasis to external effects."

There are indications at various points in his articles that Samuelson may be using the term "external effects" in a rather broader sense
than is now usual, and possibly even as a generic term to cover all
causes of market inefficiency. To make quite sure that we do not get
trapped in a semantic snarl, it may therefore be wise to begin with a
brief discussion of the meaning of external economies and diseconomies.[17]

In its narrowest modern sense the concept of external economies and
diseconomies, applied to a given good, indicates that a change in the
production and/or consumption of that good will affect the utility and/or

[15] Samuelson (1955), p. 356.
[16] See Samuelson (1955), p. 350 and especially n. 1.
[17] For a very useful summary of the subject and references to the extensive literature, see
F. M. Bator, "The Anatomy of Market Failure," *Quarterly Journal of Economics,* 1958,
sec. 2.

production functions for other goods. The "reason" usually given by economists for the existence of these external economies or diseconomies is perhaps most succinctly described by Ellis and Fellner[18] as "the divorce of scarcity from effective ownership," i.e. imperfections in property titles. Following Sidgwick,[19] we might describe the problem as one of "nonappropriability," it being impossible for private firms and individuals, through ordinary private pricing, to appropriate the full social benefits (or be charged the full social costs) arising directly from their production and/or consumption of certain goods. An identical concept to be found in the important works of Bowen and Musgrave is "impossibility of exclusion," meaning that it is impossible for private firms and individuals, through private pricing, to exclude other firms and individuals from at least some part of the benefits (or be charged the full social costs) arising directly from their production and/or consumption of certain goods. The extramarket benefits in question are here to be interpreted narrowly in terms of use or enjoyment of the product itself.

The effect of these external economies and diseconomies is to create divergences between private and social costs and benefits, and thus to prevent the satisfaction of the optimum conditions. Some economic units can enjoy some of the benefits of certain activities without having to pay for them, and it would of course be grossly unrealistic to expect them to contribute voluntarily. These activities will therefore be underexpanded, and government expansion of them is justified. Similarly, where the full social costs cannot be charged to an economic unit through the pricing process, again voluntary contributions by way of compensation or expenditures to reduce the costs in question cannot reasonably be expected. Overexpansion of these activities is therefore likely, and their restraint is a legitimate economic function of government.

But for these ownership difficulties encountered by the consumer or producer of the good in physically excluding other users, there is no reason inherent in the external economies concept, why a competitive market could not ensure optimum output of it. The external economies concept in this sense is clearly not a generic term covering all causes of market inefficiency.

Do Samuelson's public goods exhibit external economies in this sense? Perhaps the easiest way of seeing that they do, is to notice the resemblance between Samuelson's definition and the Bowen and Musgrave concepts of goods for which price-exclusion is completely im-

---

[18] H. S. Ellis and W. Fellner, "External Economies and Diseconomies," *American Economic Review,* 1943, p. 511.

[19] Henry Sidgwick, *Principles of Political Economy,* 3rd ed. (London, 1883), pp. 406–7.

possible,[20] and which therefore exhibit external economies to an extreme degree. These goods are referred to by Bowen as "social goods" and by Musgrave as goods satisfying "social wants." According to Musgrave, "Social wants are those wants satisfied by services that must be consumed in equal amounts by all. People who do not pay for the services cannot be excluded from the benefits that result; and since they cannot be excluded from the benefits, they will not engage in voluntary payments. Hence the market cannot satisfy such wants."[21]

In this definition the equal consumption requirement and the impossibility of exclusion appear side by side. Samuelson on the other hand does not explicitly refer in his definition to the possibility or otherwise of price-exclusion. On reflection, however, it should be clear that impossibility of exclusion is a direct implication of his formulation of the equal consumption condition for public goods. The latter is clearly to hold by definition in all situations, optimal and nonoptimal alike; public goods, once produced, not only *can* but *must* be made equally available to all. If exclusion were possible, however, consumption would not be equal for all individuals in innumerable nonoptimal situations of private pricing, since those unwilling to pay the inefficient private price would be excluded.

The second implication of the equal consumption requirement which defines Samuelson's public good is therefore that such a good exhibits external economies, i.e. exclusion or appropriability difficulties, to an extreme degree. As we shall see, it is this characteristic alone which accounts for the failure of the market mechanism to ensure revelation of true preferences.

Are there many goods which would appear to exhibit this characteristic? The answer would seem to be that there are none. Exclusion is never completely impossible, even in such obvious cases as national defense, flood control and public health programs.

Samuelson does not explicitly consider this question.[22] Both Bowen and Musgrave appear, however, to employ the concept only to emphasize the essential feature of this particular market weakness. A less extreme usage is fairly clearly indicated, if perhaps underemphasized, in both cases.[23]

There are in fact innumerable goods which will pose price-exclusion

---

[20] H. R. Bowen, *Toward Social Economy*, pp. 172–73; and R. A. Musgrave, *The Theory of Public Finance* (New York, 1959), pp. 8–9. Our definition of "impossibility of exclusion" above is less restrictive than this.

[21] Ibid., p. 8.

[22] In the passages referred to in sec. 3.1 above, and in other places, he seems much more concerned to acknowledge that his jointness concept requires modification in the light of such considerations as capacity limits and quality variations.

[23] Bowen, ibid., pp. 196–97; and Musgrave, ibid., p. 8.

problems, and thus exhibit external economies (and diseconomies) in the less restrictive sense without approaching complete impossibility of exclusion. A theory of public expenditure based on this less restrictive, and hence more realistic and important concept, is itself correspondingly more realistic and important, with the general conclusion still justified, that, because of exclusion difficulties, true preferences will be understated, and the market will therefore fail to secure optimum production and consumption of the goods in question.

## 4. The Relationship Between Jointness, External Economies and Other Concepts in the Theory of Public Policy

We have distinguished two important properties of Samuelson's public goods, namely jointness and external economies. Are they, however, conceptually quite distinct, or are they related in some way, or perhaps even identical? And what is the relationship between them and the various concepts of the more familiar theories of public policy? We shall consider these two questions in turn.

### 4.1 Jointness and External Economies

In the light of Samuelson's own definition and that of Musgrave, quoted earlier, and indeed of the whole traditional public good literature, in all of which the two characteristics appear to be merged, it is clearly important to ask whether they are in fact independent, somehow related, or one and the same.

#### 4.1.1

We shall begin by considering whether the existence of jointness necessarily implies the existence of external economies and thus of price-exclusion problems. In other words, does it follow from the fact that a good *can* be made equally available to all, that it *must* be made equally available to all? Most public good concepts exhibit both characteristics, but does the one necessarily entail the other in this manner?

It is certainly true that some of the best examples of goods with jointness characteristics also pose the most difficult exclusion problems. National defense, flood control and public health programs are excellent examples of goods exhibiting both characteristics to a high degree.

The fact remains, however, that goods and services with jointness aspects may, and in fact often will, pose no price-exclusion problems. Bus, train and tram fares are too obvious to need comment, though in each case elements of jointness in the public good sense certainly exist.[24] Tolls are common in the case of roads and bridges. Fees are charged in the case of the courts, postal and telephone services, hospitals, etc., and could easily be extended, if necessary, to a host of similar services. Concerts, football matches and circuses (even outdoor ones!) can usually be fenced off and admission charges levied. Unscrambling devices may be perfectly feasible in the case of television and radio programs and the services of lighthouses. In short, the existence of jointness in no way necessarily entails the existence of price-exclusion problems. This point is explicitly recognized by both Samuelson and Musgrave.[25]

This is not of course to suggest that the imposition of charges will not occasionally, or even frequently, be extremely costly to the private firm and/or inconvenient to the user. In these cases it is perfectly possible that a socially superior service could be provided "free" by the government. We would therefore agree that there are often important exclusion problems coexisting with jointness, which may enormously reinforce the case for government intervention, without conceding that exclusion is the only problem involved, or, for that matter, that exclusion is in any literal sense "impossible."

### 4.1.2

Although joint supply or indivisibility in our present sense in no way necessarily implies the existence of price-exclusion difficulties, it is important to recognize that it does create a very similar problem for the effective functioning of political choice or voting mechanisms.

We have seen that there is no necessary problem in principle of ensuring, under a price system, that individuals will reveal their true preferences for goods exhibiting Samuelsonian jointness characteristics. Market inefficiency arises here because of the independent phenomenon of jointness.

If, however, the government steps in to promote, by extramarket means, more adequate provision of the service in question, the prob-

---

[24] The last bus can be made available to sixty people, etc.

[25] Samuelson (1954), p. 389, and (1958), p. 335; and Musgrave, p. 10, n. 1. Musgrave, however, fails to see the point stressed by Samuelson, and perhaps the distinguishing feature of his whole theory, that jointness as such (and the consequent need for multiple pricing) gives rise to market inefficiency. Indeed he appears to suggest the contrary. This is in curious contrast to his account in the introduction (with A. T. Peacock) to *Classics in the Theory of Public Finance*, p. xiv. The point is, however, clearly recognized by Bator, p. 371 and p. 376, n. 5.

lem of determining true preferences immediately becomes acute. Whatever the nature of the political system, individuals and small groups will know that, if prices are not to be charged, the supply to them of this service "equally available to all" will depend overwhelmingly upon what the rest of the community is induced or forced to contribute, and to only the slightest extent on their own contributions. Each therefore has an enormous incentive to try to minimize his own contribution by understating his true preferences in public statements, bargaining, voting or other political activity relevant to the determination of the sharing of the burden. With large numbers behaving in this way, there is clearly a grave danger of underexpansion of the service when provided "free" by government.

This is precisely Wicksell's overwhelming objection to even the relatively refined benefit theory of Mazzola as a practical solution to the problem of securing adequate provision of public goods,[26] and the same point is also to be found in the articles by Benham, Musgrave, Bowen, and Peacock referred to in section 1.[27] Samuelson also emphasizes in all three articles "the inherent *political* difficulty of ever getting men to reveal their tastes" for public goods.[28]

It is important to stress again that this difficulty is a consequence of jointness, and arises whether price-exclusion is possible or not, and it applies to almost any conceivable voting mechanism, including that suggested by Wicksell. The problem is, however, considerably exacerbated where price-exclusion is impossible, since this removes the possibility of using previous market choices as some check on true preferences in the political activity following the switch to "free" government provision of the service.[29]

[26] Wicksell, in Musgrave and Peacock, pp. 81–82.

[27] See note 3 above. As some of these later writers have pointed out, the objection applies also, though much less forcefully, to the "Positive Solution" of Lindahl, which represents the final development of the benefit theory. Lindahl's theory is intended to be descriptive as well as prescriptive, and he depicts the political mechanism in a democracy as a bargaining process between major parties with equal power. Since large parties are involved, supply of public goods will now depend significantly on own contributions, and the incentive to understatement of true preferences is correspondingly much weaker. If his theory were valid as description, the problem of switching from private to tax-financed government provision of public goods would, therefore, be a comparatively minor one. Since, however, it is not, it remains merely a rather quixotic prescription for political organization in a democracy.

[28] Like these other writers, and even Musgrave in *The Theory of Public Finance* (p. 10), he fails to make it clear, however, that this difficulty is basically a consequence of jointness, rather than of price-exclusion difficulties.

[29] Musgrave, ibid., overstates, however, when in making substantially this point, he implies that it is the impossibility of price-exclusion which is the fundamental reason for preference-revelation problems in the political process.

### 4.1.3

If joint supply does not necessarily entail price-exclusion problems, why do writers such as Bowen and Musgrave bring the equal consumption requirement with its implications of jointness into the forefront of definitions of public goods, the essential characteristic of which is apparently intended to be complete impossibility of price-exclusion?

The answer suggested by Musgrave[30] is that, although jointness does not necessarily entail exclusion problems, the existence of exclusion problems does imply the existence of elements of jointness. If no economic unit can be price-excluded from any part of the good, it follows ipso facto, that each unit of the good is, and hence can be, made equally available to all, i.e. we have Samuelsonian jointness.

In many cases of extreme exclusion difficulties, it is true, as we have already noted, that joint supply is also involved. It is far from clear, however, that the exclusion problems in any way necessarily imply the existence of jointness. Oil wells drawing on a common pool would appear to be a case in point. New wells in the neighborhood of a strike may drastically reduce output from the original well, with the firm which made the original strike possibly quite unable to price-exclude others from peacefully expropriating a significant part of its "property." The good in question, oil, is however strictly "private" in Samuelson's sense of being "like bread whose total can be parcelled out among two or more persons with one man having a loaf less if another gets a loaf more." If one economic unit gets more oil, there is a corresponding reduction in the quantity which can be made available to others. Other similar examples could be cited. It is of course perfectly true, that all can take part in the scramble for the scarce supply, but this is the only sense in which "equal potential availability" can be claimed. In a sense, that is, the good is "indivisible," in so far as secure property titles to the individual units of it are difficult to grant, and this problem of parcelling out the total for purposes of legal ownership has doubtless contributed to the misunderstanding.[31] Such "equal availability" or "indivisibility" is clearly in no way related to Samuelsonian jointness.

From the above analysis we can conclude that jointness and external economies are conceptually quite distinct properties of Samuelson's public good, and are in no way related. A clear differentiation between them is therefore extremely important to preserve.

---

[30] Ibid., p. 10, n. 1.
[31] It is possible that Bowen (1948, p. 173) intended initially to use the term *indivisibility* in this sense only, though he goes on to speak without qualification of equal availability.

## 4.2   Jointness, External Economies and Other Concepts

Finally, let us consider possible relationships between these two characteristics of a public good and the more familiar concepts of Pigovian and Keynesian theories of public policy. We have already seen that the external economies which characterize the public good are simply an extreme category of external economies in the narrowest modern sense. The precise nature of jointness, however, requires further examination, as does the relationship between both these characteristics and the other elements which go to make up modern theories of market inefficiency.

### 4.2.1

What, first of all, is the precise relationship between jointness, which is the distinguishing characteristic of the Samuelson concept,[32] and these other theories of public policy?

The answer seems to be the obvious one suggested by the occasional use of the term *indivisibility* in this connection, namely that we are dealing here with a special case of decreasing costs.

This is perhaps most easily seen by recognizing that one of the most traditional examples of decreasing cost problems discussed in the public finance literature dealing with pricing policies for nationalized industries,[33] namely that of a bridge, is a perfect example of a good exhibiting jointness characteristics. Up to a point it is possible for some individuals to have more, without the need for anything like a corresponding reduction in the service available to others.

With a uniform toll being charged in a given period, as under private pricing, to (say) cover average cost in that period, it is quite likely that the bridge would not be used to "capacity," and some individuals who would be willing to pay marginal social cost would be excluded by the average cost price. As has been pointed out again and again in the literature, this is not Pareto-efficient pricing and, in a world in which all other optimum conditions are satisfied, the position could

---

[32] In contrast, as we have seen, to the superficially very similar concepts of Bowen and Musgrave where impossibility of exclusion is the essential feature.

[33] This literature dates back at least to Jules Dupuit's celebrated article of 1844, now reprinted in English translation in *International Economic Papers*, no. 2. The lively controversy of the 1940s was sparked off by Hotelling's classic, "The General Welfare in Relation to Problems of Taxation and of Railway and Utility Rates," *Econometrica*, 1938. For an excellent critical summary of this controversy, see I. M. D. Little, *A Critique of Welfare Economics*, 2nd ed. (Oxford, 1957), chap. 11. Also Nancy Ruggles, "Recent Developments in the Theory of Marginal Cost Pricing," *Review of Economic Studies*, 1949–50. Wicksell's brilliant 1896 discussion (for which see Musgrave and Peacock, pp. 97–105) is another landmark which is well worth attention.

be substantially improved by lowering the uniform price towards the true marginal social (opportunity) cost of supplying the service to the last user. In the case of the bridge this will be zero if we neglect wear and tear, and lowering price to this level will therefore necessarily result in substantial losses, since overheads will be uncovered. Clearly these losses are due to spectacularly decreasing costs. In the absence of government action in the form of a subsidy or complete takeover, this financially disastrous but socially ideal pricing policy can clearly not be expected of a private firm. Whatever the form of the action taken, the losses should be covered by non-(or not too-) distorting taxation.

Alternatively, and this is the familiar verbal conclusion which Samuelson has effectively demonstrated mathematically and geometrically in his articles, a system of multiple pricing[34] or multipart tariffs could be employed, mulcting the consumer surplus of intramarginal users to cover overheads. Under this system, each user would be charged a price which would equate his individual demand for the service with the fixed supply equally available to all. This is of course nothing more than a careful application of the general rule, familiar from the pricing debates referred to above, that where all other optimum conditions are satisfied, price, in the particular industry under consideration, should be set at marginal social cost and equate supply with demand.[35] It is also familiar, at least by implication, from this branch of the literature, that no decentralized pricing system can compute this multiple pricing solution, and indeed that only the very roughest approximation to such a solution such as a two- or few-part tariff could, let alone would, be attempted by a central (private or public) pricing authority.[36] It has always been clear, in addition, that this problem is in no way related to exclusion difficulties in the narrow external economies sense.

The case of a bridge is only one of a number of cases of decreasing costs discussed in the literature, which are basically examples of Samuelsonian jointness. Wicksell[37] lists roads, ports, canals, railways,

---

[34] Or, more strictly, as Samuelson's demonstration clearly shows, an infinite set of such systems, corresponding to the infinite set of conceivable post-policy distributions of welfare. See his objection (1955, p. 354), on precisely this point, to the formulations of Wicksell, Lindahl, and Bowen. Only if we adopt the Bergson-Samuelson "Social Welfare Function" version of the New Welfare Economics, is one of these systems likely to be better than the others. This is also the point which lies at the heart of Musgrave's contention (pp. 8 and 84) that Samuelson's normative theory is indeterminate "if we apply the criterion of efficiency as understood in the determination of market price . . . a more specific welfare function is needed to secure an optimal solution."

[35] Optimum price and output are thus, of course, mutually determined.

[36] See Little, pp. 199–200, on the feasibility of such a solution.

[37] Wicksell, pp. 99–100.

postal services, and public squares as well as bridges. Little,[38] writing more than fifty years later, mentions museums, parks, passenger trains and buses, broadcasting, water supply, and roads. In all these cases the decreasing cost problem is due very largely to elements of jointness, in the sense that at least up to a point, once a given unit of the good has been produced, additional consumption by one individual does not imply a corresponding reduction in the quantity which can be made available to others.

The decreasing cost implications of Samuelson's public good concept should indeed be evident on reflection from his definition, which implies very directly, even if it does not state, that the opportunity cost of supplying more of the service, and more specifically of supplying the same unit to more users, is zero. Modified in the direction of realism to take account of capacity limits, quality variations, and minor wear and tear effects due to additional use, the essential point remains, that opportunity cost is likely to be almost negligible and certainly very low in relation to average cost, i.e. we have sharply decreasing costs. In all these Samuelsonian cases, as long as any individual is excluded who has paid or is willing to pay any necessary "marginal customer cost" (the cost of installation of the telephone, the price of the television or radio receiver or vehicle, etc.), and who is also willing to pay the relatively small marginal social cost due to wear and tear (zero in the extreme Samuelson case), price to such users should be lowered.[39,40] It is unlikely that even a private firm in a monopoly position could do this without incurring losses, and in the absence of public policy it would therefore never be done.[41]

These are not of course the only examples of decreasing cost industries. Other cases traditionally quoted, such as steel and other heavy industries, are due to indivisibility of factors with no elements of

[38] Little, p. 195.

[39] Most economic functions of government are necessarily desirable individually, only if all other functions necessary to achieve the optimum are simultaneously performed. Where marginal cost is actually zero, however, as in the extreme Samuelson formulation, the general case for satisfying this condition no longer depends upon the simultaneous satisfaction of all other optimum conditions.

[40] In some instances, and particularly in certain periods, demand will already be pressing up against the capacity limit, and marginal social cost, properly interpreted, may be well above an average cost price. Consumption is then no longer in the decreasing cost range, and there is no apparent need for either multiple pricing or the financing of deficits by nondistorting taxation under marginal cost pricing. No problem remains—except to expand capacity to an adequate level, ration existing capacity efficiently by charging the marginal cost price which will equate supply and demand, and dispose of the surplus by multiple pricing (lower prices to intramarginal users) or nondistorting subsidies!

[41] It is interesting to note the similarity between this problem and that posed by an uneven time-pattern of demand, the so-called problem of the peak. Peak and off-peak services, like the services of public goods to different individuals in the same period, are essentially joint. Charging a uniform average cost (or even long-run marginal cost) price

jointness of product in our sense.[42] There can be little doubt, however, that Samuelsonian cases are amongst the most numerous and important. It is also clear, both from the theory and from practical experience, that the resulting economic function of government is likely to be far from easy to perform efficiently even without price-exclusion difficulties.

It seems then that in terms of the usual theories of public policy, what is perhaps the essential characteristic of Samuelson's public good, namely its jointness of supply or indivisibility in the sense of equal potential availability, gives rise to a very important category of decreasing cost problems. It is interesting to observe the growing appreciation of this crucial point in his three articles. In the original mathematical exposition there is no mention whatever of decreasing costs. In the geometrical version we find, in the penultimate paragraph, the completely enigmatic statement that "whether or not I have overstated the applicability of this one theoretical model to actual governmental functions, I believe I did not go far enough in claiming for it relevance to the vast area of decreasing costs that constitutes an important part of economic reality and of the welfare economics of monopolistic competition."[43] Finally, in the third article, in the course of developing, with reference to television programs, the argument that impossibility of exclusion is far from the be-all and end-all of his public good concept, and under the general heading "Decreasing-cost phenomena," we find a brief but clear and explicit exposition of this basic point.[44]

### 4.2.2

We have now seen that the first characteristic of Samuelson's public good, viz. jointness or indivisibility, accounts for an important part

---

is likely to prevent the use of off-peak units for which someone would be perfectly willing to pay marginal social cost (e.g., labor and materials costs), whilst at the same time failing effectively to ration peak use. Public goods usually exhibit both kinds of jointness. On this problem see P. O. Steiner, "Peak Loads and Efficient Pricing," *Quarterly Journal of Economics,* 1957; and J. Hirschleifer, "Peak Loads and Efficient Pricing — Comment," *Quarterly Journal of Economics,* 1958.

[42] Though the often slightly artificial distinction between factor and product tends to obscure a fundamental similarity.

[43] Samuelson (1955), p. 356.

[44] Samuelson (1958), p. 335. He notes that broadcasting is, in a way, a perfect example of his public good, in spite of the possibility of exclusion with the help of unscrambling devices. Market inefficiency arises here because "our well-known optimum principle that goods should be priced at their marginal costs would not be realized in the case of subscription broadcasting. Why not? In the deepest sense because this is, by its nature, not a case of constant returns to scale. It is a case of general decreasing costs." And again, "what after all are the true marginal costs of having one extra family tune in on the program? They are literally zero." See also Bator, p. 376.

of the familiar concept of decreasing costs. The second characteristic, namely complete impossibility of exclusion, is a special and extreme case of the modern external economies concept.

Is there not, however, a sense in which decreasing costs and external economies are related? And is there perhaps some general relationship between these and the other major elements which go to make up modern theories of market inefficiency?[45]

**4.2.2.1**  Referring back to our earlier summary of the explanations which have been offered for the existence of external economies and diseconomies, we defined nonappropriability as that property of a good which makes it impossible for private economic units to appropriate, by ordinary private pricing, the full social benefits from their production and/or consumption of that good. So far, following the mainstream of the modern external economies doctrine, we have interpreted these "full social benefits" in a very narrow sense to refer only to use or enjoyment of the product itself. By price-exclusion problems we have therefore simply meant difficulties in physically excluding, from use or enjoyment of the product itself, other economic units who have not paid for the privilege.

Interpreting these full social benefits in the widest sense, however, it is clear that nonappropriability or impossibility of exclusion accounts for all decreasing cost problems as well as external economies in the narrow modern sense. By lowering price from (say) average cost to marginal cost in a situation in which all other optimum conditions are satisfied, a decreasing cost monopolist could provide resource-allocation benefits such that, as a result, it would be possible to make someone better off without making anyone else worse off. The firm could not, however, as a general rule, charge for these social benefits, and the individual beneficiaries could not be expected to contribute voluntarily. The possibly quite substantial losses that would be incurred by the monopolist through the lowering of price would not therefore in general be covered by other means, even though it would be possible for the community, by cooperative action, to compensate him and still enjoy a net benefit, with some members better off and none worse off than before. Since such spontaneous and voluntary cooperation cannot be relied upon, the average cost price and consequent misallocation will persist in the absence of government, and the reason is precisely the nonappropriability of these potential resource-allocation benefits. Exactly the same general argument ap-

---

[45] The analysis of this section is based upon the highly suggestive extensions of the external economies concept contained in W. J. Baumol, *Welfare Economics and the Theory of the State* (London, 1952).

plies to Samuelsonian as to other forms of lumpiness, and indeed to the much more general category of imperfections of competition from whatever cause (including decreasing cost phenomena).

**4.2.2.2** It is interesting to notice that, in this more general sense, nonappropriability or impossibility of exclusion also accounts to a considerable extent for Keynesian and post-Keynesian vagaries of aggregate demand and supply and their associated inefficiency concepts of unemployment "equilibrium" and inflation. An economic unit increasing its consumption- or investment-spending, or accepting a substantial money-wage cut in a situation of unemployment equilibrium, can by no means appropriate to itself, through private pricing, the full social benefits in the form of multiplier and real balance effects on the incomes and profits of other economic units. Instead, the individual consumption-spender risks severe later hardship and insolvency; the investment-spending firm risks heavy losses and ultimate bankruptcy; the single trade union or employee accepting a wage cut loses both absolutely and relatively to less socially-minded employee groups; and the small nation risks international insolvency and consequent further employment difficulties. With the signs changed, a similar argument applies to the inflation case, where again the full benefits from reduced inefficiencies of all sorts are not appropriable. The nonappropriability case for government activity in the stability field is therefore clear.

Again, in the case of suboptimal economic growth, the full benefits in terms of rising real wages from growth-promoting behavior, such as thrift, risk-bearing, dividend- and wage-restraint, are seldom anything like fully appropriable from the point of view of the economic unit which must bear the full cost of such behavior. Competitive depreciation and tariff and export-subsidy wars, including beggar-my-neighbor remedies for unemployment, provide further examples of cases in which socially responsible behavior fails to receive anything like its just reward.

In all these cases it would be possible for the community, by means of voluntary cooperative action, to compensate potential losers from socially desirable changes, and still enjoy a net benefit with some members better off and none worse off. Such cooperative effort will seldom be forthcoming in the absence of coercion and the inefficiency due to nonappropriability will therefore persist.[46]

---

[46] It might be suggested that this extension of the nonappropriability concept to cover so many causes of market inefficiency robs it of all explanatory significance, and reduces it to a synonym for such inefficiencies. There can be little doubt, however, that the approach does yield valuable insights into the persistence of these malfunctions, and the extension therefore seems well justified.

In a broad but very real and important sense then, domestic and international economic stability, domestic and international allocation of resources in accordance with consumers' wishes and an optimal rate of growth can all quite properly be regarded as public goods, for adequate provision of which public policy must be relied upon.

**4.2.2.3** Of the most important elements in the usual theories of market inadequacy only such slippery, though undoubtedly vital, concepts as inequitable income distribution (including therefore important aspects of economic stability and growth), imperfect knowledge and irrational motivation remain outside this wider nonappropriability net, and even here some part of the problem can undoubtedly be ascribed to exclusion difficulties.[47]

The most important of these concepts, namely the gross inequalities of income which result from the free functioning of the market, is a concept which is largely alien to the New Welfare ethical foundations on which the whole of the above theory is based.

In our account we have adopted a goal of economic organization in the Kaldor-Hicks "hypothetical-compensationist" tradition of a situation in which it is impossible to make someone better off without making someone else worse off, and have regarded any resulting redistributions of income as of negligible importance. Alternatively, in the "actual-compensationist" tradition we could have postulated the same goal, but insisted at the same time that losers from any policy leading to the goal be compensated in costless lump-sum fashion, thus making the policy implications of the theory "more generally acceptable." Following this latter approach still further, we could insist in addition that the government's first policy act be to correct any initial (prepolicy) inequities in the distribution of income.[48] A further extension of this approach would be the Bergson-Samuelson formulation, under which it is the post-policy distribution of income in the "bliss state" which is to be made ideal (or "swung to the ethical observer's optimum") using costless lump-sum taxes and subsidies. Finally, in the limit, we could demand that the government ensure that the initial

[47] For a detailed analysis of these problems, see chapter 10 below.
[48] This is the approach followed by Wicksell and Lindahl, and adopted also by Musgrave in *The Theory of Public Finance*. It is this form of the theory which Musgrave (ibid.) and Musgrave and Peacock have noted as indeterminate, though this also applies a fortiori to the two previously mentioned variants. The point here is that, even given the prepolicy distribution of welfare, there is still an infinite set of postpolicy distributions, which will satisfy the requirement that someone has been made better off and no one worse off. The suggestion by Musgrave, and Musgrave and Peacock, that this indeterminacy problem is in some way peculiar to the provision of "public goods," narrowly defined, is, however, unjustified and highly misleading. The ambiguity lies in the welfare criterion itself.

distribution of income is ideal, and also that, in implementing the policies necessary for "efficiency," incomes be simultaneously redistributed to maintain an ideal income distribution throughout the process.

In other words, it is possible in various ways to graft considerations of income distribution on to the formal framework of a basically New Welfare theory of public policy. The operation is, however, rather artificial, and the crucial questions regarding the appropriate distribution of income are either ignored or begged, in accordance with the fundamental tenet of New Welfare that the economist qua economist has little to contribute on this important but controversial subject.[49]

---

[49] For an excellent critical survey of the New Welfare literature, see Little, *A Critique of Welfare Economics*.

# 9. Externality and Public Policy

## 1. Introduction

The recent revival of interest in the basic Continental public policy concept of a public good has gone hand in hand with an equally remarkable upsurge of interest in the traditional Anglo-American public policy concept of external economies and diseconomies, or externalities.[1] In the course of this discussion, the meaning, effects, and policy implications of the externality concept have been intensively reexamined, and the standard analysis by Pigou in *The Economics of Welfare* has been subject to continual and very sharp criticism.[2] It is the aim of this paper to discuss some of the main features of the emerging theory of externalities and to relate this discussion, wherever possible, both to the standard Pigovian doctrine and to the parallel developments in the theory of public goods.

We shall begin, in section 2, with a discussion of the meaning and forms of externality. Then, in section 3, we shall examine the effects of externality on the allocation of resources. Finally, in section 4, we shall consider the policy implications of externality. Section 5 contains a brief summary of the main conclusions.

Reprinted without significant change from *Rivista di diritto finanziario e scienza delle finanze* 28, no. 3 (September 1969): 383–414. The author is indebted to Carl Shoup for helpful comments.

[1] Although a number of authors have made highly significant contributions to this recent development, the original and most comprehensive treatment is that of Coase (1960). This article appears to have been a crucial source of inspiration for subsequent contributions.

[2] The Pigovian analysis is particularly severely criticized in the original contribution by Coase (1960).

## 2.  The Meaning of Externality

### 2.1  The Essential Characteristics

In Pigou's classic discussion, externalities are defined to arise where ". . . one person $A$, in the course of rendering some service, for which payment is made, to a second person $B$, incidentally also renders services or disservices to other persons . . . of such a sort that payment cannot be exacted from the benefited parties or compensation enforced on behalf of the injured parties" (1932, p. 183).

These uncompensated services and disservices are external economies and diseconomies respectively.

It seems clear that this definition establishes "unenforceability of compensation"[3] as the central criterion or characteristic of an externality. In the case of an external economy, this concept corresponds closely to the crucial public goods concept of "impossibility of exclusion," viz. "people who do not pay for the services cannot be excluded from the benefits that result" (Musgrave [1959], p. 8), which obviously implies that those who provide such services cannot exact payment from the beneficiaries. In the case of an external diseconomy, there is a similar relationship with the concept of a "public bad": those who render such disservices cannot be charged for the damage they inflict.

Compensation may evidently be exacted either ex ante, in the form of prior agreement to pay or compensate for the rendering of a service or disservice, or ex post, in the form of ability to recoup for benefits provided or damage suffered (see, for example, Demsetz [1966], p. 65). In the case of external economies, the main emphasis in the literature seems to have been placed on the difficulty of enforcing prior payment from all the benefited parties. In the case of external diseconomies the possibility of ex post recoupment is, of course, clear.

There are two obvious differences between the enforcement problem, as it appears in connection with the externality concept, and the exclusion problem in the case of a public good. First, in the case of an external economy, the "incidental services" rendered need not be descriptively identical in nature or quantity, or even generically similar, to the "service for which payment is made." For example, afforestation may not only increase the supply of timber for which payment may be exacted, but may also arrest erosion and improve the climate for surrounding farm land; or, in another classic example, the production

---

[3] For convenience we use the term *compensation* here to cover payment for services as well as compensation for disservices.

of apples may provide unchargeable nectar for the honey industry. In the case of a pure public good, however, the descriptive identity in nature and quantity of the services provided is an essential characteristic.[4] It is interesting to notice that some of Pigou's illustrative examples fall in the one category and some in the other. The example of lighthouse services, borrowed from Sidgwick, evidently falls in the public goods category.[5]

A second difference is that, in the case of an external economy, the "incidental service" may extend to only one or a few "other persons." Depending upon the precise legal position, the fence which I build on my property may provide incidental unchargeable privacy to my neighbor, but to no one else. In the case of a pure public good the incidental services extend by definition to all other persons in the relevant group.[6]

There are two distinct types of reasons why enforcement may be difficult, technical and legal. Thus, for example, it may be technically difficult, or very costly, to ensure prior payment by excluding those who do not pay. In Sidgwick's time this was evidently true in the case of lighthouse services. Alternatively, the problem may be legal, as in the case of exploitation of a natural resource under a regime of communal ownership of property (see, for example, Demsetz [1967], pp. 354–57). Except in this and certain other examples of rigid legal barriers, enforcement is of course seldom literally impossible, but only more or less costly and uneconomic.[7] This is recognized by Pigou, who, in introducing his practical examples, refers to technical "difficulty" rather than "impossibility" and proceeds at once to quote Sidgwick's lighthouse example in which "no toll could be *conveniently* levied" (1932, p. 184, my italics). This point has also been stressed as a criticism of the pure public goods concept in the recent literature (see, for example, chapter 8, pp. 171–73 above). The relatively neglected possibility of ex post compensation serves to reinforce this criticism.

A further essential characteristic which should be distinguished,

---

[4] See Chap. 3, pp. 77–78 above. Even in this classic polar case, the descriptively identical services will generally, of course, be evaluated differently by different individuals. See also the original contributions to the analysis of this case by Samuelson (1954, 1955) and Musgrave (1959). In the case of a public bad, the "service for which payment is made" must in general be different in nature, since a pure "bad" will not otherwise be produced at all.

[5] See Pigou (1932), p. 184. Sidgwick in turn seems to have borrowed the example from Mill. See J. S. Mill, *Principles of Political Economy,* Ashley ed., p. 976.

[6] In Musgrave's well known definition a pure public good (his "social want") ". . . must be consumed in equal amounts by all." See Musgrave (1959), p. 8.

[7] Enforcement costs include costs and inconvenience to the consumer as well as to the externality-producer. They are referred to as "police costs" in an interesting recent discussion by Demsetz (1964).

at least in the case of an external diseconomy, is "unavoidability." For an external diseconomy to exist, it is necessary not only that those who render such disservices cannot be charged for the damage they inflict, but also that the third parties affected should be unable to avoid injury. Like enforcement, avoidance is seldom literally impossible, but only more or less costly and uneconomic.[8] Crop losses inflicted by engine sparks might be reduced by switching to fire-resistant varieties. The effects of smoke may be reduced by air conditioning. At worst the injured party might move to a different locality. Since not all external economies will necessarily be regarded as "beneficial" by all affected parties over all relevant ranges, it appears that the concept of unavoidability may have a place here also. A fence may represent privacy to an immediate neighbor but an eyesore to a passer-by. A similar characteristic has been noted in the public goods literature, where it has been assumed that individuals must consume the services of a pure public good fully and equally, even if "one man's circus is another man's poison" (see Samuelson [1955], n. 1). This further characteristic has been referred to as "nonrejectability" or "impossibility of rejection" (see chapter 3, pp. 82–83 above; and Shoup [1969]).

## 2.2   A Taxonomy of Externalities

In the recent literature a number of distinctions have been drawn between different types of externalities.

### 2.2.1   Positive and negative

As we have already seen, the basic distinction between positive and negative externalities, i.e. between external economies and diseconomies, is firmly embedded in the original Pigovian formulation (1932, especially pp. 183–88). However, some blurring of this simple classification occurs where person A, in the course of rendering some service to B, renders incidental services to some third parties and incidental disservices to others.

### 2.2.2   Production and consumption

A second distinction turns on whether the externality stems from production or consumption activity, and on whether third parties are affected in their capacity as producers or consumers. The smoke from a factory chimney, which increases the costs of a nearby laundry, stems from a production activity and accrues in the first instance as a disservice to the producer of laundry services. These distinctions suggest

---

[8] This point has been particularly emphasized by Coase (1960).

a fourfold classification of externalities into producer-producer, producer-consumer, consumer-producer, and consumer-consumer varieties.[9] However, the classification becomes more complicated in practice, where, for example, a disservice such as air pollution may stem from both production and consumption activities, and may affect people in both their consumer and producer capacities.

### 2.2.3 Joint and separate supply

A distinction may also be drawn between cases in which the incidental service is such that consumption by some third parties does not correspondingly reduce the benefit to others, and cases in which increased consumption by some correspondingly reduces the benefits available to others. The improved climate for surrounding farm land resulting from afforestation falls in the first category, as does the example of lighthouse services. The nectar made available to honey producers by apple producers falls in the second category, along with congested roads and bridges, and natural resource discovery and exploitation under communal ownership conditions. Examples in the first category may be said to involve "joint supply" in the Samuelsonian public goods sense, whilst those in the second category are, in the same sense, separately supplied.[10]

### 2.2.4 Small and large numbers

It is also important to distinguish between cases in which the incidental service or disservice extends to only one or a few "other persons" and the case in which a large number of other parties are involved.[11] In terms of some of our preceding examples, the number of farms affected by a given afforestation project, or the number of honey producers affected by apple production, or the number of shipping companies affected by a "well-placed lighthouse" may evidently be large or small depending upon the precise circumstances.

### 2.2.5 Marginal and inframarginal

Another distinction turns on whether or not variations at the margin of an externality-producing activity affect third parties.[12] Pigou was particularly concerned with divergences between the private and

---

[9] The basic distinctions here were first put forward by Scitovsky (1954).

[10] This distinction is familiar in the public goods literature. See, for example, Chap. 8, p. 175 above. Note, however, that even where, as in the example of scarce nectar, there is no joint supply in the public goods sense, the nectar is nevertheless a joint product with apples in the traditional Marshallian sense.

[11] In the modern externality literature this distinction was first emphasized by Baumol (1952), chap. 11.

[12] This distinction was first developed in detail by Buchanan and Stubblebine (1962).

social net product of a marginal change in the volume of resources devoted to a particular activity. Although he does not explicitly draw this particular distinction, it therefore appears that he would concentrate attention on marginal externalities. It is perfectly conceivable, however, that an externality-producing activity may affect third parties for inframarginal changes but not at the margin. Once my fence reaches a certain height, my neighbor's desire for privacy may be fully satisfied; marginal changes beyond that level have no effect on his utility (see Buchanan and Stubblebine [1962]). Such externalities are inframarginal.

### 2.2.6  Separable and nonseparable

A further distinction depends upon whether or not the amount of the incidental service or disservice which accrues to third parties as consumers or producers varies with their own consumption or production activity. If the increase in total costs of a laundry due to the smoke from a nearby factory chimney varies with marginal changes in the output of laundry services, then marginal costs of the laundry are affected by the factory and the externality is said to be nonseparable. If the increase in total costs is unaffected by marginal changes in own output, marginal costs are unaffected and the externality is classified as separable.[13] It should also be noted that the externality may vary with inframarginal but not with marginal changes in own activity of the affected party.

### 2.2.7  Reciprocal and nonreciprocal

It is, of course, possible not only that the externality-producing activities of one party to an exchange, say A, may affect a third party C, but also that similar activities on the part of C may exert external effects on A. A's smoke may raise C's costs and vice-versa. In such a case the externality is said to be reciprocal. Where the relationship runs in one direction only, it is said to be nonreciprocal.[14]

### 2.2.8  Private and governmental

A final distinction turns on whether the externality is generated by private or governmental activity, and on whether the third parties affected are private economic units or governments.[15] Educational

---

[13] This distinction was first developed by Davis and Whinston (1962).

[14] This distinction was first developed by Meade (1952).

[15] It is evident from Pigou's examples that the "persons" mentioned in his basic definition may include juridical persons, such as firms and governments, as well as natural persons or households. In the case of intoxicants, for example, he notes that "the investment should, as Mr. Bernard Shaw observes, be debited with the extra costs in policemen and prisons which it indirectly makes necessary." See Pigou (1932), p. 186.

outlays by one state or local government may provide a flow of highly skilled and socially responsible migrants thus, say, increasing tax revenues and reducing police costs of some other state or local government. Similarly, defense spending by one national government may reduce defense costs of "friendly" governments. Mixed private-governmental externalities are also easy to imagine, as where private educational outlays reduce the costs of free public education. This distinction therefore suggests a classification of externalities into intergovernmental, mixed private-governmental, and purely private.[16]

In the following analysis of the effects and policy implications of the externality phenomenon we shall have marginal and purely private externalities particularly in mind. Wherever possible, however, we shall endeavour to point out the differing effects and policy implications of all the different categories of externalities which we have just distinguished.

## 3.   The Effects of Externality

According to Pigou the effect of an externality arising from a particular activity is to create a divergence between the marginal social and marginal private net product of resources devoted to that activity. As he had demonstrated earlier, abstracting from certain complications, an optimum allocation of resources is achieved where the marginal social net products of resources are equal in all uses (1932, pt. 2, chap. 3). Self-interest, however, will tend to bring about equality of marginal private net products. "When there is a divergence between these two sorts of marginal net products, self-interest will not therefore tend to make the national dividend a maximum . . ." (Ibid., p. 172). The effect of an externality is therefore to cause a misallocation of resources. Modern optimum conditions analysis has generally supported Pigou's findings. Regarding the direction of the misallocation, Pigou argues that industries generating external economies will be underexpanded, whilst those generating external diseconomies will be overexpanded (Ibid., p. 224).

There are, however, a number of difficulties and complications which have been pointed up in the recent debate.

---

[16] This distinction has long been familiar. In recent discussions particular attention has been focused on the intergovernmental category through the contributions of Weisbrod (1964) and Williams (1966).

## 3.1   The Market Optimum with "Costs of Movement"

In the first place, as Pigou himself had recognized, there are conditions under which equalization of the marginal social net products would reduce rather than increase the size of the national dividend, i.e. worsen rather than improve the allocation of resources. Thus, where costs are involved in moving resources from one place or occupation to another, an appropriate degree of inequality between marginal social net products may represent a market optimum. In particular, if the social net product of a unit of resources in one activity exceeds the social net product in another activity by no more than the social "costs of movement" for that unit, then a market optimum is already at hand; and a transfer of resources from the second activity to the first to equalize the marginal social net products would distort allocation.[17]

Pigou seems to have overlooked the possible relevance of this argument for his analysis of the externality problem. In the case of an externality it is, by definition, "technically difficult," i.e. very costly, to remove the divergence between marginal private and social net products by enforcing "payment from the benefited parties" or "compensation of the injured parties," and thus ensuring an appropriate movement of resources. Following Pigou's own argument, it would therefore seem that a market optimum is already at hand; and, in the absence of further special considerations, a bounty on enforcement devices (e.g. a scrambling device for lighthouse signals) which would tend to move resources in such a way as to equalise marginal social net products would evidently distort resource allocation.[18] The existence of an uncompensated externality need not therefore imply that resources are misallocated.[19] The market optimum may not represent

---

[17] Ibid., pp. 138–39. Pigou no doubt had such items as transport cost particularly in mind. It is interesting to note, however, that he explicitly mentions the cost of middlemen in connection with the movement of capital from one occupation to another. See ibid., p. 158.

[18] See Pigou's excellent statement of this particular point in his discussion of the effects of eliminating obstacles to resource movement. Ibid., pp. 147–48.

[19] In the recent debate this general point was first developed and strongly emphasized by Demsetz (1964), pp. 13–14. Conventional optimum conditions analysis has followed the Pigovian tradition in concluding that in the presence of an uncompensated externality the market fails to achieve a full Pareto optimum. As it stands, however, this conventional theory of market failure is somewhat misleading. What optimum conditions analysis actually shows is that, where there are external economies, the market fails to make everyone as well off as they would be with costless marketing of the nonmarketed product. By assumption, however (and ignoring the possibilities explored in the following sections), such marketing is very costly. A market optimum therefore requires that certain benefits and costs should remain external to the market. Whether the political mechanism could be expected to improve on this market optimum is a separate question to be discussed in sec. 4 below.

the best possible arrangement in an absolute sense, since, if enforcement were costless, a better arrangement would be possible; but it is the best market arrangement given the costs of enforcement.[20]

## 3.2    Exchange as a Substitute for Enforcement

Another significant problem not explored by Pigou arises from the fact that an externality relationship is necessarily two-sided. As a result, the fact that it is very costly to "exact payment from the benefited parties" or "enforce compensation of the injured parties" is not in general sufficient to create a divergence between marginal social net products. Where, for example, it is impossible to force the smoke-producing firm to compensate the laundry for damage caused by its activities, it may nevertheless be possible for the laundry to bribe the factory to curtail its smoke-producing activities.[21] Similarly, in the case of an external economy, although it may be impossible for the externality-producer to price-exclude those who benefit from the incidental service, it is nevertheless possible that those who stand to benefit may contribute voluntarily, i.e. initiate an agreement to pay the "producer" for the extension of the externality-producing activity.[22] If such exchanges can be made without cost, it is evident that, in contrast to the analysis of the preceding section, the appropriate transfer of resources towards or away from the externality-producing activity

[20] This statement simply applies Pigou's conclusion regarding the effects of costs of movement to the externality problem. See Pigou (1932), p. 138.

[21] This possibility has been particularly stressed by Coase (1960). It could even be argued that the possibility is not entirely neglected by Pigou. Thus he discusses at great length the problem of designing compensation schemes for improvements under tenancy contracts to avoid the positive or negative externalities which might otherwise result from a tenant's decision to improve a property or allow it to deteriorate; and in the course of this discussion he clearly recognizes that otherwise inevitable externalities may often be avoided by voluntary adjustment of the terms of the original contract. Where competition is imperfect, however, compensation laws may be required. See Pigou (1932), pp. 174–83. The central externality problem, however, arises where the external benefits or costs accrue not to one of the contracting parties but to third parties. Referring to these latter cases, he argues (p. 192) that "it is plain that divergences between private and social net product of the kinds we have so far been considering cannot, like divergences due to tenancy laws, be mitigated by a modification of the contractual relation between any two contracting parties, because the divergence arises out of a service or disservice rendered to persons other than the contracting parties." In going straight on to advocate public intervention, he appears, however, to overlook the possible emergence of a separate contractual relationship between third parties and the externality-producer—or he assumes implicitly that an agreement would necessarily be too costly, perhaps because large numbers are so frequently involved.

[22] Some caution is evidently necessary in interpreting the following well known statement by Musgrave (1959, p. 8): "People who do not pay for the services cannot be excluded from the benefits that result; and since they cannot be excluded from the benefits, they will not engage in voluntary payments."

to equalize marginal social net products can be achieved without encountering "costs of movement." In this case a market optimum clearly requires equality of the marginal social net products; and it is obvious that the existence of externalities will not serve to obstruct the resource movements necessary for such equalization.[23] Where "exchange costs" are zero, high "enforcement costs" thus provide no effective barrier to the achievement of a Pareto optimum. From an allocative (though not from a distributional) point of view, exchange is a perfect substitute for enforcement.[24]

## 3.3   Some Determinants of Exchange Cost

Although "exchange" provides a possible substitute for "enforcement," it is obvious that the market agreements in question cannot in general be completely costless.[25] Bargaining, as Pigou, amongst others, has pointed out, absorbs resources.[26] To an important degree the magnitude of these exchange costs will vary with the nature of the particular externality under consideration. Considerable attention has been devoted to this problem in the recent literature.

Thus, for example, there are likely to be important differences between small- and large-number externalities.[27] Where the incidental service or disservice extends to a large number of "other parties," we encounter the problem, familiar from public goods analysis (see, for example, Chapter 3, Section 2.2.2.3 above), that the benefit to any particular party from an agreement to extend or contract the relevant externality-producing activity tends to be almost completely independent both of his own participation and of that of any other individ-

[23] Considerations of this sort have led Buchanan and Stubblebine (1962) to distinguish between "Pareto-relevant" and "Pareto-irrelevant" externalities. As a result of exchange, the externality-producing activity may be expanded or contracted to the point where the marginal social net products are equalised and no further mutually profitable exchanges are possible. At this point, as Coase (1960) and Buchanan and Stubblebine (1962) have emphasized, marginal externalities may well remain but are balanced by internal economies or diseconomies and are therefore Pareto-irrelevant. See also Turvey (1963).

[24] If we could abstract from the effects of the differences in income distribution under regimes of costless exchange and costless enforcement, the allocation of resources would not only be Pareto-optimal in both cases but also descriptively identical. This possibility is particularly stressed by Coase (1960). The effect of the differences in income distribution in destroying the descriptive identity of resource allocation in the two cases is emphasized by Mishan (1967).

[25] This point is clearly recognized by even the most ardent advocates of the possibility of exchange. See, for example, Coase (1960), p. 15.

[26] Indeed, according to Pigou, bargaining is itself a prime source of divergence between marginal social and private net products. See Pigou (1932), pp. 200-3.

[27] In the modern externality literature these differences were first analyzed in detail by Baumol (1952), chap. 11.

ual party.[28] Under these conditions no party has any incentive to engage in bargaining with other potential beneficiaries in an attempt to exploit the mutually profitable opportunities which must exist. Any party attempting nevertheless to initiate such exchange agreements therefore faces formidable exchange costs. In a small-number setting this particular problem does not arise.[29]

Even where numbers are small, however, exchange costs may be far from negligible, and the magnitude of these costs will vary with further characteristics of the externality. The simplest case would appear to be that of a single nonreciprocal externality involving just one "other party." To bring about the resource movements necessary to equalize marginal social net products, all that is required here is a simple two-party exchange agreement between the externality-producer and the "third party" affected. The basic problem in this case is that, although each party knows its own cost or utility function, it does not know the cost or utility function of the other party. As a result, the bargaining process itself becomes a crucial source of information.

In one recent discussion (see Davis and Whinston [1965]), a simple iterative two-party bargaining procedure has been examined under which the affected party provisionally offers to pay a certain amount per unit for an extension or contraction of the externality-producing activity for an externality of the consumption-consumption variety. It is easy to show how such a process may generate information and produce agreements leading to desirable resource movements (see ibid.). Even here, however, problems arise. (i) If, for example, the consumption activity giving rise to an external economy is "inferior" to the consumer (though not to the externally-affected party), a simple per-unit payment will not, beyond a point, produce the necessary extension of the activity if the income effect comes to outweigh the substitution effect.[30] The bargaining process may therefore converge to an agreement which falls short of full Pareto optimality. It is interesting

---

[28] It is interesting to notice that this problem arises whether the externality under consideration is of the "joint supply" or "separate supply" variety. Where, for example, a large number of honey producers are affected by the nectar output of an apple producer, there is the same basic difficulty that the benefits to any single honey producer from a joint agreement with the apple producer to expand production is likely to be virtually independent of his own participation or that of any other single honey producer.

[29] The basic large-number dilemma which we have just discussed should be clearly distinguished from the simple point that exchange cost will be greater the larger the number of individual transactions required, as in the case of numerous identical small-number externalities.

[30] See ibid., pp. 120–22. The problem is perhaps more serious in the case of an external diseconomy, since a similar problem arises precisely where the externality-generating activity is not inferior.

to notice that this problem does not arise in the case of externalities which stem from production activities. (ii) A second problem is that this or any other iterative process takes time and absorbs resources. Because of the costs involved, the process may have to be truncated short of a Pareto optimum. (iii) The most fundamental difficulty, however, is that the parties have an incentive to behave strategically, concealing information on their true cost or preference functions and revealing false information, in an attempt to extract the maximum net benefit from the bargaining process. The "information" generated by bargaining may therefore leave much to be desired. Such strategic behavior and the possibility of threat-making may enormously increase exchange costs and thus obstruct otherwise desirable resource movements. It is this sort of behavior to which Pigou refers when he remarks that resources devoted to bargaining are "wasted" (1932, p. 201).

Where the externality is both reciprocal and nonseparable, the problem may be even more complicated. To illustrate, let us take the case, considered from a somewhat different viewpoint by Davis and Whinston (1962), of a reciprocal externality relationship of the production-production variety in which two competitive firms are related through their cost functions. Since the externality is nonseparable, the marginal cost function of each firm will depend upon the output of the other firm. As a result, for each firm, there is no unique output which would maximize its profits regardless of the output of the other firm. In this situation there is in general no firm status quo or initial equilibrium from which the bargaining process can proceed.[31] Under these conditions the problems of bargaining are evidently greatly increased.

Finally, it should be noted that any hard-won exchange agreement must in general be renegotiated with every change in taste or technology affecting the parties involved.

## 3.4  Merger as a Substitute for Exchange

Even where it is too costly to secure an otherwise allocatively desirable resource movement through an exchange agreement with the externality-producer, it is nevertheless possible that a divergence between marginal social net products may be eliminated through the

---

[31] An equilibrium may not exist, and even if it exists it may be almost impossible to achieve. See Davis and Whinston (1962). This problem does not arise if the externality is reciprocal but one or both of the relationships are separable. Suppose the external effect of firm A's output on firm B is separable. B's marginal cost function is then independent of A's output, and B's profit-maximizing output is uniquely determined. Although the external effect of B's output on A is nonseparable, A's profit-maximizing output is nevertheless uniquely determined by the given equilibrium output of B.

market by a merger or takeover, or what Coase calls "extension of the firm."[32] In the intractable case, which we have just considered, of two firms linked by reciprocal and nonseparable externalities, agreements to extend or contract outputs may well be too complicated and costly to consider. While the externalities remain, there is, however, a profit to be made by combining the activities of the two firms either by merger, by a takeover of one firm by the other, or by a takeover of both firms by a third firm.[33] This would then allow the management of the combined entity to secure the necessary resource movements between activities by an administrative decision made in the light of pooled data on cost functions and the externality relationship. "The rearrangement of production then takes place without the need for bargains between the owners of the factors of production" (Coase [1960], p. 16). If such arrangements were costless, it is evident that neither high enforcement costs (i.e. the existence of externalities) nor high exchange costs could obstruct the resource movements necessary to equalize marginal social net products. From this point of view, merger or "extension of the firm" represents a perfect substitute for both enforcement and exchange.

In fact, however, resource movements secured through "extension of the firm" are unlikely to be costless.[34] Where, for example, the firms involved in the externality relationship are engaged in very different activities, the administrative costs of a single organization combining these activities may be very high.[35] The standard case of air pollution provides a good example. Where, by contrast, the firms involved are engaged in the same or similar activities, the possibility arises that the necessary merger will produce (or increase) monopoly elements, leading to resource movements which may offset or more than offset any tendency to equalization of marginal social net products through administrative allowance for the externality. Even where competition exists initially, a large-number externality relationship can readily be envisaged which would require a monopoly-creating merger. Sidgwick's lighthouse problem, for example, might require a merger or takeover of an entire competitive shipping industry.[36] Finally, it is

[32] In the recent debate this possibility was first emphasized by Coase (1960), pp. 16–17. See also Davis and Whinston (1962) and Demsetz (1964).

[33] The possibility of a merger solution in this difficult case has been particularly stressed by Davis and Whinston (1962).

[34] Most of the following problems have been clearly recognized by advocates of the merger solution. See, for example, Coase (1960), p. 17; Davis and Whinston (1962), p. 244.

[35] These are what Davis and Whinston (1962) call the "costs of decentralized administration" and Demsetz (1964) calls "underspecialization costs."

[36] These effects through an increase in the degree of monopoly are themselves externalities which might be overcome through exchange or extension of the firm. But where there are large numbers of consumers this may not be possible because of the high costs involved.

evident that a merger or takeover cannot be negotiated without cost. The initial merger or takeover agreement is, of course, an exchange transaction, and will be subject to some degree to the strategic behavior and large number problems discussed in the preceding section. In contrast to the exchange solution, however, there is the great advantage that the initial merger agreement need not be renegotiated with every change affecting the cost functions of the firms involved.

The merger or takeover possibility evidently applies mainly to externalities of the production-production variety. There may, however, also be some limited application in the case of production-consumption and consumption-production externalities. Consumers suffering the external costs of monopoly pricing might conceivably get together to purchase the assets of the offending firm and enforce the necessary change in price and output policy.

## 3.5   The Direction of Misallocation

Even ignoring all of the above complications, great care must also be exercised in interpreting Pigou's apparent contention that where external economies arise from the activities of a particular industry, the volume of resources devoted to the industry, and the output of the industry, will be less than they would be in a situation where the marginal social net products were equalized.[37]

In the first place the use of the concept of an "industry" and its "product" may involve us in problems of aggregation. An externality example of the consumption-consumption variety analyzed in a recent discussion illustrates the problem very well.[38] In this example the purchase and utilization of health service inputs by B, e.g. immunization shots, besides providing healthy days to B, provides incidental health benefits to A, but the relationship is nonreciprocal. This is a case in which the "incidental service" is descriptively similar to the "service for which payment is made." In the health service "industry" we therefore have two superficially similar but economically quite different activities: utilization of health service inputs by B which generates external economies, and utilization of health service inputs by A which does not. In this situation, a careful interpretation of Pigou would suggest only that resources devoted to the externality-producing activity (viz. utilization of shots by B), and the corresponding output (healthy days consumed by B), would be underexpanded. And even this conclu-

---

[37] And, of course, the corresponding overexpansion thesis for external diseconomies. See Pigou (1932), especially pp. 224–25.

[38] See Buchanan and Kafoglis (1963). The same example is further discussed by Baumol (1964) and Olson and Zeckhauser (1967).

sion may not hold if the good is inferior, or if the externality is non-separable and the amount of benefit varies directly with A's own consumption.

The looser interpretation that "the volume of resources devoted to health services will be too small" is still more hazardous. Due to the externality, utilization of inputs by B provides health services to A, and is therefore a substitute for utilization by A. In so far as utilization by B is reduced by the externality, A will have to purchase more direct inputs himself. Thus even where resources devoted to the externality-producing activity itself are reduced by the externality, it is quite possible that resources devoted to the health-service industry as a whole may not be reduced and may even be increased. This possibility is evident where utilization of an input unit by B is a perfect or more-than-perfect substitute for utilization by A (see Buchanan and Kafoglis [1963], pp. 405–407).

Further complications arise where there is more than one externality relationship in the system. Although Pigou's long list of examples clearly demonstrates the widespread incidence of externality relationships, his statement of their effects strictly refers to a single externality and abstracts from the possible existence of other externalities.[39] He explicitly recognizes this limitation, however, and indicates the modifications which may be required in the more general case (see ibid., p. 225). For the general case he suggests that the relative magnitude of the externalities is likely to be a consideration of prime importance. Where, for example, there are numerous external economy relationships in the system, but the divergences between marginal social and private net product vary widely, the only general statement possible is that those activities for which the divergence is greatest are likely to be underexpanded; though even this general presumption may not hold in particular cases. An interesting and important special case of multiple externalities is that of a reciprocal externality of the sort where the "incidental service" is descriptively similar to the "service for which payment is made." Purchase of health service inputs by B improves A's health and vice-versa.[40]

In such a case it is obviously possible that, over certain ranges, B's purchase of an input unit may be much more beneficial to A than A's purchase is to B. Remembering, from our previous discussion of the nonreciprocal form of this case, that utilization of an input unit by B allows A to reduce his own purchases and vice-versa, our general pre-

---

[39] This is true both of his formal statement (ibid., p. 224) and also of his discussion of particular examples.

[40] This case is analyzed by Buchanan and Kafoglis (1963), pp. 407–12. For further discussion, see Baumol (1964) and Olson and Zeckhauser (1967).

sumption would suggest that utilization of inputs by B will tend to be underexpanded and utilization by A will tend to be overexpanded as a result of the particular externality relationships assumed. As in the corresponding nonreciprocal case, the possibility evidently arises that the volume of resources devoted to the health service industry as a whole may be overexpanded.[41] Here again the results reflect the relative inefficiency and waste involved in producing health services through utilization of inputs by A.

## 4.   The Policy Implications of Externality

Having made the point that the effect of an externality is to create a divergence between the marginal private and social net products of resources devoted to that activity, and hence to prevent the equalization of marginal social net products required for maximization of the national dividend, Pigou goes straight on to point out that ". . . consequently, certain specific acts of interference with normal economic processes may be expected, not to diminish, but to increase the dividend" (1932, p. 172). More specifically, "it is . . . possible for the State, if it so chooses, to remove the divergence in any field by 'extraordinary encouragements' or 'extraordinary restraints' upon investment in that field. The most obvious forms which these encouragements and restraints may assume are, of course, those of bounties and taxes" (ibid., p. 192). Though, "it should be added that sometimes, when the interrelations of the various private persons affected are highly complex, the Government may find it necessary to exercise some means of authoritative control. . ." (ibid., p. 194). In the case of an activity generating external economies, the proximate objective of policy would presumably be to increase the volume of resources devoted to that activity, and, in the case of external diseconomies, to reduce resources employed.

Here again, however, there are many difficulties and complications, most, but not all, arising from the problems involved in determining the effects of externality, which we have just discussed.

### 4.1   Political Optimum versus Market Optimum

An obvious difficulty would seem to arise from our earlier demonstration that where there are "costs of movement" the achievement of a

[41] Where the good is inferior or the externality is nonseparable, even B's utilization of inputs and consumption of healthy days may be overexpanded.

market optimum may require certain inequalities in marginal social net products. On Pigou's own arguments, the only resource movements which are obstructed by externalities are those which do not justify the very high "enforcement costs" involved; a market optimum is therefore already at hand. This argument might appear to suggest that Pigovian policies to promote these resource movements must necessarily distort rather than improve allocation.

The essential point, however, is that the costs of securing a given transfer of resources through the political mechanism are not necessarily as great as securing the same transfer through the market. If, for example, an appropriate Pigovian policy to eliminate all divergences between marginal private and social net product could be designed and implemented without cost, it is evident that, in contrast to the market situation, the relevant transfers of resources towards or away from externality-producing activities could be achieved entirely without "costs of movement." In such a case public policy becomes a perfect substitute for "enforcement," "exchange" or "extension of the firm." Where "political costs" are zero, high "market costs" (of enforcement, exchange or merger) thus provide no effective barrier to the equalization of marginal social net products.[42] The market optimum does not here represent the best possible arrangement; the political optimum is superior.

An interesting special case here is that of the "legal" externality created by the existence of a rigid legal barrier to enforcement or avoidance. A natural resource may have to be exploited under a regime of communal ownership of property; a railway may be freed by statute from legal liability for damage caused by engine sparks; or individuals may be legally obliged to consume certain products into the range of negative marginal evaluation. In such cases the achievement of a political optimum may simply require the repeal of the offending legislation.

## 4.2   The Concept of Political Cost

In general, of course, resource movements secured through the political mechanism are unlikely to be costless. The design of appropriate policies requires information which is costly to acquire and may, beyond a point, be unobtainable. For this and other reasons, such policies will be more or less costly to administer. "Feasible best" Pigo-

---

[42] As pointed out in note 19 above, modern optimum conditions analysis effectively compares market performance with a Pareto optimum based on costless marketing of nonmarketed products. The resulting theory of market failure is therefore of immediate relevance for public policy only if "political costs" are zero.

vian policies may therefore look very different from "ideal" Pigovian policies. This seems to be the essential meaning of the well-known demonstration by Coase that an imperfect Pigovian policy may produce results inferior to those of the market.[43]

There is also the problem that the policy-maker may not even *try* to devise and implement "feasible best" Pigovian policies. Under majority voting, for example, "feasible best" policies may run counter to the interests of his supporters. Indeed he may be motivated to create new inequalities between marginal social net products where the policies in question provide private net benefits to his supporters; for such policies, private net benefit evidently exceeds social net benefit. The attempt to eliminate divergences between private and social net products by resort to the political process may therefore merely introduce new divergences of a precisely analogous character.[44]

It is therefore clear that there will be a variety of "political costs" associated with any attempt to eliminate divergences between private and social net product through the political mechanism. Intervention for this purpose is therefore justified on efficiency grounds only if these "political costs" do not exceed such allocative benefits as result.[45] This is unambiguously the case if the actuality locus with such public intervention lies entirely outside the actuality locus without such public intervention.[46]

---

[43] Coase is extremely critical of Pigou's analysis and appears, at first glance, to be trying to show that even an ideal Pigovian scheme may do more harm than good. On closer examination, however, it becomes evident that the compensation and tax-subsidy schemes considered are not properly based upon the minimum economic loss involved for the injured party. See Coase (1960), pp. 31–34 and 41–42. The real significance of his arguments therefore lies elsewhere.

[44] This point is developed in detail by Buchanan (1962). The magnitude of the resulting "political failure" in relation to the familiar benchmark of a full Pareto optimum will, of course, vary with the precise nature of the political mechanism considered. Recognition of this problem has led to the development of a general theory of constitutional choice. See Buchanan and Tullock (1962).

[45] Note that the familiar benchmark of a full Pareto optimum does not directly enter into this calculation. The theory of market failure based on a comparison of market performance with a Pareto optimum, like a theory of "political failure" based on a comparison of political performance with a Pareto optimum, is of no direct relevance for public policy. The ultimate comparison required for policy purposes is a direct one between market performance and political performance. These points were first clearly formulated by Buchanan and Tullock (1962). This is also presumably what Coase (1960, p. 34) means when he states that "the comparison of private and social products is neither here nor there." And again (ibid): "The Pigovian analysis shows us that it is possible to conceive of better worlds than the one in which we live. But the problem is to devise practical arrangements which will correct defects in one part of the system without causing more serious harm in other parts."

[46] As we know from the welfare debate of the 1940s, a simple test in terms of "cost" or "value of production," as suggested by Coase and others in the recent debate, may be ambiguous. See, for example, Head and Shoup (1969).

Contrary to the impression left by the recent debate, the general problem involved here is in fact well recognized by Pigou, particularly in connection with his discussion of public intervention in industry. As he puts it:

> It is not sufficient to contrast the imperfect adjustments of unfettered private enterprise with the best adjustment that economists in their studies can imagine. For we cannot expect that any public authority will attain, or will even whole-heartedly seek, that ideal. Such authorities are liable alike to ignorance, to sectional pressure and to personal corruption by private interest. A loud-voiced part of their constituents, if organized for votes, may easily outweigh the whole. [1932, p. 332]

And in the particular context of tax-subsidy schemes to correct divergences between private and social net product, he points out that

> ... in real life considerable administrative costs would be incurred in operating schemes of this kind. These might prove so large as to outweigh the benefit even of the optimum scheme, and, *a fortiori*, of the others. Again, it must be clearly understood that, unless the rates of taxes and bounties imposed fall within certain determined limits, more harm than good will be done even though there are no administrative costs.[47]

In fact much of *The Economics of Welfare* is devoted precisely to the analysis of the distortions and costs produced by a variety of possible forms of public intervention in economic life.

## 4.3  Information Costs of Tax-Subsidy Schemes

Even if we assume that the policy-maker will try to devise appropriate policies, we have seen that he may lack the necessary information. It is interesting to notice, however, that the amount and kind of information required, and hence the magnitude of this component of political costs, will vary to an important degree with the nature of the externality. This point can readily be illustrated by reference to the information requirements for an "ideal" tax-subsidy scheme which have been analyzed at some length in the recent debate.

The simplest case would seem to be that of a single nonreciprocal externality, say, an external diseconomy involving just one "other party." Assuming with Pigou that the existence of the external dis-

---

[47] Pigou (1929), p. 124. Similarly he is at least as sceptical as Coase regarding the probable efficiency of court-administered compensation schemes. See Pigou (1932), pp. 174–83. Like Coase, he explicitly points out the dangers of overcompensation. See ibid., pp. 178–79.

economy creates an otherwise ineradicable divergence between marginal social net products, the central requirement for an ideal corrective tax policy is the imposition of a tax on the externality-producing activity with the marginal rate equal to the marginal damage imposed at the optimum level of output. Pigou himself speaks in terms of a single rate of tax or bounty, and must therefore have envisaged a linear tax function satisfying this central requirement. In order to design a suitable tax function, however, the policy-maker must have sufficient information on the relevant cost and demand functions in order to be able to determine both the optimum level of output for the externality-producing activity and the marginal damage·imposed on the other party at that level of output. Thus, for example, in the case of two competitive firms related nonreciprocally but nonseparably through their cost functions, the policy-maker must somehow obtain accurate knowledge of both cost functions over the relevant ranges — the given product prices would provide sufficient information on the demand side.[48] Similarly, in the case of two consumers with (non-reciprocally) interrelated preference functions, the relevant portions of these functions must somehow be determined. In contrast to the relatively modest informational requirements of a perfectly functioning market mechanism, it is obviously insufficient for each economic unit to know only his own preference or cost function along with the relevant prices signalled by the market; these functions must somehow be determined by the policy-maker. Both parties will, however, be motivated to provide inaccurate information in order to maximize their net gain or minimize their net loss from the policy. And, in any case, complicated econometric studies may well be required. Even in the simplest case, then, it seems that serious information problems arise.

The problem becomes even more complicated, however, when the externality relationship between the two parties is both reciprocal and nonseparable. In the case of two competitive firms related reciprocally and nonseparably through their cost functions, Davis and Whinston (1962) have shown that the profit-maximizing output for each firm depends upon the level of output chosen by the other. In this situation there is in general no unique equilibrium, and actual output will depend upon the strategies adopted by the managers. In attempting to

---

[48] If the externality is separable, knowledge of the cost function of the externality-producer, together with knowledge of the external damage inflicted at various levels of the externality-generating activity, is sufficient, since the marginal damage inflicted is independent of the output of the affected firm. If we depart from the standard Pigovian conception of a linear tax function, an informationally less demanding alternative in this simple case would be the imposition of a schedule of marginal tax rates equal to the marginal external damage inflicted at each level of the externality-generating activity.

design a tax-subsidy scheme capable of achieving a Pareto optimum, the policy-maker therefore requires knowledge of the strategies which will be adopted in response to alternative policies. Some knowledge of the psychological characteristics of the decision-makers is therefore required in addition to the relevant cost functions (see ibid., p. 256).

Even if the relevant information could be obtained, it is interesting to notice that the natural procedure for the design of an ideal tax-subsidy policy in general requires the determination of the optimum level for the relevant activities. If this information must anyway be obtained, it would seem pointless to bother with the refinements of a tax-subsidy scheme. The parties involved could simply be directed to set their activities at the ideal level (see Davis and Whinston [1966], p. 306).[49]

As the number of "other parties" involved in a particular externality relationship is increased, the number of cost and preference functions which must somehow be ascertained by the policy-maker is increased. For a large-number externality the information cost involved in designing an ideal tax-subsidy scheme may well be infinite. The situation is similar in a world containing many different externality relationships. Here again numerous cost and preference functions must in general be known.

The formidable information problems involved in designing an ideal tax-subsidy scheme by the natural procedure, even in the context of small-number externalities, have led to the development of informationally-decentralized policy alternatives which are analytically related to the bargaining procedures discussed earlier. Thus Davis and Whinston have suggested a simple iterative procedure which eliminates the need for knowledge on the part of the policy-maker of the relevant cost or demand functions and, in the difficult reciprocal and nonseparable case, of the relevant strategic decision rules (see ibid., sec. 3). Taking the example of two competitive firms related reciprocally and nonseparably through their cost functions, the policy-maker begins by announcing to each firm that it can set the output of the other at whatever level it chooses. These outputs are compared with those freely chosen by the producing firm itself, and the policy-maker announces provisional per unit taxes or subsidies arbitrarily related to the difference, the tax on one firm's output to be paid as a subsidy to the other firm and vice-versa. In this new situation each firm is again asked to set the output of the other, and these outputs are compared with those which would now be chosen voluntarily by the producer. The original set of taxes and subsidies is then adjusted accord-

---

[49] As pointed out in n. 48 above, the informational demands of the ideal tax-subsidy scheme can in simple cases be reduced by departing from the requirement of a constant marginal rate of tax or subsidy. The above argument therefore requires some modification.

ing to a simple rule based on the differences. This process is continued until the provisional taxes and subsidies announced produce output choices on which both firms are agreed. These outputs should maximize joint profits and hence produce a Pareto optimum. This set of provisional taxes and subsidies is therefore ideal and is enforced.

The central feature of schemes of this sort is that the government acts as an intermediary in a quasi-bargaining situation, imposing taxes on one party to be paid as subsidies to the other. As in a bargaining scheme, the iterative process for the determination of the appropriate taxes and subsidies in effect generates the necessary information on cost and utility functions. The procedure is not, however, likely to be costless. The iterative process takes time and may therefore be quite costly to operate; and, as in a bargaining scheme, the process may be prolonged by strategic concealment of true cost and preference functions aimed at maximizing net gain or minimizing net loss from the resulting policy.[50] Furthermore, where there are many such small-number externality relationships, many iterative procedures of this sort must be administered and coordinated. The ideal system is therefore correspondingly more costly to produce. Finally, in the case of a genuine large-number externality, the quasi-bargaining procedure, like the bargaining process itself, may well fail completely. Each "other party" knows that the benefit he receives is independent of his own participation in any bargaining or quasi-bargaining scheme. In the iterative process described above, each might therefore tend to choose the existing zero activity levels for himself and others, which would minimize the chance that he would be taxed. As a result, no corrective tax-subsidy scheme whatever would emerge.

## 4.4  Some Implications of Exchange or Merger

The foregoing analysis of the information costs of devising an ideal tax-subsidy scheme followed Pigou in assuming that the existence of an externality creates an otherwise ineradicable divergence between marginal social net products. We saw, however, in our earlier analysis of the effects of externality, that this is not necessarily the case. Even where enforcement is too costly, the necessary resource movements may nevertheless be effected through the market by exchange or merger. If the relevant exchange or merger agreements could be reached without cost, all inequalities between marginal social net

[50] In the case of externalities stemming from consumption activities, it may simply be impossible to devise an ideal policy along these particular lines, since the income effect of the tax may come to outweigh the substitution effect. As mentioned above, this problem has been noted by Davis and Whinston (1965) in connection with a pure bargaining scheme.

products would be eliminated. From an allocative point of view, Pigovian policies to remove divergences between private and social net products would not therefore be required; and, if political costs were positive, such policies would be allocatively harmful. The externalities are not Pareto-relevant.

In general, of course, as we have seen, exchange or merger agreements cannot be completely costless. It is interesting to notice, however, that it is precisely where the political costs of devising an appropriate Pigovian policy are least, that the possibilities for exchange and extension of the firm are greatest. Thus, as we have just seen, the political costs of designing an ideal tax-subsidy scheme are likely to be least where the number of externalities in the system is small and where any given externality relationship involves only a small number of "other parties." As we saw earlier, however, these are precisely the conditions under which appropriate exchange or merger agreements are most likely to be achieved. Over a wide range of externality problems the comparison of political costs and market costs therefore seems likely to be close and difficult. Only if political costs are less than market costs can government intervention be justified on allocative grounds.

Finally, it should be noted that the possibility of exchange or merger has some interesting implications for the design of an ideal tax-subsidy scheme. Where exchange is possible, it is no longer sufficient to impose an appropriate per unit tax or subsidy on the externality-producing activity. For example, in the simple case of an external diseconomy affecting just one other party, the solution, according to Pigou, would be to impose a per unit tax on the externality-producing activity equal to the marginal damage inflicted at the optimum level of that activity. In this situation, however, the affected party has an incentive to reduce the damage still further by offering to pay the externality-producer some amount less than the marginal damage for further reductions in his activity level. In the presence of a unilateral Pigovian tax, exchange will therefore tend to lead the system away from a Pareto optimum. This effect can only be avoided if the per unit tax on the "producer" is paid as an equivalent per unit subsidy to the affected party. Where exchange is possible, a bilateral tax-subsidy system is therefore required. Such a system is, of course, analytically equivalent to a pure exchange solution. A unilateral tax or subsidy is appropriate only where, as envisaged by Pigou, exchange or merger is impossible.[51]

[51] The problem discussed in this paragraph was first recognized by Buchanan and Stubblebine (1962), pp. 382–83. They erred, however, in suggesting that the initial situation produced by a properly calculated unilateral Pigovian tax is not Pareto optimal, and that

## 4.5  Conditions for an Improvement

In view of the formidable information problems involved in designing an ideal scheme of public intervention, some comfort may perhaps be drawn from the thought that the proximate objective of policy is after all simply to push more resources into activities generating external economies and to pull them out of activities generating external diseconomies. As long as we are not too ambitious, some improvement in allocation should not be too difficult to achieve.

Here again, however, some care is necessary, as can be seen from our earlier finding that the volume of resources devoted to an "industry" generating external economies may under certain circumstances be too large relative to the optimum.[52] Under these circumstances it would evidently be wrong to think that the immediate objective of policy should be to channel resources indiscriminately into the "industry." It is only the particular activity generating the external economies which should in general be expanded. Moreover, where there are several such activities in the same industry, this presumption applies, if at all, only to those for which the divergence between social and private net product is greatest.[53]

Even where there are multiple externalities of varying magnitude, it can, of course, still be said of any Pareto-relevant external economy or diseconomy that a small expansion or contraction of the relevant activity will necessarily improve allocation.[54] This is small comfort, however, since, even disregarding the possibility of exchange or merger, it is no longer sufficient to observe the existence of a particular externality in order to justify a modest piecemeal policy of encouraging or discouraging the relevant activity. To determine Pareto-relevance, an informationally extremely demanding cost-benefit calculation is in general indispensable.

the effect of exchange is to lead the system towards a true Pareto optimum. The correct solution was subsequently stated by Turvey (1963), pp. 310–11 and Davis and Whinston (1965), p. 122. This problem should be clearly distinguished from that discussed by Coase (1960), where a unilateral tax equivalent to marginal damage actually inflicted must be matched by a tax on the affected party. This "double tax" scheme is necessary only where damage is calculated on an "actual" rather than an opportunity cost basis, and where exchange is impossible.

[52] See sec. 3.5 above.

[53] As noted earlier, where the good is inferior or the externality is nonseparable, even these conclusions may not hold.

[54] Baumol (1964, p. 359) goes much further and argues that in independent adjustment equilibrium any external economy is necessarily Pareto-relevant. Under multiple externalities this is evidently incorrect. It cannot even be said that transferring a unit of resources to the relevant activity from a nonexternality-generating activity will improve allocation.

Moreover, even if the Pareto-relevance of, say, a particular external economy could somehow be determined and a small expansion justified, the achievement of an optimum may nevertheless require a contraction of the relevant activity.[55] A piecemeal policy of expansion, although constituting an improvement, may therefore lead away from the optimum. A series of Pareto-desirable piecemeal policies, although it must ultimately lead to an optimum, may therefore do so only by a very circuitous and politically unacceptable route.[56]

## 4.6   The Second-Best Problem

The distinction between the requirements for an improvement in allocation and the requirements for an optimum is, however, of more general significance for policy in the presence of multiple externalities. Thus, abstracting from costs of movement, the achievement of an allocative optimum requires equality of marginal social net products and hence, in general, the elimination of all divergences between marginal social and private net products. A policy eliminating all divergences is therefore not only allocatively desirable but allocatively optimal.

Recognizing the impossible informational demands of such a policy, it might be thought that eliminating some of the more obvious and readily measurable divergences should at least constitute an improvement. It is, however, an immediate implication of the negative corollary of the well-known General Theorem of the Second Best that a policy which eliminates the divergence for one particular activity may or may not produce an improvement in allocation. Short of the optimum, satisfying more optimum conditions is not necessarily better than satisfying fewer (see Lipsey and Lancaster [1956], pp. 11–12). Thus even if the policy-maker could diagnose the existence of one or a few externality relationships and devise policies which would precisely eliminate the relevant divergences between private and social net product, there is no guarantee that the implementation of these policies would improve allocation. Only if there is some prospect that the policy-maker may be able subsequently to eliminate all other divergences, can a naive policy of eliminating particular divergences be supported.

The distinction between the requirements for an improvement and

---

[55] This possibility theorem is demonstrated by Baumol (1964), sec. 2. Contrary to Baumol, this goes beyond anything demonstrated by the matrix example developed by Buchanan and Kafoglis (1963). At their equilibrium point M, a further shot for B generates Pareto-relevant external economies. Their optimum at E, however, requires no contraction in B's shots.

[56] In a dynamic context an optimum will therefore remain far from fully achieved.

the requirements for an optimum is clearly recognized by Pigou, and he shows no sign of advocating a naive piecemeal policy of eliminating particular divergences between private and social product. Thus, with particular reference to the possibility of a tax-subsidy solution, he states:

> ... under conditions of simple competition, for every industry in which the value of the marginal social net product is greater than that of the marginal private net product, there will be certain rates of bounty, the granting of which by the State would modify output in such a way as to make the value of the marginal social net product there more nearly equal to the value of the marginal social net product of resources in general, thus ... increasing the size of the national dividend ... ; and there will be one rate of bounty, the granting of which would have the optimum effect in this respect. [1932, p. 224]

## 4.7 The Second-Order Problem

A final fundamental policy problem arises from the complication, clearly recognized by Pigou, that, under certain conditions, the equalization of marginal social net products, though necessary, may not be sufficient to ensure the achievement of an allocative optimum. As Pigou puts it:

> ... if several arrangements are possible, all of which make the values of the marginal social net products equal, each of these arrangements does, indeed, imply what may be called a relative maximum for the [national] dividend; but only one of these maxima is the unequivocal, or absolute, maximum (ibid., p. 140).

The possibility of a multiplicity of local optima arises when generalized diminishing returns, and hence the second-order conditions for a maximum, somewhere fail to hold; and in the recent debate it has been emphasized that there is a strong connection between externalities and the second-order conditions (see Baumol [1964], section III). For example, in the presence of multiple externalities (all external economies or all external diseconomies), if the externalities are sufficiently strong, the second-order conditions will necessarily be violated (see ibid., p. 364). This important relationship should, however, be no great surprise to the careful reader of Pigou, who points out the relationship between increasing returns and the second-order conditions (1932, p. 139), and subsequently proceeds to discuss increasing returns in a competitive industry as a special case of external economies, one in which the incidental service is rendered to producers in the same industry (see ibid., pt. 2, chap. 11).

The possible existence of a number of local optima obviously further complicates the problem of devising appropriate policies under multiple externalities. Even if all externality relationships could somehow be measured and a set of policies designed which would precisely eliminate the relevant divergences between marginal private and social net products, there is now no guarantee that such a policy set will produce results which are allocatively desirable let alone allocatively ideal. In particular the result might very well be the achievement of a local optimum rather than a global optimum;[57] and, if so, it is even possible that this local optimum might be allocatively inferior to an initial situation not too far removed from the global optimum. Similarly, depending upon the starting point, a series of Pareto-desirable piecemeal policies can no longer be guaranteed to lead, however circuitously, to a global optimum, but may lead instead to a local optimum. To achieve the allocative ideal the policy-maker must be able to determine and compare all local optima. For this purpose even more comprehensive knowledge of the relevant cost and demand functions is required, thus placing inordinate informational demands on the policy-maker.

## 5. Conclusions

The main results of the above analysis can be summarized briefly as follows:

**1.** *Meaning.* The central characteristic of the externality concept is "unenforceability of compensation" for services rendered or damage inflicted. Enforceability is, of course, seldom, if ever, literally impossible, but rather more or less costly and uneconomic. A significant development in the modern literature has been the recognition and classification of different types of externalities which may have different effects and policy implications.

**2.** *Effects.* The effect of an externality is to create a divergence between the marginal private and social net product of resources devoted to the externality-generating activity, and hence to prevent the equalization of marginal social net products usually thought to be required for allocative efficiency. Since enforcement is, by definition, uneco-

---

[57] It is interesting to notice, as pointed out by Baumol (1964), that the achievement of a local optimum may require an increase in an activity which, for a global maximum, may need to be cut back. This is a case in which overexpansion is not a problem of relative spillovers. Here again, however, Baumol is incorrect in implying that this possibility is demonstrated by Buchanan and Kafoglis (1963).

nomically costly, the resulting inequalities may be perfectly consistent with the achievement of a market optimum. In some cases, however, these inequalities may be eliminated through the market itself by exchange or merger. The externalities are thus effectively internalized. Exchange or merger are, however, costly; and these costs may vary markedly from one type of externality to another. Even abstracting from the possibility of exchange or merger, it should be noted that industries generating external economies (diseconomies) may not be underexpanded (overexpanded) relatively to an "ideal" situation in which marginal social net products are equalized.

**3.** *Policy implications.* Where externalities are observed and marginal social net products are not equalized, public intervention may be possible to improve resource allocation — or it may not. Such intervention inevitably involves a variety of "political costs," and is therefore justified on efficiency grounds only when these costs are outweighed by the allocative benefits. It was shown, for the Pigovian tax-subsidy scheme, how one important category of these costs, namely information costs, may vary widely from one type of externality to another. In view of the formidable informational requirements of an ideal scheme, it is somewhat disturbing to find that, under multiple externalities, the simple "Pigovian" rule of pushing more resources into industries generating external economies cannot be relied upon to produce even a modest improvement.

**4.** *Genealogy.* In our analysis the modern theory of externality was deliberately presented in an explicitly Pigovian terminology and setting, and continually compared with the traditional Pigovian findings. In this way it is easy to see that, contrary to a widespread impression, the modern theory represents no sharp break with the Pigovian tradition, but rather represents an elaboration, refinement and extension of Pigou's classic analysis.

# References

Baumol, W. J., *Welfare Economics and the Theory of the State* (Cambridge, Mass., 1st ed. 1952, 2nd ed. 1965).

Baumol, W. J., "External Economies and Second-Order Optimality Conditions," *American Economic Review,* June 1964.

Buchanan, J. M., "Politics, Policy and the Pigovian Margins," *Economica,* Feb. 1962.

Buchanan, J. M., and Kafoglis, M. Z., "A Note on Public Goods Supply," *American Economic Review,* June 1963.

Buchanan, J. M., and Stubblebine, W. C., "Externality," *Economica,* Nov. 1962.

Buchanan, J. M., and Tullock, G., *The Calculus of Consent* (Ann Arbor 1962).

Coase, R. H., "The Problem of Social Cost," *Journal of Law and Economics,* Oct. 1960.

Davis, O. A., and Whinston, A., "Externalities, Welfare, and the Theory of Games," *Journal of Political Economy,* June 1962.

Davis, O. A., and Whinston, A., "Some Notes on Equating Private and Social Cost," *Southern Economic Journal,* Oct. 1965.

Davis, O. A., and Whinston, A., "On Externalities, Information and the Government-Assisted Invisible Hand," *Economica,* Aug. 1966.

Demsetz, H., "The Exchange and Enforcement of Property Rights," *Journal of Law and Economics,* Oct. 1964.

Demsetz, H., "Some Aspects of Property Rights," *Journal of Law and Economics,* Oct. 1966.

Demsetz, H., "Toward a Theory of Property Rights," *American Economic Review,* May 1967.

Head, J. G., "Public Goods and Public Policy," *Public Finance,* no. 3, 1962. [Chap. 8 above.]

Head, J. G., "The Theory of Public Goods," *Rivista di Diritto Finanziario e Scienza delle Finanze,* June 1968. [Chap. 3 above.]

Head, J. G., and Shoup, C. S., "Public Goods, Private Goods and Ambiguous Goods," *Economic Journal,* Sept. 1969.

Lipsey, R. G., and Lancaster, K., "The General Theory of Second Best," *Review of Economic Studies,* no. 63, 1956.

Meade, J. E., "External Economies and Diseconomies in a Competitive Situation," *Economic Journal,* Mar. 1952.

Mill, J. S., *Principles of Political Economy,* Ashley ed. (London, 1909).

Mishan, E. J., "Reflections on Recent Developments in the Concept of External Effects," *Canadian Journal of Economics and Political Science,* Feb. 1965.

Mishan, E. J., "Pareto Optimality and the Law," *Oxford Economic Papers,* Oct. 1967.

Musgrave, R. A., *The Theory of Public Finance* (New York 1959).

Olson, M., Jr., and Zeckhauser, R., "Collective Goods, Comparative Advantage and Alliance Efficiency," in *Issues in Defense Economics* (New York 1967).

Pigou, A. C., *A Study in Public Finance,* 2nd ed. (London 1929).

Pigou, A. C., *The Economics of Welfare,* 4th ed. (London 1932).

Samuelson, P. A., "The Pure Theory of Public Expenditure," *Review of Economics and Statistics*, Nov. 1954.

Samuelson, P. A., "Diagrammatic Exposition of a Theory of Public Expenditure," *Review of Economics and Statistics*, Nov. 1955.

Scitovsky, T., "Two Concepts of External Economies," *Journal of Political Economy*, Apr. 1954.

Shoup, C. S., *Public Finance* (Chicago 1969).

Turvey, R., "On Divergences between Social Cost and Private Cost," *Economica*, Aug. 1963.

Weisbrod, B., *External Benefits of Public Education* (Princeton 1964).

Wellisz, S., "On External Diseconomies and the Government-Assisted Invisible Hand," *Economica*, Nov. 1964.

Williams, A., "The Optimal Provision of Public Goods in a System of Local Government," *Journal of Political Economy*, Feb. 1966.

# 10.  On Merit Goods

## 1.  Introduction

Professor Musgrave's great treatise *The Theory of Public Finance*[1] is based on the welfare foundations provided by his "multiple theory of the public household."[2] Apart from providing much the most elegant version of a post-Keynesian welfare framework familiar from the public finance literature of the postwar period,[3] the central contribution of Musgrave's multiple theory is to be found in the twin concepts of "social wants" and "merit wants" which dominate his discussion of the Allocation Branch.[4] Of these, most attention has so far been paid to the social wants concept which, on examination, proves to be identical with the concept of a public good which has figured so prominently in Continental discussions. Following the pioneering work of Baumol, it has been shown that the public good concept, although of little significance in itself even in relation to allocation problems, can readily be generalized into Sidgwick's concept of nonappropriability (or externality) to become an important contributing factor to domestic and international misallocation of resources, economic instability, and suboptimal rates of economic growth.[5]

Reprinted without significant change from *Finanzarchiv* 25, no. 1 (March 1966): 1–29. The research for this paper was carried out while the author was a Visiting Fulbright Scholar at Columbia and Princeton Universities in the United States during the academic year 1964–65. He is particularly indebted to Richard Musgrave and Carl Shoup for helpful discussions.

[1] R. A. Musgrave, *The Theory of Public Finance* (New York, 1959).
[2] Ibid., chap. 1. Some readers will be familiar with the earlier version of this theory contained in his article "A Multiple Theory of Budget Determination," *Finanzarchiv*, n.s. 17 (1956–57). See also his paper "Principles of Budget Determination," in Joint Economic Committee, *Federal Expenditure Policy for Economic Growth and Stability* (Washington, 1957).
[3] For a general discussion of this post-Keynesian framework and its relationship to modern welfare economics, see chap. 1, sec. 4 above.
[4] Musgrave, *Theory of Public Finance,* chap. 1, sec. B.
[5] For a detailed discussion and further references, see chap. 8 in this volume.

The considerable interest which has been shown in the clarification and further development of the social wants concept stands, however, in sharp contrast to the comparative neglect of merit wants. It might perhaps be thought that this neglect simply reflects the relative simplicity or unimportance of the merit wants concept, or the completeness of Musgrave's own discussion. On close examination, however, the apparent simplicity of the concept soon disappears, and its importance becomes increasingly obvious. Similarly, as in the case of social wants, Musgrave's own discussion, though extremely interesting and stimulating, is somewhat unclear, and he makes no attempt to relate the concept to more familiar theories of public policy. It is therefore the aim of the present article to examine the meaning of the merit wants concept as it appears in Musgrave's theory, and to relate it to more familiar Pigovian, Keynesian and post-Keynesian theories of public policy. In this way it is hoped to contribute to the clarification and further development of this important but rather enigmatic public finance concept.

We shall begin (section 2) with a brief outline of Musgrave's merit want theory. Then (section 3) we shall set out and examine in detail the main characteristics of merit goods. In section 4 we shall attempt to relate a generalized concept of merit goods to other important concepts in modern theories of market failure. In section 5 we shall compare the resulting merit goods theory of market failure with the generalized public goods theory which has emerged from recent discussions. The political problem of improving on market performance in the case of merit goods will be discussed in section 6. Section 7 contains a brief summary of the main conclusions.

## 2.  Musgrave's Theory of Merit Wants

In the case of social wants or public goods, the need for public policy arises from the failure of the market to allocate resources in accordance with given individual preferences.[6] In contrast, in the case of merit wants, the preference maps of individuals are no longer taken as given, but are themselves subject to critical scrutiny. Public policy in

---

[6] It is easy to show that pure public goods, defined as those which must be consumed in equal amounts by all, exhibit to an extreme degree special forms of two conceptually quite distinct and independent characteristics, namely joint supply and external economies. As a result, it is impossible for decentralized market institutions to achieve a Pareto optimum based on the existing pattern of factor ownership, technology, and individual preferences. See again chap. 8 above.

this area is justified by the need to correct individual preferences. As Musgrave expresses it, ". . . the satisfaction of social wants falls within the realm of consumer sovereignty, as does the satisfaction of private wants. The satisfaction of merit wants, by its very nature, involves interference with consumer preferences."[7]

Since merit goods are those satisfying merit wants, merit goods may be defined as those of which, due to imperfect knowledge, individuals would choose to consume too little. In such cases the government should intervene to encourage consumption. As possible examples of corrective interference to satisfy merit wants, Musgrave mentions publicly provided school luncheons, subsidized low-cost housing and free education.[8] Symmetrically, "demerit" goods may be defined as those of which, due to imperfect knowledge, individuals would choose to consume too much. Here the government should intervene to discourage consumption. Musgrave suggests liquor taxation as a possible example of such intervention.[9]

To justify interference with consumer sovereignty for the purpose of satisfying merit (or demerit) wants, and thus to justify the place of the merit wants concept in his welfare framework, Musgrave offers three arguments.[10] According to the first, "wants that appear to be merit wants may involve substantial elements of social wants." Educational services and health measures are mentioned as examples. Secondly, under certain conditions, an "informed group" may be justified in "imposing its decision upon others." Examples suggested include education, health services, protection of the interests of minors, avoidance of undesirable discrimination, and control of the sale of drugs. Finally, due to persuasive advertising, "the ideal of consumer sovereignty and the reality of consumer choice in high-pressure markets may be quite different things."

## 3. The Properties of Merit Goods

Turning now to more detailed consideration of the merit goods concept, it appears that merit goods may raise as many as three distinct problems, namely preference-distortion problems, distributional problems, and public goods problems.

---

[7] Musgrave, p. 13.
[8] See ibid.
[9] See ibid.
[10] Ibid, pp. 13–14.

## 3.1  Preference-distortion Problems

It is evident from Musgrave's discussion that distorted preferences constitute the essence of the merit goods problem; individuals find the benefits from merit goods particularly difficult to evaluate. By contrast, the most striking common characteristic of modern welfare theories is the uncritical acceptance of given individual preferences as the foundation of welfare economics; and the rather vague notion of consumer sovereignty has been given more precise expression in the crucial concept of a Pareto optimum.[11] The critical attitude to individual preferences which is the central feature of the merit wants approach thus represents a striking departure from the modern welfare tradition.

### 3.1.1  Preference-distortion arguments in the literature

Nevertheless, this critical attitude to individual preferences has a long history in the economics literature. An interesting classical example is provided by the distinction between productive and unproductive consumption. Further examples include Marshall's well known classification of wants into the natural and the artificial, and the more systematic criticisms of the given wants approach to be found in the works of J. M. Clark and F. H. Knight.[12] In the more recent literature the critical attitude to the given wants approach has been very forcefully represented by such writers as Galbraith and Scitovsky.[13]

In traditional public finance discussions, preference-distortion arguments for government intervention are commonplace. Typical examples concern the treatment of minors and lunatics, lower-class education, drug addiction, and the choice between luxuries and necessities.[14] Indeed it is hardly too much to say that arguments regarding erroneous individual preferences and the superior knowledge of some

[11] In its most general form, the "Social Welfare Function" version of modern welfare theory allows, at least conceptually, for the possibility of rejecting or modifying individual preferences. Nevertheless, practitioners of this approach have usually accepted individual preferences without serious question. For a very stimulating discussion of the problem by a leading welfare theorist, see, however, T. Scitovsky, *Papers on Welfare and Growth* (London, 1964), pt. C. Also J. Rothenberg, "Consumers' Sovereignty Revisited and the Hospitability of Freedom of Choice," *American Economic Review, Papers and Proceedings,* 1962.

[12] For an excellent survey and analysis of the earlier literature on this subject, see H. Myint, *Theories of Welfare Economics* (London, 1948), chap. 11.

[13] See, for example, J. K. Galbraith, *The Affluent Society* (Boston, 1958), and Scitovsky, pt. C.

[14] Such examples figure prominently even in Mill's classic liberal analysis of the economic functions of government. See J. S. Mill, *Principles of Political Economy,* book 5.

elite group or government dominate public policy discussions in most of the older literature. Perhaps the most celebrated example of a merit goods discussion to be found in the public finance literature is, however, Pigou's argument regarding the irrational discount which individuals place on future as compared with present consumption and the consequent bias against capital accumulation and growth.[15]

### 3.1.2 The causes of distorted preferences

What are the main causes of distorted preferences? From the diversity of Musgrave's own examples and others to be found in the literature, it appears that there are important distinctions to be drawn between the different types of imperfect knowledge which may be involved. In particular, it seems desirable to distinguish between preference distortions due to uncertainty (i.e. incomplete or inaccurate information) and those due to irrationality.

**3.1.2.1** *Uncertainty.* The overwhelming importance of uncertainty in individual behavior has often been noted. Individual preferences for most goods are inevitably based on incomplete information, the degree of incompleteness varying with such factors as the complexity of the item, the indirectness or remoteness of the benefits, and the frequency of purchases. Additional information is costly to acquire, and a substantial degree of ignorance will therefore usually be completely rational. The difficulties facing the individual in the purchase of the modern array of technically complex and often potentially dangerous consumer durables provide an obvious illustration of the problem. A more traditional example is to be found in the attitude of the uninformed to the benefits of education and preventive health services. Incomplete information is also a crucial factor in all intertemporal choices.

Moreover, much information which is reasonably readily available is persuasive and misleading rather than informative. This clearly applies to most types of advertising. Galbraith's point regarding the inherent bias against public sector products due to high-pressure advertising of private products merely provides the most graphic of many possible applications of this general argument.

In all these cases it may be possible for the government, acting on the advice of technical experts or other "informed groups," to reduce many of the most important uncertainties, including the flow of misleading information, or otherwise to correct the distorting effects on individual choices. Possible examples of such government intervention

[15] A. C. Pigou, *A Study in Public Finance* (London, 1928), pt. 2, chap. 8, sec. 4.

might include pure foods acts, apprenticeship and registration requirements governing entrance to certain trades and professions, various
types of safety legislation, regulations controlling the sale of dangerous drugs, standards legislation of all sorts, many subsidy programs,
sumptuary excises, and the taxation and regulation of advertising.

Experience of increased or reduced consumption·of certain qualities
of particular products as a result of appropriate government intervention will here tend to result in the eventual correction of distorted
preference structures. The individual should himself be able to recognize the relative inferiority of his preintervention choices. The subsidy,
tax or regulation used to redirect consumption of a particular good
could therefore eventually be removed. In a pure comparative statics
framework this would seem to imply that merit goods policies of this
sort should be largely self-eliminating in the long run. In a dynamic
world of new commodities and new individuals, new merit goods
problems must, however, continually arise. Existing measures may
therefore have to be retained and new measures introduced.

The case for regarding the correction of preference distortions due
to uncertainty as a legitimate economic function of government is
obviously a strong one. Indeed such functions can scarcely be regarded
as lying outside the consumer sovereignty tradition. The acceptance
of actual choices or "revealed preferences," however remote from true
preferences, clearly requires a value judgment at least as controversial
as the merit goods approach.

**3.1.2.2** *Irrationality.* Even where information is complete and accurate, however, a concept of distorted preferences is still possible.

Thus it is conceivable that an individual may make an erroneous
choice even when he is in possession of all the relevant information.
Such a choice we may define as irrational. Obvious examples are
provided by the preferences of the psychologically disturbed and the
immature. In these cases, preferences for a wide range of goods may
be involved, and the irrationality arises less from the inherent nature
of the good than from the particular class of consumer. The habit-
forming drugs, however, provide an example where the irrationality
tends to be associated more narrowly with the nature of the good
itself. In any actual case, including the examples mentioned, it is of
course extremely difficult to disentangle apparent irrationality from
incomplete and incorrect information as a source of distorted preferences.

Apart from the somewhat extreme cases quoted above, the concept
of pure irrationality poses obvious problems. This can easily be seen
by considering Pigou's argument regarding the merit goods charac-

teristics of future consumption, which is much the most famous and most carefully stated irrationality argument which has been levelled at the behavior of mature adults in the public finance literature. As he expresses it, "Broadly speaking, everybody prefers present pleasures or satisfactions of a given magnitude to future pleasures or satisfactions of equal magnitude, *even when the latter are perfectly certain to occur*. But this preference for present pleasures does not — the idea is self-contradictory — imply that a present pleasure of given magnitude is any *greater* than a future pleasure of the same magnitude. It implies only that our telescopic faculty is defective, and that we, therefore, see future pleasures, as it were, on a diminished scale."[16] The promotion of capital formation and economic growth can therefore be regarded as a legitimate economic function of government.

In its pure form as stated by Pigou, this argument, although intuitively quite appealing, has proved extremely controversial, and has been widely criticized as authoritarian and contrary to democratic principles; if everyone really prefers present to future pleasures, who is the economist to object?[17] This is an inevitable welfare weakness of a pure irrationality argument appealing for its moral authority to experts, elites or informed groups. Indeed, on closer examination, much of the superficial attractiveness of the argument turns out to derive from the overwhelming importance of uncertainty in intertemporal choices.

The concept of erroneous preferences in a world of complete and accurate information is therefore fraught with difficulties; and the problem clearly cannot be avoided by appealing to majority tastes rather than an informed group or ethical observer as arbiter, since majority preferences are often (and quite rightly) what practitioners of the approach are most concerned to criticize.[18] In spite of these difficulties associated with the irrationality concept, however, it could still quite reasonably be argued that uncritical acceptance of the "true preferences" of individuals cannot provide a really adequate and comprehensive welfare framework for public finance theory.[19]

---

[16] Ibid., p. 117. (First set of italics mine.) The same argument is also to be found in *The Economics of Welfare* (London, 1920), pp. 24–25. The suggestion that individuals prefer present to future satisfactions had of course been made earlier by such writers as Menger and Böhm-Bawerk. Pigou's formulation is of particular importance for its emphasis on the welfare implications of this preference.

[17] See, for example, Myint, pp. 175–76.

[18] See, for example, Scitovsky, pp. 245–47. Others would no doubt prefer a majority decision in this area. For an extremely interesting example of the latter argument, see Erik Lindahl, "Tax Principles and Tax Policy," *International Economic Papers*, 10 (London and New York, 1960). See also Musgrave, p. 14.

[19] Welfare theories, by their very nature, cannot of course be "proved" or "disproved" in any usual scientific sense. Their whole aim is rather to influence policy, and their "validity" must therefore depend upon the persuasiveness of the arguments in terms of general

## 3.2  Distributional Problems

Although distorted preferences are clearly the essential characteristic of Musgrave's merit goods concept, his discussion and choice
of examples suggest the existence of further characteristics. Thus the
examples of low-cost housing, education, school luncheons, and health
services all suggest that important distributional problems may be
involved.

This impression is confirmed in the course of his discussion of distribution, where he observes that ". . . the satisfaction of merit wants
is associated frequently with distributional considerations. Subsidies
in kind, for instance, may be given for the satisfaction of certain
private wants. Free charity clinics may be furnished, or subsidies may
be given to low-cost housing, the benefits of which will accrue to
low-income families. Such programs have a dual nature. They may be
looked upon as operations of the Allocation Branch in the satisfaction
of merit wants and as operations of the Distribution Branch in the
redistribution of income."[20] In his later discussion of public sales, he
analyses the case of low-cost housing in rather more detail as follows:
". . . the government may wish to sell at a loss . . . to subsidize the
buyer of particular products. Such is the case with public operations
in low-cost housing. . . . In the efficient system, a loss operation in
low-cost housing involves (1) a policy of distributional adjustment in
favor of low incomes, since only *low*-cost housing is involved; (2)
recognition of *housing* as a merit want, since the distributional adjustment is not made in cash . . ."[21]

If, as suggested in the above argument, housing in general is a
merit good, one might wonder why only low-cost housing is mentioned
in Musgrave's merit want discussion. Again, a loss operation in low-
cost housing may be allocatively efficient, but in terms of Musgrave's
own familiar conception of the proper state of distribution in terms of
horizontal and vertical equity it appears that the operation must be
distributionally inefficient. In particular, the program discriminates
between different low-income individuals according to their expenditures on housing, and significant horizontal inequities are therefore
practically unavoidable. For horizontal equity in the conventional
sense, the distributional adjustment would have to be made in cash,
even where distorted preferences are involved. The cost of the Allocation Branch operation in low-cost housing should be charged to the

acceptability, community advantage, social justice, objective rationality, etc. which can
be mustered in support.

[20] Musgrave, p. 21.
[21] Ibid., p. 49.

low-income individuals concerned, and the purchase made compulsory. To avoid the apparent inconsistency in Musgrave's discussion, the obvious conclusion would seem to be that in a number of significant cases merit goods pose distributional problems of a rather special sort; in these cases the distributional objective is defined partly in terms of the distribution of these particular goods, and not merely in terms of "income."

Although this may not have been Musgrave's explicit intention, such a conception has considerable merits. Conceptions of equity or the proper state of distribution seldom run solely in terms of Lorenz-curves of income. Indeed, in relatively conservative democracies such as the United States, distributional objectives frequently seem to be formulated in terms of particular goods rather than income.[22] Thus there may be strong support for a certain degree of equality (or at least high minimum standards) of access to education and health services, even where there is little interest in more orthodox public finance concepts of horizontal or vertical equity formulated in terms of Lorenz-curves of income. These are also cases in which it is easy to construct strong arguments regarding the importance of individual benefit-evaluation problems and consequent distorted preference structures, particularly amongst the lower income groups. It is an important contribution of Musgrave's merit goods concept to focus attention on this important relationship.

Is there, however, any necessary relationship between distorted preferences and distributional objectives applied to particular goods? In principle it seems clear that the two characteristics are conceptually quite distinct, and need be in no way related. Distributional objectives may be applied to goods which pose no particular preference-formulation problems. A low-income housing project would appear to provide an excellent example! Similarly the so-called sumptuary excises on demerit goods such as liquor and tobacco provide examples where no distributional problem of the special sort under consideration here (or indeed any other!) has generally been recognized. It is therefore of the greatest importance to preserve a clear distinction between these characteristics.

## 3.3  Public Goods Problems

The third important characteristic of the merit goods concept is that public goods (or social wants) problems appear to be involved. This is

---

[22] Compare Scitovsky's recent suggestion (chap. 16) that equity is mainly a question of the distribution of "necessities." More generally, it appears that, in concepts of equity, different weights are assigned to the distribution of different classes of commodities.

evident from the following passage containing the first of the three arguments which Musgrave puts forward to justify the place of the merit goods concept in his normative framework: "To begin with, situations arise that seem to involve merit wants but on closer inspection involve social wants. Certain public wants may fall on the border line between private and social wants, where the exclusion principle can be applied to part of the benefits gained but not to all. Budgetary provision for free educational services or for free health measures are cases in point. Such measures are of immediate benefit to the particular pupil or patient, but apart from this, everyone stands to gain from living in a more educated or healthier community. Wants that appear to be merit wants may involve substantial elements of social wants."[23] Since this argument is presumably intended to justify the merit wants rather than the social wants concept, it seems reasonable to conclude that merit goods typically exhibit public goods characteristics.

Although once again Musgrave's intentions are not entirely clear from his discussion, the idea that goods with merit aspects also typically, or at least frequently, exhibit public aspects has much to commend it, as his own merit goods examples of health and educational services clearly show. The existence of such a relationship has in fact been widely claimed in the traditional public goods literature. Indeed, the very essence of the public goods problem has usually been held to be not the external economies or joint supply characteristics emphasized in recent Anglo-American discussions, but the impossibility of individual evaluation of the benefits involved. The benefits of public goods have been said to be too indirect, too delayed or too complicated to be susceptible of accurate appraisal by the vast majority of uninformed individuals. In these matters individuals must rely upon the superior knowledge of the bureaucracy or government, i.e. "experts" or some informed elite. More democratic versions of the same argument assert the value of "collective" consideration of such difficult matters. However this may be, it is clear that many goods pose both preference-formulation and public goods problems, and a concept of merit goods embodying both characteristics serves to focus attention on a most important phenomenon.

Once again, however, it is extremely important to consider whether there is any necessary relationship between distorted preferences and public goods problems. It has recently been shown that a pure public good, defined as one which must be consumed in equal amounts by all, exhibits to an extreme degree special forms of two distinct and inde-

[23] Musgrave, p. 13.

pendent characteristics, namely joint supply and external economies.[24] Neither of these characteristics, however, is either implied by, or implies, the existence of individual benefit-evaluation problems. Thus classic examples such as a bridge or theatrical performance demonstrate clearly that significant elements of joint supply or indivisibility of product in the public goods sense may exist without involving any obvious problems of benefit evaluation.[25] Similarly, in the case of a large fireworks display, most individuals are surely capable of appreciating the benefits involved, in spite of the existence of extreme external economies or price-exclusion problems. In the same way it seems clear that incomplete information, misleading advertising or elements of irrationality may lead to severely distorted preferences even in the case of otherwise purely private goods. Thus although recent Anglo-American theories of public goods, such as that of Samuelson, probably go too far in completely ignoring the overwhelming problems facing the individual in attempting to assess the benefits he is likely to derive from some of the most important public goods,[26] the traditional identification of public goods problems with preference-formulation problems is clearly incorrect and extremely misleading. The two sets of problems are conceptually quite distinct and independent.

From the above analysis it thus appears that merit goods pose three conceptually quite distinct and independent problems, namely individual evaluation problems, distributional problems, and public goods problems. Although there is no necessary relationship between these problems, the merit goods concept is extremely useful in focusing attention on the empirically very significant coincidence that goods posing the most difficult preference-formulation problems frequently exhibit pronounced public goods characteristics and at the same time involve special but particularly important problems of distribution.

## 4. The Relationship between Merit Goods and Other Concepts in the Theory of Public Policy

Let us now consider more general relationships between the three characteristics of the merit goods concept and other important con-

---

[24] For a detailed discussion, see chap. 8 in this volume.

[25] For a celebrated statement of this argument, see Antonio de Viti de Marco, *First Principles of Public Finance* (London, 1936), p. 118, n. 1.

[26] These difficulties have not, however, been ignored by all writers in the individualistic tradition. Such great pioneers of this approach as Sax, De Viti, Wicksell, and Lindahl all concede that public goods frequently pose extremely difficult individual benefit-evaluation problems.

cepts in modern theories of market failure. As in the case of the public goods concept, it appears that Musgrave's merit goods concept may lend itself to considerable and very fruitful generalization.

## 4.1  Distribution

We have seen that, although merit goods pose special redistributive problems, there is no necessary entailment relationship between the special problem of distributional objectives applied to particular goods and the individual benefit-evaluation problems which are the essence of the merit goods concept. It appears, however, that there are extremely important relationships between distributional objectives and the generalized problem of imperfect knowledge.

### 4.1.1  Uncertainty and income-insurance measures

Thus individual uncertainty concerning the future may play an important role in the formulation of conceptions of the proper state of distribution and the need for redistributive measures. The individual's own future income, not to mention that of his family, is usually subject to a considerable degree of uncertainty. Even in relatively stable societies, incomes of individuals of the same age, and even of similar educational background and other socioeconomic characteristics, show considerable dispersion.[27] In societies which have been ravaged by great wars, revolutions, depressions, hyperinflations, and other political or social upheavals, such uncertainty may clearly be intense. At least to a substantial degree, such income-uncertainty is likely to be privately unavoidable and uninsurable; and in a society in which most individuals are risk-averters, this uncertainty may be reflected in redistributive government policies and mildly egalitarian conceptions of the proper state of distribution, either of income in general or of particularly important commodities (as in the case of merit goods). Thus an economic policy objective of a proper state of distribution may to some extent reflect individual attitudes towards privately unavoidable and uninsurable risk.

The government can perform its redistributive function in this field in two main ways, either by acting preventively to reduce the risk itself, or reparatively by providing some form of insurance. Thus, in the case of nonappropriability problems involving large numbers of economic units, where the individual himself is unable to reduce the risk by unilateral action and where voluntary cooperative action is

[27] For the United States, see, for example, J. Morgan, "The Anatomy of Income Distribution," *Review of Economics and Statistics*, 1962.

difficult to organize and inherently unstable, preventive government action may nevertheless be possible. Economic stabilization policies of all sorts are important examples of preventive activities affecting income generally. Public health measures would appear to be a good example in the field of particular commodities. Free education is an example with important implications both for the distribution of income and for the distribution of the particular service. It should be noted that such activities may be desirable even where private insurance arrangements exist, since the latter may be costly and are seldom fully adequate. Hence the case for such activities as fire protection and police services.

The second obvious method is the provision of some form of insurance. At least beyond a point, preventive government action to reduce a particular risk may be impossible or relatively very costly. If private insurance is inadequate, the promotion of more adequate insurance arrangements may be attempted. By providing appropriate facilities itself or by subsidizing and regulating private insurance arrangements, the government can considerably increase the risk-pooling facilities available to individuals, and at the same time, perhaps by making membership compulsory, achieve significant economies of scale not normally possible for unaided private organizations. Social security schemes, such as old age, survivors', disability, and unemployment "insurance," provide obvious and extremely important examples of governmental income-insurance. Most price stabilization schemes for primary commodities also possess significant income-insurance aspects. Even progressive income taxation may be justified in part as an income-insurance measure. Medical insurance schemes, including also a national health service and more or less generous deductions for medical expenses from tax liability, provide excellent examples for a particular commodity.[28] From the few examples quoted it is clear that these public "insurance" arrangements may bear little resemblance to private insurance.[29] This is not of course in itself a defect of the public arrangements. On the contrary, the well known and often criticized departures of "social insurance" schemes from well-established private insurance principles can be regarded as an attempt to broaden the narrow range of risks which can be pooled efficiently through private schemes.

[28] For an excellent recent discussion of the role of uncertainty in the field of medical care, see K. J. Arrow, "Uncertainty and the Welfare Economics of Medical Care," *American Economic Review*, 1963.

[29] On the departures from private insurance principles in the field of social security, and the largely public relations function of the term *insurance* in this context, see the classic study by A. T. Peacock, *The Economics of National Insurance* (London, 1952), especially chap. 3.

It is obvious that action to reduce the incidence of a particular risk and action to promote more adequate insurance arrangements are to a considerable extent substitutes. Thus, up to a point, efficient stabilization policy may substitute for unemployment benefits and indextied pensions, and public health measures may substitute for medical insurance. The choice between the two approaches should, of course, be made on efficiency grounds.

As in the corresponding but much narrower merit goods problem of individual benefit-evaluation difficulties, the present redistributive economic function of government is clearly quite consistent with the individualistic or consumer sovereignty tradition. Whereas the present function is one of reducing the dispersion of individual income or of the consumption of items of particular distributional significance, the earlier merit goods function was essentially one of reducing the dispersion of utilities derivable from certain categories of purchases.

The insurance function of government has of course long been recognized in the public finance literature, most notably by some of the earlier benefit theorists.[30] The relation to the general redistributive function has, however, until recently been largely overlooked.[31,32]

### 4.1.2  Ethical authoritarianism and the proper state of distribution

Many of the best known statements of the case for redistribution as an economic function of government make no reference whatever to individual attitudes to risk. In the Anglo-American public finance literature, this is obviously true of the powerful utilitarian tradition with its various sacrifice theories of equitable taxation;[33] and, to take a more recent example, it is equally true of Henry Simons's famous and very influential statement of the case for progressive taxation, according to which "the case for drastic progression in taxation must be rested on the case against inequality — on the ethical or aesthetic judgment that the prevailing distribution of wealth and income reveals a degree (and/or kind) of inequality which is distinctly evil or unlovely."[34] In these and many similar arguments, there is frequently

---

[30] From a vast literature, see, for example, A. Thiers, *De la propriété* (1848).

[31] A remarkable exception is to be found in Edgeworth's celebrated argument for utilitarian welfare objectives in terms of expected utility maximization. See F. Y. Edgeworth, "The Pure Theory of Taxation," *Economic Journal*, 1897, reprinted in R. A. Musgrave and A. T. Peacock, eds., *Classics in the Theory of Public Finance* (London and New York, 1958), pp. 120–21.

[32] In the more recent literature, the relationship between uncertainty and redistributive measures has been particularly emphasized in J. M. Buchanan and G. Tullock, *The Calculus of Consent* (Ann Arbor, 1962), chap. 13.

[33] With the notable exception of Edgeworth. See n. 31 above.

[34] H. C. Simons, *Personal Income Taxation* (Chicago, 1938), pp. 18–19.

a strong element of ethical authoritarianism. To the intellectual elite supporting it, the distributional value judgment in question seems intuitively obvious, requiring only to be clearly stated to convince all except the perverse or irrational.

There is clearly a close relationship between this tradition of ethical authoritarianism in discussions of distribution, and the irrationality concept in the merit goods discussion. In both cases there is the same appeal to the authority of experts, elites, and informed groups rather than to individual preferences or even majority preferences. Thus, in a very real and important sense, equity may be said to provide a classic example of a merit good of the authoritarian type. In this connection it is interesting to notice that Pigou's famous argument regarding the defective telescopic faculty also has extremely important (inter-generation) equity aspects. For most writers, distribution is clearly not a matter which can safely be left to be determined by individual preferences.

The welfare weakness of the authoritarian approach to equity as an objective of economic policy is the same as that of the irrationality argument for merit goods. Any value judgment relying virtually entirely upon the moral authority of some enlightened elite or in-formed group is bound to be controversial, and the resulting theory of public policy is to that extent less likely to influence action and opinion. This is of course precisely the reason for the general abandon-ment of utilitarian welfare economics and the development of modern welfare theories. As in the case of the irrationality argument, how-ever, it is still possible to argue that uncritical acceptance of indi-vidual preferences, including attitudes to risk and uncertainty, cannot provide an adequate welfare framework for public finance theory, least of all in the field of equity.[35]

## 4.2  Allocation

We have seen that, although some of the best examples of public goods pose extremely difficult preference-formulation problems, there is no necessary relationship between preference-formulation prob-lems and the special forms of joint supply and external economies which characterize pure public goods.

It is easy to show that Samuelsonian joint supply (or indivisibility of product) accounts for a particular category of decreasing cost prob-lems,[36] which in turn represent a special but extremely important case

[35] For a critique of modern welfare theory along these lines, see chap. 1, sec. 2.4 above. See also p. 220, n. 19.
[36] See chap. 8, sec. 4.2.1.

within the general category of problems of imperfect competition. Similarly, the external economies or extreme exclusion problems characteristic of a pure public good are simply a special case of the general problem of external economies and diseconomies. External economies and diseconomies, and imperfections of competition, including those due to decreasing costs, together constitute the major concepts in the traditional Pigovian theory of market failure in the field of resource allocation. The Pigovian theory can therefore be regarded as a generalized public goods theory.

Are there not, however, extremely important relationships of a more general sort between these crucial Pigovian inefficiency concepts and the problems of imperfect knowledge?

### 4.2.1  Uncertainty and imperfect competition

The first of these relationships concerns the role of uncertainty in promoting and preserving imperfections of competition.[37] Thus where, for example, the technical complexity of a merit good makes it difficult for the consumer to appreciate genuine quality differences, the incentive to effective quality competition in this market is significantly reduced. Moreover, under conditions of uncertainty, consumers tend to regard price, along with the size, age, and reputation of the firm, as an important index of quality.[38] Since a lower price may therefore be taken as an indication of inferior quality, demand elasticities tend to be low and the incentive to price competition is therefore also reduced.

At the same time, uncertainty enormously increases the scope for emotive advertising and superficial "quality variations" embodied in "new models" as weapons of competition. As well as representing a waste of resources and misleading consumers, advertising tends to exhibit increasing returns to scale, thus operating as a significant barrier to the entry of new firms. Similarly, due to decreasing costs, the need to provide adequate service arrangements as a form of insurance in the case of expensive and technically complex consumer durables also poses a serious problem for new entrants. The most important uncertainty-related obstacle to entry, however, is the ignorant consumer's habit, already mentioned above, of judging quality by the size, age and reputation of the seller.[39] The new entrant

---

[37] The following analysis is based on Scitovsky's excellent discussion (chap. 12).

[38] For a penetrating analysis of the habit of judging quality by price, see Scitovsky, chap. 11.

[39] Scitovsky (p. 207) has pointedly observed that established firms "often pursue an advertising policy that seems deliberately aimed at impressing the consumer with his own ignorance. . . . All such advertising carries the suggestion that the consumer, a mere layman, would be unwise to judge quality unaided, by mere inspection, and should rely instead on the guarantees offered by the reputation of established manufacturers." See also p. 194.

must therefore purchase existing goodwill, or create its own by means of a large-scale advertising campaign. This same habit is also largely responsible for the capital market imperfections which particularly affect small new firms.

In short, by restricting quality and price competition among existing firms and by obstructing the entry of new firms, consumer uncertainty is a prime cause of imperfect competition.

### 4.2.2  Uncertainty, external economies, and decreasing costs

A very different but also extremely important relationship between uncertainty and the Pigovian inefficiency concepts can be seen from our discussion in section 4.1.1 above, where it appears that many Pareto-relevant uncertainty problems can be traced to the existence of external economies and decreasing costs. In particular, due to generalized public goods problems, private economic units may find themselves unable, either unilaterally or through voluntary cooperation, to reduce a certain type of risk at reasonable cost; efficiency considerations may indicate that the risk-reducing service should be provided in partially nonexcludable form and/or under conditions of decreasing cost. This would certainly seem to be the case for such general risk-reducing services as defense, public health measures, police services, and fire protection, where the risk is not narrowly associated with the purchase of particular commodities. Similarly, where preventive action to reduce the incidence of the risk is too costly and private insurance is inadequate, we saw that the government may be able to provide a much wider range of risk-pooling facilities whilst at the same time achieving the spectacular economies of scale technically possible but often not privately available without some form of government intervention. Health insurance provides a good example.[40]

In our discussion of merit goods in the narrow Musgrave sense, we have also considered the general category of uncertainties associated with the purchase of particular commodities, which may provide a possible justification for such measures as standards and safety legislation of all sorts. In fact, of course, many forms of risk-reducing and insurance services for particular commodities can be provided quite profitably through the market.[41,42] It is only in so far as the risk-

[40] See Arrow, p. 963.

[41] Thus, for example, guarantees (of varying duration) and service contracts are commonplace in the field of the more expensive and technically complex consumer durables. Likewise it is obvious that many safety features and quality controls require no legislation, but are adopted in response to market pressures. Similarly, voluntary cooperation in such ventures as consumer associations can also do much to reduce uncertainty in an otherwise inexpert market.

[42] It should be noted that much advertising and public relations activity reduces subjec-

reducing or insurance service must be provided in partially nonexcludable form and/or under conditions of decreasing cost[43] that a prima facie case for government intervention can be established. As in the case of the general risk-reducing and insurance services, however, there can be little doubt that these Pigovian inefficiency factors are frequently very important in the field of particular commodities, and efficient unilateral or cooperative action by private economic units cannot therefore be relied upon.

### 4.2.3  Irrationality and external economies

Even in the case of the pure irrationality concept there is an important relationship with a generalized concept of external economies. Thus it is possible to argue that objections by "informed groups" to the true preferences of other individuals represent simply a special form of the general external economies and diseconomies phenomenon. In many of the examples frequently quoted of the inferior tastes of less educated groups, it is easy to discern the external diseconomies suffered by a sophisticated elite regularly exposed to the sights and sounds of an uncongenial popular culture. Even where the relationship is slightly less straightforward, as in the case of scholarly (as distinct from interest-group) conceptions of the proper state of distribution, or in the case of judgments of an elite such as a priestly caste substantially isolated from the rest of the community, it is nevertheless quite clear that in a very real sense the consumption choices or utilities of other individuals enter as arguments into the preference functions of the informed group. To the extent that irrationality problems can be treated as a special case of external economies and diseconomies, it thus appears that at least some part of this apparently authoritarian conception can in fact be reconciled with the individualistic or consumer sovereignty tradition.

To suggest that the concept of irrational preferences can be completely explained in terms of external economies and diseconomies would, however, be extremely misleading. In particular, there is always a strong implication in irrationality arguments that the judgments concerned are in some sense completely objective and disinterested. In such cases the external economy or diseconomy element is by definition very weak or nonexistent; or the same point might

tive uncertainty without in any way affecting objective uncertainty. The "special personal relationship" established with customers (or patients in the case of the medical profession), now largely replaced by advertising and "brand images" in most fields, falls in this category.

[43] One very special example particularly emphasized by Scitovsky (chaps. 13 and 15) is the threat to the traditional educational function of elite tastes represented inter alia by the overwhelming importance of economies of scale under modern conditions.

alternatively be expressed by saying that externalities of this particular sort are defined to be Pareto-irrelevant. Strictly defined in this way, the irrationality concept remains completely authoritarian and is irreconcilable with the individualistic tradition.

## 4.3  Economic Stability

There are also obvious and important relationships between uncertainty and the Keynesian and post-Keynesian theories of unemployment and inflation. According to orthodox Keynesian theory, crucial factors contributing to the instability of the economic system include interest-elasticity of the liquidity preference schedule, interest-inelasticity of the investment-demand schedule, and elastic price and interest expectations.[44] As emphasized by Keynes himself, these factors are essentially phenomena of a highly risky and uncertain world.

Thus the role of uncertainty in the theory of liquidity preference is immediately evident from Keynes' discussions of the precautionary and speculative demands (and of course from the terms themselves).[45] The precautionary demand is analysed in terms of risk-aversion, and the speculative demand in terms of differing opinions held with subjective certainty. A major feature of more recent discussions has been the increasingly rigorous analysis of liquidity-preference as behavior towards risk.[46]

Similarly, the interest-inelasticity of the investment-demand schedule has been explained largely in terms of the overwhelming importance of risk in investment decisions, and the consequent relative unimportance of feasible changes in rates of interest compared with the large risk premium demanded by investors. The phenomena of elastic price and interest expectations along with highly unstable liquidity-preference and investment-demand schedules are also clearly the product of an unstable and consequently uncertain world.[47] Problems of uncertainty and speculation in the foreign exchange market, together with unemployment and inflation, are also crucial causes of some of the worst balance-of-payments problems.

---

[44] See, for example, the classic analysis of a generalized Keynesian system by Don Patinkin, *Money, Interest, and Prices* (Evanston, Ill., 1956), chap. 14.

[45] J. M. Keynes, *The General Theory of Employment, Interest, and Money* (London, 1936), pp. 168–70.

[46] See, for example, the excellent analysis by J. E. Tobin, "Liquidity-Preference as Behaviour towards Risk," *Review of Economic Studies*, 1957–58.

[47] See, for example, Keynes's celebrated discussion of the "state of long-term expectation" (chap. 12).

Due to nonappropriability problems, direct action to reduce economic instability is in general impossible for private economic units[48] —hence the case for economic stabilizing fiscal, monetary, wages, price-control and exchange-rate policies. Effective economic stabilization policy maintained over a period may reduce markedly the need for further government action by mitigating some of the most important destabilizing factors such as elastic expectations and unstable demand functions.

## 4.4   Economic Growth

The classic problem of imperfect information is, however, that of economic growth.

### 4.4.1   Uncertainty and economic growth

Nowhere does uncertainty arise in such an acute and obvious form as in choices concerning the future; and, in the case of growth, intertemporal choices are the very essence of the problem. The basic choices in a growth context are those between present and future consumption and between alternative types of investment including investment in research and in the development of new products and processes. In making these savings and investment choices the private economic unit (household or firm) must, in addition to knowing current alternatives, attempt to forecast the future pattern of demand and supply in the relevant markets, which will in turn depend upon the choices made by other private economic units. The availability of refined market-research forecasts, the possibilities of risk-reduction through diversification, the existence of well-developed futures markets in money and certain basic commodities and the possibility of long-term contracts all help to reduce the intrinsic uncertainties. In most markets, however, even the best estimates are inevitably subject to extremely wide margins of error, and the scope for private action to reduce or avoid these uncertainties is usually strictly limited. In a world of risk-averters it is evident that savings, investment and growth rates would tend to be relatively too low.

Some of the most serious privately unavoidable risks facing the firm or household in its savings and investment choices are those represented by recessions and inflations. As we have seen in the preceding section, government stabilization policies can contribute greatly to the reduction of these risks. Even with effective stabilization measures

---

[48] See chap. 8, sec. 4.2.2.2 in this volume.

guaranteed, however, the privately unavoidable uncertainties involved in savings and investment decisions would still be immense, and these uncertainties would particularly affect decisions of crucial importance for growth, such as investment in research and in the development of new products and processes.

Since these privately-unavoidable risks may vastly exceed socially-unavoidable risks, specific growth-oriented policies may be justified. Thus, for example, private uncertainty can be further reduced by the techniques of so-called "indicative planning," essentially a vast socialized market-research and public-relations project. In particularly important fields such as research and development, socialization of investment decisions or government subsidies may make possible a much more effective and economical pooling of risks and the achievement of more conventional scale economies. Many policies familiar to the public finance specialist, such as generous depreciation and loss-offset provisions, also find their major justification in their risk-reducing effects. Loss-offset provisions under the income tax, for example, can be regarded as a special type of coinsurance arrangement. Action to broaden the coverage and increase the stability of private "insurance" arrangements such as futures markets, and of risk-spreading facilities such as the stock exchange, may also be possible. One of the most important justifications of socialism is similarly to be found in the growth benefits to be derived from the socialization of investment decisions in a fully planned economy.

### 4.4.2 Irrationality and economic growth

We have seen earlier[49] that Pigou's famous argument regarding the merit goods characteristics of future consumption provides one of the best examples of a pure irrationality argument which has been directed at the behavior of mature adults in the public finance literature. This argument regarding the existence, even in a world of certainty, of an irrational preference for present pleasures over equal future pleasures has its immediate application in the field of growth, and suggests a case for government promotion of capital formation and economic growth generally. Amongst the policies most directly suggested by the Pigovian argument would be compulsory savings schemes for the young and compulsory social insurance.

The irrationality case for growth-promotion is further supported by the equally well known intergeneration equity argument that time-preference is not only irrational but immoral. According to this argument, the preferences of present and future generations should on

---

[49] See above, sec. 3.1.2.2.

ethical grounds be weighted equally in determining the allocation of resources over time. Like most equity discussions to be found in the public finance literature, this intergeneration equity argument makes the same sort of appeal to the moral authority of elites as the Pigovian irrationality argument.[50] The two arguments thus illustrate very well the importance of the authoritarian tradition in the growth literature. In spite of their undoubtedly controversial nature, they constitute a critique of the individualistic tradition in a growth context, which has considerable intuitive appeal to many "informed groups" and cannot safely be ignored in any comprehensive welfare framework.

The importance of such considerations has also been recognized in the more recent public finance literature, notably in cost-benefit discussions where an important role has been assigned to the concept of a "social rate of discount" based at least in part on these authoritarian or merit goods considerations.[51]

# 5. Information Problems versus Nonappropriability Problems

We have seen that individual benefit-evaluation difficulties or preference-distortion problems constitute the essential characteristic of the merit goods concept. Generalizing this essential characteristic to cover all types of imperfect information, we have found that the information problem plays an extremely important role in more familiar Pigovian, Keynesian and post-Keynesian theories of market failure; maldistribution of income, misallocation of resources, eco-

---

[50] Indeed the intergeneration equity argument is often not clearly distinguished from the Pigovian irrationality argument. This is true, for example, of S. A. Marglin's otherwise excellent discussion, "The Social Rate of Discount and the Optimal Rate of Investment," *Quarterly Journal of Economics*, 1963. Pigou himself does not in fact employ this further argument. His well known contention (*The Economics of Welfare*, 4th ed., p. 29) that the government must act as "trustee for unborn generations" in the field of conservation policy is based on an argument regarding capital market imperfections (and hence uncertainty), not intergeneration equity. See ibid., pt. 1, chap. 2, sec. 4.

The irrationality and intergeneration equity arguments have also led to some confusion regarding the "true meaning" of consumer sovereignty in an intertemporal context. According to some writers, consumer sovereignty requires that the preferences of present individuals should be decisive. Others maintain that the preferences of all consumers, future as well as present, must be fully represented. It seems simpler and less confusing to define consumer sovereignty in terms of the preferences of present individuals, and to recognize its possible welfare defects in terms of rationality and intergeneration equity.

[51] For an interesting recent discussion and further references, see M. S. Feldstein, "The Social Time-Preference Discount Rate in Cost Benefit Analysis," *Economic Journal*, 1964.

nomic instability, and suboptimal rates of economic growth are all to some extent ascribable to problems of uncertainty and irrationality. Thus, in a generalized sense, the familiar objectives of the post-Keynesian multiple theory of the public household, namely equity, efficiency, stability, and growth, all exhibit important merit goods characteristics.

In recent discussions it has become clear that the *public* goods concept can also be generalized into a comprehensive theory of market failure via Sidgwick's concept of nonappropriability or Baumol's generalized external economies.[52] The analysis of section 4 above shows that nonappropriability problems, such as those of external economies and decreasing costs, play an extremely important role in market failure of uncertainty origin. In particular, market failure problems due to uncertainty can only arise where, for maximum efficiency, the risk-reducing or insurance service must be provided in partially nonappropriable form and involves large numbers of economic units. There is thus an extremely important connection between the two theories obtainable by generalizing the public goods and merit goods concepts.

The two approaches are, however, by no means identical. Although there are no Pareto-relevant uncertainty problems which do not involve nonappropriability, there are other imperfect knowledge concepts, notably that of irrational preferences, where some attempt is made to abstract completely from nonappropriability problems; and there are nonappropriability problems in which uncertainty or irrational preferences do not seem to be significant. It may therefore be interesting to consider at least in general terms the relative importance of uncertainty and irrationality problems compared with pure nonappropriability problems in the development of a general economic theory of the public household (or theory of market failure).

## 5.1   Distribution

The main relatively pure nonappropriability problem in a distributional context would appear to stem from the possibility that members of the middle- and upper-income groups may derive altruistic satisfaction from increased consumption by the lower-income groups.[53] A member of the upper-income group unilaterally transferring income to

---

[52] See chap. 8 above.
[53] See the highly suggestive analysis by W. S. Vickrey, "One Economist's View of Philanthropy," in F. G. Dickinson, ed., *Philanthropy and Public Policy* (New York, 1962), pp. 40–44.

the lower-income groups may thus provide altruistic benefits to other high-income individuals. As a result, private philanthropy will tend to be restricted because of nonappropriability problems, even though any given high-income individual might be willing to contribute significantly more for the benefit of the low-income group if other high-income individuals would agree to do likewise. If the number of economic units involved is large, however, voluntary cooperation is likely to be of only very limited adequacy. It may thus be possible to justify a substantial redistributive tax-transfer system for the benefit of the lower-income groups imposing proportionate sacrifice on all members of the higher-income groups.

Although equity has seldom been recognized as an important nonappropriability problem, there can be little doubt that attitudes of this sort contribute significantly to the relative general acceptability of redistributive welfare schemes for depressed groups and of progressive income taxation itself.

From our discussion of section 4.1.1 above, it is clear that the uncertainty problem is also likely to be a powerful if sometimes rather subtle force affecting attitudes to distribution in a market economy. Although a clear separation of motives in individual attitudes may be almost impossible to achieve, it seems that uncertainty-related attitudes would usually be no less important than purely altruistic or aesthetic egalitarian attitudes. To judge from their importance in the literature, the various authoritarian approaches to the equity question likewise cannot be neglected.

## 5.2   Resource Allocation

We have already cited cases such as a fireworks display, a bridge, or theatrical performance, in which important elements of external economies or joint supply in the public goods sense may exist without necessarily involving any significant problems of individual benefit evaluation.[54] Other examples of external economy or diseconomy problems frequently analysed or quoted in the literature, such as the familiar case of apples and nectar, or smoky chimneys, likewise involve no obvious problems of uncertainty or irrationality. Similarly, information problems play no obvious role in many of the most familiar examples of decreasing costs (steel, chemicals, electricity generation, etc.) due to elements of lumpiness or indivisibility of factors (rather than the product indivisibility peculiar to the public goods case).

---

[54] See above, sec. 3.3.

As indicated in section 4.1.1, there are, however, many nonappropriability problems in which information problems are a crucial ingredient. Thus some of the best examples of public goods are to be found in the field of general risk-reducing services, such as defense, police services, and fire protection, where the risk is not narrowly associated with the purchase of particular commodities. In some of these cases, such as defense, the uncertainty problem even extends to the evaluation of the benefits from the service itself. We have also found many examples of uncertainties more narrowly associated with the purchase of particular commodities, providing a possible justification for pure foods acts, and other standards and safety legislation. Extremely significant examples of conventional decreasing costs associated with uncertainty are to be found in more formal insurance arrangements in such fields as hospital and medical care, as well as in the case of many of the preventive services already mentioned.

It is therefore clear that there are important examples of both pure and uncertainty-related nonappropriability problems in the field of allocation. Many alleged examples of irrational preferences are also to be found in the literature, though their existence and importance are obviously more difficult to demonstrate.

## 5.3  Economic Stability

In a stability context, the most important example of a nonappropriability problem in which uncertainty does not seem to be an essential factor is provided by cost-inflation.[55] Even under relatively stable monetary and demand conditions, employer or employee organizations may attempt to use their market power over price to alter the distribution of factor income in their own favor. Other groups in a position to pass on such a redistributive price-increase and thus protect their factor share proceed to do so, and a cost-inflationary spiral ensues. Losing groups usually include farmers, pensioners, salary-earners, and others whose incomes tend to be relatively fixed in money terms.[56] Under these conditions, the full social benefits to be derived from price-, dividend-, and wage-restraint will not in general be appropriable by the individual union or firm, and public policy (notably an incomes policy) must be relied upon.

[55] For a very useful recent survey of cost-inflation theory, see M. Bronfenbrenner and F. D. Holzman, "Survey of Inflation Theory," *American Economic Review,* 1963, sec. 3.

[56] It is not therefore the case that only ignorance of the ability of other groups to defend their income shares can explain the original wage-push or profit-push. Although this and other imperfect knowledge problems, such as money illusion, are no doubt frequently of some importance in cost-inflation, they do not seem to be an essential ingredient.

As shown in section 4.3, uncertainty plays a crucial role in modern theories of economic instability of demand-side origin. Thus we saw that unstable demand schedules, interest-elastic demand for money, interest-inelastic investment demand and elastic expectations are all phenomena of an uncertain world. Although interest in the problem of cost-inflation has been steadily increasing over the postwar period, it still seems reasonable to suggest, in the light of the available evidence, that uncertainty-related nonappropriability problems are of overwhelming importance in a stability context.

## 5.4  Economic Growth

The pure nonappropriability problem which has been most fully analysed in a growth context is that in which the consumption of future generations enters altruistically into the utility functions of members of the present generation.[57] Activities of one member of the present generation which lead to increased consumption by future generations provide altruistic benefits to other members of the present generation. Growth-promoting activities therefore tend to be under-expanded because of nonappropriability problems. Under these conditions, an individual for whom the sacrifice involved in additional saving would not be fully justified in terms of greater consumption by future generations may nevertheless be willing to save more if other members of the present generation could be relied upon to do likewise. Since a large number of private economic units will usually be involved, voluntary cooperative solutions are likely to be seriously inadequate, and growth-promoting government policies apportioning the sacrifice of present consumption may therefore be justified.[58] This sort of "future-oriented altruism" is probably relatively unimportant in highly-developed Western societies. It may, however, be a socio-political factor of some importance in certain underdeveloped countries.

More important in most cases, no doubt, is the phenomenon of "future-oriented self-interest." Since the benefits in terms of higher real wages and consumption levels resulting from growth-promoting

---

[57] See, for example, the comprehensive analysis by Marglin.

[58] When simultaneous account is taken of future-oriented altruism and the present-oriented altruism discussed in sec. 5.1 above, the market tendency to suboptimal growth rates due to future-oriented altruism may be offset by a tendency to superoptimal growth due to present-oriented altruism. In particular, due to present-oriented altruism, individual members of the middle- and upper-income groups will tend to want fellow-members to transfer part of their savings to low-income individuals in the present generation. For some discussion of this and related points, see the "Comments" on Marglin's article by G. Tullock, R. C. Lind, and D. Usher, *Quarterly Journal of Economics*, 1964.

activities spill over onto other individuals, members of the present generation wishing to enjoy higher levels of real income and consumption in the future may be willing to bear an increased burden of saving, risk-bearing, and dividend- and wage-restraint only if others are forced to do likewise. Thus it is future-oriented self-interest, i.e. the promise of more rapid rates of growth and thus higher living standards for the present generation within a reasonably short planning period, rather than future-oriented altruism, which appears to account for a significant part of the genuine support for comprehensive growth policies in many countries.

As we have seen in section 4.4, however, uncertainty problems are of overwhelming importance in a growth context. Moreover, precisely where a significant degree of "future-oriented altruism" or "future-oriented self-interest" may be expected, notably in underdeveloped countries, the uncertainties and risks associated with savings and investment decisions are frequently the greatest. In general, it seems safe to suggest that uncertainty-related nonappropriability problems are much more important than pure nonappropriability problems in a growth context. From our earlier discussion,[59] it is clear that irrationality and related problems are also of considerable importance.

# 6.   Merit Goods and Welfare Politics

We have now examined the role of generalized merit goods (i.e. knowledge) problems in the economic theory of the public household and compared them with the generalized public goods (i.e. nonappropriability or externality) problems which have figured so prominently in recent discussions.

The great revival of interest in public goods as a crucial concept in the theory of market failure has, however, also been accompanied by a revival of interest in the political problem of improving on market performance. In particular, it has been increasingly recognized that, where the market fails, it does not necessarily follow that the political mechanism can reasonably be expected to do better. The economic theory of the public household, based on the theory of market failure, requires therefore to be supplemented by a *political* theory of the public household.[60]

---

[59] See above, sec. 4.4.2.

[60] Important contributions to the development of such a theory have recently been made by Downs and Buchanan and Tullock. See A. Downs, *An Economic Theory of Democracy* (New York, 1957); and J. M. Buchanan and G. Tullock, *The Calculus of Consent* (Ann Arbor, 1962). Increasing attention has also been paid to the pioneering work of Wick-

## **6.1**  Information Problems and Welfare Politics

It appears that there is in fact a very close relationship between the central inefficiency concepts in the generalized merit goods theory of market failure and those in the theory of political failure. Thus the theory of welfare politics suggests two major reasons for the failure of the political mechanism: the government may not *try* to achieve the welfare objectives postulated in the economic theory of the public household; and even if it tries, it may lack the knowledge necessary for even approximate success. These problems broadly correspond to the irrationality and uncertainty problems of the generalized merit goods theory of market failure.

### **6.1.1**  Irrationality

The problem of governmental "irrationality" is well illustrated by the case of absolutist or totalitarian forms of government. In such cases it would obviously be a pure coincidence if governmental objectives happened to correspond to the post-Keynesian welfare objectives. Thus there will usually be only the loosest connection between such histori- cally typical absolutist objectives as retention of power, individual or national prestige, the establishment of empire, the propagation of the faith, etc., and such welfare objectives as equity, efficiency, stabil- ity, and growth.[61] This, of course, partly explains the sceptical attitude to government which is traditional in conservative and liberal circles. A naive faith in the political mechanism per se as a panacea for market failure is clearly completely unjustified historically.

This is not, of course, to suggest that no political mechanism can reasonably be expected to improve on market performance unless the government is directly inspired by an interest in the common good. Thus in Downs' theory of the democratic political mechanism,[62] poli- ticians are assumed to be motivated only by the desire to be elected. Competition between political parties tends, however, to force the adoption of Pareto-optimal policy programs in order to maximize elec- toral prospects.[63] It was in fact a familiar argument in the public

sell and Lindahl; see, for example, chap. 6 in this volume. For a general survey of the contributions of Wicksell, Lindahl, Downs, and Buchanan and Tullock, see chap. 1, sec. 5, above. On Lindahl and Downs, see also E. Liefmann-Keil, "Zur Entwicklung der Theorie der Bewilligung öffentlicher Einnahmen und Ausgaben," *Finanzarchiv*, n.s. 19, 1958–59.

[61] As Scitovsky has pointedly remarked (p. 242), "For many centuries, food, clothing, and shelter symbolized market goods, while cathedrals, palaces, and armies were the sym- bols of collective spending."

[62] See Downs.

[63] For a careful analysis of this tendency, see Downs, pp. 178–82.

finance literature of the late nineteenth century (e.g. Sax, De Viti de
Marco, and Mazzola) that some approach to the achievement of a Pareto optimum is a necessary condition for political equilibrium in a
democracy.[64]

### 6.1.2  Uncertainty

The problem of uncertainty is obviously no less important. Thus,
even where the government is directly or indirectly motivated by a
concern for welfare objectives, government uncertainty regarding
given individual preferences, the nature of existing inefficiencies and
the effects of alternative policies, together with individual uncertainty
regarding the nature and effects of government activities, may seriously weaken the link between political aims and achievements.

Downs, for example, has emphasized that it is only on the completely
unrealistic assumption of perfect knowledge that his majority voting
model can conceivably be expected to produce Pareto-optimal economic
policies. In the more general case, uncertainties of all sorts will prevent the system from achieving any more than the roughest approach
to Pareto-optimality. Under these circumstances, Pareto-efficiency
will no longer be a necessary condition for maximization of electoral
prospects.[65] Within fairly wide limits, government programs can thus
come to reflect the private motives and prejudices of political parties
and the empire-building tendencies of the bureaucracy; and the electoral problem becomes one of "selling" these political programs to an
uncertain electorate utilizing all the techniques of modern advertising, emphasizing simple and obvious selling points and appealing to
all sorts of irrelevant emotions.

## 6.2  Merit Goods and the Political Mechanism

In spite of these general limitations of the political process, is there
perhaps some reason for assuming that the political mechanism is
uniquely capable of improving on market performance in the case of
merit goods?

Curiously enough, some such assumption does seem to be implicit
in much of the traditional public finance literature. As pointed out in
section 3.3 above, individual benefit-evaluation difficulties have frequently been held to constitute the crucial problem posed by the existence of public goods. Thus it is argued that the concept of individual

---

[64] De Viti's discussion (book 1, chap. 1, sec. 7) is perhaps the most suggestive.
[65] For Downs's analysis of the effects of uncertainty, see chap. 10, secs. 2C-2F; also "Why
the Government Budget is Too Small in a Democracy," *World Politics*, 1959–60.

benefit shares is not applicable in the case of public goods where the benefits accrue collectively, i.e. to society as a whole, rather than to individuals.[66] Furthermore, pointing to examples such as defense, education, growth, and foreign aid, it is suggested that the benefits are anyway too indirect, long-run or technically complicated to be capable of accurate individual assessment.[67] Reliance upon the expert knowledge of the bureaucracy or government is therefore essential; or, in more democratic versions of the argument, the special value of collective decision-making in these cases is vigorously asserted.

In fact, however, there are very good reasons for supposing that the irrationality and uncertainty characteristics of merit goods pose far more difficult problems for the political mechanism than those associated with pure nonappropriability.

### 6.2.1  Irrationality

The political problem in cases of irrationality can readily be illustrated by considering the Pigovian example of an irrational preference for present over future consumption. Abstracting from all other knowledge problems, could, for example, a majority voting mechanism of the Downsian sort be expected to lead to the implementation of the growth policies required to correct the resulting inefficiency? Since the vote-maximizing political parties of the model have no interest in the achievement of welfare goals for their own sake but only for their vote-getting potential, the answer depends on whether additional votes could be attracted by promoting a rate of growth in excess of that consistent with the true intertemporal preferences of electors. It is clear, however, that each and every individual would prefer a given Pareto-optimal program excluding Pigovian growth measures to the same program plus (non-redistributive) Pigovian growth measures. The adoption of the Pigovian policies would therefore result in electoral catastrophe and could not reasonably be expected of the vote-maximizing political parties of the model.[68]

[66] As we have already seen, this argument was effectively demolished by De Viti de Marco. See n. 25 above.

[67] Carl Shoup, for example, particularly emphasizes the benefit-evaluation problems arising from the preventive nature of so many important government services.

[68] As an example of an irrational preference, the Pigovian case has the interesting peculiarity that an electorate which ex ante may unanimously oppose the required growth measures, may equally approve them ex post, if they can somehow be forced through initially. Indeed, even more Draconian measures would seem justified ex post on Pigovian arguments, since, as Pigou himself emphasizes (*A Study in Public Finance*, p. 117), the defective telescopic faculty also works in reverse (when we contemplate the past). The fact remains, however, that no government could ever be elected in a Downsian democracy on a program of Pigovian growth measures, or even on the continuation of such measures after a period of growth-oriented and ex post justified dictatorship.

The argument for reliance upon the longer views and expert knowledge of government for the performance of merit want functions of this sort is therefore politically extremely vulnerable. Since it would obviously be naive to rely upon the emergence of an absolutist government inspired by an altruistic desire to rectify irrational individual preferences, and since the democratic process, as envisaged by Downs, is evidently completely incapable of performing this function, it would appear that this aspect of merit want theory is completely nonoperational in a fundamental political sense.

Following an important line of thought in the traditional public finance literature, it might, however, be argued that the above analysis incorrectly assumes complete identity of individual preferences in the market and in the political process. According to this argument, under the influence of basic social psychological forces (e.g. the "mutualism" and "collectivism" of Sax),[69] individuals tend to take longer, more rational and more altruistic views in the context of collective (and especially democratic) decision-making than in the market.[70] Thus it is suggested as a basic sociological phenomenon that individuals take a completely different attitude to (say) growth or foreign aid in a political context from that implicit in their individualistic market behavior.[71] The vote-maximizing political parties of Downs's model-democracy would therefore be forced, by political competition, to perform these merit want functions.

Although the existence of such differences in attitude is undeniable, the argument scarcely suggests the existence of the genuine schizophrenia required in the present context. A more obvious interpretation would be that such essentially cooperative social psychological forces

---

[69] See Emil Sax, "Die Wertungstheorie der Steuer," *Zeitschrift für Volkswirtschaft und Sozialpolitik*, 1924. Most of the relevant section is available in an English translation and summary, "The Valuation Theory of Taxation," in R. A. Musgrave and A. T. Peacock, eds., *Classics in the Theory of Public Finance* (London and New York, 1958).

[70] From the public finance literature, in addition to the important work of Sax, see, for example, E. R. A. Seligman, "The Social Theory of Fiscal Science," *Political Science Quarterly*, 1926. A similar view has been persuasively advocated over a long period by Gerhard Colm. See his *Volkswirtschaftliche Theorie der Staatsausgaben* (Tübingen, 1927); *Essays in Public Finance and Fiscal Policy* (New York, 1955); "Comments on Samuelson's Theory of Public Finance," *Review of Economics and Statistics*, 1956; "In Defense of the Public Interest," *Social Research*, 1960; and, most recently, in his article "National Goals Analysis and Marginal Utility Economics," *Finanzarchiv*, n.s. 24, 1965. In his latest contribution (p. 213), Colm summarizes his position as follows: "As there is no strict comparability between the preference scales of two individuals, there is also no cogent relationship between the preference scales of the same individual as homo oeconomicus and homo politicus."

[71] The possibility of applying this argument in the field of growth is considered (and rejected) by Marglin (pp. 98–99).

as "mutualism" and "collectivism" merely help to overcome the problems of nonappropriability and large numbers which prevent the market from providing an accurate reflection of given individual preferences. The political mechanism may thus induce a more accurate expression of given individual preferences, but this in no way suggests that it can be used to correct an irrational preference. An even more obvious explanation of the undoubted differences in attitude would be that individuals are extremely uncertain regarding the benefits to be derived from changes in the output of public goods; their expressed preferences are therefore highly unstable and can be expected to change and fluctuate under the differing influences of the market and the political environment.

### 6.2.2 Uncertainty

We have already seen that government uncertainties regarding given individual preferences, the nature of existing inefficiencies and the effects of alternative policies, together with individual uncertainties regarding the nature and effects of government activities, may prevent even a rough approach to a Pareto-optimum through a Downsian democratic political mechanism. If, due to incomplete information, the individual does not know his own true preferences for some goods, a further uncertainty is added to an already formidable list. Is there any reason to suppose that the individual's true preferences for these merit goods will receive more accurate expression through, for example, the democratic political mechanism as envisaged by Downs than through the market? Here again the answer depends upon whether more adequate provision of the merit goods in question offers the prospect of additional votes. In so far as the government benefits in these cases tend to be indirect, delayed or otherwise complicated and difficult to appreciate,[72] and given a general aversion to uncertainty, it seems clear that, other things being equal, a Pareto-optimal government program including the relevant merit good policies will be regarded as inferior to a nonoptimal program providing benefits which are more obvious or more certain. Thus even if government experts or party elites could somehow determine the true preferences of individuals,

---

[72] Uncertainty regarding the benefits from merit goods need not, of course, entail uncertainty regarding the benefits of the appropriate governmental risk-reducing or insurance service. In fact, however, uncertainty does seem to be an important problem in the case of many of the most characteristic public services, particularly those of a preventive character.

the inclusion of merit goods policies would result in electoral disaster. Such policies may therefore never be tried.[73]

Writers in the democratic political tradition would presumably argue that the basic Downsian model completely ignores the crucial role of discussion and deliberation under the leadership of informed groups and party elites. According to this argument, a major merit of democracy as a political mechanism is that individual preferences can be formed and modified in the course of the free discussion which is held to be the essence of the democratic process.[74] It is, however, possible to doubt whether the competitive political advertising of the democratic process is any less misleading or any more conducive to individual self-knowledge than advertising in the market.

## 7.  Conclusions

The main results of the above analysis can be summarized as follows:

(a) Musgrave's concept of a merit good appears to exhibit as many as three distinct and independent characteristics: individuals find its benefits difficult to evaluate; it is frequently the subject of special distributional objectives; and it typically exhibits public good aspects. Although there is no necessary relationship between these characteristics, the merit goods concept is extremely useful in focusing attention on the empirically very significant coincidence that some of the best examples of goods posing individual benefit-evaluation difficulties are also the subject of special distributional objectives and exhibit important public goods characteristics. The concept thus provides a particularly striking and important illustration of compound market failure.

(b) Individual benefit-evaluation difficulties are clearly intended by Musgrave to constitute the essence of the merit goods problem. Generalizing this essential characteristic to cover all types of imperfect knowledge, it is easy to show that the information problem also plays an extremely important role in more familiar Pigovian, Keynesian and

---

[73] Appropriate merit goods policies would, however, be regarded by the electorate as fully justified ex post, if they could somehow be introduced initially. Moreover, in contrast to the Pigovian merit goods policies discussed in the preceding section (see especially n. 68 above), a government could be elected on a program of continuation of existing merit goods policies. Indeed, once introduced, such measures could not safely be omitted from the program of a party wishing to maximize its electoral prospects. It may therefore be possible for a government in office successfully to introduce appropriate merit goods policies at the cost of temporary but electorally irrelevant unpopularity. There will, however, be little or no political pressure to do so in the basic Downsian model.

[74] From the public finance literature, see, for example, De Viti de Marco, p. 118, n. 2.

post-Keynesian theories of market failure; maldistribution of income, misallocation of resources, economic instability, and nonoptimal rates of economic growth are all to some extent ascribable to problems of uncertainty and irrationality. Thus, in a more general sense, the familiar objectives of the post-Keynesian multiple theory of the public household, namely equity, efficiency, stability, and growth, all therefore exhibit important merit goods characteristics.

(c) In recent discussions it has become clear that the concept of a *public* good can also be generalized into a comprehensive theory of market failure via Sidgwick's concept of nonappropriability or Baumol's generalized external economies. Our analysis indicates that generalized public goods problems also play a crucial role in the generalized merit goods theory of market failure. In particular, market failure due to uncertainty can only occur where, for maximum efficiency, risk-prevention or insurance services must be provided in partially nonappropriable form. There is thus an extremely important connection between the two theories of market failure obtainable by generalizing the public goods and merit goods concepts.

(d) The two theories are, however, by no means identical. Although there are no Pareto-relevant uncertainty problems which do not involve nonappropriability, there are other imperfect knowledge concepts, notably that of irrational preferences, where an attempt is made to abstract completely from nonappropriability problems; and there are nonappropriability problems in which uncertainty or irrational preferences do not seem to be significant. It therefore seems desirable to preserve a clear distinction between the two types of problem. An examination of the relative importance of uncertainty and irrationality problems compared with pure nonappropriability problems clearly suggests that a general economic theory of the public household cannot afford to emphasize either set of problems at the expense of the other.

(e) It is interesting to observe the symmetry between the problems of market failure and those of political failure. Two major reasons for the failure of the political mechanism are that the government may not try to achieve the objectives postulated in the economic theory of the public household, and that, even if it tries, it may lack the knowledge necessary for even approximate success. These problems broadly correspond to the irrationality and uncertainty problems of the generalized merit goods theory of market failure. On examination, it appears that the political problem of improving on market performance is likely to be even more difficult in the case of merit goods than in the case of pure public goods.

# 11.  Merit Goods Revisited

## 1.  Introduction

The modern theory of public expenditure, as developed by Musgrave and others, offers an interesting variety of new concepts, new questions and new conclusions. The new concepts, put forward by Musgrave in *The Theory of Public Finance*, are those of social wants (or public goods) and merit wants (or merit goods).[1] In the considerable literature to which the modern theory has given rise, the public goods concept has been thoroughly analyzed and generalized.[2] The merit goods concept has, however, been rather neglected.

In a previous paper in this journal,[3] I have tried to some extent to remedy this defect with a detailed analysis and generalization of the merit goods concept. The lively comments on my paper by Charles McLure[4] suggest that some further discussion may help to clarify the main issues.

We shall begin, in section 2, with the problem of interpreting the merit goods concept as developed by Musgrave. Then, in section 3, we shall consider the possible role of the concept in a normative theory of public finance. Section 4 contains a brief summary of the main conclusions.

## 2.  The Interpretation of the Merit Goods Concept

### 2.1  The Central Characteristic

The central characteristic of a merit good is that many individuals are unable to evaluate the benefits correctly. The problem is therefore

Reprinted without significant change from *Finanzarchiv* 28, no. 2 (March 1969): 214–25.

[1] R. A. Musgrave, *The Theory of Public Finance* (New York, 1959), chap. 1, sec. B.
[2] For a recent survey and detailed references, see chap. 3 in this volume.
[3] See chap. 10.
[4] C. E. McLure, Jr., "Merit Wants: A Normatively Empty Box," *Finanzarchiv* n.s. 27, 1968.

one of imperfect knowledge, broadly interpreted. In such cases, overt preferences do not represent the individual's "true" preferences or "real interests." In relation to the benchmark of true preferences or real interests, the overt preferences of the individual are evidently "incorrect" or "distorted." Public intervention may therefore be justified to correct consumer preferences. These are the "preference-distortion problems" or "imperfect knowledge problems" of my original paper.[5]

In his interpretation of the concept, McLure lays great stress on the fact that Musgrave speaks of "interference" with consumer preferences.[6] The normative purpose of such "interference" is, however, quite obviously to improve or correct consumer choices, not worsen them. As Musgrave himself points out, "the reason . . . for budgetary action is to *correct* individual choice."[7] Hence, of course, his choice of the term *merit want* in preference to pejorative alternatives such as *interference want* or *violation want*.[8]

## 2.2   Two Categories of Incorrect Preferences

Overt preferences may be distorted by two broad influences: ignorance and irrationality.

### 2.2.1   Ignorance

Thus, on the one hand, the consumer may lack basic information on the product necessary for a correct choice between market alternatives. Available information may be very incomplete, or, in the case of advertising, positively misleading. These are the "uncertainty problems" of my original paper.[9] They account for all possible divergences between an individual's "desires" and "satisfactions," in the traditional

---

[5] Chap. 10, sec. 3.1, Preference-distortion problems.

[6] McLure, passim.

[7] Musgrave, p. 9 (my italics).

[8] The term *interference good* is referred to in this connection in the course of a discussion of metropolitan finance by Tiebout and Houston, which I had not seen when I was working on my own paper. They offer yet another interpretation of the merit goods concept. See C. M. Tiebout and D. B. Houston, "Metropolitan Finance Reconsidered: Budget Functions and Multilevel Governments," *Review of Economics and Statistics*, 1962. A further brief attempt at interpretation is to be found in J. F. Due's well known textbook, *Government Finance*, 3rd ed. (Homewood, Ill., 1963), p. 14. See also J. M. Buchanan, "The Theory of Public Finance," *Southern Economic Journal*, 1960, p. 237.

[9] Chap. 10, sec. 3.1.2.1. Uncertainty. In this context I used the term *uncertainty* in the broader nontechnical sense to include the concept of risk as well as uncertainty in the technical sense. Perhaps the term *ignorance* may be more suitable.

terminology, or between ex ante and ex post preferences.[10] Appropriate public intervention should here produce choices which the individual himself would be able to recognize as "superior," i.e. more in accordance with his real preferences. Such adjustments are therefore quite consistent with consumer sovereignty, broadly interpreted.

McLure would seem to deny any role to ignorance or inadequate information in the merit goods context.[11] Such a position seems untenable. What Musgrave explicitly emphasizes are cases in which "an *informed* group is justified in imposing its decision upon others";[12] and, with particular reference to education, he comments that "the advantages of education are more evident to the informed than the uninformed."[13] The provision of certain health facilities is also mentioned in the same context. In the following paragraph he goes on to discuss the effects of advertising on consumer choices, pointing up the possible "distortion in the preference structure" which may result.[14]

McLure's interpretation seems to founder on the well known ambiguities of the "consumer sovereignty" concept.[15] As Musgrave explicitly points out, the satisfaction of merit wants need only involve "interference with consumer sovereignty, *narrowly defined.*"[16] It was a major objective of my own discussion to show what a wide range of information problems can be handled within the framework of consumer sovereignty, *broadly defined.* Evidently McLure would agree.

## 2.2.2 Irrationality

Individual choices may be distorted not only by ignorance but also by irrationality.[17] Even where there is no particular problem of incomplete or inaccurate information, in the narrow sense, the individual may nevertheless make choices which an external observer may

---

[10] Note that Pigou's "defective telescopic faculty" provides an example of an irrational preference rather than an uncertain preference. His description of this phenomenon in terms of a divergence between "desires" and "satisfactions" is misleading. See A. C. Pigou, *The Economics of Welfare,* 4th ed. (London, 1932), pt. 1, chap. 2.

[11] McLure, passim.

[12] Musgrave, p. 14 (my italics).

[13] Ibid.

[14] Ibid.

[15] Musgrave refers repeatedly to the concept of consumer sovereignty in his merit goods discussion, but without making his precise usage clear. See, however, the remarkably divergent interpretations of this concept by leading modern welfare theorists including Scitovsky, Rothenberg, Bergson, and Baumol in *American Economic Review, Papers and Proceedings,* 1962, pp. 262–90. The concept of "individual preferences" is subject to a similar range of ambiguities.

[16] Musgrave, p. 14 (my italics).

[17] See chap. 10, sec. 3.1.2.2.

regard as "irrational," "inferior," or "contrary to his real interests."[18] At least in principle, then, incorrect choices may be made without any information problem, narrowly defined. These "irrationality problems" account for all divergences between an individual's "satisfactions" and his "welfare," in the traditional terminology, or between ex post preferences and "real interests." The consumption of habit-forming drugs provides a good example. Pigou's argument regarding the defective telescopic faculty is another.

Even in this category, some examples may be reconcilable with a broad interpretation of consumer sovereignty or Pareto optimality. Thus, some of the objections by elite groups to the "inferiority" of popular tastes in certain fields may be interpreted in terms of external economies and diseconomies. The case for adjustment of individual preferences can then be rested upon the resulting psychic benefits to the "external observer."[19] Such a reconciliation does not, however, do full justice to most of the examples usually discussed in this connection.[20] The central concept of irrational or inferior preferences thus remains to some degree elitist and authoritarian. Even here, however, some reconciliation with a very broad interpretation of consumer sovereignty may be possible in cases where consumers voluntarily surrender their sovereignty over certain types of choices to government. There are many examples which might be quoted here. The cultural dictatorship exercised by BBC radio in the United Kingdom during the 1930s would seem to be one. In many other cases, no doubt, such an interpretation is not possible.

[18] The term *irrationality* is thus used here in the broad nontechnical sense to describe a preference which, although unaffected by ignorance, is nevertheless contrary to the individual's welfare or best interests. It should not be confused with irrationality in the narrow technical sense of "intransitivity" as used, for example, in modern consumer behavior theory.

[19] See chap. 10, sec. 4.2.3. In this connection it is interesting to notice that Tiebout and Houston (p. 414) appear to define the merit goods concept precisely in terms of this particular category of externalities. A similar interpretation is to be found in M. V. Pauly, "Efficiency in the Provision of Consumption Subsidies," *Kyklos,* 1970.

It seems reasonable to suppose that many people would like to see some adjustment in the preference patterns of other groups and individuals. Note, however, that such desires may stem from a variety of motives, including envy, admiration, etc., and not merely from an altruistic concern for the welfare of others. Note also that this justification for public intervention disappears if there is a sufficiently strong and widespread "liberal" feeling that such desires represent intolerable meddling in the affairs of others. It is possible, for example, that each person may respect his own "disinterested" merit goods desires, but reject those of most others as "none of their business."

[20] In most of the traditional examples it is clearly implied that the case for intervention rests firmly on the "welfare" of the individuals concerned, not on the tastes of the "objective" and "disinterested" external observer. Such examples are by definition Pareto-irrelevant.

McLure would seem to confine the merit goods concept to those cases of irrational or inferior preferences which cannot be reconciled with consumer sovereignty or Pareto optimality, broadly interpreted.[21] I find no warrant for this in Musgrave's discussion. Indeed the general tone of his discussion strongly suggests the contrary; and he explicitly excludes all cases which cannot be reconciled with his "normative model based upon a democratic society."[22]

## 2.3   Other Characteristics

It is clear from Musgrave's discussion that incorrect or distorted preferences constitute the essential characteristic of the merit goods concept. However, as with a public good, which turns out on examination to have several quite distinct characteristics, it appears that Musgrave's merit goods may also have further characteristics.[23] In particular, merit goods may be the subject of special distributional objectives, as in the case of health or education services where some degree of equality or certain minimum standards may be desired. Moreover, merit goods frequently exhibit public goods characteristics.[24] Certain services, e.g. health and education, may therefore compound all three characteristics of preference-distortion problems, distributional problems and public goods problems.

Although Musgrave's discussion serves to draw our attention to what may well be an empirically significant phenomenon, it is quite evident, both from his own treatment and on analytical grounds, that the three characteristics are nevertheless quite distinct in principle

---

[21] McLure, passim. To illustrate the dangers of an interpretation of Musgrave based on the consumer sovereignty concept, it is interesting to notice that at least one leading welfare theorist would interpret consumer sovereignty in terms of preferences corrected for all effects of both ignorance and irrationality. See Rothenberg. The corresponding concept of a Pareto-optimum would therefore be based not on overt preferences but rather on a normalized set of consumer preferences adjusted for the effects of both ignorance and irrationality.

[22] See Musgrave, p. 14. As he puts it, "interferences with consumer choice may occur simply because a ruling group considers its particular set of mores superior and wishes to impose it on others. Such determination of wants rests on an authoritarian basis, not permissible in our normative model based upon a democratic society."

[23] See chap. 10, secs. 3.2 and 3.3 above.

[24] Due (p. 14) would appear to regard this as the main characteristic of a merit want. Buchanan (p. 237) goes even further and suggests that it is the only characteristic. Specifically he interprets the merit want concept as a confused attempt by Musgrave to cover the important intermediate cases lying between the unrealistic case of a pure public good and the case of a private good. McLure at one point makes a somewhat similar comment. See his sec. 3 (a). This does not seem, however, to be a plausible interpretation.

and often in practice.[25] It may therefore be desirable for many purposes to preserve a sharp distinction between "corrective goods," "necessity goods," and "public goods," each concept epitomizing one of the three characteristics frequently found together in the merit good.[26]

## 2.4  Merit Goods in Other "Branches"

In Musgrave's discussion, the role of the merit goods concept is essentially restricted to the allocation branch. As we have just seen, the central characteristic of incorrect preferences happens empirically to be associated with an interesting and somewhat neglected distributional problem, but the two market failure concepts remain analytically distinct. As in the case of public goods, the central merit goods problems of ignorance and irrationality are restricted to the allocation branch. Much of my original paper is devoted to showing the important role of these same problems in the other branches of distribution, stabilization and growth. Both concepts of ignorance (or uncertainty) and irrationality are shown to play a vital role in market failure problems in these other branches.[27] It is emphasized that in many, though not all, of these cases, public intervention is quite consistent with a broad concept of consumer sovereignty or Pareto optimality. The most notable exceptions are to be found in the irrationality category, for example in the distribution and growth branches,[28] though these exceptions might be further reduced if we allow for the possibility of a voluntary surrender of sovereignty.[29] In the light of the above discussion, it should be clear why I completely reject McLure's suggestion[30] that this part of my original paper is essentially unrelated to the merit goods concept.

## 2.5  A Question of Optimal Semantics

Ultimately, McLure's arguments seem to rest on what Musgrave "should have said" rather than on what he actually said or even "really

---

[25] See chap. 10, secs. 3.2 and 3.3 above.

[26] The term *necessity goods* is suggested by Tiebout and Houston, p. 415. The concept is developed in an interesting way by Scitovsky in *Papers on Welfare and Growth* (London, 1964), chap. 16.

[27] See chap. 10, sec. 4 above.

[28] See ibid., secs. 4.1.2 and 4.4.2.

[29] See sec. 2.2.2 above.

[30] McLure, passim.

meant to say."[31] There is indeed an interesting and important question
of optimal semantics involved. If, as my original paper showed, and
McLure agrees, so many cases of ignorant and irrational preferences
can be shown to be examples of Pareto-relevant nonappropriability
or externality problems, would it not be better terminologically to
include these in the general category of externality problems, and reserve the term "merit goods" for those cases in which no reconciliation
with a broad concept of consumer sovereignty or Pareto optimality is
possible? For many purposes such a usage may indeed be very convenient. Musgrave's apparent usage in *The Theory of Public Finance*
serves, however, to point up and relate certain aspects of many nonappropriability or externality problems which have become submerged
in the modern public finance discussion of the public goods concept.

## 2.6   The Technique of Public Intervention

It may be useful to consider, finally, whether provision for merit
goods presupposes any particular technique of public intervention. The
merit goods concept may perhaps be characterized not only by ignorance and irrationality but also by a particular mode of public provision.

With all merit goods problems a number of different techniques of
public intervention are presumably available, including the supply of
relevant information, fiscal inducements and penalties, public production, centralized directives setting certain standards or levels of consumption or production, etc. In the case of the demerit good of cigarette
consumption, for example, the government may supply information to
consumers and/or manufacturers on the health hazards involved, it
may tax or ban what is felt to be misleading advertising by the manu-
facturer, it may tax cigarette consumption, it may impose physical
limits on production, introduce cigarette rationing, etc. It may be
possible, at least in principle, to design measures or combinations of
measures in several of these forms, each of which would produce with

[31] In more recent writings, Musgrave certainly appears extremely uneasy about his
original concept. See, in particular, R. A. Musgrave, "Provision for Social Goods,"
presented at the International Economic Association, Proceedings of the Biarritz
Conference, 1966, Section D, and subsequently published in J. Margolis and H. Guitton,
eds., *Public Economics* (London, 1969), sec. 4. Specifically he seems to edge towards an
interpretation in terms of the psychic externalities derived from the provision of "necessity goods"! His comments are rather sketchy, however, and hardly constitute a systematically developed alternative to his original discussion. In any case, my concern in
the present context has been with the interpretation of what, to my mind, is the carefully thought out and consistent position to be found in *The Theory of Public Finance*.

similar efficiency precisely the desired adjustment of consumption. Amongst these, however, only those measures which involve some form of "physical compulsion" might be regarded as true merit goods policies. Of the alternatives mentioned, the centralized directives or quota-type provisions, and possibly the fiscal penalties, might be classed as merit goods policies. Note, however, that on the basis of this crude classification, many policies for Pareto-efficient *public* goods supply would take on merit goods characteristics.

A related but much more sophisticated alternative would be to classify as merit goods policies only those forms of public intervention which do not satisfy the Pareto test.[32] Under this approach all policies designed to deal with those merit goods problems which are not reconcilable with the broad consumer sovereignty concept would be classified as merit goods policies. Policies designed to deal with Pareto-relevant merit goods problems would, however, be regarded as merit goods policies only if they did not satisfy the Pareto test.[33] Note in this latter case that if the test is applied ex ante, the control of consumption by centralized directives, however accurate, fails to satisfy the Pareto test and thus constitutes a merit goods policy. If, however, the test is applied ex post, the individual may well feel better off and the merit goods label does not apply. Here again the problem also arises that allocatively efficient policies to supply purely public goods may likewise fail to satisfy the Pareto test. Do they thereby become merit goods policies?

Ignoring this latter problem, the central issue here seems to turn on the fact that the consumer may be "supplied with information" in different ways. One of these is to provide information or financial inducements. Another is to compel or tax him into experiencing a different level of consumption. As a result of this experience he may choose voluntarily to continue at the new level of consumption without public intervention. The choice between these alternative techniques should presumably be based largely on their relative efficiency. It therefore seems undesirable to base the merit goods classification on what ap-

[32] McLure (p. 479) explicitly considers this possibility, but appears to reject it. Taking his discussion as a whole, however, it does seem to represent the essential logic of his position.

[33] Here, as elsewhere in our discussion, it is important to distinguish clearly between the Pareto optimum (with its associated concept of "Pareto optimality") and the Pareto criterion or Pareto test (with the associated concept of "Pareto desirability"). For recent emphasis on the need for a sharp distinction here and for a very clear exposition of the difference, see C. S. Shoup, *Public Finance* (Chicago, 1969), chap. 21. Pareto relevance is different again, being determined on the basis of a hypothetical compensation test. On this concept, see J. M. Buchanan and W. C. Stubblebine, "Externality," *Economica*, 1962.

pears to be merely an ideological preference for one technique of public intervention over another.[34,35]

## 3. The Role of the Merit Goods Concept in Normative Theory

It is one thing to settle the problem of interpreting the merit goods concept. It is, of course, quite another to show that the concept, once defined, has a legitimate place in a normative theory of public policy. As the discussion of this issue in my original paper was rather sketchy and unsystematic,[36] and as McLure vigorously denies the legitimacy of the concept as he interprets it,[37] some further discussion of this crucial question seems desirable.

### 3.1   The Pareto Approach to Normative Theory

A position of extreme individualism might suggest that the Pareto criterion provides the only appropriate foundation for a normative

---

[34] Even Mill was willing to allow that more coercive methods of public intervention may sometimes be justified on efficiency grounds, in spite of his strong ideological preference for more conventional methods of supplying information. As he comments, on the case for public education, ". . . a thing of which the public are bad judges may require to be shown to them and pressed on their attention for a long time, and to prove its advantages by long experience, before they learn to appreciate it, yet they may learn at last; which they might never have done, if the thing had not been thus obtruded upon them in act, but only recommended in theory." He then goes on to state the case for compulsory education at the elementary level. See J. S. Mill, *Principles of Political Economy*, Ashley ed. (London, 1909), p. 954.

[35] In modern public goods analysis there has been a similar attempt to avoid a classification based in any way on the precise technique of public intervention. Thus, for example, a classification based on whether the good is publicly or privately *produced* has been explicitly and no doubt rightly rejected. The precise technique of public intervention should be determined on efficiency grounds, and a classification based on means tends to beg this crucial question. See, for example, Musgrave, chap. 3, sec. A. Note that Musgrave uses the term *social wants* for what are here called public goods. He uses the term *public goods* to refer to goods produced publicly, a rather unfortunate terminology.

[36] On the contested question of adjusting irrational or inferior preferences, the relevant comments are to be found in chap. 10, pp. 219–20 and 227–28 above.

[37] McLure, passim, but especially sec. 3. McLure's position is, however, obscured by his curious argument that many of the central merit wants problems of ignorance and irrationality discussed in my paper represent "cases in which the underlying assumptions of traditional welfare economics do not hold" (p. 475), "questions about which welfare economics offers no solution" (p. 482), are "not adequately treated by the theory of welfare economics" (ibid.), "do not fit very well into the framework of economic theory" (ibid.). His arguments condemning the merit wants concept from the standpoint of welfare theory thus appear to assume away the central merit goods characteristics and refer

theory of public policy.[38] According to this criterion, only those policies are desirable which make at least some people better off and none worse off. The ultimate objective of policy under this approach would be to implement all and only those policies which satisfy this test. At first glance, such a theory seems likely to be extremely conservative and quite unduly restrictive of the legitimate economic functions of government. It was, of course, in an attempt to avoid or overcome these problems that the great variety of hypothetical compensation criteria, from Kaldor to Little, were developed.[39]

As a result of more recent work by Baumol and Buchanan, however, it has become increasingly clear that the Pareto criterion is potentially much less narrow and restrictive than had been thought.[40] Within the allocation branch, the possibility of actual compensation, package deals, and longer-run interpretations of the criterion itself removes much of the apparent restrictiveness. The criterion can also quite readily be extended from the allocation branch to the other branches; it has been shown that the Pareto criterion can be used to justify a wide variety of stabilization, growth and even redistributive policies. A subsidiary objective of my merit goods paper was in fact to systematize and further extend this demonstration of the range of potentially Pareto-desirable public policies; and a major objective was to show the considerable range of merit goods policies (to deal with generalized ignorance and irrationality problems) which are potentially reconcilable with a broad interpretation of the Pareto criterion.[41]

McLure apparently identifies this Pareto approach with the consumer sovereignty concept to which Musgrave so often refers, and proceeds to base his critique of the narrow merit goods concept on this particular foundation.[42] It should not, however, be thought, as McLure

only to some completely arbitrary and authoritarian conception. In this way he seems to miss the whole point of the merit goods concept, which is precisely to recognize, and to some extent redress, these evident inadequacies in the conventional welfare framework.

[38] This approach has been particularly persuasively developed in the writings of Buchanan. See, for example, "Positive Economics, Welfare Economics, and Political Economy," *Journal of Law and Economics*, 1959. It is implicitly accepted by McLure.

[39] See chap. 1, sec. 2 in this volume.

[40] In addition to the important paper by Buchanan cited in n. 38 above, see especially, W. J. Baumol, *Welfare Economics and the Theory of the State* (Cambridge, Mass., 1952); and J. M. Buchanan, "The Relevance of Pareto Optimality," *Journal of Conflict Resolution*, 1962. It is extremely important to notice that, in spite of his own impressive demonstration of the scope of the Pareto criterion, Baumol would regard it only as a sufficient criterion for policy, not necessary and sufficient as we have interpreted it above. In Baumol's interpretation a policy which fails to satisfy the Pareto test simply cannot be judged, whereas in the influential Buchanan approach it would be rejected.

[41] See chap. 10, secs. 4 and 5, above.

[42] McLure, sec. 3.

seems to imagine, that this Pareto approach is the only possible, or even the natural, interpretation of the consumer sovereignty tradition.[43] The consumer sovereignty concept has traditionally been unconcerned with matters of income distribution. The hypothetical compensationist criteria of Kaldor, Hicks and Scitovsky are therefore the natural heirs of the consumer sovereignty tradition. The Pareto criterion is obtained only when "consumer sovereignty" is extended into the distribution branch. In this way we obtain an approach based on individual values rather than consumer sovereignty.

According to the Pareto approach, those merit goods policies which do not satisfy the Pareto test are evidently illegitimate. Since McLure restricts the merit goods concept to precisely such cases, he concludes that the concept has no place in this particular normative framework. In terms of the broader concept espoused in my paper, he would not, of course, contest the place of Pareto-relevant merit goods problems in this framework, as long as the corrective policies employed satisfy the Pareto test.[44] As the contested area is confined to the merit goods concept in the narrow sense, we shall restrict further discussion to this narrower concept.

McLure's main concern in this context appears to be to show that the narrow merit goods concept has no legitimate place in Musgrave's normative framework, which he identifies both with the notoriously ambiguous consumer sovereignty concept and, more precisely, with the Pareto approach. A careful reading of Musgrave, however, reveals little evidence that he would accept either the Pareto approach or consumer sovereignty (however interpreted) as fully equivalent to his own multibranch framework. Both in his merit goods discussion and in his discussion of equity, Musgrave clearly expresses strong reservations about the adequacy of individual preferences as the foundation for a general normative theory. His concern seems rather to elaborate an appropriate set of norms for a democratic society.[45]

---

[43] See, for example, Rothenberg, sec. 1.

[44] By contrast, the consumer sovereignty tradition, as interpreted above, would embrace all Pareto-relevant merit goods problems as long as the relevant corrective policies were *potentially* Pareto-desirable.

[45] The careful reader will notice that Musgrave refers repeatedly to democracy as an ultimate standard. Thus he refers to his "normative theory of public economy based upon the premise of individual preference *in a democratic society"* (p. 13, my italics), and to his "normative model based upon a democratic society" (p. 14). Musgrave evidently regards the concept of democracy as constraining the sway of consumer sovereignty in important respects, particularly in the fields of equity and merit wants. In itself, however, the concept of democracy seems rather too ambiguous to provide a clear set of restrictions on the already ambiguous consumer sovereignty concept. His "multiple theory" should therefore be interpreted as reflecting his own view of the "good democracy."

However, the Pareto approach has been used by other writers, notably Buchanan, to criticize not only the narrow merit goods concept but also Musgrave's multibranch framework.[46] The central problem of justifying the merit goods concept therefore remains.

## 3.2  Alternative Approaches to Normative Theory[47]

### 3.2.1  The ethical approach

The great attractions of the Pareto approach are its firm foundation in individual values and its general acceptability. To an extreme individualist the emphasis on individual values and the absence of coercion may constitute a sufficient ethical attraction. This seems to be Buchanan's position. There are, however, other ethical systems of great cogency and influence which would impose certain limits on the sovereignty of individual values.[48] In many of these systems some adjustment of irrational or inferior preferences may well be justified. Musgrave's vision of a "normative model based upon a democratic society" appears to be one such system. The mere assertion of the Pareto criterion is evidently insufficient to demolish such an ethical approach to justification of the narrower merit goods concept. When different ethical visions of the good society conflict, there is no ultimate arbiter to whom we can turn.

### 3.2.2  The acceptability approach

For many welfare theorists the general acceptability of the Pareto criterion is valued for its own sake, rather than on ideological grounds. The policy adviser understandably seeks acceptability, relevance, and influence. According to this view, a normative theory should above all generate acceptable policy proposals.

Even from this point of view, however, the Pareto approach is vulnerable. Individual values vary widely and may well conflict on many issues, notably those involving merit goods. In such cases Pareto-acceptable counsel cannot be offered.

Under these circumstances the welfare economist has two obvious alternatives: either he can accept the values of his particular client, including his views on the inadequacy of consumer choices in certain

---

[46] See Buchanan, "The Theory of Public Finance."

[47] These alternatives are developed in more detail in chap. 2 above.

[48] Wicksell, for example, was willing to apply his consensus requirement (and hence the Pareto criterion) only in the presence of a just property order. See Knut Wicksell, "A New Principle of Just Taxation," in R. A. Musgrave and A. T. Peacock, eds., *Classics in the Theory of Public Finance* (London and New York, 1958), pp. 108–9.

areas; or he must surrender his policy influence on these issues. Some welfare economists would no doubt choose the first alternative, which allows a role for the narrow merit goods concept; others, like Buchanan and Baumol, would presumably choose the second, which allows no such role. There appears to be no reason why a normative theorist concerned above all with acceptability, relevance or influence should not choose the first alternative.

### 3.2.3  The positivistic approach

Another approach is possible where, as suggested by Archibald,[49] the welfare framework is given a strictly positivistic interpretation. Recognizing that the consumption of certain drugs is regarded by some groups as irrational and contrary to the consumer's own welfare, the theorist might simply label these "demerit goods." He might then proceed to analyse the requirements for "optimal demerit goods supply" without any implication or commitment as to the desirability or otherwise of such policies. He would simply hope that such analysis would be "useful" or "interesting" in policy discussions. In contrast to the previous approach, his aim here is the more modest one of providing useful information rather than acceptable policy recommendations.

### 3.2.4  The political approach

One of the most obvious difficulties with the merit goods concept, and particularly with the irrationality aspects under consideration in this section, is that appropriate merit goods policies are seldom likely to be politically operational, except by chance.[50] And where the political mechanism does seem to be consistent with the preference adjustments required by, say, an ethical concept of merit goods, it is often equally consistent with a wide variety of other preference-adjustment policies. A theorist in the modern welfare politics tradition might therefore prefer a political approach to the merit goods concept, in which the necessary adjustments to individual preferences include all and only those which would result from an appropriately specified political system, e.g. majority voting.[51]

---

[49] See G. C. Archibald, "Welfare Economics, Ethics, and Essentialism," *Economica*, 1959.
[50] See chap. 10, sec. 6 above.
[51] Musgrave's approach has some flavor of both the ethical and the political approaches. His merit goods policies would seem to be those which would be implemented in the "good democracy." See n. 45 above.

## 3.3   A Relativistic Approach to Welfare Methodology

In the light of the above discussion it seems evident that there are various approaches to normative theory which would allow a role to the narrow merit goods concept. The position taken here is that the Pareto approach is just one of a number of alternative approaches to normative theory, each of which, whilst having possible disadvantages in terms of the other approaches,[52] is methodologically legitimate.[53] My own feeling is that the welfare framework of public finance theory should be capable of incorporating a generalized preference-adjustment concept.

## 4.   Conclusions

Although the merit goods concept, as presented in Musgrave's *Theory of Public Finance,* poses considerable problems of interpretation, I find McLure's arguments unconvincing. For Musgrave, on my interpretation, the merit goods concept serves to epitomize those problems of ignorance and irrationality which have formed the basis of traditional reservations to a narrow and dogmatic interpretation of the consumer sovereignty concept.

Such a merit goods concept clearly requires in general a broader welfare framework than that provided by the Pareto approach. Other approaches to welfare theory are, however, possible and even preferable. Bergson's recent discussion provides an excellent example.[54] I agree that in the hands of an economist, the preference-adjustment concept soon becomes superficial and speculative. In the detailed design of a general normative theory, the economist qua economist may have relatively little to contribute. I conclude, however, with Scitovsky, that "if the economist feels incompetent to make such judgements himself, he should at least admit their legitimacy and provide the analytical framework to help others to make these judgements."[55]

[52] Arrow's well known "Impossibility Theorem" can be interpreted as showing that there is no political mechanism capable of satisfying the requirements of a particular ethical ideal. There is therefore necessarily some degree of conflict between any "political approach" and what he would regard as an "ethically-impelling approach." See K. J. Arrow, *Social Choice and Individual Values,* 2nd ed. (New York, 1963).

[53] See chap. 2 above.

[54] See A. Bergson, "On Social Welfare Once More," in his *Essays in Normative Economics* (Cambridge, Mass., 1966).

[55] Scitovsky, p. 249.

# 12.  Public Goods and Multilevel Government

## 1.  Introduction

One of the most striking features of the public finance literature of the past two decades has been the development of the modern theory of public goods, due largely to the pioneering contributions of Musgrave, Samuelson and Buchanan.[1] Most of the relevant analysis has been devoted to such problems as the clarification of the basic theoretical concepts, the demonstration of market failure in public goods supply, and the possibility of centralized political provision. Some attempt has, however, been made, led by Tiebout, Williams, Breton, and Buchanan, to develop the implications of the theory for multilevel government.[2] It is the aim of the present paper to explore some of these implications.

We shall begin, in section 2, with a brief discussion of the public goods concept. In section 3 we shall discuss some implications for optimal fiscal decentralization in the absence of spillovers. In section

Reprinted without significant change from W. L. David, ed., *Public Finance, Planning and Economic Development: Essays in Honour of Ursula Hicks* (London and New York: Macmillan and St. Martin's Press, 1973), pp. 20–43. I am indebted to Geoff Brennan and Tom McGuire for helpful comments.

[1] See, in particular, R. A. Musgrave, *The Theory of Public Finance* (New York, 1959); P. A. Samuelson, "The Pure Theory of Public Expenditure," *Review of Economics and Statistics*, 1954; J. M. Buchanan, *The Demand and Supply of Public Goods* (Chicago, 1968).

[2] See, for example, C. M. Tiebout, "A Pure Theory of Local Expenditures," *Journal of Political Economy*, 1956, and "An Economic Theory of Fiscal Decentralization," in *Public Finances: Needs, Sources and Utilization* (Princeton, 1961); A. Williams, "The Optimal Provision of Public Goods in a System of Local Government," *Journal of Political Economy*, 1966; A. Breton, "A Theory of Government Grants," *Canadian Journal of Economics and Political Science*, 1965; J. M. Buchanan, "Comment" on R. A. Musgrave, "Approaches to A Fiscal Theory of Political Federalism," in *Public Finances: Needs, Sources and Utilization;* J. M. Buchanan and R. E. Wagner, "An Efficiency Basis For Federal Fiscal Equalization," in J. Margolis, ed., *The Analysis of Public Output* (New York, 1970).

4 we shall explore the fiscal coordination problems which arise when public goods benefits spill over. In section 5, we shall discuss the special problem of grants to poor unit governments. Section 6 contains a brief discussion of some of the wider implications of the theory.


## 2. The Concept of Public Goods

A pure public good, in the original formulations of Samuelson and Musgrave, is one which must be consumed in equal amounts by all. Polaris submarine deterrent provides a good example. Such a good has two main characteristics. The first is "joint supply," in the special sense that, once it is supplied to one person, equal quantities of identical quality services can be made available to other persons without limit at no extra cost. The second is "impossibility of exclusion": if the service is supplied to one person, it cannot be withheld from any other person wishing to consume it. A third characteristic, of somewhat less importance in the present context, is nonrejectability: once the service is supplied, it must be fully and equally consumed by all, including by those who would if possible reject it.

It is easy to show that the market mechanism must fail dramatically in the supply of a pure public good, due mainly to the problem of impossibility of exclusion. The joint supply characteristic also creates complicated differential pricing requirements, which no decentralized market mechanism can handle effectively. Political provision offers, by comparison, significant advantages, notably a crude exclusion device in the form of the tax power, though significant problems undoubtedly remain.[3]

The concept of a pure public good clearly represents an extreme polar case of limited empirical significance. The concept can, however, readily be generalized; and similar, though less dramatic, conclusions regarding market failure and political provision can be shown to hold for impure public goods.

The Samuelsonian joint supply characteristic can be generalized in two distinct dimensions. In the first place it is common for the benefits of a joint good to taper off in some pattern from the point of input, such as fire protection which diminishes with distance from the fire house. Other examples readily spring to mind in such areas as police services, emergency hospital services, recreational services, etc.

---

[3] For a more detailed discussion of public goods characteristics, market failure problems and public provision, see chap. 3 above.

For a given population distributed in a given pattern over a given area, the benefits from such a service are not equal, as with Polaris submarine deterrent, but vary with distance from the input unit. The location of the input unit, such as the fire house, the hospital or the park may be fixed, especially in the short run, but is in general variable, at least in the long run. Different consumers and producers will also be variously affected by other characteristics of the input unit; a given police force may be better trained and equipped to deal with some types of crime than with others.[4]

The joint supply characteristic can be generalized in a second and quite distinct dimension, as we envisage a steady increase in the population of a given area with no change in the general pattern of distribution. For a fixed facility (fire brigade, hospital establishment, park service, etc.) of given capacity, it is evident that, in contrast to Polaris submarine deterrent, it is only up to a certain point that the same standard of service can be supplied to additional persons without extra cost. Beyond that point, congestion sets in and the standard of service deteriorates.[5]

The second public goods characteristic of "impossibility of exclusion" is easily seen to be a special and extreme case of the general Pigovian concept of external economies.[6] This characteristic can therefore readily be generalized to cover empirically more significant cases such as that in which prices could readily be charged for some but not all of the benefits of a particular service. Examples might include the "vocational" as against the "cultural" benefits of educational services, and public health services such as a vaccination program. The externalities involved will generally have both spatial and other dimensions. In the case of education, for example, the cultural externalities may spill over into neighboring areas as a result of migration.

By means of these various generalizations the public goods concept can be expanded to encompass a broad spectrum of services all exhibiting important joint supply or nonexclusion characteristics, and posing varying but significant market failure problems and possibilities for public provision.

---

[4] For a general analysis of this aspect of the joint supply characteristic, see J. M. Buchanan, "Joint Supply, Externality, and Optimality," *Economica*, 1966.

[5] For a general analysis of this dimension of joint supply, see J. M. Buchanan, "An Economic Theory of Clubs," *Economica*, 1965. The various dimensions of the relevant cost functions are nicely distinguished by C. S. Shoup, *Public Finance* (Chicago, 1969), pp. 79–86.

[6] See chap. 8 above.

# 3. Public Goods and Fiscal Decentralization

Different levels of government are distinguished conventionally by the scope of the geographical area over which their respective jurisdictions extend. Central government jurisdiction extends by definition over the entire area under consideration. Regional governments administer nonoverlapping subsections of the "country." Local governments exercise responsibility over nonoverlapping areas within a region. Such governments are variously denominated in practice under different systems, federal and unitary, and in principle a much more elaborately tiered structure can readily be imagined.[7] In practice, of course, noneconomic factors have exercised considerable influence on the precise structure of multilevel government, and constitutional and other rigidities impede change. Assuming away all these problems, it is, however, interesting to consider how a system of multilevel government should be structured from the point of view of ensuring an efficient supply of the many varieties of public goods, pure and impure. For purposes of the present section we shall assume artificially that the benefits from public goods supply in a given jurisdiction do not extend (are neither sold nor spill over) to neighboring jurisdictions.

In this context the crucial dimensions of the public goods concept are clearly those relating to area and population. In the case of a pure public good such as Polaris submarine deterrent, provision should clearly be assigned to a single unit of government with jurisdiction over the entire area and population under consideration. The service does not taper off with area covered, and additional persons can be supplied at no extra cost. Per capita cost is therefore minimized by central government provision. (Even this, of course, is no absolute minimum, since with a pure public good, per capita cost falls without limit and optimum population size is literally infinite.)[8] Pareto-optimal provision clearly also requires full knowledge of individual preference functions by the central planning agency. The preference

---

[7] Indeed the standard conception of government units based on area should ideally be generalized to allow for the possibility of units based on economic ("functional"), racial, religious, linguistic and other characteristics. To simplify the discussion we shall assume conventionally that the spatial dimension is in some sense more fundamental. It might, for example, be argued that, at least in some cases where other characteristics are of particular and independent significance, generalized public goods interaction (e.g. racial, religious, or class prejudice) will tend to produce spatial groupings based on the relevant characteristic. In a more general analysis, however, the locational dimension of each public good would need to be supplemented by other dimensions in the design of an optimal structure of multilevel government.

[8] See Buchanan, "An Economic Theory of Clubs."

revelation problems involved in practice are a familiar theme in the modern public goods literature.[9]

In a world polarized between pure public goods and pure private goods, it is therefore evident that multilevel government has no economic place. Private goods should be provided by decentralized market institutions and public goods by centralized political institutions, chosen to ensure the best possible approximation to full preference revelation. As we have already seen, however, the pure public good concept is of very limited empirical significance. When the concept is generalized along the lines suggested in section 2, we find a considerable variety of "impure" goods for which public provision may be appropriate.

When we depart from the pure public goods concept, a possible case for lower level or "multibranch" provision is not difficult to construct. This is perhaps most clearly seen in a simple case in which a given and completely immobile population with the same tastes and incomes is distributed uniformly over a given area. Assume a very simple polar case of a regional or local public good, which is purely public only over a limited area (which we shall assume to be a simple fraction of the total area of the country). The same level of service can be extended to additional households, and over a wider area, up to this given limit without extra cost. Beyond this limited area the benefit "tapers off" suddenly to zero. In such a case the public good must be provided by a number of regional or local governments (or "branches," if provision is assigned initially to a single agency). The country should simply be divided into nonoverlapping jurisdictions of a size equal to the technologically fixed benefit area for the public good. In this way the per capita cost of providing a uniform Pareto-optimal level of service throughout the country is clearly minimized.

Somewhat more realistically we might alternatively assume no rigid area limit to the extension of benefits, but suppose instead that some extra cost is necessarily involved as a given and uniform level of service is extended to additional households over a wider area. Following Tiebout, it might, for example, be assumed that per capita cost per unit of service (unit cost per resident) falls initially as a larger area and population are covered, but subsequently rises, due, for example, to the impact of transport costs. Combining this relationship with, say, a conventional U-shaped relationship between unit cost and service level (for given area and population), a cost surface is obtained from which, with the aid of the preference functions, the least-cost

---

[9] See Samuelson, "The Pure Theory of Public Expenditure."

jurisdiction for the optimal level of service can readily be determined.[10] (It is assumed that there is no spillover of benefit beyond the boundaries of the least-cost jurisdiction.) Again a lower level government or multibranch agency will be required to provide a uniform Pareto-optimal level of service throughout the country.

It is not difficult to generalize this second example to cover the empirically much more significant case in which the level of service over the benefit area is not uniform but tapers off from some point of input as in the case of fire protection or recreational services. With given cost and demand conditions, the maximization of surplus in relation to cost will require the establishment of a number of service branches distinguished by points of input (e.g. antimissile sites, fire stations, police stations, hospitals, parks, etc.) at regular intervals over the area under consideration. Each local branch would ideally provide the same tapering pattern of service over a least-cost jurisdiction for that Pareto-optimal standard of service.[11]

When the simplifying assumptions of uniform tastes, incomes and population distribution are relaxed, the country-wide uniformities in Pareto-optimal service standards and least-cost jurisdictions disappear. Higher standards of service should be provided in high-taste, high-income areas; and the ideal jurisdiction will vary in size, depending upon the precise cost function for the particular service, from one part of the country to another. Within a given jurisdiction the possibilities of discrimination in the case of "tapering" services should be fully exploited to provide a higher level of service to clusters of high-taste, high-income households by appropriate location of the relevant input units (fire station, park, etc.).[12]

It should be noted that with the taste, income and area homogeneities previously assumed, there is no clear case for any genuine delegation of political decision-making powers to the local governments or branches, which need merely administer centralized decisions regarding the level of service provision.[13] We have so far justified

---

[10] For a detailed analysis, see Tiebout, "An Economic Theory of Fiscal Decentralization," pp. 82–87.

[11] For a more detailed discussion, see ibid., pp. 87–90.

[12] For the relevant optimality requirements, see Buchanan, "Joint Supply, Externality, and Optimality."

[13] This point has recently been stressed by Hartle and Bird, who note that what is involved here is the fundamental public finance distinction between public production and public provision. See D. G. Hartle and R. M. Bird, "Criteria for the Design of Governmental Decision-Making Units," Canadian Economics Association Conference, 1969. For the contrary view, see M. Olson, "The Principle of 'Fiscal Equivalence,'" *American Economic Review, Papers and Proceedings*, 1969.

only decentralized "production" not decentralized "provision" in the strict public finance sense. When these uniformities are relaxed and effective preferences vary widely, the resulting problems may well justify genuine decentralization of political decision-making. In particular, preference-revelation problems, together with constitutional or quasi-constitutional rigidities, such as geographically nondiscriminatory taxation, may drastically limit the scope for interregional variation in service levels within a given jurisdiction. As a result there may be obvious gains to be derived from political decentralization under a wide variety of circumstances.[14] This possibility is particularly evident, however, if we make the reasonable assumption that preferences tend to be much more homogeneous within given regions and localities than between them.[15] In this situation the differing preferences of different regions and localities can clearly be satisfied only under appropriately decentralized political decision-making. An optimal structure of multilevel government thus takes on a more "federal" and less "unitary" appearance.

A crucial assumption which we have so far retained is that the population is completely immobile. Relaxation of this assumption opens up interesting new possibilities. For example, in the very simple polar case of a regional or local public good, which is purely public only over a limited area, the same standard of service can be extended to additional persons at no extra cost. Per capita cost could therefore be further reduced by concentrating population through migration. Minimum per capita cost would require that the whole population be concentrated in a single jurisdiction. This case is probably of limited empirical significance, but it may have some validity for a service such as damage limitation through antimissile defense. For overall efficiency, possible reductions in per capita cost of public goods achieved through population concentration must of course be balanced against possible increases in the cost of private goods production due to diminishing returns.[16]

As we have already seen, the extreme joint supply characteristic can readily be generalized to allow for congestion phenomena such that, beyond a point, the same standard of service can be supplied to additional persons in a given area only at some extra cost. Even here it is quite possible that per capita cost could be significantly reduced

[14] The advantages of decentralized political decision-making, based on the assumption of rigid interregional uniformity of service levels under centralized provision, are analyzed by Y. Barzel, "Two Propositions on the Optimum Level of Producing Collective Goods," *Public Choice*, 1969.
[15] This assumption is strongly supported by Hartle and Bird. See ibid.
[16] See Buchanan and Wagner, "An Efficiency Basis for Federal Fiscal Equalisation."

by increased population concentration. Beyond a point, however, the total cost of maintaining a given level of service may rise so steeply that per capita cost increases.[17] As density is increased, a new least cost jurisdiction may be determined corresponding to a new and presumably somewhat higher optimal service level.

When public goods preferences vary widely (but incomes are similar), population mobility offers the further interesting possibility that an initial optimum may be improved by the regrouping of population in accordance with public goods preferences. Instead of having to consume a small volume of a given local public good in a jurisdiction dominated by low-demand people, a minority with high public goods demand may be able to move to another area dominated by high-demand people in which their preferences will clearly be better satisfied. It should be stressed that this point holds even under omniscient planning where local public goods supply is initially Pareto-optimal in each jurisdiction with tax-prices calculated on strict marginal benefit principles.

The possible advantages are, however, greatly increased when the unrealistic assumption of omniscient planning is relaxed and the preference-revelation problems in a world of diverse preferences are explicitly recognized. Thus, because of preference-revelation problems, a low-demand person may find himself paying the same high tax rates as high-demand people for the large volume of public good supplied in a predominantly high-demand area. This inefficiency in initial fiscal arrangements can, however, be removed if our low-demand person can move to a low-demand, low-tax jurisdiction. More generally, when combined with a sufficient variety in the volume and mix of public goods available in different local jurisdictions, population mobility may significantly improve resource allocation as people "vote on foot" by moving to jurisdictions in which their public goods preferences are most fully satisfied. As Tiebout first pointed out, population mobility thus offers a preference revelation mechanism for local public goods which is not available for central public goods such as Polaris submarine deterrent and applies only to a limited degree in the case of regional public goods for which the optimal number of jurisdictions is relatively small.[18]

When differences in income are allowed for, certain complications arise. High-income jurisdictions could generally be expected to offer a given standard of service at lower rates of tax. Low-income house-

[17] For a general discussion of the relevant cost relationships, see Shoup, pp. 84–86.
[18] See Tiebout, "A Pure Theory of Local Expenditures"; also G. J. Stigler, "The Tenable Range of Functions of Local Government," in Joint Economic Committee, *Federal Expenditure Policy for Economic Growth and Stability* (Washington, D.C., 1957).

holds would, of course, be attracted by these low tax rates. Various types of strategic behavior can be expected as high-income enclaves attempt to limit the entry of "undesirables," and low-income jurisdictions may find it necessary to depart from traditional tax principles of ability to pay and even from marginal benefit taxation in an attempt to retain high-income residents.[19] The efficiency of the Tiebout mechanism is in any case somewhat less than perfect due, for example, to limited population mobility and the existence of uncompensated spillovers associated with population movement.[20] On balance, however, the case for genuine decentralization of political decision-making is clearly strengthened to the extent that the Tiebout mechanism is operative.[21]

Summarizing the foregoing discussion, we see that when the concept of a public good is generalized to cover the broad spectrum of goods exhibiting varying but significant degrees of the crucial joint supply and nonexclusion characteristics, some degree of fiscal decentralization is clearly required. Some goods, like national defense, approximate the concept of a central public good and should be provided by a one-branch agency or central government. Others may be regional public goods requiring a limited number of regional branches or governments for optimal provision. University education, highways, and certain public health measures may be examples. Others again, like police and fire protection, are local public goods requiring a relatively very large number of local governments or agencies. Ideally an even more elaborate structure might well be required with a different "level" responsible for each relevant category of public good. The degree to which effective political decision-making power should be delegated to local units should depend upon the possible advantages to be derived in terms of preference revelation, which may be quite significant where taste and area heterogeneity are great. Where this is not the case, local units may simply be required to administer centralized decisions regarding the level of service provision.

## 4.  Public Goods and Fiscal Coordination

The arguments of the preceding section suggest that efficiency in public goods supply may well require a considerable degree of genuine

[19] For an interesting analysis of this possibility, see J. M. Buchanan, "Principles of Urban Fiscal Strategy," *Public Choice,* 1971.

[20] On the latter, see J. M. Buchanan and C. J. Goetz, "Efficiency Limits of Fiscal Mobility: An Assessment of the Tiebout Model," *Journal of Public Economics,* 1972.

[21] In principle a higher-level government might create a sufficient variety of local "branches" varying in the volume and mix of local public goods supplied. Constitutional

decentralization of political decision-making powers to regional and local units. An important simplifying assumption underlying the discussion has, however, been that the benefits from public goods supply in a given jurisdiction do not extend into neighboring jurisdictions. It remains to consider how the analysis is affected when this assumption is relaxed.[22]

The case for centralized provision would evidently be seriously undermined if we were to assume that, even though some benefits might be extended to neighboring jurisdictions at little or no extra cost, impossibility of exclusion does not apply for nonresidents. Even though nonexclusion applies for residents, exclusion is possible for nonresidents and fees can be charged.

In general, however, it must be recognized that where it is very difficult, costly or inefficient to price-exclude households within a given locality, there will usually be some unchargeable spillover of service to the residents of other localities. Some part of the benefit may spill over directly, as in the case of pollution control or mosquito spraying; it may spill over through commuting or migration as in the case of education, public health or road services; it may spill over through trade as in the case of cost-reducing public intermediate goods. Some spillovers of benefit are therefore inevitable even with a system of optimal boundaries designed in accordance with the general principles discussed in the preceding section. The problem is, however, enormously more significant in the case of any actual system of multilevel government, with local and regional boundaries determined historically with little regard for economic considerations. Generalized nonexclusion problems, which lead us to predict the failure of decentralized market institutions, therefore remain to plague genuinely (and, a fortiori, nonoptimally) decentralized political institutions.

Indeed the existence and geographical scope of benefit spillovers, i.e., the nonexclusion characteristic, comes to replace per capita cost (i.e., joint supply) as the essential foundation of the case for centralized provision in the arguments of the preceding section.[23] In the case of a pure public good, for example, the benefits spill over without

and other rigidities and problems of preference relevation tend, however, to produce a considerable degree of uniformity in standards of service provision within any given jurisdiction.

[22] It has also been assumed that the tax costs of public goods supplied in a given jurisdiction cannot be exported to neighboring jurisdictions. This assumption too is very unrealistic, but will be retained for simplicity in the following discussion.

[23] The crucial role of spillovers and the nonexcludability characteristic in the case for centralized provision has recently been stressed by Olson in his principle of "fiscal equivalence." See also G. Tullock, "Federalism: Problems of Scale," *Public Choice*, 1969.

geographical limit, and decentralized political institutions may fail almost completely in large-number cases. If, however, exclusion applies and the benefits can be sold to nonresidents, jointness alone provides no clear case for central provision.

By contrast, jointness or cost considerations emerge as directly relevant mainly for questions of production rather than provision in the strict sense. Per capita cost or jointness may, for example, justify a production unit serving a number of different jurisdictions. This is the point, first noted by Stigler and subsequently stressed by other writers, that "economies of scale" are of only limited relevance to the design of optimal boundaries for public goods provision, at least if we abstract from various forms of organizational rigidity.[24] Jointness may, however, play an important indirect role, notably in extreme cases where cost considerations require a high degree of interregional uniformity in service standards, thus eliminating one major disadvantage of centralized provision.

The distorting effects of benefit spillovers can be quite subtle and complicated. Take, for example, the simple case of taste, income and area uniformity (and complete immobility), in which, as we saw in the preceding section, the same standard of local government service should clearly be provided throughout the country. Any spillovers in this case will be symmetrical, with spillouts precisely matching spillins for any given jurisdiction. It is not true, however, as is sometimes suggested,[25] that such externalities necessarily cancel each other out leaving no net allocative distortion. Ignoring income effects, the spillout will probably vary directly with own output, thus in effect creating a distorting substitution effect against local production. The receipt of an equivalent spillin may not, however, create an offsetting substitution effect. In fact there will be no offset whatever if, as may well be the case, the amount of the spillin is completely independent of own output. A suboptimal standard of service should therefore be expected.[26]

Further complications arise when the assumption of interarea taste and income uniformity is relaxed and income effects are allowed for. Even retaining the assumption of symmetrical benefit-spillover functions with the asymmetrical substitution effects assumed above, it becomes possible that total output and consumption of the local

[24] See Stigler, p. 218. See also C. M. Tiebout and D. B. Houston, "Metropolitan Finance Reconsidered: Budget Functions and Multi-Level Governments," *Review of Economics and Statistics,* 1962; and G. Tullock.

[25] See, for example, Tiebout, "An Economic Theory of Fiscal Decentralization," pp. 91–92.

[26] See B. A. Weisbrod, "Comment" on Tiebout, in *Public Finances: Needs, Sources and Utilization,* pp. 131–32.

public good for the country as a whole may be *larger* than in the absence of spillovers—but still not Pareto-optimal.[27]

In any general analysis the assumption of symmetrical benefit-spillover functions must clearly be abandoned. As a result it must be recognized that production in one local jurisdiction may benefit residents in another, but not vice-versa. For example, because of prevailing winds, pollution control measures in A may benefit B's residents, but no reciprocal relationship may hold. Or, at least in the relevant ranges of production and consumption, education, public health or urban renewal measures in poverty-stricken area C may greatly benefit residents of D, with only a weak reciprocal relationship for corresponding measures in D. In such cases, the distortion takes the form of a significant relative underexpansion of service provision in the area generating the larger spillover. By distorting the location of "production," the effect of the spillover may be to cause a larger volume of resources to be devoted to the production of a lower standard of service over the country as a whole.[28]

A related problem which has been much discussed emerges in the Tiebout model of residential mobility, where high-income enclaves are able not merely to hive themselves off from a larger (city) unit, but may, by commuting, continue to receive the benefits of many city services as uncompensated spillovers. As a result the pattern of net spillovers may be highly asymmetrical between city and suburbs with consequent underexpansion of city services and charges of suburban exploitation of the city.[29]

[27] See A. Williams, "The Optimal Provision of Public Goods in a System of Local Government." Brainard and Dolbear have argued that overexpansion is possible in the Williams analysis only because his compensation scheme (to internalize the externality) would allow one local unit to be made worse off than under independent adjustment. This point was subsequently demonstrated rigorously for the case of a pure public good by Pauly. See W. C. Brainard and F. T. Dolbear, "The Possibility of Oversupply of Local 'Public' Goods: A Critical Note," *Journal of Political Economy*, 1967; and M. V. Pauly, "Optimality, 'Public' Goods, and Local Governments: A General Theoretical Analysis," *Journal of Political Economy*, 1970. Especially in the more general case of asymmetrical spillovers, however, it could well be argued that independent adjustment equilibrium may represent an inequitable and unacceptable basis for compensation or negotiation. Williams's conception of "local autonomy" may be an appealing and more acceptable alternative. If the public good can be inferior for at least one locality, the possibility arises in either framework that output and consumption may be larger, not only for the country as a whole, but also for each local unit. For a demonstration of this possibility in the Williams framework, see G. Brennan, "The Optimal Provision of Public Goods: A Comment," *Journal of Political Economy*, 1969.

[28] See J. M. Buchanan and M. Z. Kafoglis, "A Note on Public Goods Supply," *American Economic Review*, 1963. The Buchanan-Kafoglis analysis is developed for the case of two persons, but applies equally to the case of two localities.

[29] For a detailed analysis, see J. Rothenberg, "Local Decentralization and the Theory of Optimal Government," in J. Margolis, ed., *The Analysis of Public Output* (New York, 1970).

As with the market failure theorems of public goods analysis, the above discussion of the distortions to be expected under genuinely decentralized political institutions strictly applies only where large numbers of units (here local governments) are involved. Where, for example, what we have called "regional" public goods are involved, the number of governments potentially concerned, at least under optimal decentralization, is relatively small. Even in the case of local public goods, where the total number of units is much larger, the spillover benefits from local provision may be confined to a small number of contiguous units. In these small number cases, if the spillover benefits are significant, the political units involved have an obvious incentive to get together and agree on some method of compensation for spillovers to avoid underprovision. The necessary degree of "coordination" of the various area governments on a given "level" can here be achieved through voluntary agreement.[30]

This is not, however, to suggest that the voluntaristic solution is entirely without problems. Even in the simplest conceivable case of a nonreciprocal spillover involving just two contiguous units, bargaining difficulties may obviously arise.[31] Problems of strategic behavior are likely to be particularly severe in the case of spillovers which are both reciprocal and nonseparable. Here the amount of the spillin varies with the level of local provision, as may well be the case with education, and the equilibrium level of service for each local unit involved depends reciprocally upon the standard of service provided by the other units. Such small number preference-revelation problems may possibly be reduced by the voluntary amalgamation of adjacent units.[32] Amalgamation may therefore be economically justified even though service provision over the amalgamated jurisdiction would tend in other respects to be more costly, as under an initially optimal system of boundaries determined in accordance with the analysis of the preceding section.

These voluntaristic procedures break down completely where the number of local units involved in a particular spillover is large.

[30] The possibility of voluntary agreement in small-number cases has been particularly stressed in the modern externality literature stemming from the classic discussion by Coase. See R. H. Coase, "The Problem of Social Cost," *Journal of Law and Economics,* 1960. The same arguments apply equally to spillovers between local government units.

[31] For a formal analysis of some of these problems in a two-person setting, see O. A. Davis and A. B. Whinston, "Some Notes on Equating Private and Social Cost," *Southern Economic Journal,* 1965.

[32] The special problem of reciprocal and nonseparable externalities was first analyzed by Davis and Whinston who considered the case of two competitive firms related through their cost functions. They concluded that a merger of the two firms might offer the best solution. See O. A. Davis and A. B. Whinston, "Externalities, Welfare, and the Theory of Games," *Journal of Political Economy,* 1962.

Large-number preference-revelation problems arise, as the benefits from a voluntary agreement embracing all parties, seen from the point of view of a single unit, come to depend less and less on own participation.[33] Some form of compulsion, such as the "Pigovian" alternative of taxes and subsidies administered by a higher level government or central agency, must therefore be considered. In an intergovernmental context, genuine large-number cases are likely to be significant only under a rigid and grossly nonoptimal balkanized structure of multilevel government. A Pigovian solution might, however, also be considered in small-number cases, in view of the bargaining difficulties encountered under voluntaristic procedures.

As Pigou himself has warned, the tax-subsidy approach is likewise not without problems. Unless the relevant grants and taxes are appropriately designed and calculated the system may do more harm than good.[34] Information problems arise, as can readily be seen by considering the information requirements for an ideal grant system.

The simplest case, already mentioned above, would seem to be that of a nonreciprocal spillover of service from one local government unit A to a neighboring unit B and related to output by A. Assuming that no voluntary compensation agreement is possible, the distortion could be corrected if a higher level of government or centralized agency could arrange to pay a "conditional matching grant" to local government A, related to output of the service, with a uniform "matching" rate determined by the marginal collective benefit to B's citizens at the optimum level of output. In order to do this, the higher-level government must have sufficient knowledge of the cost function for the service, the spillover function, and the demand functions in A and B, to be able to determine the optimum level of output for the service and the marginal benefit to B at that level of output. Under genuinely decentralized political decision-making such information may not be at all readily available to a higher level of government. Small number preference-revelation problems may arise as each local unit attempts to obtain a more favorable or less unfavorable grant arrangement.[35]

The problem is even more complicated in the case of reciprocal and nonseparable spillovers where, as we have seen, the equilibrium level

[33] This argument is familiar both from the public goods literature and the broader externality literature. See, for example, Musgrave, p. 80; and W. J. Baumol, *Welfare Economics and the Theory of the State* (Cambridge, Mass., 1952), chap. 11.

[34] See A. C. Pigou, *A Study in Public Finance* (London, 1929), p. 124.

[35] If we depart from the standard Pigovian conception of a constant "matching" rate, a somewhat simpler but still informationally extremely demanding solution would be to pay a conditional matching grant with the marginal matching rate equal to the marginal spillover benefit at each level of output. For this purpose, "only" the spillover benefit function must be determined.

of service for each local unit depends reciprocally upon the level of service provided by the other. In this situation there is in general no unique equilibrium under independent adjustment, and actual service levels will depend upon the strategies adopted by each unit. Design of an optimal grant structure here requires knowledge of local strategies in response to alternative grant policies in addition to the relevant cost, spillover, and demand functions.[36]

Where a number of local units are involved in a given spillover relationship, or where the number of spillover relationships is large, the information requirements are still more demanding, as the number of cost, spillover, and demand functions which must be estimated is correspondingly greater. At best, therefore, only a very crude approximation to an ideally efficient grant scheme could possibly be expected.

It is interesting to notice that a conditional grant without "matching" provisions is in general totally inadequate for this purpose. Except in very special cases of corner solutions, such a grant does not have the necessary stimulating substitution effect on service provision, but only an income effect. The effect of the grant is therefore purely redistributive and no different from that of a completely unconditional grant or one tied to some other local service generating no spillovers. It is true that a somewhat larger nonmatching grant can generally be found which would have the same net stimulating effect on service provision as a matching grant of given revenue cost. The corrective substitution effect of the matching grant is, however, required to remove the disturbance to the optimum conditions represented by the divergence between marginal local benefit and marginal social benefit.[37]

To this point we have analyzed the spillover problem under multi-level government on the assumption of genuinely decentralized political decision-making. As we saw in the preceding section, an alternative structure of decentralized provision can readily be imagined in which the local units are mere branches of a central agency, and are required to administer centralized decisions regarding the appropriate level of service provision for each unit. The use of centralized directives is, of course, a possible alternative to the voluntary agreements, amalgamations and the Pigovian grant system which we have just discussed.

---

[36] For a detailed analysis of these problems in the analogous case of interfirm externalities, see O. A. Davis and A. B. Whinston, "On Externalities, Information and the Government-Assisted Invisible Hand," *Economica*, 1966.

[37] For a recent demonstration of these points in the analogous setting of interpersonal externality relationships, see M. V. Pauly "Efficiency in the Provision of Consumption Subsidies," *Kyklos*, 1970.

In this connection it is interesting to observe that the information requirements for an efficient system of uniform-rate conditional matching grants administered by a higher-level government are identical to those for an efficient system of centralized directives. In the simple case of a nonreciprocal spillover from one local government unit A to a neighboring unit B, the design of an ideal grant requires the determination of the optimal level of output for the service in A in order to calculate the marginal spillover benefit to B at that level of output. But if the optimal level of service provision in A can be determined, a centralized directive could simply be issued to establish A's output at the optimal level. In the absence of constitutional rigidities, it would therefore seem pointless to bother with the refinements of a Pigovian grant system.[38]

Summarizing the above discussion, we see that when spillovers are significant, as they may be even under optimal boundaries, some form of coordination of local units is required for optimal supply of local public goods. Such coordination may be possible on a purely voluntaristic basis through compensation or amalgamation agreements. Alternatively a Pigovian system of corrective grants administered by a "higher level of government" may be employed. A fourth and final possibility is a system of centralized directives. All these coordination devices involve costs which vary with the nature of the spillover and the number of local units involved. From an efficiency point of view the least costly approach should obviously be chosen, though the comparison may frequently be close and difficult.

In general it seems clear that the efficiency case for genuine decentralization of political decision-making in local or regional public goods supply is weakened by the existence of significant spillovers. It is not, however, completely demolished, since the benefits in terms of preference revelation for local public goods may well justify a combination of local decision-making and a voluntaristic compensation or Pigovian coordination device in preference to central provision. Only where there is considerable interarea uniformity of demands for local public goods, or in special cases of extreme jointness where cost considerations either require or heavily favor a high degree of uniformity of consumption standards, do we find a clear case for a higher-level monopoly of effective political decision-making to internalize significant spillovers. In the more general case, optimal boundaries

---

[38] This argument is developed in relation to interfirm externalities by Davis and Whinston (1966). As we have seen in n. 35 above, however, the information demands of the grant approach can be reduced by departing from the standard requirement of a uniform matching rate. The above argument therefore requires some modification, at least in the simpler cases of spillover interaction.

for political decision-making should be determined by balancing the advantages of a small unit in terms of preference-revelation for local public goods against the advantages of a larger unit in terms of minimizing spillovers and the consequent need for costly and inaccurate coordination devices.[39]

In order to justify a relatively simple three- or four-level structure of multilevel government on the basis of the factors so far considered, we would evidently have to assume a significant clustering in the spectrum of public goods in terms of the geographical scope of spillovers, preference homogeneities and jointness, suitably combined.[40] There seems, however, to be little justification for such an assumption. Indeed, even this assumption would not generally be sufficient, as a variety of single-purpose governments on a given level might in principle offer scope for a more detailed registration of voter preferences. Other factors, such as voter information costs, opportunities for log-rolling or political trading and administrative economies, may, however, help to justify something like the political conglomerates we observe in practice.[41]

## 5. Public Goods and Fiscal Equalization

Grants to low-income regional or local governments have traditionally been justified in the literature mainly on grounds of equity. The best-known and most sophisticated approach is that of Buchanan, who attempts to show that a system of grants to low-income units can be derived from the fundamental horizontal equity principle that equals should be treated equally.[42] Buchanan begins by assuming that all governments at all levels treat equals equally within their own jurisdictions, both on the tax side and on the benefit side. He then proceeds to demonstrate that the fiscal residuum (benefits minus taxes) of individuals residing in low-income areas will be smaller than that of their equals in high-income areas, provided only that the budgets of the regional or local governments are redistributive. He concludes that unconditional grants to poor governments, administered by an appropriate higher level government, may provide the best feasible means of reducing these inequalities. Efficiency considerations are not stressed, but the important point is made that, if

[39] For an elegant formal synthesis of most of the relevant factors, see W. E. Oates, *Fiscal Federalism* (New York, 1972), chap. 2.
[40] Some such clustering is assumed, for example, by Breton, p. 178.
[41] See, for example, Tullock; Olson; Hartle and Bird.
[42] See J. M. Buchanan, "Federalism and Fiscal Equity," *American Economic Review*, 1950.

the private sector allocation of resources is initially ideal, the introduction of an effectively decentralized fiscal system provides an allocatively distorting incentive to factor flows out of low-income jurisdictions. Equalizing grants would serve to reduce this incentive.[43]

Both the equity and efficiency aspects of Buchanan's analysis have been criticized. The well known Scott-Buchanan debate focused, for example, on the treatment of private-sector allocation.[44] For our present purposes, however, we shall confine ourselves to the treatment of public-sector benefits. In his original formulation total spending by each government is simply distributed over the relevant citizens in proportion to the assumed (equal) sharing basis, and the resulting money amount is taken as the measure of total individual benefit. In general, however, this method of benefit imputation has a clear rationale only in the case of welfare payments. In the case of public goods, such as health and education services, it becomes at best a mere "cost imputation" and could not conceivably serve as a measure of individual benefits received.

Two of Buchanan's major propositions seem, however, to depend crucially on this simple approach to benefit imputation. The first is that an individual will be indifferent between two jurisdictions in which his fiscal residuum is the same even though the level of public service provided is quite different. The second, which is simply a special case of the first, is that, if no redistribution is attempted and taxes are imposed on a strict benefit basis in proportion to benefits received, fiscal residua in different jurisdictions will be equal at zero. In both cases there is therefore no horizontal inequity and no distorting incentive to factor movement.[45]

In fact, as Buchanan himself points out in a subsequent paper, fiscal residua based on cost imputations must, in the case of public goods, be sharply distinguished from a true measure of taxpayer's surplus.[46] Equality of fiscal residua at zero, or at any other value, may conceal substantial differences in taxpayer's surplus. In any relevant welfare sense there may therefore be both horizontal inequities and incentives to factor movement where fiscal residua are equalized.[47] Except perhaps to the extent that public services take the form of

[43] Ibid., sec. 3.
[44] See J. M. Buchanan, "Federal Grants and Resource Allocation," *Journal of Political Economy,* 1952; A. D. Scott, "Federal Grants and Resource Allocation," ibid.; and J. M. Buchanan, "A Reply," ibid.
[45] See Buchanan, "Federalism and Fiscal Equity."
[46] See Buchanan, "Comment" on Musgrave, "Approaches to A Fiscal Theory of Political Federalism."
[47] See J. F. Graham, *Fiscal Adjustment and Economic Development* (Toronto, 1963), pp. 176–78. Also A. D. Scott, "The Economic Goals of Federal Finance," *Public Finance,* 1964, pp. 254–55.

welfare payments, no clear justification for fiscal equalization in terms of "residua" therefore emerges.

It might be thought that if the concept of the fiscal residuum was to be replaced by that of taxpayer's surplus the original propositions might still hold. Public goods analysis suggests, however, that substantial modifications may be necessary. Thus, for example, it has become clear that benefit taxation can only be interpreted meaningfully in terms of an equality of marginal benefit and marginal taxation. Under strict benefit taxation by all governments, taxpayer's surplus would not therefore be equalized at zero or indeed at any other figure. The second proposition must therefore be completely abandoned.[48]

More fundamentally, however, public goods analysis casts some doubt on the basic proposition that the taxpayer's surplus of equals in different jurisdictions should be equalized. In particular, although this objective may well be appropriate from the point of view of equity, it is doubtful whether it can be justified from the point of view of efficiency.[49]

As in the case of the fiscal residuum the taxpayer's surplus can generally be expected to be greater in high-income than in low-income jurisdictions. Even assuming a Pareto-optimal supply of local public goods with taxes based on strict marginalist benefit principles, it is still generally true that a high-income jurisdiction will tend to provide a higher level of service at somewhat lower rates of tax. If, Lindahl-like, we can ignore differences in tastes for public goods, the basic requirement is simply some positive elasticity of the marginal utility of income (or private good) schedule. As in Buchanan's original model, individuals in low-income areas would therefore have a fiscal incentive to move to high-income areas.

From the point of view of public goods supply, however, it is not at all obvious that such movement is necessarily inefficient. This is particularly evident in the simple polar case of a pure local public good where additional households can be provided with the same level of service at no extra cost. Per capita cost, and hence the tax rate in a high-income jurisdiction, could therefore be lowered as the result of an inflow of population from a low-income jurisdiction. Indeed, as we have already seen, minimum per capita cost of local public goods supply would here require that the whole population of the country be concentrated in a single local government area; though population immobility and considerations of efficiency in private goods production

[48] See Buchanan, "Comment."
[49] See Buchanan and Wagner, "An Efficiency Basis for Federal Fiscal Equalisation."

under diminishing returns no doubt rule this out as an overall allocative objective.[50]

The essential point, however, is that population movement produces
spillovers on the cost side of public goods supply. People attracted to
a high-income jurisdiction by the greater taxpayer's surplus take no
account of the reduced cost of public goods supply and still lower tax
rates for existing residents which their presence makes possible. If,
therefore, we were to begin with an interjurisdictional distribution
of population determined largely by considerations of efficiency in
private goods supply, the efficient provision of local public goods may
well require the preservation or even some widening of differentials in
taxpayer surplus between low- and high-income jurisdictions. Here
there is no efficiency case for fiscal equalization.

This conclusion is to some extent modified when the polar concept of
a local or regional public good is generalized to allow for congestion
phenomena. Beyond a point the addition of further residents, attracted
by the higher taxpayer's surplus in a high-income jurisdiction, may
cause per capita cost to rise. Migration may thus produce a spillover
cost rather than a spillover benefit in the high-income area. The prospective migrant takes no account of the resulting increase in costs and
taxes for existing residents, and migration may therefore tend to be
excessive. If, say, for constitutional reasons, it is necessary to avoid
formal fiscal or other barriers to internal migration, a fiscal equalization grant might in principle be used to offset any distorting tendency.
The aim of such grant would be to narrow initial taxpayer surplus
differentials just sufficiently to compensate for the externality.[51]

Considerations of efficiency in the supply of local or regional public
goods therefore suggest a possible case for some measure of fiscal
equalization between high- and low-income units. The relevant circumstances are, however, quite narrowly restricted, and the degree
of equalization justified on these grounds would fall far short of the
original Buchanan conception of full equality of either fiscal residuum
or taxpayer's surplus.

## 6.  Public Goods and Other Functions

The discussion of the preceding sections has focused attention on the
traditional and narrowly economic allocation branch problems which

[50] See ibid., sec. 2.
[51] See ibid., sec. 3.

have been the central concern of modern public goods theory. The analysis can, however, be considerably extended by further generalization of the public goods concept.

To begin with, it is possible to take account of some of the most important "noneconomic" factors which complicate the application of economic analysis to problems of multilevel government. For example, the previous discussion deliberately abstracted from troublesome problems of local or regional nationalism. Regions or localities with distinctive historical, ethnic, linguistic, religious or cultural background commonly show great concern with the preservation or enhancement of local or regional identity. In such cases "group identity" can obviously be regarded as a local or regional public good in a generalized sense. Since a high degree of political autonomy may be essential to the preservation of group identity, decentralization of political decision-making may legitimately be extended well beyond what might seem justified by narrowly economic considerations.[52]

It is also possible to extend the analysis into other branches of the well known Musgrave trinity.[53] Following Baumol, economic stabilization can be regarded as a generalized externality or public goods problem with an important spatial dimension. The antirecession fiscal policies of one local unit, for example, would generally provide significant spillover benefits in the form of increased income and employment in neighboring localities. The relevant multiplier (and induced investment effects) would be greater at the regional than at the local level, and greater again at the national level. Precisely analogous arguments hold for the corresponding anti-inflationary policies. Effective fiscal stabilization policy is therefore out of the question at the local level, would at least require a very high degree of voluntary coordination at the regional level, and is evidently best performed by the central government. This is not, of course, to suggest that such policies should not take account of the uneven regional or local incidence of economic instability.

Even the redistribution function can to some degree be regarded as a generalized public goods problem. Middle- and upper-income individuals derive satisfaction from the relief of poverty, and charitable donations by one person therefore provide external benefits to others.[54] Under these circumstances the relief of poverty by redistributive fiscal measures in one locality may provide spillover benefits to better-off

---

[52] For a detailed analysis, see Hartle and Bird; also Olson.
[53] See chap. 8, sec. 4.2, above.
[54] See, for example, H. M. Hochman and J. D. Rodgers, "Pareto Optimal Redistribution," *American Economic Review*, 1969.

sections of the community across the country.[55] There is therefore a strong case here for assigning basic responsibility for the redistributive function to higher-level government. A similar argument can obviously be used to justify a program of redistributive grants to low-income provinces and localities administered by higher levels of government. Much so-called regional policy can also be justified in the same way. Where, however, the benefits of redistributive measures in a given locality are confined largely to middle- and upper-income residents of the same locality, redistribution takes on the characteristics of a local public good and lower-level provision may be justified.[56]

Fiscal harmonization too is a generalized public goods problem. In the absence of some form of central coordination, including an appropriate assignment of the various tax types to the different levels of government, tax competition between different localities may cause serious misallocation of resources, both in the public sector and in the private sector. A cut in income tax rates by one locality may inflict heavy external costs on other localities by attracting mobile capital or skilled labor; or, with mutually destructive retaliation, the result may be little change in private-sector allocation, but a massive starvation of the public sector. Central coordination of local and regional tax rates, and higher-level control of interregionally more potent tax sources such as the income taxes, find much of their justification here.

Some of the functions of multilevel government are admittedly relatively less amenable to public goods analysis than others. This is particularly true of those functions which lie in part outside the consumer sovereignty tradition of modern public goods theory. The general redistributive function provides the most important example. In Musgrave's classic discussion the concept of a merit good is employed to epitomize these further problems.[57] In contrast to the public good, the central problem here is that, due to ignorance or irrationality, individual preferences may be distorted and unacceptable. Some services, such as health and education or the control of addictive drugs, may exhibit both public goods and merit goods characteristics. In the traditional literature on intergovernmental fiscal relations, strong merit goods overtones are frequently to be detected in arguments for specific grants-in-aid to lower levels of government. Although it is true that

[55] This argument is reinforced by the further consideration that the better-off residents of the given locality may decide to enjoy their altruistic or other benefits at a safe fiscal distance by removing themselves or their capital to a less welfare-oriented locality.

[56] This latter possibility has been explored in some detail by Pauly in "Income Redistribution as a Local Public Good," *Journal of Public Economics,* 1972.

[57] See Musgrave, *The Theory of Public Finance,* pp. 13–14.

many alleged merit goods problems can be reformulated in terms of a generalized externality or public goods concept, not least in the field of intergovernmental fiscal relations, it may be doubted whether all such problems can be adequately explained in this way.[58]

The broader implications of the theory of public goods for the problems of multilevel government should be evident from the foregoing discussion. There are relatively few problems in the design of a fiscal constitution for multilevel government which cannot be significantly illuminated by the application of modern public goods analysis.

---

[58] See chap. 11 in this volume. For some discussion of merit goods problems in the context of multilevel government, see Tiebout and Houston, "Metropolitan Finance Reconsidered: Budget Functions and Multi-Level Governments." In the case of involuntary redistribution, for example, it is a familiar conclusion that central government provision is required, since high-income residents will otherwise relocate in more congenial fiscal surroundings. If some involuntary redistribution must be undertaken at the local level, the size of the optimal jurisdiction should be determined on the basis of some compromise between the advantages of a small unit in terms of preference-revelation for local public goods and the distributional advantages of a large unit which may serve to ensure the inclusion of a reasonable proportion of high-income residents. On this latter point, see Rothenberg.

# Index

## Author

## Subject